MASTERPLOTS
FIFTEEN-VOLUME
COMBINED EDITION

Volume Eight
Last-Mard

MASTERPLOTS

15-Volume Combined Edition
FIFTEEN HUNDRED AND TEN
Plot-Stories and Essay-Reviews
from the
WORLD'S FINE LITERATURE

Edited by
FRANK N. MAGILL

Story Editor
DAYTON KOHLER

VOLUME EIGHT—LAST-MARD

SALEM PRESS
INCORPORATED
NEW YORK

This work also appears under the title of
MASTERPIECES OF WORLD LITERATURE IN DIGEST FORM

THE LAST CHRONICLE OF BARSET

Type of work: Novel
Author: Anthony Trollope (1815-1882)
Type of plot: Domestic realism
Time of plot: Mid-nineteenth century
Locale: "Barsetshire," England
First published: 1867

Principal characters:
    MR. CRAWLEY, Curate of Hogglestock
    MRS. CRAWLEY, his wife
    GRACE CRAWLEY, their daughter
    MR. PROUDIE, Bishop of Barchester
    MRS. PROUDIE, his wife
    HENRY GRANTLY, Grace's suitor
    LILY DALE, Grace's friend
    JOHN EAMES, Lily's suitor

Critique:

To readers who are familiar with Trollope's novels the shire of Barset undoubtedly exists and should be shown on the maps. Barchester and its towers, Plumstead Episcopi, and Hogglestock seem as real as if they had actually stood for a thousand years. Mrs. Proudie, the Thornes of Ullathorne, Archdeacon Grantly and his wife, and the weak Quiverfuls are among Trollope's characters who make up an ever-living community. The genius of Anthony Trollope lies in his understanding of human wisdom and human ignorance.

The Story:

In the community of Hogglestock the citizens were upset because Mr. Crawley, the curate, had been accused of stealing a check for twenty pounds. In Archdeacon Grantly's home, where there was concern lest Henry Grantly might marry Grace Crawley, the curate's schoolteacher daughter, feeling was high.

Bishop Proudie and his wife were set against the unfortunate Crawley. Mrs. Proudie, who exerted great power over her husband, persuaded the bishop to write a letter forbidding Mr. Crawley to preach in his church until the case should

have been settled one way or another. Mr. Crawley refused the injunction. Mr. and Mrs. Proudie quarreled over the answer, and Mr. Proudie sent for Mr. Crawley to attend him in the bishop's palace at once. When Mr. Crawley arrived, he was hot and tired from walking. He repeated what he had stated in his letter and left the bishop and his wife amazed at his boldness.

Mr. Crawley was not kept from performing his duties on Christmas morning. Since he could not recall how he had come into possession of the money in question, he informed his wife that he had but two choices—either to go to jail or to bedlam.

At last Henry Grantly decided to ask Grace Crawley to marry him, even though he should be going against his parents' wishes. At the same time Lily Dale, Grace Crawley's friend, was being wooed by young John Eames, a clerk in the Income Tax Office in London and a suitor, once rejected, whom Lily's mother favored. Eames was the friend of a London artist named Conway Dalrymple, who was painting a portrait of Miss Clara Van Siever, a mutual friend, in the sitting-room of Mrs. Dobbs Broughton. Meanwhile the aged Mrs. Van Siever was engaged in forcing Dobbs Broughton to pay money he owed to her.

Not long afterward John Eames met Henry Grantly. Neither liked the other at first. John, meeting Lily in Lady Julia de Guest's home, where Grace was also a guest, discussed his unfavorable meeting with Henry ·Grantly in front of Grace. When Henry proposed to Grace, she refused him and returned home to be with her father during his trial. Lily told John that she planned to die an old maid, her heart having been broken by Adolphus Crosbie, a former suitor.

Mr. Toogood, a distant relative, was to defend Mr. Crawley. John Eames was brought into the Crawley case by Mr. Toogood, who wanted John to go to Florence and attempt to persuade Mr. Arabin, an influential clergyman, to come to Mr. Crawley's rescue. There was another reason why Arabin should return to England. Mrs. Arabin's father, Mr. Harding, was ailing and growing weaker each day.

Conway Dalrymple worked on Miss Van Siever's picture, which was still a secret from Dobbs Broughton, in whose house it was being painted. Although Broughton had ordered the artist out of his house, Mrs. Broughton wanted the picture painted, regardless of her jealous husband's reactions.

The clerical commission summoned by Bishop Proudie reached no decision concerning Mr. Crawley. It was resolved that nothing should be done until the civil courts had decided his case.

Archdeacon Grantly tried to engage the help of Lady Lufton to prevent the marriage of his son to Grace Crawley, but Lady Lufton refused. The archdeacon finally promised that he would no longer oppose the marriage if Mr. Crawley should be found innocent of any crime.

Dobbs Broughton was being pressed hard for money by old Mrs. Van Siever. Clara Van Siever was to marry Mussel-

boro, Broughton's former partner. Dalrymple, still hoping to marry Clara, was putting the last touches to the canvas when Mrs. Van Siever entered the Broughton house. At her word he destroyed the portrait. Over Clara's objections, Mrs. Van Siever announced that her daughter was to marry Musselboro. After the Van Sievers left, Musselboro arrived with news that Dobbs Broughton had killed himself that morning. Clara and Dalrymple resolved to face Mrs. Van Siever's wrath together.

Mrs. Proudie continued her fight to have Mr. Crawley removed. After a quarrel between the bishop and Mrs. Proudie, she retired to her room and there died of a heart attack. True to the resolution imposed upon him by Mrs. Proudie before her death, Mr. Crawley preached a final sermon in his church and never again entered it as the curate.

On the continent John Eames learned from Mrs. Arabin the cause of Mr. Crawley's troubles. Mrs. Arabin, who had received the check from a tenant, had turned it over to Mr. Crawley without telling her husband, the dean, of the transaction. She had only recently heard of the charges and she was hurrying home to England to do what could be done to straighten out the matter. In the meantime Mr. Toogood traced the theft of the check to the tenant who had forwarded it to Mrs. Arabin.

Mr. Toogood and Henry Grantly took the good news to Mr. and Mrs. Crawley. When she heard their story, Mrs. Crawley, who had defended her husband from the beginning, broke into tears. The messengers had to explain the situation carefully to Mr. Crawley, who could not at first believe that his innocence was about to be proved. Then Mr. Harding, the aged incumbent in St. Ewold's, died. Archdeacon Grantly offered the living to Mr. Crawley as a recompense for all he had suffered. In midsummer Grace Crawley became Mrs. Henry Grantly.

John Eames did not marry Lily Dale

after all, for Lily was unable to make her decision, but Dalrymple married Clara Van Siever as he had planned. Musselboro, who had lost Clara, proceeded to marry the widow of his old partner and thus Mrs. Broughton's sorrows were brought to an end.

THE LAST DAYS OF POMPEII

Type of work: Novel
Author: Edward George Earle Bulwer-Lytton (1803-1873)
Type of plot: Historical romance
Time of plot: A.D. 79
Locale: Pompeii
First published: 1834

Principal characters:
GLAUCUS, a wealthy young Greek
ARBACES, Egyptian priest of Isis
IONE, his Greek ward
APAECIDES, her brother
NYDIA, a blind flower girl

Critique:

This novel has found many readers among those who are interested in the classical civilization which ended when barbarians took over the Mediterranean world. Bulwer-Lytton's handling of plot, character, and passion followed a tradition which has not maintained its hold. It is the tradition of nineteenth-century drama, direct, obtuse, fiery. Concerned with indirection today, the reader finds the descriptions of the characters' thoughts unrealistic. Their passions are too apparent, their actions too much explained. Cast in a different mold from novels of today, *The Last Days of Pompeii* offers one of the longest, most sustained views of the world we call classic.

The Story:

Late one afternoon in the ancient city of Pompeii the fashionable rich young men were congregating for the daily rite of the public baths. Among them were Clodius, a foppish Roman, and Glaucus, a popular young Greek. Together the two strolled toward the baths, mingling with slaves bearing bronze buckets, idlers gowned in purple robes. Along the way they saw the beautiful blind flower girl, Nydia. She, too, was from Greece and for that reason Glaucus took an interest in her. It was still too early for the baths, and the two friends walked along the sea front as Glaucus described a Neapolitan girl of Greek birth with whom he had fallen in love. Unfortunately, he had lost contact with the girl and was now morose. While they talked, Arbaces, the evil-looking Egyptian priest of Isis, intercepted them. The two young men were barely able to conceal their dislike for the Egyptian.

Arbaces secretly defied the Romans and the Greeks, and prayed for the day when Egypt would once more be powerful. He revealed to a lesser priest his interest in the brother and sister, Apaecides and Ione, his wards. He hoped to make a priest of Apaecides, and he planned to marry Ione. They had been in Naples, but recently he had brought them to Pompeii, where he could influence them.

Glaucus met Ione at a party. She was the girl he had seen and lost in Naples. At the same time Arbaces developed his hold over Apaecides, who was growing more and more confused after coming in contact with the sophistries of the corrupt priest of Isis. Meanwhile the blind flower girl, Nydia, was falling hopelessly in love with Glaucus.

It happened that Glaucus and Clodius were loitering in the establishment of Burbo, the wine-seller, when the innkeeper and his wife were beating Nydia, whose slave she was. Glaucus, hearing the girl's cries, bought her; he planned to give her to Ione. Nydia realized Glaucus could never love her after he gave her a letter to deliver to Ione. In this letter he accused Arbaces of false imputations. On reading his letter, Ione decided to go at once to Arbaces' palace and to face him with Glaucus' charges.

Knowing the danger to Ione at Arbaces' palace, Nydia warned both Ione's brother and Glaucus. Glaucus hurried to the palace to confront the priest. An earthquake interrupted the quarrel between the two men. When the goddess Isis fell from a pedestal, striking Arbaces, Glaucus and Ione ran from the building to join the throng in the street. Alone, deserted, the blind slave wept bitterly.

The next day, the earthquake having passed with but little damage, the people of Pompeii took up again the threads of their varied lives. Apaecides became a convert to Christianity. Glaucus and Ione remained together.

Julia, daughter of a wealthy freedman named Diomed, was also in love with Glaucus and sought to interfere between him and Ione. She went to the house of Arbaces, where the two plotted together. Arbaces had a drug prepared which was administered to Glaucus. The drug drove him into a demented stupor so that he ran from his house into a cemetery. To this cemetery came Apaecides and Arbaces. They quarreled and Arbaces stabbed Apaecides, killing him. Then, hoping to kill Glaucus indirectly, the priest summoned the crowd and declared that Glaucus in his drunken rage had killed Apaecides. Glaucus and a Christian who attempted to defend him were arrested. They were condemned to be given to wild beasts at the public games.

After the funeral of her brother, Ione resolved to declare her belief in the innocence of Glaucus. But before she could carry out her plan Arbaces had seized her and carried her off to his palace. The only one who knew of Arbaces' guilt was a priest who was also his prisoner. But Arbaces reckoned without Nydia, who as a dancing girl had learned most of the secrets of his palace. Nydia, contacting the priest imprisoned by Arbaces, agreed to carry his story to the authorities. Unfortunately, she too was captured. She persuaded a slave to carry the message to Sallust, a friend of Glaucus. But the message was delivered while Sallust was drunk and he refused to read it.

The last day of Pompeii arrived. It was also a day of celebration in the arena, for which the populace had been waiting. The games began with gladiatorial combat which the audience watched listlessly, bored because the deaths did not come fast enough or with enough suffering. After one combat an unpopular gladiator was condemned to death by the action of the crowd. His body was dragged from the arena and placed on the heap with those previously slain. Unfortunately for the crowd's amusement, the lion turned loose in the arena with Glaucus crept with a moan back into its cage. Before the lion could be prodded into action Sallust appeared demanding the arrest of Arbaces. A slave had called his attention to Nydia's letter, which he had thrown aside the night before. Reading it, he had hurried to lay his information before the praetor. The mob, not to be cheated after Glaucus had been set free, demanded that Arbaces be thrown to the lion.

Then the famous fatal eruption began. The whole gladiatorial scene became chaos as terrified thousands poured out of the doomed amphitheater, crushing the weakest in their hurry to escape. Looting began in the temples. Nydia reached Glaucus. Together they hurried to the house of Arbaces to discover and save Ione. It was too dark to see, but Nydia, accustomed to darkness, was able to lead Ione and Glaucus through the streets. Arbaces was killed in the earthquake. At last Glaucus, Ione, and Nydia gained the safety of the seaside and put out to sea in a small ship.

All night they slept in the boat. In the morning Glaucus and Ione discovered that before they had awakened, the heartbroken Nydia had cast herself into the sea.

THE LAST OF SUMMER

Type of work: Novel
Author: Kate O'Brien (1897-   )
Type of plot: Naturalism
Time of plot: 1939
Locale: Eire
First published: 1943

Principal characters:
ANGÈLE MAURY, an actress
HANNAH KERNAHANS, her aunt
TOM KERNAHANS, and
MARTIN KERNAHANS, Hannah's sons
NORRIE O'BYRNE, in love with Tom

Critique:

Against a background of imminent war, Angèle Maury struggled against the iron will of the aunt who had never admitted her existence and who was determined to keep this stranger out of her family and her life. The story is a dramatic one, tense and stark, but told with great restraint and simplicity. The personal struggle between Angèle and Hannah seems only to reflect the greater struggle between those peoples who wanted to be free and the political despots who would not let go their hold.

The Story:

Angèle Maury was an actress, half French, half Irish, who had taken her mother's name as her stage name in preference to Kernahans, her Irish father's name. Both her parents were dead. On an impulse she stopped to visit her father's people when her company toured Ireland. She found her aunt, Hannah Kernahans, strangely hostile to her and learned that Aunt Hannah had never told her three children of their uncle's marriage or of his daughter.

It was obvious that Aunt Hannah was fiercely jealous of any intruders from the outside world. She loved all her children, but Tom, the oldest son, was tied to her by a silver cord so strong it seemed unlikely the bond would ever be broken. Tom had long been loved by Norrie

O'Byrne, but he was not sensitive to her love. Martin, the second son, had grown up quite independent. A student, he had traveled all over Europe on scholarships and had lived wildly at times. His mother either could not or did not care to tie him to her so closely.

What none of the children knew, and Angèle did not learn, was that her father and their father had both loved Aunt Hannah. She had accepted Angèle's father, but before the wedding he had discovered her steel will and had asked to be released from the engagement. She then married his brother, giving the impression that it was she who had changed her mind. But she never forgave Angèle's father for embarrassing her, and she would never forgive Angèle for being her father's child. She sensed in Angèle an enemy to the isolated life she lived with Tom.

Soon after her arrival Martin told Angèle that he wanted her and offered her anything but marriage; he was not yet ready for those ties. Angèle, not taking him seriously, thought that she was only someone new whom he would soon forget. The fact that they were first cousins also stood in the way of a serious proposal. But Martin brooded over her treatment of him and worried also about the impending war. Hitler, having taken Czechoslovakia, stood on the threshold

THE LAST OF SUMMER by Kate O'Brien. By permission of the author's agent, Ann Watkins, Inc. Published by Doubleday & Co., Inc. Copyright, 1943, by Kate O'Brien.

of Poland. Ireland was neutral, but Martin knew that he could not stand idly by while the world blew up under his feet. Only Martin and Angèle took the war seriously. Knowing that her mother's people would be deeply affected by the war, she was annoyed to see Aunt Hannah brush aside the whole affair with a shrug. Tom refused to see that no one could remain completely neutral when war finally came.

One day Tom told Angèle that he loved her. Unused to strong emotion, he had not recognized his feelings until they were too intense to ignore. Angèle, returning his love, realized that Aunt Hannah would not like their engagement, lest Tom get away from her. Aunt Hannah was clever enough to make Tom believe she was delighted, but she subtly put obstacles in their way. Since they were first cousins, they would have to get special dispensations from Rome. Angèle wanted to return to France on their honeymoon, in spite of the dangers of war. Aunt Hannah used her weapons cleverly, fooling Tom but not deceiving Angèle at all. She sensed that it would take more will power than Tom had ever shown for him to overcome these obstacles and see his mother's hold on him. Angèle's hope was that Tom would shake off his chains and be free and independent.

Martin brought matters to a head. It angered him to hear Angèle talk of returning to France before war broke out, for he realized that Germany would soon march into Poland. If Angèle wanted to see France, to act like a Frenchwoman, she should return to her people and help them in their time of crisis. Aunt Hannah encouraged the idea, all the time acting considerate and loving. She knew that if she could once get Angèle away from Tom, he would come back to the fold easily enough. Martin, of course, hoped for the separation so that he could have time to make Angèle love him. He knew that she could never win against his mother, and he sincerely felt that she and Tom were not suited to each other.

When Church officials failed to hurry dispensation proceedings, Angèle fretted at the time lost. She even considered going by herself to France. Aunt Hannah tried to goad her into leaving alone, but she did not wish to hurt Tom just to please his mother. Tom kept promising Angèle that he would find a way to hurry matters, but she took little hope; fast action was not in his nature.

Martin, too Irish to sign up with the British, prepared to leave to join the French army. Angèle even wished that she were a man so that she would have to go back to France. Then the issue would be clear, not muddled in emotional reactions. Before he left, Martin told Angèle again that he loved her. He told her too that she did not really love his brother, that she was too strong a person to love anyone as weak as Tom. He warned her that Hannah would win, that she would never let Tom go. Martin begged her to return to France with him the next day. Although she rejected the plan, Angèle thanked Martin for his honesty and allowed him to kiss her goodbye.

In the meantime Hannah made her final play for Tom. Pretending to feel sorry for Angèle because she was so torn between Tom and France, she told him that Angèle and Martin were the same kind, that Martin was desperately in love with his cousin. She said also that Angèle had fallen in love with Tom because he was attractive and because she thought that he and Martin were much alike. Although it hurt her to tell him, Hannah declared, she knew that Angèle would never be happy with Tom in Ireland, and it was only the girl's sense of obligation that made her stick to her promise. Hannah, knowing that she could handle that problem when she got to it, played too on the suitability of Norrie O'Byrne.

Shortly after his talk with his mother Tom saw Martin and Angèle kissing goodbye. He thought then that his mother had been right, as usual. He went to Angèle, released her from her betrothal to him, and apologized for being a selfish fool in taking her love. Angèle knew then that she was beaten. She told Tom that she really loved him but that she realized their marriage would never work out. It was futile to try to make him see his mother as she really was.

Angèle also told Aunt Hannah why she was leaving—that she did love Tom but knew she could never fight the bond or restore Tom's confidence in himself. She went away with Martin, to return for good to France, and left Tom lost forever, the silver cord unbroken.

1966

THE LAST OF THE BARONS

Type of work: Novel
Author: Edward George Earle Bulwer-Lytton (1803-1873)
Type of plot: Historical romance
Time of plot: 1467-1471
Locale: England
First published: 1843

Principal characters:
EARL OF WARWICK, the kingmaker
ISABELLA, his older daughter
ANNE, his younger daughter
KATHERINE DE BONVILLE, his sister
EDWARD IV, King of England
WILLIAM DE HASTINGS, a royal chamberlain
ADAM WARNER, an alchemist
SIBYLL, his daughter
NICHOLAS ALWYN, a goldsmith
MARMADUKE NEVILE, kinsman of the Earl of Warwick

Critique:

The Last of the Barons is a complex, involved, and fascinating novel of a troubled period in English history. After the Wars of the Roses the House of York seemed secure, the leaders of the House of Lancaster being dead or in exile. Edward IV was a popular ruler who might have enjoyed a peaceful reign if he had not insulted the Earl of Warwick, the last of the great lords whose power overshadowed the king's. A dramatic moment in history has been recaptured by Bulwer-Lytton in this novel.

The Story:

Just outside London a crowd had gathered to watch an archery contest. Several shot at the white cloth on the butt, but no one hit the mark squarely. Then in a haughty and preoccupied way a commoner stepped up, fitted his arrow, and pierced the center of the white field. While his fellow tradesmen applauded, he dropped back into the crowd.

A young noble, who was not entered in the contest, borrowed a bow. With sure aim he hit fairly the little peg that secured the cloth to the butt. Gallantly he returned the bow and strode away. As he was leaving, the commoner who had hit the cloth stopped him. At once

their recognition was mutual, and they began to talk delightedly of past times.

The commoner was Nicholas Alwyn, a goldsmith who had been the younger son of a good family. He had rejected the monk's habit, the usual lot of younger sons, and had chosen to go into trade. He was shrewd enough to see that the future greatness of England lay in the prosperous middle class and that the day of feudal nobility was nearly over. He had taken part in the tournament simply to advertise his profession, not through love of decadent sport. The young noble, who was his foster brother, was Marmaduke Nevile. He had come from his northern estate to seek service with his kinsman, the powerful Earl of Warwick, who was known as the kingmaker.

On Alwyn's advice, Marmaduke went up to Lord Montagu, the Earl of Warwick's brother, and made known his errand. The nobleman repulsed Marmaduke in full view of his retinue, for Marmaduke's father had fought on the side of Lancaster in the recent wars, and the Warwicks had successfully supported the Yorkists.

Feeling abashed, Marmaduke accompanied Alwyn into the city. Alwyn advised him to go to see the earl in person, and Marmaduke resolved to do so the very next day.

On the road to his inn he met a gentle girl surrounded by a screaming mob of women who earned their living by dancing and playing timbrels for fair crowds. Accusing the girl of trying to earn money by playing her gittern at the tournament, they would have harmed her if Marmaduke had not come to her rescue. He escorted the frightened girl away, but through faint-heartedness he did not take her all the way home. As soon as he left her, the women set upon her again. She was rescued by an older man, a true knight who saw her to her ruined dwelling.

It was dusk when Marmaduke left the city. Shortly afterward he was attacked by a band of robbers who slashed him severely and left him to die. He managed to make his way to a nearby house, and there he was cared for by the girl whom he had deserted a short time before. She was Sibyll Warner, daughter of Adam Warner, a philosopher and alchemist who spent all his time in his laboratory. He had, after years of labor, nearly completed a crude model of a small steam engine. In those superstitious days Adam was accounted a sorcerer and his daughter was suspected of witchcraft.

During his convalescence Marmaduke was greatly attracted to Sibyll, but her superior learning was a barrier between them. Alwyn, who came to the house many times, also fell in love with the girl. But Sibyll thought always of the great knight who had brought her to her door.

When Marmaduke was well and able to leave the house, he at once sought an audience with the mighty Earl of Warwick. Warwick welcomed him and made him a courtier. There he met Isabelle, Warwick's haughty older daughter, and Anne, her gentle young sister.

Warwick was preparing to go to France on a mission to the court of Louis XI. On Warwick's advice, King Edward IV had agreed to marry his sister Margaret to one of the French princes. During Warwick's absence Marmaduke served in the king's household.

As soon as Warwick had left the country, Edward's wife and all her kinsmen of the Woodville family began to work on the king's pride. The Woodvilles, intensely jealous of Warwick, encouraged the king to defy the king-maker's power. They proposed that Edward hastily affiance his sister to the Duke of Burgundy. Edward, persuaded by his wife, at once invited the illegitimate brother of the Burgundian ruler to England and concluded the alliance.

Warwick, hurrying back when he heard the news, felt keenly the slight to his honor. When he found Edward at a hunting party, he immediately demanded Edward's reasons for his step. Edward was frightened, but he assumed an air of confidence and declared that he had followed what seemed the best policy of diplomacy. Although he was much mortified, Warwick magnanimously forgave the king and withdrew. His many followers sought him out and offered to rebel, but Warwick withdrew entirely from court and went into seclusion on his own estate.

Meanwhile Adam Warner had been brought to the court as alchemist to the Duchess of Bedford. Sibyll fitted in well with court life, and Lord Hastings became attached to her. In time they became engaged, and Lord Hastings awaited only the king's permission to marry her. Katherine de Bonville, Warwick's sister, had been his first love, but Warwick had refused his consent to a marriage because Lord Hastings then was not powerful enough to aspire to a connection with the Warwicks. Although Katherine had later married another, Lord Hastings still loved her; his attachment to Sibyll was only temporarily the stronger.

As Warwick had foreseen, the Duke of Burgundy proved an unworthy ally of England and the incensed French king never ceased to make trouble for the

English. At last Edward had to confess that he could not rule the kingdom without Warwick to advise him. The king swallowed his pride and invited Warwick back to London with more honors and power than he had held before. The gallant earl, as a gesture of friendship, brought his daughter Anne to live in the queen's retinue.

Anne chose Sibyll as her companion and the two girls became close friends. One night the lecherous Edward accosted Anne in her bedroom. The girl screamed with fright and ran to Adam Warner for help. There the king found her and abjectly begged her pardon, but Anne was still hysterical. Marmaduke smuggled Anne out of the castle and told her father what had happened.

Warwick at once put Marmaduke at the head of a hundred men who tried to capture the king, but Edward stayed secure in his tower. Warwick then withdrew his followers from the court and embarked for France.

In London, Lord Hastings and Sibyll continued to meet. Then Katherine de Bonville's husband died and she was free once more. Lord Hastings' old love revived and he married her secretly in France.

Margaret of Anjou, the Lancastrian queen in exile, joined forces with Warwick in France. When the mighty earl returned to England, the people welcomed him and joined his cause. Edward fled without fighting a battle. Warwick restored Henry VI to the throne.

The success of his kingmaking made Warwick careless. Edward's power lay not with the nobles but with the merchants, and a coalition of the rich merchants and the adherents of the House of York soon put Edward back into power. On the battlefield of Barnet Warwick was killed and his chiefs were either executed or exiled. Somehow Adam Warner and Sibyll died together in the same fight. Alwyn, an adherent of Edward, took Marmaduke prisoner but later tried to secure his freedom. History does not tell whether he succeeded.

THE LAST OF THE MOHICANS

Type of work: Novel
Author: James Fenimore Cooper (1789-1851)
Type of plot: Historical romance
Time of plot: 1757
Locale: Northern New York State
First published: 1826

Principal characters:
NATTY BUMPPO, a frontier scout known as Hawkeye
CHINGACHGOOK, Hawkeye's Indian friend
UNCAS, Chingachgook's son
MAJOR DUNCAN HEYWARD, an English soldier, Hawkeye's friend
MAGUA, a renegade Huron
CORA MUNRO, daughter of the commander of Fort William Henry
ALICE MUNRO, her sister

Critique:

The battles and exciting pursuits which constitute the plot of *The Last of the Mohicans* are rounded out by interesting Indian lore and the descriptive style of the author. In spite of Cooper's awkward characterizations, this novel remains the most popular of the Leatherstocking Tales, a classic story of the French and Indian wars.

The Story:

Major Duncan Heyward had been ordered to escort Cora and Alice Munro from Fort Edward to Fort William Henry, where Colonel Munro, father of the girls, was commandant. In the party was also David Gamut, a Connecticut singing-master. On their way to Fort William Henry they did not follow the military road through the wilderness. Instead, they placed themselves in the hands of a renegade Huron known as Magua, who claimed that he could lead them to their destination by a shorter trail.

It was afternoon when the little party met the woodsman, Hawkeye, and his Delaware Mohican friends, Chingachgook and his son Uncas. To their dismay, they learned they were but an hour's distance from their starting point. Hawkeye quickly decided Magua had been planning to lead the party into a trap. His Mohican comrades tried to capture the renegade, but Magua took alarm and fled into the woods.

At Heyward's urging the hunter agreed to guide the travelers to their destination. The horses were tied and hidden among some rocks along a river. Hawkeye produced a hidden canoe from among some bushes and paddled the party to a rock at the foot of Glenn's Falls. There they prepared to spend the night in a cave.

That night a band of Iroquois led by Magua surprised the party. The fight might have been a victory for Hawkeye if their supply of powder and ball had held out. Unfortunately, their ammunition had been left in the canoe which, unnoticed until it was too late, was stolen by one of the enemy who had ventured to swim the swirling river. The only hope then lay in the possibility of future rescue, for the capture of the rock and the little group was a certainty. Hawkeye, Chingachgook, and Uncas escaped by floating downstream, leaving the girls and Major Heyward to meet the savages.

Captured, Cora and Alice were allowed to ride their horses, but Heyward and David were forced by their captors to walk. Although they took a road paralleling that to Fort William Henry, Heyward could not determine the destination the Indians had in mind. Drawing close to Magua, he tried to persuade him to betray his companions and deliver the party safely to Colonel Munro. The Huron agreed, if Cora would come to live with him among his tribe as his wife. When she refused, the enraged Magua had everyone bound. He was threatening Alice with his tomahawk when Hawkeye and his friends crept silently upon the band and attacked them. The Iroquois fled, leaving several of their dead behind them. The party, under David's guidance, sang a hymn of thanksgiving, and then pushed onward.

Toward evening they stopped at a deserted blockhouse to rest. Many years before it had been the scene of a fight between the Mohicans and the Mohawks, and a mound still showed where bodies lay buried. While Chingachgook watched, the others slept.

At moonrise they continued on their way. It was dawn when Hawkeye and his charges drew near Fort William Henry. They were intercepted and challenged by a sentinel of the French under Montcalm, who was about to lay siege to the fort. Heyward was able to answer him in French and they were allowed to proceed. Chingachgook killed and scalped the French sentinel. Then, through the fog which had risen from Lake George, and through the enemy forces which thronged the plain before the fort, Hawkeye led the way to the gates of the fort.

On the fifth day of the siege, Hawkeye, who had been sent to Fort Edward to seek help, was intercepted on his way back and a letter he carried was captured. Webb, the commander of Fort Edward, refused to come to the aid of Munro.

Under a flag of truce, Montcalm and Munro held a parley. Montcalm showed Webb's letter to Munro and offered honorable terms of surrender. Colonel Munro and his men would be allowed to keep their colors, their arms, and their baggage, if they would vacate the fort the next morning. Helpless to do otherwise, Munro accepted these terms. During one of the parleys Heyward was surprised to see Magua in the camp of the French.

He had not been killed during the earlier skirmish.

The following day the vanquished English started their trip back to Fort Edward. Under the eyes of the French and their Indian allies they passed across the plain and entered the forest. Suddenly an Indian grabbed at a brightly-colored shawl worn by one of the women. Terrified, she wrapped her child in it. The Indian darted to her, grabbed the child from her arms, and dashed out its brains on the ground. Then under the eyes of Montcalm, who did nothing to discourage or to hold back his savage allies, a monstrous slaughter began.

Cora and Alice, entrusted to David Gamut's protection, were in the midst of the killing when Magua swooped down upon them and carried Alice away in his arms. Cora ran after her sister, and faithful David dogged her footsteps. They were soon atop a hill, from which they watched the slaughter of the garrison.

Three days later, Hawkeye, leading Heyward, Munro, and his Indian comrades, traced the girls and David with the help of Cora's veil which had caught on a tree. Heyward was particularly concerned for the safety of Alice. The day before the massacre he had been given her father's permission to court her.

Hawkeye, knowing that hostile Indians were on their trail, decided to save time by traveling across the lake in a canoe which he discovered in its hiding place nearby. He was certain Magua had taken the girls north, where he planned to rejoin his own people. Heading their canoe in that direction, the five men paddled all day, at one point having a close escape from some of their intercepting enemies. They spent that night in the woods and next day turned west in an effort to find Magua's trail.

After much searching Uncas found the trail of the captives. That evening, as the party drew near the Huron camp, they met David Gamut wandering about. He told his friends that the Indians thought him crazy because of his habit of breaking into song, and they allowed him to roam the woods unguarded. Alice, he said, was being held at the Huron camp. Cora had been entrusted to the care of a tribe of peaceful Delawares a short distance away.

Heyward, disguising his face with paint, went to the Huron camp in an attempt to rescue Alice, while the others set about helping Cora. Heyward was in the camp but a short time, posing as a French doctor, when Uncas was brought in, a captive. Called to treat an ill Indian woman, Heyward found Alice in the cave with his patient. He was able to rescue the girl by wrapping her in a blanket and declaring to the Hurons that she was his patient, whom he was carrying off to the woods for treatment. Hawkeye, attempting to rescue Uncas, entered the camp disguised in a medicine man's bearskin he had stolen. Uncas was cut loose and given the disguise, while the woodsman borrowed David Gamut's clothes. The singer was left to take Uncas' place while the others escaped, for Hawkeye was certain the Indians would not harm David because of his supposed mental condition. Uncas and Hawkeye fled to the Delaware camp.

The following day Magua and a group of his warriors visited the Delawares in search of their prisoners. The chief of that tribe decided the Hurons had a just claim to Cora because Magua wished to make her his wife.

Under inviolable Indian custom, the Huron was permitted to leave the camp unmolested, but Uncas warned him that in a few hours he and the Delawares would follow his trail.

During a bloody battle Magua fled with Cora to the top of a cliff. There, pursued by Uncas, he stabbed and killed the young Mohican, and was in his turn sent to his death by a bullet from Hawkeye's long rifle. Cora, too, was killed by a Huron. Amid deep mourning by the Delawares, she and Uncas were laid in their graves in the forest. Colonel Munro and Heyward conducted Alice to English territory and safety. Hawkeye returned to the forest. He had promised to remain with his sorrowing friend Chingachgook forever.

THE LAST OF THE VIKINGS

Type of work: Novel
Author: Johan Bojer (1872-   )
Type of plot: Regional realism
Time of plot: Early nineteenth century
Locale: Norway
First published: 1921

Principal characters:
KRISTÀVER MYRAN, owner of the fishing boat *Seal*
LARS, his son
ELEZEUS HYLLA,
HENRY RABBEN,
KANELES GOMON, and
ARNT AWSON, fishermen with Kristàver
PETER SUZANSA, owner of the *Sea-fire*
JACOB DAMNIT-ALL-WITH-A LIMP, owner of the *Sea-bird*

Critique:

The Last of the Vikings tells the story of a Lofoten fisherman, Kristàver Myran, as simply as Knut Hamsun tells the story of Isak, the farmer and builder in *Growth of the Soil*. Both types are obsolete in the modern world since the fisherman now goes to sea in a motor-driven ship and the farmer has little new land to break to his plow, but both characters are powerfully drawn. It is hard to forget the rigors of the Lofoten fishing season after reading about Kristàver and his crew. The novel is as simple in design and style as it is compelling in its picture of people, local in time and place, but universal in their qualities of courage and endurance.

The Story:

When Kristàver Myran brought home his own Lofoten boat, his oldest son Lars was tall and strong enough to join the next fishing trip to the islands off the coast of Norway. Lofoten men thought of their boats as descendants of dragon-prowed Viking ships, and Lars dreamed that he was an early Norseman who would do battle when the time came to sail north.

Kristàver had bought the *Seal* cheaply at auction, though even that low price was more than he could pay without guarantors. People said he must want to die early, to have bought that boat which had capsized during the last three winters. Kristàver was sure he could tame her.

His crew consisted of Lars; Elezeus Hylla, a brother-in-law; Henry Rabben, who was always combing his beard; Kaneles Gomon, boyish except for his yellow mustache; and Arnt Awson, a shoreman who had never before sailed on a Lofoten boat. The boats to travel with them were Peter Suzansa's *Sea-fire*, Andreas Ekra's *Storm-bird*, and Jacob Damnit-all-with-a-limp's *Sea-bird*. Kristàver has some trouble keeping the *Seal* up with the other boats as they sailed through the fjord to the open sea. As he and the rest lay in the long bunk on deck after their first day's sailing, he slept, but even in sleep he was working on his problem. Half-awake, he got up and moved some of the cargo back a few yards. The next day the boat, in better humor, pleased Kristàver's crew as she plowed steadily past the other boats. For days they sailed through the snow and anchored at night. The men began to look alike, snow-covered, and to learn to stand wind and cold.

As they passed Helgeland, the Nordland boats came out to join them. Soon the waters were covered with sailing ships and a few steamers. Held over by the weather at Bodö, Jacob was nearly killed in a fight. Henry Rabben carried him on board and the next day Jacob was sailing along with the rest. Whenever the Southlanders met the Nordlanders, there was likely to be a fight in which everybody joined.

One day, across the West Fjord, they sighted Lofoten, a long chain of snow-streaked mountains. At the foot of the mountain wall lay the fishing station from which rose the odor of fish-oil, pitch, and fish. Peter's crew and Kristàver's were to share a hut there for the winter.

When the Inspector raised the signal-flag for the first sea-going day, everybody was ready to head for the banks. It was a great day when they first put out the nets. Each man knew that only plenty of cod in those nets could make it worth while to bear the wind, snow, and sea for months in that frozen place. The first day's catch was poor, and the men were discouraged when bad weather kept them imprisoned at the station. They slept all day. When it was time for supper, each man went to his own chest to take out the flat bread, cheese, and butter his own wife or mother had put in for him; the fishermen felt that they were paying a short visit home. After the storm they found their nets torn and tangled; a bad beginning.

When the cod came, there was no time for rest. The men pulled on their nets and filled their boats until they lay far down in the water. There was hardly time to rest after cleaning the fish before Kristàver had the men out for the next day's fishing. Even with their big woolen gloves, their hands were rubbed raw, and ice clung to their clothes. But, with fourteen hundred cod in a day, each man figured he would be wealthy by spring. They worked until Saturday night, when they dropped into a heavy sleep that lasted until dark on Sunday. Then, rousing themselves, they called for "Melja," a dish fit for a wedding. They broke flat bread, put boiled fish-liver over it, then grated goat's milk cheese, and long streams of treacle. They had lived on coffee and bread for so long they could not get enough "Melja," and Henry Rabben had to make more and more for them.

Lars was not yet a full-fledged Lofoten man; he was a "scaurie" until he stood treat. To save him embarrassment, his father gave him money to buy French brandy for all who came to the hut. Then he could hold up his head among the fishermen.

As the fishing slackened, the men began to wonder whether this would be a golden year after all. After weeks passed with no cod running, Kristàver listened to the inner voice that had led him right before; this time it told him to turn east. He spoke to Peter about it and then led his men silently down to the *Seal* at night to row away. As dawn came, they saw a host of boats coming out of harbors, all hurrying as though they had news of fish. Then they saw a whale spouting. Where there is a whale, there are herring; where there are herring, there are cod.

After the whale had been driven into a fjord, trouble began because the steamers came and blocked the entrance to keep the fishermen out. The fishermen, seeing shoals of fish just inside the fjord, were frantic to get them. The cod were gold just outside their reach. Men cannot stand back under such circumstances, and so they began to fight the men on the steamers. Driven back by streams of boiling water from hoses, the fishermen were about to give up when Kaneles swam under the steamer and came up on the other side to turn the hoses on the steamer men. Then the fight started all over the ships until the fishermen drove their little boats past the steamers. Soon the fjord was packed with boats. The fish were so thick that nets filled immediately, but the boats were so close that the nets fouled. Not until the next day, when the Inspector brought law into the fjord, could the fishermen pull in their nets. Then Arnt came into his own. He built a cabin on the shore so that Kristàver's men would not freeze while they slept at night. Elezeus was nearly frozen that first night and he never recovered, but Henry Rabben gave him the sacrament and he died in peace.

Sailing back to the fishing station, the Seal heeled over in a storm. Kaneles was knocked unconscious, but Kristàver held him while the others clung to the keel.

Peter Suzansa, in the Sea-fire, was swept by them in the storm. Jacob Damnit-all-with-a-limp was able to tack around and drive his boat over the keel while his own men pulled in the survivors, all but Kaneles.

When his boat was recovered after the storm, Kristàver put his new mast four inches farther aft than it had been before. After that he was able to make her stand up. When he sailed home in the fair spring winds, he felt that she was a Viking ship and he a chieftain.

1975

THE LAST PURITAN

Type of work: Novel
Author: George Santayana (1863-1952)
Type of plot: Social criticism
Time of plot: Early twentieth century
Locale: Connecticut, Massachusetts, England
First published: 1936

Principal characters:
OLIVER ALDEN, the last puritan
PETER ALDEN, his father
HARRIET ALDEN, his mother
FRAULEIN IRMA SCHLOTE, Oliver's governess
JIM DARNLEY, Oliver's friend
ROSE DARNLEY, Jim's sister
MARIO VAN DE WEYER, Oliver's cousin
EDITH VAN DE WEYER, another cousin
BOBBY, Jim's illegitimate son

Critique:

Although he is best known as a philosopher and essayist, George Santayana has invaded the field of fiction with great success. *The Last Puritan* is his first novel; but, unlike most first novels, it is the work of a mature mind. In the story of Oliver Alden, Santayana has given us a character sketch of an almost extinct type of American, a puritan.

The Story:

Young Peter Alden was educated in America but left Harvard before he had completed his studies and went abroad with a tutor. After he had come of age and had inherited his money he wandered aimlessly about the world, studying occasionally. He was in his early middle years before he completed any one course. Licensed to practice medicine, his practice was limited to himself, for he had burdened himself with many ills, some real but most of them imaginary. Once he consulted Dr. Bumstead, a psychiatrist whose main concern was Peter's money. Dr. Bumstead convinced Peter that a home and a wife would be the best treatment possible and, as a consequence, Peter married the doctor's daughter Harriet. Oliver was their only child.

Little Oliver was a puritan from the beginning. He accepted things as they were, never complaining, never wondering why. There were no other children with whom he could play because his mother feared that other children might be dirty or vulgar. And there were no stories, songs, or prayers for the boy, as Mrs. Alden would not have him filled with nonsensical ideas. His father was no more than a polite stranger to little Oliver, for he spent most of his time traveling about the world.

Fraulein Irma Schlote, a German, became Oliver's governess, and from her he had what little brightness there was in his childhood. On their long walks together, Irma instilled in Oliver his first love of nature and a love for the German language. But even with Irma, Oliver remained a stoical little puritan. If he were tired or his foot hurt, there was no use to complain. They had come for a walk, and they must finish that walk. One must do his duty, even an unpleasant one. As he grew older, Oliver hated human weakness with the hatred of a true puritan.

When Oliver was fifteen, he went to high school, where he excelled in scholarship and in athletics because it was his duty to keep his body strong and because it was his duty to do everything that the school demanded.

During one holiday season Oliver joined his father on his yacht. There he met Jim Darnley, the captain, who had been a British sailor before he became involved in a scandal. Jim was an entirely new type of person in Oliver's world. Oliver knew that the sailor was worldly and had no sense of duty, but strangely enough Oliver was always to consider Jim his dearest friend.

After his graduation from high school, Oliver joined his father and Jim in England. There, while visiting Jim's family, he learned to respect Jim's minister father and to enjoy the company of Rose, Jim's young sister. He learned also that Jim had an illegitimate child, Bobby, who lived with Mrs. Bowler, his tavern-keeping mother.

While in England, Oliver also met his distant cousin, Mario Van de Weyer, a worldly young man dependent upon his rich relatives for his education and livelihood. Mario also puzzled Oliver. Mario had nothing, not even much real intelligence, yet he was happy. Oliver, who had everything, was not consciously happy; he merely lived as he felt it his duty to live.

Before they left England, Oliver's father committed suicide. He felt that Oliver needed to be free of him and as much as possible of his own mother. Rather than see the boy torn between his conflicting duties to both parents, Peter took his own life.

Back in America, Oliver entered Williams College. While playing football, he broke his leg. In the infirmary he was visited by his cousin Mario and another cousin, Edith Van de Weyer. Mario, who attended Harvard on Oliver's money, seemed to feel no reluctance about living extravagantly on his cousin's bounty. Oliver began to think of Edith as a possible wife. Like his father, he did not consider love an important element in marriage, but he felt it his duty to marry and have children.

In his last year of college, Oliver transferred to Harvard University. There he spent much time with Mario, until that young man was forced to leave college because he had been found in his room with a young woman. When he went to Edith's home to tell her about Mario, Oliver found that Edith's family had already heard the story from Mario and had forgiven him. Oliver also learned that Edith had great affection for Mario. But because he thought a match between himself and Edith a sensible one, he proposed to her anyway, forgetting to mention love. Edith refused him. She knew that marriage with Oliver would be a dutiful experience only, and she wanted more than duty.

When he had finished college, Oliver took a cruise around the world. Then he settled in England and lived for a time near Jim Darnley's family. War was coming closer, but Oliver felt no duty toward either side. Mario enlisted at once, for Mario was romantic. The war became more personal for Oliver when he learned that Jim had been killed. Jim's death seemed proof of war's useless waste. More practically, Jim's death meant that Bobby and Rose were now Oliver's responsibility.

When the United States entered the war, Oliver felt that it was his duty to go home and join the army. After his training he was sent to France. Before he went to the front, he wrote to Rose Darnley, asking her to marry him at once, so that she would be his wife and would be cared for if he were killed. But Rose, like Edith, wanted love, and she refused to marry him. She knew, too, that Oliver should never marry, because love should be unreasoning and illogical at times, conditions which Oliver could never accept.

After Rose's refusal, Oliver seemed free for the first time. No one needed him any longer. Jim was dead. Mario was in the army and provided for in case of Oliver's death. Bobby had been made secure financially. Edith was engaged to be married. Rose was provided for in Oliver's will. All his life he had acted in accordance with duty, in his parental relations, in school, in the army. At least he would not be a dutiful husband. Now he need be true only to himself. That night he slept peacefully.

Oliver was killed, but not in battle. He was a post-Armistice casualty, the victim of a motorcycle accident. His will told the story of his life. He had left adequate, but not extravagant, provisions for Mario, Rose, Mrs. Darnley, Fraulein Irma, and Bobby. The bulk of his fortune he left to his mother because he had believed it his duty to provide for her.

So Oliver Alden ended his life a true puritan, doing what must be done without flinching, taking little pleasure in worldly things, yet not withdrawing from the world. He did not believe in puritanism, for he knew that those who lived selfishly were often more happy than he. He was not a prig. He had been a puritan in spite of himself, and for that reason, perhaps, the last true puritan.

THE LAST TYCOON

Type of work: Novel
Author: F. Scott Fitzgerald (1896-1940)
Type of plot: Social criticism
Time of plot: The 1930's
Locale: Hollywood
First published: 1941

> *Principal characters:*
> MONROE STAHR, a film producer
> KATHLEEN MOORE, his mistress
> PAT BRADY, Stahr's partner
> CECILIA BRADY, his daughter

Critique:

This unfinished novel is perhaps the most highly regarded fragment in American literature, for in it Fitzgerald's prose is said to have achieved its greatest power, flexibility, and economy. As edited by Edmund Wilson, *The Last Tycoon* has six completed chapters (about half the book), a summary conclusion, and a selection of the author's notes; but since Fitzgerald was a painstaking reviser, it is by no means certain that the completed chapters are in their final form. Nevertheless, it is clear that the heart of the novel is the deathly tired Stahr's poignant love affair with Kathleen. Of considerable technical interest is the use of Cecilia as a narrator who is allowed to imagine fully events she does not actually witness.

The Story:

Cecilia Brady was flying to California for a summer vacation from college. On the plane she met Wylie White, an alcoholic screenwriter, and Schwartz, a ruined producer. Monroe Stahr, the partner of Cecilia's father, was also aboard, though traveling as Mr. Smith. When the plane was grounded at Nashville, Schwartz sent a note to Stahr, warning him about Pat Brady, Cecilia's father. When the plane took off again, Schwartz stayed behind and committed suicide.

Stahr had been the boy wonder of the film industry. He had been in charge of the studio in his twenties, almost dead from overwork at thirty-five. Indeed, he was half in love with death for the sake of his dead wife, Minna Davis, a great star with whom he had been deeply in love. Since her death he had increased his work load, often remaining in his office around the clock. In contrast to Stahr's highly developed sense of responsibility, Brady was mean and selfish. Lacking taste and understanding little of the technical end of the industry, Brady had acquired his share of the studio through luck and had retained it through shrewdness.

One night, while Cecilia was visiting the studio, there was an earthquake. Stahr, working with his trouble-shooter, Robinson, to clear away the mess, saw a sightseer perched on top of a floating idol. The girl reminded him of his dead wife, and he tried to discover her identity. That night Cecilia also fell in love with Stahr, but she felt that her attachment was hopeless.

A self-made, paternalistic employer, Stahr personally managed almost every detail at the studio, from picking the stories to passing on the rushes. Though not an educated man, he had raised the artistic level of the movies and did not hesitate to make good pictures that would lose money. As a result he had incurred the distrust of the stockholders, exploiters who saw the movies only as a business. Their distrust, however, was mixed with a genuine respect for the producer's many abilities. In addition to the opposition of the stockholders, Stahr was concerned because Communists were trying to organize the writers; he worked closely with his writers and wanted them to trust him. Wylie White, in particular, enjoyed his favor, although White resented him. At this time White hoped to marry Cecilia for the sake of her father's influence. Typical of Stahr's interest in his employees was his investigation of the attempted suicide of a cameraman, Pete Zavras. Stahr learned that Zavras had been unable to find work because of a rumor that he was going blind. Stahr was able to scotch the rumor by providing Zavras with a statement from an oculist.

By this time Stahr had succeeded in locating the girl who resembled his wife. She was Kathleen Moore. Though she was at first reluctant to meet him, they later had a brief, passionate affair. Stahr learned that she had been the mistress of a deposed monarch who had undergone a personality deterioration and that now she was about to marry an American who had rescued her from that situation. Stahr realized that marriage to Kathleen could give him the will to go on living. While he hesitated, her fiancé arrived ahead of schedule, and she went through with the marriage from a sense of obligation.

Cecilia, knowing nothing of these matters, was still desperately hoping to attract Stahr, her pull toward him increased by a break with her father after she had discovered him with his nude secretary. At Stahr's request she arranged a meeting with a Communist organizer. Then Stahr got drunk and tried to beat him up.

At this point the manuscript ends, but the rest of the story may be pieced together from the author's notes. Because the studio had been in financial difficulties, Brady had tried to push through a wage cut. Stahr, opposing this plan, had gone east to convince the other stockholders to postpone the wage slash. Brady cut the salaries and betrayed the writers while Stahr was sick in Washington. Although he broke with Brady after that, Stahr agreed to go along with Brady's plan for a company union, chiefly because Stahr felt personally responsible for the welfare of his employees. Wylie White had also turned on Stahr.

In the meantime Kathleen and Stahr resumed their relationship. When Brady tried to blackmail Stahr, the producer threatened him with some information about the death of Brady's wife. At one time Fitzgerald had considered having Brady persuade Robinson to undertake Stahr's murder; however, Fitzgerald rejected this idea in favor of having Brady inform Kathleen's husband, a movie technician involved with the union organizers, of Kathleen's affair with Stahr. An alienation-of-affection suit resulted from that, but Stahr was somehow saved by Zavras, the cameraman.

Stahr became alienated from Kathleen and was no longer able to dominate his associates at the studio. Nevertheless, he continued to oppose Brady. Finally Stahr felt that he had to eliminate Brady before Brady had him killed. After hiring gangsters to murder Brady, Stahr flew east to provide himself with an alibi; but he changed his mind on the plane and decided to call off the killers at the next airport. The plane crashed before he could carry out his intention.

Fitzgerald was uncertain about including an episode in which the plane's wreckage was plundered by three children who discovered it, the idea being that each child's personality was reflected by the items he stole. Stahr's funeral would have been a powerful, detailed, ironic arraignment of Hollywood sham. It would have included the incident of a has-been cowboy actor who was invited to be a pallbearer by mistake and consequently enjoyed a return of good fortune.

Cecilia later had an affair, probably with Wylie White, and then suffered a complete breakdown. At the end of the novel the reader was to learn that she was telling the story while a patient in a tuberculosis sanitorium.

THE LATE GEORGE APLEY

Type of work: Novel
Author: John P. Marquand (1893-1960)
Type of plot: Simulated biography
Time of plot: Late nineteenth and early twentieth centuries
Locale: Boston
First published: 1937

Principal characters:
GEORGE APLEY, a proper Bostonian
JOHN, his son
ELEANOR, his daughter
CATHARINE, his wife
MR. WILLING, George Apley's biographer

Critique:

Satire has been said to require the utmost of great minds. In a sense it requires a man to have two visions: one of society as it might be and one as it is. The range between those two points offers the opportunity for satirical comparisons. In The Late George Apley the satire is double-edged because of the method of telling the story. The novel is sub-titled "A Novel in the Form of a Memoir." Mr. Willing, the supposed biographer of these memoirs, is as much a source of satire as George Apley himself, for without Mr. Willing, the staid, polished, and politely-dull annotator, the book would be only one more realistic novel.

The Story:

George William Apley was born on Beacon Hill, on January 25, 1866. The Apleys were an old family in Massachusetts. Thomas, known in the old records as Goodman Apley, had emigrated from England to America and settled in Roxbury in 1636. Goodman Apley's son, John, had graduated from Harvard in 1662. From his time there had been an Apley in Harvard in each succeeding generation. John Apley's son, Nathaniel, established himself in Boston. A later Apley, Moses, became a shipping master and laid the foundation of the Apley fortune. Moses Apley was George Apley's grandfather.

George Apley grew up in a quiet atmosphere of wealth and social position. He learned his parents' way of living calmly and with fortitude. In an orderly way he was introduced to the polite world, at first through visits to relatives; later, through study at Harvard.

His Harvard days were probably the high point of his life. He was sent to Harvard to weld those qualities of gentlemanly behavior which private grammar school and parents together had tried to encourage. His parents were anxious that he should make friends with the right people. George was carefully instructed in the ways of high-minded gentlemen. His training was indicated by a theme in which he wrote a description of a Boston brothel in terms expressing his repulsion and shock. In the gymnasium George won distinction as a boxer. Moreover, he became a member of the Board of the Harvard Lampoon. He was taken into the Club, an honor his father appreciated greatly. In his junior and senior years he took part in the musical extravaganzas of the Hasty Pudding Club. In spite of these activities he never neglected his studies and he was known as a respectable student with grades placing him in the middle of his class at graduation.

While in college, he fell in love with

an impossible girl, Mary Monahan. The affair was cut short by the Apleys and never referred to publicly. Shortly thereafter his family prescribed a sea voyage for him. When he returned home he took up the study of law, and became a member of the board for the Boston Waifs' Society.

George was instructed in the shrewd businesslike manners and knowledge of tne Apleys. He was sent to work with his Uncle William for one summer. William sensed that his nephew would never make a good businessman and advised that George should be put into law or made a trustee of other peoples' money, not his own. As a result George, like many of his friends, never went actively into business, but spent his lifetime clipping coupons.

In February, 1890, George followed his parents' wishes and suitably became engaged to Catharine Bosworth. Both his father-in-law and his own father saw to it that the young couple had a summer cottage and a house for the winter. The two mothers were equally solicitous. George discovered that he had married not only Catharine but also her family.

As the years passed, George devoted his time to charitable groups, learned societies, and to writing for his clubs. One of his papers, "Jonas Good and Cow Corner," was said to be among the best papers read before the Browsers in fifty years.

His first child's name was a subject for debate in his own and Catharine's family. The name, John, common to both families, was finally chosen. His second child was a daughter, Eleanor.

Shortly after his sister Amelia's marriage, George's father died of an apoplectic stroke. He left a million dollars to Harvard, other large sums to his charities, and the remainder of his fortune in trust for his family. George had to pay a sum of money to a woman who claimed she had borne a son to his father. Although he did not believe the charge, he paid rather than cause scandal in the

family.

George invested in a place known as Pequod Island and there he took his friends when he wanted to get away from Boston. On the island he and his friends condescended to share the campfire with their guides. Planned as a male retreat, the island was soon overrun with literary lights of the times invited by George's wife and sister.

As his son grew up, George noted an increasing desire on the part of the younger generation to be wild and careless with money. Later, George began to realize that he and his generation had let much slip and that Boston was going to the Irish. He gave his name to the "Save Boston Association" as he considered his membership an Apley duty. He also interested himself in bird lore and philosophy and took as much personal concern as possible in the affairs of his children. When his mother died in 1908, George counted her death one of his most poignant tragedies.

When George's son entered Harvard, George took a new interest in the university and noted many changes he did not like.

Old Uncle William, now over eighty, still controlled the Apley mills and held out successfully against the new labor unions. One day the old man shocked his family by marrying his nurse, a Miss Prentiss.

His daughter Eleanor's marriage was completely unsatisfactory to George because she did not induce her husband to give up his job for a position in the Apley mills and to take up residence near her family. But George was proud of his son John for his service at the front. George himself belonged to the Home Guards. When John married a girl of good connections after the war, George was doubly pleased.

At last George came into opposition with a man named O'Reilly, whom George planned to have brought before criminal court on charges of extortion. However,

O'Reilly tricked George into a scandal. George intended to have the whole case cleared in court, but before the trial he received a note from his one-time sweetheart, Mary Monahan. After an interview with her, he settled the case quietly and bought off his opponents.

In 1928 he became a grandfather. As soon as the baby had been born, Georg telegraphed Groton to include his grand son's name among the entrance ap plicants.

In his last years George took interest in the new novels, condemning those too blatant in their description of sex and fighting against the inclusion of some of them in the Boston libraries. His own copy of *Lady Chatterly's Lover* he hid in the silver safe to keep his daughter from seeing it. He defied pro hibition as an abuse of his rights and kept a private bootlegger on principle because he thought it important to help break the prohibition law.

He thought, too, that the colossal fortunes being gathered by the unedu cated should be handed over to the gov ernment. In the autumn of 1929 he and his wife made a trip to Rome, where they visited Horatio Apley, recently ap pointed to a diplomatic post there. George was absent from America when the stock market crash came. His financial affairs did not suffer greatly, but, his health breaking, he began to plan his will and his funeral.

George Apley died in December, 1933.

THE LATE MATTIA PASCAL

Type of work: Novel
Author: Luigi Pirandello (1867-1936)
Type of plot: Psychological realism
Time of plot: Early twentieth century
Locale: Italy
First published: 1904

Principal characters:
MATTIA PASCAL, a young Italian
ROBERTO PASCAL, his brother
ROMILDA PESCARONE, Mattia's wife
MALAGNA, manager of the Pascal estates
ADRIANA, a young girl in love with Mattia

Critique:

Outside of Italy, Pirandello has been much better known for his dramas than for his novels, although his fiction has always been highly regarded in his native land. In this particular case, part of the plot of the novel was also used in a play, as the first part of the novel formed the basis for Pirandello's Sicilian comedy, Liola. When the novel appeared, some critics objected to it, saying that the action was impossible in terms of real life. In 1921, Pirandello wrote a preface to the book in which he pointed out that a similar happening had actually occurred in Buffalo, New York, in that same year. He went on to state that it was his opinion this type of criticism should not be used in evaluating a work of the creative imagination; he said that the novel, like any other medium of art, dealt not with individuals but with mankind and all of the incidents and individuals which make up the total composite of man. He felt that the illusion of the present might very possibly be the reality of the future.

The Story:

As boys, Mattia Pascal and his brother Roberto lived an easy life with their wealthy widowed mother. While the boys were growing up, however, the fortune their merchant father had left them was gradually acquired by a dishonest man named Malagna, to whom the moth-er confided all her business affairs. One by one the farms and city property belonging to the Pascals were mortgaged and then sold. Everyone except the widow Pascal realized how dishonest Malagna was. Her confidence in her agent enabled him to rob her of everything over a period of many years.

When he was in his teens, Mattia Pascal fell in love with a beautiful young girl, Romilda Pescarone. Unfortunately for the affair, Malagna, whose two wives had failed to give him any children, had his eye on Romilda for himself. A bad situation developed when Romilda became pregnant; her mother, a termagant who seized any opportunity to improve her position, saw a chance to capitalize on the evil. She advised Romilda to take Malagna as her lover and let him think the child was his. The mother thought that he would be so happy to have his impotence seemingly disproved that he would at least make Romilda, her mother, and the child very comfortable.

Although Romilda told Malagna the truth, the two kept the whole affair a secret. Malagna's wife discovered, through Mattia Pascal, what had happened. In revenge on her husband, whom she had suspected of playing her false, she in turn became pregnant by Mattia. The husband, realizing what had happened as soon as his wife told him of her pregnancy, was furious. In his anger he refused to help Romilda, saying it was bad enough that he should be compelled to support one of Mattia Pascal's bastards. In a way the prospect pleased him, for the Pascal fortune he had stolen would now go eventually to Mattia's child by Malagna's wife.

Mattia and Romilda were married, but their marriage was a most unhappy one. Because Malagna had foreclosed on the last bit of property owned by the Pascals, the newlyweds and Mattia's mother were forced to move into the hovel owned by Romilda's mother. Mattia's aunt finally took pity on his mother and took her away, but Mattia, who was unable to find a job, and his wife continued to live with his shrewish mother-in-law. Their situation was relieved somewhat by Mattia's success in getting a political appointment as the caretaker of a municipal library in the town. The post was a sinecure; Mattia spent most of his time reading and catching rats that infested the place.

Mattia's mother and his child both died suddenly and within a day of one another. A few days after his mother's burial Mattia received several hundred lire from his brother, who had married into a rich family. The funeral expenses were already paid for and Mattia put the money away. One day he suddenly decided to travel. He took the money his brother had sent and went to Monte Carlo. There he won a fortune. Although he lost most of it again, he stopped playing after seeing the corpse of a destitute young gambler who had shot himself.

On his way home with the eighty-two thousand lire he had won, Mattia read in a newspaper an account of his death and burial. The people in his village, it appeared, had discovered a body some days after his secret departure, and his relatives had identified it as his. When the shock of the story wore off, Mattia realized how lucky he was: he had been released suddenly from an unhappy mar-

riage and a mountain of debts; in addition, he had enough money in his pockets to live comfortably for many years.

Instead of going back to his native village, Mattia went to Rome and assumed a new identity. He shaved off his beard, had his hair cut shorter, and called himself Adriano Meis. The only part of his appearance he could not change was a crossed eye; to disguise that identifying characteristic, he began wearing dark glasses.

As Adriano Meis, Mattia rented a room in a private home and spent his days walking and reading. But he gradually discovered that his lack of a past was bothersome; he hated to live a literal lie. He discovered also that without an official record, any proof of identity, he was limited in his activities. He could not even buy a dog, lest he get into trouble in buying a license for it. At the same time he could not afford to have his real identity become known because he would be sent to prison for deserting his wife and evading his debts. Most discouraging of all, he fell in love with the daughter of his landlord, a girl named Adriana. He could not marry her, however, for he could not prove his own existence. His life was that of a shadow in the world of men.

The circumstance which finally convinced him that he could not go on masquerading as Adriano Meis was the theft of twelve thousand lire by his landlord's son-in-law. Everyone knew that the man had taken the money, but the victim was unable to go to the police, for fear they would investigate him and ask embarrassing questions. When he did not go to the police, everyone became suspicious, even the girl who loved him. Mattia took his money one evening and wandered about town while he tried to decide what to do with himself. He realized that his position was untenable; he could not go on living as he had.

As he was about to leap into the river and commit suicide, Mattia had a brilliant idea. Deciding to die as Adriano Meis and return to his identity as Mattia Pascal, he left his hat and other evidence to make it seem as if Adriano Meis had jumped into the river. Within a day or two the newspapers carried accounts of the suicide of Adriano Meis. Quite happy to regain his original identity, Mattia went to visit his brother Roberto. At his brother's home Mattia learned that Romilda had married a childhood sweetheart and had had a child. Mattia was even more disconcerted to learn that he would have to take his wife and her mother back again. According to the law, his return from the dead voided the second marriage.

Disturbed by that news, Mattia returned to his native village. There he found his wife and her new husband quite happy and his hateful mother-in-law alive. In spite of the law they all decided that it was best for the current arrangements to continue, and so Mattia relinquished unofficially his marital rights and responsibilities. He found himself some rooms in the village and lived there quietly, spending his days reading and preparing an account of his strange adventures, a story which was to be published after what he termed his third and final death.

LAVENGRO

Type of work: Novel
Author: George Henry Borrow (1803-1881)
Type of plot: Simulated autobiography
Time of plot: Nineteenth century
Locale: England, Scotland, Ireland
First published: 1851

> *Principal characters:*
> LAVENGRO, a scholar, journalist, and tinker
> JOHN, his brother
> JASPER PETULENGRO, his gipsy friend
> MRS. HERNE, an old crone
> THE FLAMING TINMAN, a bully of the roads
> ISOPEL BERNERS, Lavengro's companion
> PETER WILLIAMS, an evangelist
> WINIFRED, his wife

Critique:

Lavengro; The Scholar—The Gipsy—The Priest is a long novel, in part fiction and in part the autobiography of its eccentric author, which gives an interesting and unusual picture of England during the early part of the last century. The autobiographical method of the narrative has aroused the interest of scholars as to what is fact in the book and what is pure imagination. To the general reader, *Lavengro* is most interesting for its accounts of nomadic gipsy life and character studies of tinkers, beggars, and thieves who roamed the English highways more than a hundred years ago.

The Story:

Lavengro was the son of an army officer who had fought against Napoleon, and the boy spent his early years at army garrisons in various parts of England, Scotland, Ireland, and Wales. When he was six years old, Lavengro discovered *Robinson Crusoe,* a book which stimulated his imagination and aroused in him a desire to read and to study languages. One day, wandering on the outskirts of a garrison town, he met a group of gipsies who threatened to do him harm. They drew back, however, when he showed them a tame snake which he was carrying. The gipsies, becoming friendly, nicknamed him Sapengro, or snake tamer. A young gipsy named Jasper declared that

they would always be brothers. He met also at the gipsy camp a Romany whom he saw hanged fifteen years later at Newgate.

A few years later he began the study of Latin. About the same time his father was ordered to Edinburgh. In Scotland, Lavengro took part in several bickers, or fights, with his schoolmates and learned mountain climbing. Then in 1815 his father was ordered to Ireland. Lavengro went to a seminary at Clonmel and studied more Latin and Greek and, in an incidental fashion, learned to speak Irish. His brother John was made an ensign and transferred to a post some few miles away. After peace was signed with the French, opportunities for military employment were few. John had always wanted to paint; therefore, his father allowed him to go to London to study his art.

Lavengro again met Jasper, his gipsy friend, and discovered that Jasper's last name was Petulengro. Jasper was now a Romany Kral—or gipsy king—a horseshoer, pugilist, jockey, and soothsayer. Through Jasper, Lavengro made the acquaintance of a malignant old crone named Herne, who hated him because she believed that he was stealing the Romany tongue. It was Jasper who named him Lavengro, which means "word-master," because he learned the gipsy language so rapidly. All of the gipsies departed for London, except Mrs. Herne, who went to Yorkshire. Lavengro remained at home with his parents while his father tried to decide what to do with him. It was finally agreed that Lavengro would enter a solicitor's office to study law. But Lavengro neglected his Blackstone while he studied Welsh and translated the poetry of Ab Gwilym. About the same time, Lavengro obtained a Danish book and learned to read it by first studying the Danish Bible. One day Lavengro was sent to deliver a thousand pounds to a magistrate with whom he had a very entertaining conversation concerning the manly art of self-defense. In spite of the magistrate's fondness for boxing, however, he refused a place on his land for a match.

Lavengro met Jasper again and put on the gloves with him for a friendly bout. Later he returned home and discovered that his father was seriously ill. His brother John also arrived home just before his father died. Shortly afterward Lavengro went to London to seek his fortune as a writer, taking with him a letter of introduction to a noted publisher. The publisher seemed delighted to be able to employ him, but was not interested in such things as Lavengro's translations of the songs of Ab Gwilym and his translations of Danish songs. Lavengro was informed that the reading public scoffed at works like these. Instead, the publisher recommended a story somewhat along the line of The Dairyman's Daughter.

While walking through Cheapside one day, Lavengro climbed upon the balustrade of a bridge in order to see something below. An old woman selling apples nearby thought he was trying to commit suicide and begged him not to fling himself over. The old lady had a partiality for a book about the "blessed" Mary Flanders. Lavengro returned from time to time to see her and to talk with her.

Lavengro, invited to dinner at the publisher's house one Sunday, discovered that the publisher did not believe in eating meat or drinking wine. After dinner Lavengro heard what was to be his new assignment since the publisher had now decided not to publish anything like The Dairyman's Daughter. He was to prepare a collection of the stories of the lives and trials of famous criminals incarcerated at Newgate. In addition, he was to translate the publisher's book of philosophy into German and to write an article about it for the Review.

In the company of an acquaintance named Francis Ardry, Lavengro visited many of the underworld spots of London and this experience, together with the series on criminals which he was preparing, gave him a wide and practical knowledge of the underworld. Then Lavengro's brother came to London and introduced him to a painter of the heroic. The peculiar thing about this painter's pictures was the short legs of the people in his paintings. When Lavengro's stories of crime were finished, he took them to the publisher. But the publisher was displeased because Lavengro had omitted several of the publisher's favorite criminal histories.

Lavengro went to visit the apple-woman again and his despondent appearance led her to think that he had been caught stealing. The apple-woman never became aware of Lavengro's profession. He talked her into letting him read her cherished copy of the life of Mary Flanders.

The publisher's speculations failed and left Lavengro without money, but Lavengro finally obtained all the wages that were due him. Taggart, the publisher's assistant, told Lavengro that Glorious John, another printer, would publish his ballads and the songs of Ab Gwilym. But Lavengro never offered his ballads to Glorious John. In midwinter he went again to visit the apple-woman and found that she had moved her stall to the other side of the bridge. He promised to take her book and trade it in for a Bible. However, he lost the book and had nothing to trade. He decided to purchase a Bible and never let her know about his negligence.

About this time Lavengro saved an Armenian from pickpockets. The Armenian wished him to translate some Armenian fables into English, but Lavengro refused. The Armenian, who had inherited a hundred thousand pounds from his father, was intent upon doubling the amount through his speculation. The Armenian ran into a bit of luck and came into possession of two hundred thousand pounds. Lavengro's advice to the Armenian was to take his fortune and fight the Persians.

Lavengro decided, when his money got short, to do the translations for the Armenian but the man had already departed to invest his money in a war against the Persians.

Lavengro left London after having some small success writing fiction. He met and talked with many and various people on his travels about England. On his rambles he heard the stories concerning the Flaming Tinman, who held a great repute as a fighter and who had forced Jack Slingsby, another tinker, out of business on threats of death. Lavengro met Slingsby and bought him out. He decided to become a tinker himself in the hope of meeting the Flaming Tinman.

One day, while he was mending pots and pans, he encountered Mrs. Herne and Leonora, a thirteen-year-old girl who was traveling with the old woman. Leonora brought him cakes made by Mrs. Herne. He ate one of them and that night became seriously ill. When the evil old crone came to gloat over him, he realized that the cakes had been poisoned. Then the sound of wheels frightened the old woman away, and Lavengro was saved by the timely arrival of Peter Williams, a traveling Welsh preacher, and Winifred, his wife. Peter Williams told Lavengro the sad story of his life

and related how he had been led to commit the sin against the Holy Ghost, a sin for which there was no redemption. Peter had become a preacher to warn other people against the unforgivable sin. Lavengro journeyed with Peter and his wife as far as the Welsh border, where he left them to join Jasper Petulengro and his band of gipsies.

Jasper told Lavengro how Mrs. Herne had hanged herself because of her failure to poison him. Since Jasper was a blood-kinsman of Mrs. Herne, it was required by Romany law that he obtain revenge from Lavengro. Lavengro, however, was really only indirectly responsible for the old woman's death, a fact of which Jasper was well aware. They retired to a place where they could fight, and there Jasper received full satisfaction when he made Lavengro's nose bleed.

Soon after his friendly tussle with Jasper, Lavengro met the Flaming Tinman, Moll, his wife, and Isopel Berners, child of a gipsy mother and a noble father and now a free woman of the roads. Isopel was responsible for Lavengro's victory in a brawl with the Flaming Tinman, for she had told him to use his right hand and to strike at the bully's face. The Flaming Tinman and Moll departed, leaving the territory to Lavengro the tinker, but Isopel remained behind with her belongings. The story of the Flaming Tinman's defeat was soon known throughout the neighborhood, and Lavengro became a hero of the roads. At a public house he met a priest whom he called the Man in Black. He and Lavengro had many conversations concerning religion and the attempt to establish Catholicism as the religion in England.

On a wild stormy night Isopel and Lavengro helped a coachman right his coach which had overturned. Later the coachman told them the story of his life, and his tale was proof that in those days romance journeyed on the highways and adventure waited around the turn of any English lane.

THE LAY OF THE LAST MINSTREL

Type of work: Poem
Author: Sir Walter Scott (1771-1832)
Type of plot: Semihistorical romance
Time of plot: Mid-sixteenth century
Locale: The Scottish Border
First published: 1805

Principal characters:
LADY BUCCLEUCH, widow of the Lord of Branksome
MARGARET, her daughter
THE MASTER OF BUCCLEUCH, her son
LORD CRANSTOUN, Margaret's lover
SIR WILLIAM OF DELORAINE, a knight in Lady Buccleuch's service
THE DWARF, an evil magician
THE GHOST OF MICHAEL SCOTT, a wizard

Critique:

As Scott himself tells us in his introduction to *The Lay of the Last Minstrel,* his purpose was to describe the manners and the scenery of the Scottish Border country during the middle of the sixteenth century. He was concerned more with these than he was with the story itself and often left the narrative for several stanzas in order to portray customs of the Scottish clans. As in his other metrical romances, Scott had here the touch of the artist; the scenes he painted are as real to us as if we were seeing them for ourselves. Scott's ability to tell a picturesque, rousing story in verse is almost as great as his achievement in the novel.

The Story:

As an old minstrel, the last of his kind, wandered through the country, he was treated kindly by a duchess at whose mansion he asked food and shelter. Later he rewarded her by singing a song of days gone by. This is the tale he sang:

Bold Lord Buccleuch had been killed in battle with the English, but his widow and children were well protected in their castle at Branksome by a group of brave knights who had followed their dead leader. Although a truce had been declared, there were skirmishes between the English and the Scots throughout the Border country.

The widow, Lady Buccleuch, was the daughter of a magician; before he died he had taught her to talk with the spirits. One night she heard the spirits predicting that the stars would show no favor to Branksome castle until pride should die and make love free. Lady Buccleuch knew this omen was meant for her, for her daughter Margaret loved the young Lord Cranstoun, who had fought against Lord Buccleuch. But Lady Buccleuch swore that Margaret should never wed a foeman, no matter what the spirits might say. She sent William of Deloraine to Melrose Abbey, there to secure the mystic book of Michael Scott, a wizard long dead and buried in the abbey crypt. She ordered William of Deloraine not to look into the book on peril of his life.

The monk at the abbey, although he quavered at the request made by Deloraine, obeyed without question Lady Buccleuch's command. Leading him deep into the vaults, he took the knight to the wizard's tomb. Deloraine, bravest of knights in battle, shivered with dread as he looked at the body of the magician. The man lay as if he had not been dead a day, and when the knight took the book from his hand, he seemed to frown. As Deloraine left the vault, he heard noises like the laughter and sobbing of fiends.

On the same day, while Deloraine went to the abbey, Margaret slipped out of the castle to meet her lover, Lord

Cranstoun. Cranstoun was accompanied by a Dwarf, who had some time before attached himself to Cranstoun and now would not leave his side. Since the Dwarf served him well, Cranstoun had ceased his efforts to rid himself of the little page. The Dwarf warned the lovers of the approach of a horseman. The traveler was Deloraine, returning from his mission, and while Margaret fled, the two knights battled. Deloraine was seriously wounded. Cranstoun ordered the Dwarf to take Deloraine to Branksome Hall so that his wounds could be properly tended. The Dwarf found the book but could not open it until after he had smeared the cover with the blood of Deloraine, who was almost an infidel. While he was reading one of the spells described in the book, an unseen hand struck him on the cheek and knocked him to the ground. The book snapped shut and could not be opened again. The Dwarf, hiding it under his cloak, proceeded to Branksome Hall with the wounded Deloraine.

At the castle the Dwarf spied the young Master of Buccleuch. Changing himself and the boy into dogs, he led the child into the woods. There, after they had resumed their real shapes, the child was captured by the English soldiers patrolling the Border. At the castle his absence was not known, for the Dwarf returned there and, taking the child's shape, made mischief for everyone. Lady Buccleuch, busy tending the wounds of her faithful Deloraine, failed to notice the child's strange behavior.

Suddenly watchers in the castle sighted signal fires. Their meaning was clear; the English were gathering to attack the Scots. From the castle messengers were sent hurriedly to summon friendly clans of the Border to the defense of Branksome Hall. In the confusion the Dwarf, still in the form of the Master of Buccleuch, escaped from the knight assigned to watch him.

The English, arriving before the castle, made their demands. They wanted Deloraine turned over to them, for they accused him of murdering the brother of one of their group. They also demanded that two hundred English knights be quartered in Branksome, to prevent the Scotsmen from making raids on the English side of the Border. If these demands were not met, they declared, the castle would be stormed and the young heir of Buccleuch, who was held by the English, would be sent to the English court to serve as a page.

Lady Buccleuch would not meet the demands. She could not send her faithful knight to his doom, though her deed might cost her her son, her castle, and perhaps her life. She proposed that Deloraine meet the brother of the slain man in combat and settle the dispute in that knightly fashion. The English leaders, refusing to accept these terms, were preparing to attack the castle when one of their number brought word that strong Scottish clans were approaching the castle. Fearful of a trap, the English agreed to accept the proposal for a settlement by mortal combat between the two knights concerned, or by the wronged man and a substitute for Deloraine should his wounds not be healed by the next day. Then English and Scots joined together in feasting and revelry until the time appointed for the combat.

As the time approached, other knights argued over the right to represent Deloraine, who was still weak from his wounds. But at the last minute Deloraine appeared in full armor, ready to defend himself. The fighting was long and fierce, and both knights lost much blood before the Englishman fell wounded. Deloraine, standing triumphantly over his victim, did not remove his visor. Then the spectators saw with amazement that Deloraine was approaching from the castle. Quickly the supposed Deloraine was uncovered. In his place stood young Lord Cranstoun. He had stolen Deloraine's armor so that he might defend the home and save the brother of Margaret. At first Lady Buccleuch would not greet him, but at last she thought of the prophecy of the spirits and knew that she must forget pride and allow love to prevail. Yielding, she gave her daughter to the knight who had been her husband's enemy. She also swore to herself that she would return the book to Michael Scott's tomb.

At the wedding feast the Dwarf continued to make trouble. In order to undo the mischief he caused, all the minstrels sang songs of days gone past. As the last song died away, the banquet hall grew suddenly dark. A great flash of lightning streaked through the room and struck the Dwarf. The evil page was seen no more. Deloraine was terrified, for in the unearthly light he had seen the shape of the dead wizard. Lady Buccleuch renounced forever the magic of her father, and all the knights made pilgrimages to pray for peace and rest for Michael Scott's soul.

Thus ended the song of the ancient minstrel.

LAZARILLO DE TORMES

Type of work: Novel
Author: Unknown
Type of plot: Picaresque romance
Time of plot: Sixteenth century
Locale: Spain
First published: 1553

Principal character:
LAZARILLO DE TORMES, an adventurer

Critique:

This early work is the first of many picaresque tales. *The Life of Lazarillo de Tormes* antedates Cervantes, and LeSage in *Gil Blas* drew heavily on this entertaining story of a rogue. The narrator, in a series of brief sketches, gives a vivid picture of the stratagems used by the poor merely to stay alive. Without a trace of self-pity he shows us the humorous side of continual penury and want. The tales are scarcely developed into a unified whole. This novel was once credited to the sixteenth-century writer, Diego Hurtado de Mendoza, but his authorship is now regarded as extremely doubtful.

The Story:

Lazarillo's surname came from the peculiar circumstance of his birth. His mother happened to stay the night at the mill where his father was employed. Lazarillo was born on the mill floor just over the river Tormes, after which he was named.

He had reached his ninth year when his father was caught taking flour from customers' sacks. After being soundly punished, the father joined an army getting ready to move against the Moors. He became a mule driver for a gentleman soldier and was killed in action.

Lazarillo's mother opened an eating house near a nobleman's estate. The widow soon made the acquaintance of Zayde, a colored groom who frequently visited them. At first Lazarillo was afraid of the black man, but he quickly learned that Zayde's visits meant food and firewood. One consequence was a bit displeasing: Lazarillo acquired a small, dark brother to look after.

The nobleman's steward began to miss horseshoes and brushes as well as other supplies. When he was asked directly about the thefts, Lazarillo told all he knew of Zayde's peccadillos. Zayde was soundly flogged and boiling fat was poured on his ribs. Lazarillo's mother, to avoid further scandal, set up a new eating house in a different neighborhood.

When Lazarillo was fairly well grown, his mother apprenticed him to a blind man who wanted a boy to lead him about. Though old, the blind man was shrewd and tough. As they were leaving the city, they passed by a stone bull. When the blind man told the boy to put his ear to the statue and listen for a peculiar noise, Lazarillo obeyed. Then the old man knocked the boy's head sharply against the stone, hard enough so his ears rang for three days. Lazarillo was forced to learn a few tricks for himself in order to survive.

The blind man, when they squatted over a fire to cook a meal, kept his hand over the mouth of his wine jug. Lazarillo bored a tiny hole in the jug, and, lying down, let the liquid trickle into his mouth. Then he stopped up the hole with beeswax. But when the suspicious old man felt the jug, the wax had melted and he found the hole. Giving no sign, the next night he again put the jug in front of him and Lazarillo again lay down expecting to guzzle wine once more. Suddenly the blind man raised the jug and brought it down with great force in Lazarillo's face. All the boy's teeth were loosened.

On another occasion Lazarillo seized a roasting sausage from the spit and substituted a rotten turnip. When the blind man bit into his supposed sausage he roared with rage and scratched the boy severely with his long nails. Resolved to leave his master, Lazarillo guided him to the shores of a brook. Telling the blind man he must run and leap, he placed his master behind a stone pillar. The old man gave a mighty jump, cracked his head on the stone, and fell down senseless. Lazarillo left town quickly.

His next master was a penurious priest who engaged him to assist at mass. Unfortunately, the priest watched the collection box like a hawk, and Lazarillo had no chance to filch a single coin. For food, the priest allowed him an onion every fourth day. If it had not been for an occasional funeral feast, the boy would have starved to death.

The priest kept his fine bread securely locked in a chest. Luckily, Lazarillo met a strolling tinker who made him a key. Then to avoid suspicion, he gnawed each loaf to make it look as if rats had got into the chest. The alarmed priest nailed up the holes securely, but Lazarillo made new holes. Then the priest set numerous traps from which Lazarillo ate the cheese. The puzzled priest was forced to conclude that a snake was stealing his bread.

Fearing a search while he was asleep, Lazarillo kept his key in his mouth while he was in bed. One night the key shifted so that he was blowing through the keyhole. The resulting whistle awoke the priest. Seizing a club, he broke it over Lazarillo's head. After his head had been bandaged by a kind neighbor, Lazarillo was dismissed. Thinking to find employment in a larger city, he sought further fortune in Toledo.

One night while his pockets were full of crusts he had begged on the city streets, a careless young dandy, a real esquire, engaged Lazarillo as a servant. Thinking himself lucky to have a wealthy master, Lazarillo followed him to a bare, mean house with scarcely a stick of furniture.

After waiting a long time for a meal, the boy began to eat his crusts. To his surprise his master joined him. So the days went by, both of them living on what Lazarillo could beg.

At last the esquire procured a little money and sent Lazarillo out for bread and wine. On the way he met a funeral procession. The weeping widow loudly lamented her husband and cried out that the dead man was going to an inhospitable house where there was no food or furniture. Thinking they were going to bring the corpse to his esquire's house, Lazarillo ran home in fear. His master disabused him of his fear and sent him back on his errand.

At last the master left town and Lazarillo was forced to meet the bailiffs and the wrathful landlord. After some difficulty he persuaded the bailiffs of his innocence and was allowed to go free.

His next master was a bulero, a dealer in papal indulgences, who was a most accomplished rogue. Rumors began to spread that his indulgences were forged, and even the alguazil accused him publicly of fraud. The wily bulero prayed openly for his accuser to be confounded, and forthwith the alguazil, falling down in a fit, foamed at the mouth and grew rigid. The prayers and forgiveness of the bulero were effective, however, and little by little the alguazil recovered. From that time on the bulero earned a rich harvest selling his papal indulgences. Lazarillo, now wise in roguery, wondered how the bulero worked the trick; but he never found out.

Four years of service with a chaplain who sold water enabled Lazarillo to save a little money and buy respectable clothes. At last he was on his way to some standing in the community. On the strength of his new clothes he was appointed to a government post which would furnish him an income for life. All business matters of the town passed through his hands.

The archpriest of Salvador, seeing how affluent Lazarillo had become, gave him a wife from his own household. The woman made a useful wife, for the archpriest frequently gave them substantial presents. Lazarillo's wife repaid the holy man by taking care of his wardrobe. But evil tongues wagged, and the archpriest asked Lazarillo if he had heard stories about his wife. Lazarillo disclosed that he had been told that his wife had borne three of the archpriest's children. The archpriest advised him sagely to think of his profit more and his honor less. So Lazarillo was content, for surely the archpriest was an honorable man.

Lazarillo was now so influential that it was said that he could commit any crime with impunity. His happiness increased when his wife presented him with a baby daughter. The good lady swore that it was truly Lazarillo's child.

LEAVES OF GRASS

Type of work: Poetry
Author: Walt Whitman (1819-1892)
First published: 1855

The total effect of Walt Whitman's *Leaves of Grass* has been compared to that of a symphony, with interwoven and recurring themes that are scored for a full orchestra, from gentle strings to raucous brass; actually, if one compares his poetry to music, Whitman's work seems closer to a Wagnerian opera, for Wagner employs not only the great melodic themes and the contrast of soft and harsh music but also a human element, the actors and singers on the stage. And while Whitman is famed as a champion of democratic ideas, he rarely presents them in the abstract, rarely strays from the individual man or woman. Even the *en-masse* "I" of his "Song of Myself" becomes particular in the dramatic incidents of the runaway slave who is "limpsy and weak" from his journey, of the woman who peeks from behind the blinds of her windows and mentally projects herself among the twenty-eight young men who splash naked on the seashore, and of the brave captain in the sea battle who has just begun to fight. Whitman is also like Wagner in that his triumphs and failures are similar to those of the composer; both are capable of unmatched eloquence and both fail when they become overblown and pretentious.

So broad is Whitman's scope in *Leaves of Grass* that any short discussion of his work must be divided into compartments (which may be arbitrary and incomplete) or degenerate into random comments. Because of his breadth, Whitman may be considered as four men: philosopher, propagandist, humorist, and poet.

Whitman the Philosopher: In the short poem which opens *Leaves of Grass* Whitman bluntly states the core of his philosophy:

One's-Self I sing—a simple, separate
  Person;

Yet utter the word Democratic, the
  word *En-masse.*

Of Physiology from toe to toe I sing;
Not physiognomy alone, nor brain
  alone, is worthy for the muse—I say
  the Form complete is worthier far;
The Female equally with the male I sing.

O Life immense in passion, pulse, and
  power,
Cheerful—for freest action form'd, under
  the laws divine,
The Modern Man I sing.

Having stated the paradox, the dilemma, Whitman expands upon this theme so persuasively that by the time the reader has finished the volume he accepts the paradox as reasonable and true. In the strident "Song of the Open Road," Whitman seems to emphasize the individual at the expense of society, telling us to throw off all conventions and responsibilities, to strike out on our own:

Afoot and light-hearted I take to the
  open road,
Healthy, free, the world before me,
The long brown path before me, leading wherever I choose.

Henceforth I ask not good fortune—I
  am good fortune,
Henceforth I whimper no more, postpone no more, need nothing,
Strong and content, I travel the open
  road.

The earth—that is sufficient,
I do not want the constellations any
  nearer,
I know they are very well where they
  are,
I know they suffice for those who belong to them.

Still here I carry my old delicious
  burdens,

I carry them, men and women—I carry
them with me wherever I go,
I swear it is impossible for me to get
rid of them,
I am filled with them, and I will fill
them in return.

In "Crossing the Brooklyn Ferry," the
individual merges into crowds that in
turn merge with the stream of life. When
Whitman examines his position in "I
Hear It Was Charged Against Me," he
seems to evade the paradox by proclaiming that he has nothing to do with any
institution except that "of the dear love
of comrades"; but the reader may reflect
that these comrades are the individuals
who make up a complex world society.

Many themes appear in *Leaves of
Grass*. Whitman celebrates the brotherhood of man, democracy, America as a
symbol of both brotherhood and democracy, and Lincoln as a symbol of the
lonely individual deeply involved in humanity; as natural outgrowths of these
themes come Whitman's insistence on
the "normality" of sex, the equality of
male and female, and the oneness of
man with all things in the universe, from
great stars to tiny ants. All these ideas
are consistent with the poet's viewpoint,
all a part of the primary dilemma. One
of his greatest poems, "When Lilacs Last
in the Dooryard Bloom'd," presents Lincoln as the solitary figure who is also the
man of the people; and when the funeral
train slowly bears his body across the
country, Whitman describes not only the
great grief of the masses but also the
mourning of the poet, the individual:

Coffin that passes through lanes and
streets,
Through day and night, with the great
cloud darkening the land,
With the pomp of the inloop'd flags,
with the cities draped in black,
With the show of the States themselves,
as of crapeveil'd women, standing,
With processions long and winding,
and the flambeaus of the night,
With the countless torches lit—with the

silent sea of faces and the unbared
heads,
With the waiting depot, the arriving
coffin, and the sombre faces,
With dirges through the night, with
the thousand voices rising strong and
solemn;
With all the mournful voices of the
dirges, pour'd around the coffin,
The dim-lit churches and the shudder-
ing organs—
Where amid these you journey,
With the tolling, tolling bells' perpetual
clang;
Here! coffin that slowly passes,
I give you my sprig of lilac.

Whitman the Propagandist: In this
role, Whitman, like his contemporary
Whittier, seems least successful. While it
is natural for a poet in a time of crisis to
feel his responsibilities, to turn his talent
to a cause, only rarely does he produce
great poetry in so doing. The section of
Leaves of Grass called "Memories of
President Lincoln" is above the realm of
propaganda and ranks with the finest
elegies written in the English language;
but many of the selections in "Drum-
Taps," which is concerned with the Civil
War, are "forced" poems, written as if the
poet felt himself compelled to comment
on the events taking place. For instance,
in "Beat! Beat! Drums!" the first few
lines are:

Beat! beat! drums!—Blow! bugles! blow!
Through the windows—through doors
—burst like a force of ruthless men,
Into the solemn church, and scatter the
congregation;
Into the school where the scholar is
studying:
Leave not the bridegroom quiet—no
happiness must he have now with
his bride;
Nor the peaceful farmer any peace,
ploughing his field or gathering his
grain;
So fierce you whirr and pound, you
drums—so shrill you bugles blow.

Here Whitman is merely superimposing
the spirit and technique of "Song of the

Open Road" on an entirely different subject. However, in a few of the war poems —such as "Come Up from the Fields Father" and "Give Me the Splendid Silent Sun," in which Whitman is writing about the fringes of the war—he seems more at ease and is consequently more successful.

Whitman the Humorist: This aspect of Whitman's talent is rarely recognized and almost never discussed fully. *Leaves of Grass* contains much sly humor, many passages in which the reader suspects Whitman of poetic playfulness. Although Whitman wrote no purely comical poems, he often expresses his ideas in a witty manner. In "To a Common Prostitute" he seriously accepts the girl as a part of the human scene, but surely in the last line he has his tongue in his cheek: "Till then I salute you with a significant look that you do not forget me." The first line of "Salut au Monde"—"O take my hand Walt Whitman"—and the other passages in which the poet talks to himself and makes poetry of his own name are certainly the affectation of a "character." Even the justly celebrated section in "Song of Myself" about the nature of grass can become, with a slightly unsympathetic reading, a deadpan masterpiece of comic simplicity. And Whitman's humor is intentional. In Richard Chase's *Walt Whitman Reconsidered*, the poet is quoted as having said to his Camden friends: "I pride myself on being a real humorist underneath everything else." Here is a poet who is alternately comic and serious—and sometimes both at the same time. Whitman will always be chiefly remembered as a poet of force and eloquence, a prophet of high ideals, but his wit must also be reckoned a part of his genius.

Whitman the Poet: The range of Whitman's skill in poetic technique is remarkable. In his carol in praise of death, from "When Lilacs Last in the Dooryard Bloom'd," he creates an effect as soft as a summer night; and in the love song of the grieving bird in "Out of the Cradle Endlessly Rocking" the music is gentle, poignant, haunting:

Soothe! Soothe!
Close on its wave soothes the wave behind,
And again another behind, embracing and lapping, every one close,
But my love soothes not me.

Low hangs the moon—it rose late,
O it is lagging—O I think it is heavy with love.

O madly the sea pushes upon the land,
With love—with love.

O night!
O do I not see my love fluttering out there among the breakers?
What is that little black thing I see there in the white?

. . . .

O rising stars!
Perhaps the one I want so much will rise with some of you.

At other times he sounds his "barbaric yawp," which many casual readers have labeled the uncontrolled outpourings of an undisciplined poet. True, there are times when the repetition, the ceaseless cataloguing, the too Biblical rhythms, the artificial combination of Quakerisms and first-reader French seem hardly worth wading through; but these passages contain the flaws to be found in the collected works of any poet. At his best Whitman is a master of precise diction. The opening twenty-two lines of "Out of the Cradle Endlessly Rocking" not only contain a stirring rhythm and a perfectly timed climax but also are characterized by an exquisite choice of words. In a much shorter poem, "When I Heard the Learn'd Astronomer," Whitman's form is the usual heavily accented free verse, but here again there seems hardly a word that could be changed or omitted.

Whitman has been called a "line poet" because among his many virtues is the ability to pack the memorable into a single line. Frequently these lines open his poem and he lets them double as titles: "As Toilsome I Wander'd Virginia's Woods," "Give Me the Splendid Silent Sun," "I Hear America Singing," "Good-bye My Fancy," and "I Sing the Body Electric." Whitman is so famed as the breaker of tradition, the iconoclast who broke the way for the "modern poetry" of our time, that we tend to forget his rank among the master craftsmen of English verse. Whitman underestimated himself when he said, in "Poets To Come,"

I but write one or two indicative words for the future,
I but advance a moment, only to wheel and hurry back in the darkness.

I am a man who, sauntering along, without fully stopping, turns a casual look upon you, and then averts his face,
Leaving it to you to prove and define it,
Expecting the main things from you.

Many of these "main things" are already fulfilled in *Leaves of Grass*.

THE LEGEND OF GOOD WOMEN

Type of work: Poem
Author: Geoffrey Chaucer (c. 1343-1400)
First transcribed: 1380-1386

Principal characters:
    CHAUCER, the dreamer
    CUPID
    ALCESTE, wife of Admetus, King of Pherae
    CLEOPATRA, Queen of Egypt
    THISBE, loved by Pyramus
    DIDO, Queen of Carthage
    HYPSIPYLE, Queen of Lemnos, betrayed by Jason
    MEDEA, princess of Colchis, betrayed by Jason
    LUCRETIA, Roman matron ravished by Tarquin
    ARIADNE, Cretan princess betrayed by Theseus
    PHILOMELA, Athenian princess ravished by Tereus
    PHYLLIS, Greek maiden betrayed by Demophon
    HYPERMNESTRA, daughter of Danaüs, King of Egypt

The Legend of Good Women, a poem recounting the stories of women from history and myth who were martyrs to love, is written in the tradition of medieval love poetry. Unlike Chaucer's masterpieces, *Troilus and Criseyde* and *The Canterbury Tales,* this work only occasionally rises above the limitations imposed by the artificial conventions of the times and is, therefore, inferior to these other works. Chaucer's greatness as a poet resulted not so much from his ability to perfect the current modes of writing as it did from his capacity to transcend them. Although his debt to contemporary thought and literary practice was considerable, his high position among English writers depends largely on his gift for bringing reality to a literature that was customarily unrealistic. In *The Legend of Good Women,* however, he constructed a framework so restricting that he was unable to infuse it with the richness and subtle shadings of human existence.

The most engaging part of the poem is the prologue, in which Chaucer revealed his elation at the arrival of spring. He delighted in roaming through the meadows, listening to the small birds, and gazing at the flowers. He was especially attracted to the daisy, which he could observe for hours without becoming bored. One spring day, after a walk in the fields, he fell asleep and had a vision in which the God of Love and the beautiful Alceste, dressed in the colors of the daisy, appeared before him. Cupid denounced the dreamer for committing heresy against the laws of love by writing of Criseyde's infidelity and by translating *The Romance of the Rose* with its disparaging remarks about womankind. But Cupid's companion (the same Alceste whom Hercules rescued from Hades after she had given her life to redeem her husband from death) rose to the poet's defense by contending that he, having appropriated his plots from other writers, acted out of ignorance, not malice. She concluded that he might gain Cupid's forgiveness by writing a legendary of wives and maidens who had been faithful in love all their lives.

The prologue is filled with literary devices popular in the fourteenth century. The religion of love—with its sins, penances, self-abnegation, and sanctity, with its Cupid and Alceste analogous to God and the Virgin Mary—closely paralleled the Christian religion. The daisy, having recently replaced the rose, was the symbol of love. The question of whether the flower or the leaf was superior, apparently a hotly debated issue in courtly circles, Chaucer touches upon, but without committing himself. The dream-vision used here had been a very popular device ever since the appearance of *The Romance of the Rose*, Chaucer himself employing it in several works. Despite this elaborate machinery, which today is mainly of historic interest, the prologue has about it a universal appeal; cheerfulness, humor, and a tinge of ironic detachment preserve it from mediocrity. Also of special excellence is Chaucer's expression of his delight in nature.

According to the prologue, Chaucer planned to write twenty tales concerning good women. He finished eight and left a ninth just short of completion. The theme of all the legends is the fidelity of women in love. All the heroines suffer for, and the majority die for, their love. All are treated as wholly admirable, even saintly, without regard to the illicit nature of some of the relationships presented. Events in their lives not concerned with their fidelity are omitted or hastily summarized. With the exception of the first two legends, the women suffer as the result of the treachery of men, who generally are as thoroughgoing in their villainy as the women are in their virtue.

The longest and one of the best of the legends retells the story of Dido's love for Aeneas. After Aeneas had landed on the Libyan coast, he met Venus, his mother, who instructed him to go to the court of Dido, Queen of Carthage. Dido greeted him cordially and, knowing his flight from Troy, felt great pity for the disinherited hero. And with her pity, came love. For comfort and entertainment during his visit, she provided everything riches could command.

One day, when Aeneas, Dido, and her retinue were hunting, a thunderstorm burst upon them. Everyone rushed for shelter, and Dido and Aeneas found themselves in the same cave. There the perfidious Aeneas protested his love for her; and she, upon much importuning, had pity and yielded herself to him. For a time, Aeneas performed all the duties of a courtly lover, but finally, becoming

weary, he made plans to leave. When Dido, noting his lessened ardor, asked what was wrong, he told her of a vision (a pure fabrication, Chaucer implied) in which his father reminded him of his destiny to conquer Italy. Ignoring her pleas, Aeneas stole away to his ships without her. As soon as she discovered his absence, she had her sister build a funeral pyre upon which, using Aeneas' sword, she stabbed herself.

Chaucer's principal source for this tale was Vergil's *Aeneid*. With slight modifications of the plot, Chaucer made substantial changes in characterization. Dido, who did not escape Vergil's censure, was made blameless by Chaucer, mainly by his elaboration of the scene in the cave. With a minimizing of the intervention of the gods and a degrading of his motives, the pious Aeneas of Vergil became in Chaucer's hands a mere seducer. Thus a story of tragic struggle between love and duty was transformed into one of man's treachery and woman's loyalty.

Chaucer's source for "The Legend of Lucretia" was Ovid's *Fasti*, which he followed rather closely. To prove the virtues of his wife Lucretia, Collatinus offered to accompany Tarquin, the king's son, to Rome to see her. Secreted outside her chamber door, they found her spinning among her servants and expressing concern for her husband's safety. Tarquin, observing her natural beauty, conceived a great desire for her. The next day, his lust increasing, he determined to return to Collatinus' house and make Lucretia his lover. Stealing into her room at night, he threatened her at sword's point and, while she lay in a swoon, ravished her. After he had left, Lucretia dressed in mourning, called her friends about her, and revealed to them the vile deed. Telling them that her husband should not gain a foul name from her guilt, she brought forth a knife and stabbed herself.

"The Legend of Hypsipyle and Medea" recounts the double treachery of Jason. On his expedition to recover the Golden

Fleece, Jason, accompanied by Hercules, stopped at the island of Lemnos, where they met Queen Hypsipyle, and conspired in capturing her affections for Jason. While Jason counterfeited modesty, his virtues were extolled by Hercules. Thus Hypsipyle was ensnared and consented to marry him. After making use of her wealth and begetting two children upon her, he left. Although he ignored her letter imploring him to return, she remained true to him and died of a broken heart.

Arriving at Colchis, Jason was entertained by King Aeëtes. Medea, the king's daughter, became enamored of Jason and revealed to him that the Golden Fleece could be secured only with her help. They agreed to marry, and Jason made a solemn promise never to be untrue. Later, after the expedition had been successful, Jason again proved false and left her to marry Creüsa.

Toward the end of *The Legend of Good Women,* Chaucer indicated a definite weariness with his subject. By adhering to his original plan, he wrote tales that have a tiresome sameness about them. Committed to perfect women and, in most instances, evil men, he found it difficult to develop his characters. A further deterrent to good characterization was his effort to keep the tales brief; some, as a result, are little more than plot summaries. Upon Dido he lavished more attention than on his other heroines, and she is his most lifelike portrait. There are good touches in other female characters; for example, the pathos of Lucretia in her death scene and the mingled fear and courage of Thisbe. His men, however, are little more than abstractions.

These tales mark a step toward Chaucer's later work, for in this poem he first used the decasyllabic couplet, afterward employed so successfully in *The Canterbury Tales.* His juxtaposing of *The Legend of Good Women* with *Troilus and Criseyde* prepared him for the more subtle contrasts of the Marriage Group. The work may have been left unfinished because of Chaucer's growing absorption with *The Canterbury Tales.* Although *The Legend of Good Women* is not without merit, this redirection of his efforts can hardly be regretted.

THE LEGEND OF SLEEPY HOLLOW

Type of work: Tale
Author: Washington Irving (1783-1859)
Type of plot: Regional romance
Time of plot: Eighteenth century
Locale: New York State
First published: 1819-1820

Principal characters:

ICHABOD CRANE, a schoolteacher
KATRINA VAN TASSEL, a rustic heiress
ABRAHAM VAN BRUNT, known as Brom Bones

Critique:

Washington Irving, the first professional writer in America, was by inclination an amused observer of people and customs. By birth he was in a position to be that observer. Son of a New York merchant in good financial standing, he was the youngest of eleven children, several of whom helped him to take prolonged trips to Europe for his health and fancy. He was responsible for two trends in American literature: one, toward the local color, legendary tale; the other, toward the historical novel. "The Legend of Sleepy Hollow" belongs to the first trend. It was first published in Irving's *The Sketch Book of Geoffrey Crayon, Gent.*, the book which established his reputation at home and abroad.

The Story:

Near Tarry Town on the Hudson is a little valley which, years ago, was the quietest place in the world. A drowsy influence hung over the place and people so that the region was known as Sleepy Hollow, and the lads were called Sleepy Hollow boys. Some said that the valley was bewitched. True it was that marvelous stories were told there.

The main figure to haunt the valley was one on horseback, without a head. Some said the specter was the apparition of a Hessian horseman who had lost his head to a cannon ball, but, whatever it was, it was often seen in the valley and adjacent countryside in the gloom of winter nights. The specter was known to all as the Headless Horseman of Sleepy Hollow.

In the valley, years ago, there lived a schoolteacher called Ichabod Crane. He looked like a scarecrow because of his long, skinny frame and his snipe-like nose.

As was the custom in that fertile Dutch countryside, he boarded with the parents of his pupils a week at a time. Fortunately for him the Dutch larders were full and the tables groaning with food, for the schoolmaster had a wonderful appetite. He was always welcome in the country homes because in small ways he made himself useful to the farmers. He was patient with the children, and he loved to spend the long winter nights with the families of his pupils, exchanging tales of ghosts and haunted places while ruddy apples roasted on the hearths.

Ichabod believed heartily in ghosts, and his walks home after an evening of tale-telling were often filled with fear. His only source of courage at those times was his voice, loud and nasal as it made the night resound with many a psalm tune.

The schoolteacher picked up a little odd change by holding singing classes. In one of his classes he first became aware of a plump and rosy-cheeked girl named Katrina Van Tassel. She was the only child of a very substantial farmer, and that fact added to her charms for the ever-hungry Ichabod. Since she was not only beautiful but also lively, she was a great favorite among the lads in the neighborhood.

Abraham Van Brunt was Katrina's favorite squire. The Dutch first shortened his name to Brom, and then called him Brom Bones when he became known for the tall and powerful frame of his body. He was a lively lad with a fine sense of humor and a tremendous amount of energy. When other suitors saw his horse hitched outside Katrina's house on a Sunday night, they went on their way. Brom Bones was a formidable rival for the gaunt and shaggy Ichabod. Brom would have liked to carry the battle into the open, but the schoolteacher knew better than to tangle with him physically. Brom Bones could do little but play practical jokes on lanky Ichabod.

The whole countryside was invited one fall evening to a quilting-frolic at Mynheer Van Tassel's. For the occasion Ichabod borrowed a horse from the farmer with whom he was then living. The horse, called Gunpowder, was as gaunt as Ichabod himself, but the steed still had a fair amount of spirit. The two of them were a sight as they jogged happily along to the party.

Ichabod was well pleased by every prospect he saw on the Van Tassel farm, the most prosperous holding for miles around. Perhaps Ichabod might be able to sell it and, with the proceeds, go farther west. It was a pretty picture he saw as he passed fields full of shocks of corn and pumpkins, granaries stuffed with grain, and meadows and barnlots filled with sleek cattle and plump fowls.

The party was a merry one with many lively dances. Ichabod was at his best when he danced with Katrina. After a time he went out on the dark porch with the men and exchanged more Sleepy Hollow ghost stories. But the food was best of all. Ichabod did credit to all the cakes and pies, meats and tea.

After the others left, he tarried to pay court to Katrina, but it was not long before he started home crestfallen on the gaunt Gunpowder. All the stories he had heard came back to him, and as he rode along in the darkness he became more dismal. He heard groans as the branches of the famed Major André tree rubbed against each other. He even thought he saw something moving beneath it.

When he came to the bridge over Wiley's Swamp, Gunpowder balked. The harder Ichabod urged him on, the more the horse bucked. Then, on the other side of the marsh, Ichabod saw something huge and misshapen.

The figure refused to answer him when he called. Ichabod's hair stood straight on end. Because it was too late to turn back, however, the schoolmaster kept to the road. The stranger—it looked like a headless horseman, but it seemed to hold its head on the pommel—kept pace with him, fast or slow. Ichabod could not stand going slowly and he whipped Gunpowder to a gallop. As his saddle loosened, he nearly lost his grip, but he hugged the horse around the neck. He could not even sing a psalm tune.

When he reached the church bridge, where by tradition the headless specter would disappear in a flash of fire and brimstone, Ichabod heard the horseman close in on him. As he turned to look, the spirit threw his head at him. Ichabod tried to dodge, but the head tumbled him into the dust.

In the morning a shattered pumpkin was found near the bridge. Gunpowder was grazing at the farmer's gate nearby. But Ichabod was never seen in Sleepy Hollow again. In the valley they say that Brom Bones, long after he had married the buxom Katrina, laughed heartily whenever the story was told of the horseman who had thrown his head at the schoolteacher during that ghostly midnight pursuit.

LEGEND OF THE MOOR'S LEGACY

Type of work: Tale
Author: Washington Irving (1783-1859)
Type of plot: Folklore
Time of plot: Seventeenth century
Locale: Granada, Spain
First published: 1832

Principal characters:
PEDRO GIL, called PEREGIL, a water carrier
HIS WIFE
A MOORISH SHOPKEEPER
PEDRILLO PEDRUGO, a prying barber
THE ALCADE
A CONSTABLE

Critique:

In 1829, during his first visit to Spain, Washington Irving lived for three months in the Alhambra, the historic fortress from which the Moors had been expelled by Ferdinand and Isabella in 1492. Irving's interest in Spanish history and legend appears in many of his writings, but his Spanish material received its most finished form in *The Alhambra*, published in 1832. The book, a collection of stories drawn from actual history and from folk imagination, includes the well-known "Legend of the Moor's Legacy." Like the more familiar "Rip Van Winkle" and "The Legend of Sleepy Hollow," this tale shows Irving's love of the picturesque and his interest in the fantastic and legendary stories of many lands. The combined qualities of reverie, genial humor, and romantic imagination made him a perfect writer of traveler's tales. This legend undoubtedly goes back beyond its Spanish origins to the unknown storytellers of *The Arabian Nights' Entertainments.*

The Story:

In the Square of the Cisterns, fronting the royal palace in the fortress of the Alhambra, was a deep Moorish well of clear, cold water. So famous was the well throughout all Granada that to it repaired water carriers from every quarter of the city, some bearing great earthen jars on their own sturdy shoulders, others, more prosperous, driving donkeys similarly burdened. The well was also a great place for meeting and gossip. Each day housewives, lazy servants, beggars—idlers of every age and condition—gathered on the stone benches to talk over the doings of their neighbors and to exchange rumors which were afloat in the city.

Among the carriers who drew water from the ancient well of the Alhambra there was once a strong-backed, bandy-legged little fellow named Pedro Gil, called Peregil for short. He had begun his trade with only a single water jar, but since no one in all Granada was more industrious than he, it was not long before he was able to purchase a donkey to do his carrying for him. All day long he trudged the streets calling his wares, and for every woman, old or young, he had a merry smile and a pleasing compliment. It was not surprising that everyone thought him the happiest of men. But Peregil's heart was often heavy and sad. He had a brood of ragged children who were ravenous as young birds, so that it was all he could do to fill their mouths with food. His wife, grown slatternly and fat, nagged poor Peregil even while she spent his hard-earned money for fripperies they could not afford. Subdued to patience by his matrimonial yoke, Peregil made the best of things and concealed his frequent dejection with merry quips and songs.

Late one summer night he made one last trip to the well in hopes of adding to his small store of coppers for meat to put in the Sunday pot. He found the square empty except for a stranger in Moorish dress. When the man said that he was a traveler taken suddenly ill, Peregil, touched with compassion, gave the stranger a ride back to the city on his donkey. On the way the man confessed that he had no lodgings in the town, and he asked that he be allowed to rest under Peregil's roof. He promised that the carrier would be well repaid.

Peregil had little desire to deal in this manner with an infidel, but in the kindness of his heart he could not refuse aid to the stranger. Ignoring his wife's protests, the carrier spread a mat in the coolest part of his hovel for the sick man. Before long the Moor was seized with convulsions. Knowing that his end was near, he gave Peregil a small sandalwood box and told him that it contained the secret to a great treasure. He died before he could reveal the nature of the secret.

Peregil's wife, afraid that the body would be found in their house and that they would be charged with murder, railed at her husband for his folly. Equally disturbed, the carrier tried to mend matters by taking the dead Moor, under cover of darkness, to the bank of the river and there burying it.

Now it happened that Peregil lived opposite to a barber named Pedrillo Pedrugo, whose greatest pleasure was to spy on his neighbors and tattle their affairs. Having seen Peregil arriving with the Moor, he was still on watch when the carrier took away the body of the dead man. Following stealthily, he spied on the secret burial. Early the next morning he hurried off to the alcalde, who was one of his daily customers, and told what he had seen.

The alcalde, who put so high a value on justice that he sold it only for gold, sent a constable to bring Peregil before him. Frightened, the water carrier called upon the saints to witness his innocence and frankly related the whole story. When he produced the sandalwood box, the alcalde expected to find it filled with gold or jewels. Instead, it contained only a parchment scroll and the end of a wax taper. Disappointed, he returned the box to Peregil, but kept the carrier's donkey to pay for the trouble the poor wretch had caused.

At home, Peregil became so disgusted with his wife's taunts over the loss of his donkey that he threw the sandalwood box to the floor. When the parchment rolled out, he picked it up and found on it some writing in Arabic. Curious to know what the meaning might be, he took it to a Moorish shopkeeper of his acquaintance. The Moor said that the scroll contained an incantation for the recovery of a treasure hidden under the Alhambra.

At first Peregil was skeptical. Several days later, however, he heard loiterers by the well talking about a treasure supposed to be buried under the Tower of the Seven Floors in the old fortress. Once more he went to the Moor and proposed that they search for the treasure together. The Moor replied that the incantation was powerless without a magic candle to burn while the charm was being read. Peregil said that the taper was also in his possession.

Later that night he and the Moor went secretly to the Tower of the Seven Floors and descended into the damp, musty vault beneath. There they lit the taper and the Moor began to read the words on the parchment. As he finished, the floor opened with a noise like thunder. Descending the steps thus revealed, they found themselves in another vault, where stood a chest and several great jars filled with gold coins and precious stones, over which two enchanted Moorish warriors stood guard. Amazed and fearful, they filled their pockets with valuables. Then they climbed the stairs and blew out the taper. The floor closed again with a ponderous crash.

Peregil and the Moor hoped to keep their secret safe, but the carrier could conceal nothing from his wife. She bought herself expensive clothing and put on so many fine airs that her neighbors became curious. One day the barber saw her after she had decked herself with some of the jewels Peregil had found. Once more Pedrillo hurried to the alcalde to tell his story. The alcalde, convinced that Peregil had tricked him, ordered the trembling water carrier dragged into his presence.

After Peregil's story had been confirmed by the Moor, the alcalde's greed for gold became almost more than he could bear. That night, taking Peregil and the Moor with them as prisoners, the alcalde, the constable, and the prying barber went to the tower. With them they took the donkey Peregil had once owned. There in the vault the taper was lighted and the Moor read the incantation. Again the floor rolled aside, revealing the treasure vault beneath. The alcalde and his friends were too frightened to descend, but they ordered Peregil to bring up two immense jars filled with gold and gems and to strap them on the donkey which they had brought to carry away the spoils. When they learned that the vault also contained a chest filled with treasure, the alcalde, the constable, and the barber overcame their fears sufficiently to go down the stairs to secure the riches for themselves. After they had entered the lower vault, the Moor blew out the taper, and the floor closed over the men below, leaving them entombed in darkness. The Moor, assuring Peregil that such was the will of Allah, threw away the magic taper.

Peregil and the Moor divided the treasure equally between them. A short time later the Moor returned to his native city of Tangier. Peregil, with his wife, his brood of children, and his sturdy donkey, went to Portugal, where his wife used his riches to make him a man of consequence, known to all as Don Pedro Gil. As for the greedy alcalde, the constable, and the prying barber, they remain under the Tower of the Seven Floors to this day.

THE LEGEND OF TYL ULENSPIEGEL

Type of work: Novel
Author: Charles Théodore Henri de Coster (1827-1879)
Type of plot: Historical romance
Time of plot: Sixteenth century
Locale: The Low Countries
First published: 1867

Principal characters:
>TYL ULENSPIEGEL, the wanderer
>CLAES, his father
>SOETKIN, his mother
>NELE, his wife
>LAMME GOEDZAK, his companion
>KATHELINE, a midwife
>HANS DUDZEELE, Katheline's betrayer
>PHILIP, King of Spain

Critique:

The glorious adventures of Tyl Ulenspiegel and Lamme Goedzak are well-known to readers of most countries of the world. De Coster's book is a heroic epic based on folk legend and history, a story complete with visions, high adventures, traitors, and heroes. Ulenspiegel was the spirit of his native land, and he had been born to deliver her from her oppressors. Always the parallel between him and King Philip is carefully drawn: Philip a destroyer and Ulenspiegel a savior. De Coster preserved the old legends of Flanders, and his account of the Flemish hero maintains its great popularity even today.

The Story:

Tyl Ulenspiegel was born with two marks, one the sign of a lucky star, the other the print of the devil's finger. Katheline, the midwife, had a vision in which she saw Ulenspiegel as the incarnated spirit of his native Flanders. At the same time Philip of Spain was born. In her vision Katheline saw Philip as the butcher of Flanders. She was afraid.

As a boy Ulenspiegel roamed the fields of Flanders. His playmate was Nele, illegitimate daughter of Katheline the midwife. But as the children played, gloom gathered over the lowlands. The father of Philip fished in the pockets of the people, and each day new edicts announced torture and death for heretics. The Inquisi-

tion was beginning, and neighbor turned against neighbor in order to inherit half his possessions. Katheline was tortured as a witch on the complaint of a neighbor. As a result of this experience the poor woman went mad.

Ulenspiegel, as a young man living by his wits, traveled into many lands. Sometimes he was hard pressed to escape with his life, but his high spirit and great strength served him well. When he returned at last to his homeland he had to put his youthful follies behind him, for trouble had come to his family. Claes had been convicted of heresy on the testimony of a fishmonger who wanted to inherit part of his wealth. The good man was tortured and burned to slow death. Soetkin and Ulenspiegel wept, helpless to save him. Ulenspiegel took ashes from Claes' heart and wore them in a bag around his neck after swearing eternal vengeance upon the murderers. Because Soetkin and Nele had hidden Claes' money, the searchers looked for it in vain. Then Soetkin and Ulenspiegel were put to torture, but although they were broken on the wheel and burned they would not reveal their secret. Meanwhile Claes' ashes beat against Ulenspiegel's heart.

In spite of their courage the money was lost. Mad Katheline told Hans, her evil lover, and Nele's father, where the money was hidden. Hans and a friend robbed the widow and son of their inheritance. Then Hans, not knowing that mad Katheline watched him, killed his accomplice. Ulenspiegel, meeting the lying fishmonger, threw his enemy into the water. Philip, now King of Spain, robbed and murdered his people and the people of Flanders.

After Soetkin died of her grief and her torture, Ulenspiegel vowed to avenge her and Claes and all of his loved homeland. Mad Katheline conjured up a vision from which Ulenspiegel learned that he could be avenged if he sought and found the Seven. Not knowing who the Seven were, he left Nele to seek them. With him went Lamme Goedzak, a fat buffoon seeking his wife, who had left him because she had been told by a monk to give up lusts of the flesh and enter a nunnery. Lamme drowned his grief in food and wine, but the ashes of Claes burned against Ulenspiegel's heart. Knowing no peace, he looked only for the Seven.

He and Lamme joined the army of William of Orange, leader of the forces against Philip and the Inquisition. They traveled over many lands, sometimes alone and sometimes with Prince William's troops. Often they were in danger of death by torture, but God protected them and kept them safe. Several times Lamme or Ulenspiegel caught glimpses of Lamme's wife, but Lamme could not catch up with her. The two friends saw much blood spilled, until they were weary of war and torture. Still Ulenspiegel looked for the Seven.

Ulenspiegel served Orange well. In spite of all resistance, however, Philip conquered all of the Low Countries and the people suffered and starved. When Hans returned to Katheline for more money, the mad woman, not knowing what she did, accused him of witchery. He was tortured and condemned to slow death by fire. Katheline, too, was given a witch's trial by water. Although she sank to the bottom, proving her innocence, the poor madwoman died three days later from the chill and the shock.

Nele, now an orphan, left Flanders and traveled to Holland. There she saved the life of Ulenspiegel, who was on the gallows for accusing his commander of false promises. The two lovers were married. Together they traveled with Lamme, who continued to seek his wife. Still the robbery and killings went on, and still Ulenspiegel searched for the Seven who could tel him how to avenge his family and save Flanders. William of Orange began to gain victories. Philip, enraged, demanded more and more bloodshed.

Ulenspiegel was placed in command of a ship, with Lamme for his cook. After a battle in which Lamme was injured, they brought on board a captive monk who was fat and lustful. His torture was that he must eat all that Lamme prepared for him, seven times a day, and he must live in a cage just big enough to enclose his great bulk. Before Lamme could get the monk fat enough to burst, Lamme's wound reopened and in his delirious condition he had to be tied to the ship so that he would not fall into the sea.

One night Lamme's wife came aboard the ship, treated his wound, and cured it. He pursued her as she fled in her boat, caught her, and heard her story. A monk, the one whom Lamme had imprisoned in a cage, had preached to her and ordered her to give up lusts of the flesh and follow him. In her innocence she had deserted her husband and gone away with the monk. Lamme feared that she had given herself to the monk, but when he learned that she had not, he took her again as his wife. The two happy lovers left Ulenspiegel and Nele and went to restore their lost home.

After William of Orange lost his life, his son carried on the battle for liberty and the lowlands were soon freed. In a vision Nele and Ulenspiegel saw at last the Seven that were and the Seven that should be, if their native land was to be free. The Seven that were now were Pride, Gluttony, Idleness, Avarice, Anger, Envy, and Lust. In the vision Ulenspiegel was told to burn the Seven. When he burned them, they were reduced to ashes and blood ran. Then from Pride came forth Noble Spirit; from Gluttony, Appetite; from Idleness, Reverie; from Avarice, Economy; from Anger, Vivacity; from Envy, Emulation, and lastly from Lust sprang forth Love. Then a mighty hand hurled Nele into space and came again and hurled Ulenspiegel into space after her. Nele awoke from the vision, but Ulenspiegel lay as one dead for two days and two nights. When a priest passed by on the way to a burial, he ordered a grave dug that Ulenspiegel might be buried by the church. But Ulenspiegel rose up from the grave and threw off the dirt, for he knew that his motherland was free at last. The new Seven would be her salvation. He knew, too, that Nele was the heart and he was the spirit of the new Flanders, and that they could never die.

LETTERS FROM AN AMERICAN FARMER

Type of work: Epistolary essays
Author: Michel-Guillaume Jean de Crèvecœur (1735-1813)
First published: London, 1782; Philadelphia, 1793

When, in 1759, Voltaire published his *Candide*, Crèvecœur was already planning to cultivate his garden, hewn out of the Pennsylvania frontier. Like Voltaire's naïve hero, he had seen too much of the horrors of the civilized world and was more than ready to retire to his bucolic paradise, where for nineteen years he lived in peace and happiness until the civilized world routed him and his family with the outbreak of the American Revolution. The twelve essays that make up his *Letters from an American Farmer* are the crude, occasionally eloquent, testimony of a man trying desperately to convince himself and his readers that it was possible to live the idealized life advocated by Rousseau.

With a becoming modesty, appropriate to a man who had learned English at sixteen, Crèvecœur begins with a confession of his literary inadequacy and decides simply to write down what he would say. But his style is not smoothly colloquial. Except in a few passages in which conviction generates enthusiasm, one senses the strain of the unlettered man wielding an unfamiliar pen. The opening letter presents the central theme quite clearly: the decadence of European civilization makes the American frontier one of the great hopes for a regeneration of mankind. He wonders why men travel to Italy to "amuse themselves in viewing the ruins of temples . . . half-ruined amphitheatres and the putrid fevers of the Campania must fill the mind with most melancholy reflections." By contrast, he delights in the humble rudiments and embryos of societies spreading everywhere in the colonies, men converting large forests into pleasing fields and creating thirteen provinces of easy subsistence and political harmony. He has his interlocutor say of him, "Your mind is . . . a *Tabula*

rasa where spontaneous and strong impressions are delineated with felicity." Similarly, he sees the American continent as a clean slate on which men can inscribe a new society and the good life. It may be said that Crèvecœur is a Lockian gone romantic, but retaining just enough practical good sense to see that reality is not rosy. "Men are like plants;" he says, "the goodness and flavour of the fruit proceeds from the peculiar soil and exposition in which they grow."

The first image Crèvecœur presents is perhaps a bit too idyllic for modern taste. He dandles his little boy on the plow as his wife sits at the edge of the field knitting and praising the straightness of the furrows, while birds fill the air with summer melodies. "Who can listen unmoved to the sweet love tales of our robins told from tree to tree?" Nevertheless, this is the testimony of a man who for nineteen years actually lived at the edge of the wilderness, three hundred miles from the Atlantic. He was no Thoreau at Walden Pond within easy walking distance of friends, family, and a highly developed New England culture at Concord. He was, instead, a responsible man, who cleared 371 acres of virgin land and raised enough crops and animals to provide for his family, Negro hands, and all peaceful strangers who chanced to appear at his door. Also unlike Thoreau (with whom he inevitably invites comparison), he was acutely aware of his social responsibilities and enormously proud of the superior way in which they could be fulfilled in the New World. No doubt it was the third epistle, "What Is An American?" that caught the attention of Benjamin Franklin and the Europeans of the Age of Enlightenment:

[America] is not composed, as in Europe, of great lords who possess everything, and of a herd of people who have nothing. Here are no aristocratical families, no courts, no kings, no bishops, no ecclesiastical dominion, no invisible power giving to a few a very visible one; no great manufacturers employing thousands, no great refinements of luxury. The rich and the poor are not so far removed from each other as they are in Europe. . . . We are the most perfect society now existing in the world.

Enthusiastic as this description is, it is not as extravagant as it might be; Crèvecœur does not claim that the colonies had founded the best of all possible worlds. He is, for example, acutely aware of the paradox that religious influence gradually declines as one goes west; instead of liberating men, it reduces them to a perfect state of war, man against man. Yet he rejoices that there are almost no concentrated religious sects preying upon each other: "Zeal in Europe is confined . . . a grain of powder enclosed; here it burns away in the open air, and consumes without effect."

Furthermore, not every man succeeds after arriving in the New World—only the sober, the honest, the industrious. In his "History of Andrew, the Hebridean," Crèvecœur presents a case history of the Horatio Alger hero in primitive America, the story of a simple illiterate Scotchman who after four years of sweat and toil became a prospering freeholder. Franklin had occasion to caution his friends in France that Crèvecœur's was a highly colored account.

Part of the coloring is contributed by the pervasive nature imagery. The freedom and beauty of birds seem to symbolize the condition man might achieve when he immerses himself in nature. Crèvecœur describes hours spent in quiet admiration of the hummingbirds, tells regretfully of shooting a kingbird to rescue bees (of 171 removed from its craw, 54 returned to life), describes the feeding and care of quail in the winter. Insects, too, fascinated him; he kept a hornet's nest in the house. The letter on rattlers and copperheads is as horrendous and awesome as anything in Bartram. Here Crèvecœur tells of copperheads enticing birds by the power of their eyes, of a defanged rattler trained as a pet, of a pair of snakes in mortal combat. Most curious of all is the account of a farmer who kicked away a snake that had thrust its fangs into his boot. After pulling off his boots that night, he suddenly became violently ill, writhed horribly, and d ed. His son, inheriting the boots, suffered the same fate. A neighbor, next in succession, almost died, too, but was saved when a shrewd doctor located the poison-filled fangs stuck in the boot. Crèvecœur in these passages reveals an exciting narrative power.

Apart from the agricultural life inland, Crèvecœur praises most the industry and sobriety of the coastal fishing communities at Nantucket and Martha's Vineyard, where "perfect equanimity prevails." At Nantucket (which, oddly, he locates north of Boston), five thousand prosperous people inhabited a place which in Europe would have housed a few simple fishermen. Their Yankee ingenuity and sound business sense had enabled them to build—beginning with one whale boat —a whaling fleet that ranged even to the South Seas. And Martha's Vineyard was already the "nursery" of seamen for the entire east coast. So detailed is Crèvecœur's description of the chase, the ferocity of the whale's struggle, the dangers from sharks and thrasher whales, the processing of blubber into whale oil —in short, the entire experience, that one wonders how Melville could have overlooked it in compiling the extracts in *Moby Dick* (1851).

Crèvecœur found Nantucket such a model community that it contained only one minister (a Presbyterian, for the Quakers, much to Crèvecœur's delight, do not have special ministers), two doctors, one lawyer (seldom employed), no soldiers, no governors. "Happy the people who are subject to so mild a government; happy the government which has to rule over such harmless and such industrious subjects! . . . I wish I had it in my power to send the most persecuting bigot I could find in —— to the whale fisheries; in three or four years you would find him a much more tractable man and therefore a better Christian." But colonial Nantucket was apparently not perfect; the Quakers persisted in their ungrammatical English, did not tolerate any deviation from their sober customs and homespun dress, sternly prohibited music, singing, and dancing. "Such an island . . . is not the place where gay travellers should resort in order to enjoy the variety of pleasures the more splendid towns of this continent afford." Crèvecœur also reports, obviously misled by some notorious gossip, that the women were addicted to opium. "But," he philosophizes, "where is the society perfectly free from error and folly?"

Crèvecœur's criticism is reserved for the most European of American cities, Charles-Town, "gayest in America . . . centre of our beau monde." Lawyers, planters, and merchants make up the population, all addicted to dangerous excesses of all kinds. At the heart of this social corruption, Crèvecœur finds the brutal institution of slavery. He tells the horrifying tale of his chance encounter with a Negro who had been driven to kill an overseer. As his punishment he had been suspended from a tree in a cage for two days. Vicious birds had already plucked out his eyes and bared his cheekbones. No sooner were the birds dispersed than swarms of insects covered him. The miserable man begged for water and hoped it was poisoned. "Gracious God!" cries Crèvecœur, "to what end is the introduction of so many beings into [such] a mode of existence! . . . Is there then no superintending power who conducts the moral operations of the world?"

Some of Crèvecœur's faith is restored by the spectacle of the humble, kind, and generous aspect of William Bartram, the Quaker botanist, whose Negroes were salaried free men, workers on his plantation, companions at his table, and worshipers at the Friends' meeting house.

But the *Letters from an American Farmer* end in ominous tones of impending tragedy. Unwilling to commit his allegiance to either the British or the colonists, Crèvecœur finds it necessary to flee: "Must I in order to be called a faithful subject, coolly and philosophically say it is necessary for the good of Britain that my children's brains should be dashed against the walls of the house in which they were reared; that my wife should be stabbed and scalped before my face; that I should be either murdered or captivated?" To escape such a fate, Crèvecœur develops an intricate plan to take his family to join an Indian settlement in the uncultivated wilderness (a plan which he never actually carried out). It is, of course, tragically ironic that this mild Frenchman's absolute certainty of the blessings of life in the colonies should be so violently shattered after nineteen years of expending all his energies to make a decent life possible. But it is also ironically appropriate that his final impulse is to immerse himself deeper into nature by joining the Indians. Whatever flaws it may have, *Letters from an American Farmer* is the most sympathetic and thoughtful of all eighteenth-century analyses of frontier life and its shaping influence on the emerging American character.

LETTERS FROM THE UNDERWORLD

Type of work: Novel
Author: Fyodor Mikhailovich Dostoevski (1821-1881)
Type of plot: Impressionistic realism
Time of plot: Mid-nineteenth century
Locale: St. Petersburg, Russia
First published: 1864

Principal characters:
THE NARRATOR
SIMONOV, his acquaintance from school days
ZVERKOV, a young Russian officer
LIZA, a prostitute

Critique:

Letters from the Underworld, sometimes called also Notes from Underground, is actually more than an extended and bitter prose fiction. The first part constitutes a philosophical statement; the second part is the morbid illustration from life of this statement. The "underworld" of the title apparently is the depths of degradation and humiliation to which the too acutely conscious human being can descend because of a perverse human quality, a factor which, according to Dostoevski, scientists will never neatly label. This quality resists fruition, completion, and whatever we tend to call the normal state of happiness. Dostoevski's arrestingly paradoxical affirmation, in the first part of this work, of the stupendous force of individuality in human nature may provide consolation for the present-day man who feels that modern social forces are molding him more and more into an uncomfortable sameness with his neighbors. The book was written after Dostoevski's return from exile in Siberia. It serves as an arrow to point the direction of his later novels.

The Story:

The Narrator, addressing an imaginary group of acquaintances, declared that after many years of life as a rude and spiteful government official, and after many years as a recluse, he was not really bitter in his heart. Something perverse in him,

his acute consciousness, had led him to find pleasure in the pain of humiliating experiences.

From experience, he advised against intellectual acuteness. The intellectual, when faced with revenge, surrounded himself with a legion of doubts; then he would crawl into his self-imposed rat's nest and torture himself with petty spite. The direct man, in wreaking revenge, might with dispatch hit his head against a wall, but he would accept the wall. But the intellectual would not accept the wall. Indeed, he would feel responsibility for the presence of the wall.

The Narrator declared that he had always had to feign taking offense and that he had had, in the face of life's transiency, to pretend to love. Life to him was a colossal bore. He could never avenge wrongs done him because the culprit, the culprit's motives, and the very misdeed itself were all phantoms in his doubting intellect.

Given another chance at life, he would have chosen a career of complete laziness, one in which he might have reveled among good and beautiful things. He declared that even if man knew absolutely what things in life were to his best advantage, he would perversely avoid these things.

The Narrator advanced the idea that man may be destined for creativeness, and for this reason, conscious of his fate, he perversely practiced destruction to individuate himself. Perhaps man was fearful of completion, of perfection; perhaps he found final attainment distasteful: life consisted in the attaining, not in the attainment. He concluded his philosophical soliloquy by pointing out that conscious inertia was the ideal state. He provocatively insisted that he did not believe a word he had written, that he had written only because the written word seemed imposing and dignified. He was oppressed by memories which were evoked by the fall of snow outside.

At the age of twenty-four the Narrator had an inchoate character. He talked to no one. His intense self-consciousness caused him to be vain at one moment and self-loathing the next. He tried to look intelligent and feared any eccentricity in himself. This acute awareness of self made him lonely, yet he felt superior to others. He became a recluse. He read voraciously and began to walk the streets at night.

One night he saw a man thrown out of the window of a billiard parlor. In envy, he went into the parlor in the hope that he, too, might be thrown out. He was humiliated when an officer shoved him aside without noticing him. He returned the next night, but, morally fearful that all the fools in the parlor would jeer at his being thrown out, he did not enter. Dedicated to revenge, he followed the officer about for months. He learned the officer's name and wrote a satirical novel in which the officer was the principal character. The novel was rejected; its style was out of date.

Two years passed. He wrote a letter challenging the officer to a duel, but he did not mail the letter. Instead, he began to take regular walks along the river promenade, where he reveled in his resentment. One Sunday he was rudely pushed aside by the officer. Maddened at his weakness, he conceived the idea of not giving way next time. He gloated over his idea. He practiced pushing aside an imaginary officer. His courage had failed him once, but he finally stood his ground when the officer tried again to push him aside.

Actually, the officer did not notice him at all, but he was delirious with happiness in having gained back his self-respect.

The Narrator now began to daydream. In his fantasies, he brought beauty and good to the world. During the fever pitch of his dream life, feeling the need of companionship, he visited his immediate superior, Anton, and sat in silence with Anton's family for hours.

He called on an old schoolmate, Simonov, and found Simonov planning, with two other old schoolmates, a farewell dinner for Zverkov, a fellow student of the direct, not too acutely-conscious type, whom he hated. Zverkov, a wealthy man, was successful in the army. The Narrator, greeted coldly by his boyhood acquaintances, invited himself to the dinner party. The other young men agreed reluctantly; he was obviously not a favorite with them. Later he detested himself for consciously having opened himself up to humiliation, but secretly he rather enjoyed having discomfited his companions.

The next day he dressed for the dinner with doubt and misgiving. He wanted to make a great impression; he wanted to eclipse the popular Zverkov. Yet he knew that he really did not want to do this either. He arrived too early and was humiliated by his wait. During the dinner he antagonized everyone and drank incontinently. Having thoroughly degraded himself, he offered conciliation and sought the love of his companions. When he apologized to Zverkov for insulting him, Zverkov humiliated him by saying that such as he could not possibly insult him. Filled with a wild, unreasonable intention of slapping Zverkov and fighting a duel with him, he followed the others to a brothel.

Here, a young girl was brought into the parlor to him; he was pleased with the prospect of being repulsive to her. He slept off his drunkenness, awoke, and delivered a bookish, insincere sermon to Liza, the prostitute, on the hazards of her profession. He was attitudinizing and he knew it to his shame. He told her of the importance of human love, something about which he actually knew nothing. Liza, to prove to him that she was not entirely lost, showed him a love letter that she had received from a young gentleman. He gave her his address and left her.

The next day he regretted having given Liza his address. He hated himself for his insincerity with her; he feared her coming. But she did not come. He imagined an idyllic relationship between himself and Liza. He would be her tutor and would mold her into a perfect creature.

When Liza finally came, she was confused by the wretched conditions in the poor Narrator's rooms. She said that she had left the brothel. Alarmed, he confessed his insincerity and declared that he had sought power over someone because he himself had been humiliated. Liza understood his inner turmoil and took him in her arms.

Liza's intuition soon told her, however, that he was despicable and that he was incapable of love. After she left his rooms, he ran after her to seek her forgiveness, but he never saw her again. He derived some consolation from the thought that her resentment of him would give her pleasure for the rest of her life.

THE LETTERS OF WALPOLE

Type of work: Letters
Author: Horace Walpole (1717-1797)
Collected editions published: Letters, edited by Peter Cunningham, 1857-1859 (9 vols.); Letters, edited by Mrs. Paget Toynbee, 1903-1905 (16 vols.); *The Yale Edition of Horace Walpole's Correspondence,* edited by W. S. Lewis, 1937-continuing

No student, not even a general reader, interested in the eighteenth century and its culture in England can afford to overlook Horace Walpole and his works. Walpole's life spanned eighty years of that century, and the man himself engaged in most of the activities of the times in one way or another. His interests lay in many areas—political, literary, artistic, antiquarian, horticultural, architectural, and social. He was novelist, playwright, historian, member of Parliament, the son of a prime minister, an arbiter of artistic excellence, a publisher, a collector, and, among other things, an inveterate letter writer. It is anticipated that the monumental collected edition of the letters, the Yale edition now in progress, will eventually reach a total of fifty volumes.

In the realm of literature alone, Walpole had an amazing record of production, even for an age notorious for its prolific writers. Walpole wrote a novel, a comedy, a tragedy, some poetry, memoirs of the eighteenth-century Hanoverian kings of England, a volume on the career of the infamous Richard III, a catalogue of royal and noble English authors, a work on painting in England, and other writings. Although his novel, *The Castle of Otranto,* has always had some vogue, his letters have received more attention in the past hundred years. Walpole would probably approve, for he himself said that letters were the best key to the history of an age. Indeed, it seems that he wrote his correspondence with posterity in mind and according to something resembling a plan. That the letters have had continued popularity is due to their intrinsic worth, as well as their historical significance. Walpole had a pleasant style, and it must have been a pleasure to have been a recipient of his letters, as Horace Mann was, for example, over a period of more than forty years.

The language of Walpole's letters seems modern, for the idiom is attractive and anything but dated. And they are never boring. One reason for their effect is the fact that the letters are seldom about the author himself. Walpole wrote, rather, about the world, its main outlines as he knew them and its details as he observed them. He saw the world in its larger relationships, but he also had an eye and mind that were cognizant of little things. A chronic victim of the gout in later life, he seldom used his letters to indulge in self-pity. Though a thoughtful man, he did not inject into the letters a mass of subjective philosophizing; though an active man, he did not expatiate upon his activities from a personal point of view. There is always a conversational tone to the letters. They read much the same way that an eighteenth-century salon conversation probably sounded. Occasional improprieties, slight bursts of anger, the gossip, the wit, even the diction, are those which one probably would have heard among the well-bred people with whom Walpole was familiar.

The subject matter of the letters is almost universal, though centered in the strata of the world that Walpole knew, the world of the Whig aristocracy of eighteenth-century England, a gay, intelligent, if somewhat superficial world from the twentieth-century viewpoint.

Certain letters have achieved eminence above others. In the main, they are those letters frequently referred to as "set pieces." They include the letters describing the trial of rebellious Jacobite peers, after the abortive revolution of 1745, of which Walpole gives an almost day-to-day account. They include a description of the executions, which Walpole apparently did not witness, of Balmerino and Lord Kilmarnock. Two funerals are also famous in Walpole's correspondence: one the funeral of George II of England, the other the funeral in Paris of the Duke de Tresmes, governor of Paris and a marshal of France.

While the "set pieces" have their place, it is the very bulk and scope of subject matter that is most important in Walpole's letters, a bulk which is impossible merely to catalogue, for somewhere in the letters Walpole seems to have hit upon almost every subject significant (and some not so significant) in his time. Highwaymen, prisons, slavery, Strawberry Hill, the ins and outs of politics, London gossip, dueling, Benjamin Franklin, George Washington, General Howe and his army, marriages, divorces, masquerades, dinner parties, the weather (usual and unusual), balloons, Captain Cook's voyages, sea-bathing, the French Revolution—all these and many more are to be found as subjects in the letters. Some readers may argue that the correspondence is too large in bulk and too slightly organized, but perhaps those supposed weaknesses are the very strength of the *Letters*. Plato wrote his philosophy in the form of dialogues so that the reader would have to participate and learn actively; in somewhat similar fashion the reader of Walpole's letters must in a sense participate in the writer's account of eighteenth-century life, filling in the larger outline from the smaller items presented.

Walpole's purposes in writing the letters now seems clear. He was reporting the age to selected friends, many of whom were recipients of his letters for many years. At the same time Walpole seems to have been careful to write so that a larger audience might eventually appreciate what he wrote. He lived in an age when letter writing was decidedly an art, and yet the polish of his letters, the careful selection of details, and the superb control of the prose rhythms in many of them indicate that extraordinary care was lavished upon his correspondence, so that it became in Walpole's mind the best means for presenting a history of his time, being immediate, flexible, and open to varying levels of formality and tone. The letters were written in the main to selected people, a circumstance which made it easier for him to write what he did and as he did. And scholars have pointed out, in a sense Walpole's correspondence substituted space for time. The largest number of letters went to Horace Mann, British envoy at Florence. Writing to a man he met but once, a man who lived at considerable distance, culturally as well as geographically, Walpole had a fine recipient for letters containing what may be termed the main strand of his social history.

In the letters to Mann, the outlines of the social history could be given, while specific areas of interest could be, and apparently were, allotted to other recipients of portions of the correspondence. The various friends who received large numbers of Walpole's letters were each written to from a somewhat different viewpoint. Thomas Gray, the poet, a lifelong friend of Walpole (despite occasional differences), received letters on matters of artistic and antiquarian interest. When Gray died, the man who became his biographer, the Reverend William Mason, became the recipient, so that the thread was not broken. Lady Ossory received letters containing gossip, especially after the death of George Montagu, who had for some years been a Walpole correspondent.

Although there is a certain element of satire in the letters, Walpole was almost never bitter. He had the well-bred man's ability to see the humor and the absurdity in human conduct without having to regard foolishness as wickedness. For more than fifty years Walpole recorded what he saw, and in such a manner that the reader feels the immediacy of what happened long ago. On the scene himself at the time, Walpole was able to write for the modern reader, as well as for the eighteenth-century recipients of the correspondence, and in such fashion that the glow of reality lights up the history.

LETTERS TO HIS SON

Type of work: Courtesy letters
Author: Philip Dormer Stanhope, Lord Chesterfield (1694-1773)
First published: 1774

On the periphery of literature exists a valuable and fascinating genre, the personal letter which, like the private diary, reveals a man and an age far more intimately than any other form of writing. Probably no era practiced the epistolary art more widely than the eighteenth century and no man more skillfully than the fourth Earl of Chesterfield. Though the good earl had served his country unimpeachably as a member of Parliament, Lord Lieutenant of Ireland, and ambassador to Holland, and though his name designates an overcoat and a couch, it is generally conceded that Lord Chesterfield would have remained an inconspicuous figure in the eighteenth-century historical scene had it not been for the unintended publication of some four hundred letters to his illegitimate son, Philip Stanhope. No doubt the very fact that these letters were strictly private, intended to develop the education and manners of a young man who was expected to take a significant place in government and cultivated society, endows them with a frankness and honesty that betrays the cultivated self-seeking and the hypocritical morality of the upper-class society of the time. Eugenia Stanhope, whose secret marriage with young Philip was only one of the many disappointments Lord Chesterfield suffered at the hands of his intractable son, was so incensed at being excluded from the earl's will that against the family's wishes she sold the *Letters* to Dodsley for £1,575, thus infuriating English society and securing for Lord Chesterfield minor but recognized importance in the history of English prose.

The early letters are charmingly didactic essays addressed to a pre-adolescent mind, expected to become "not only the best scholar but the best bred boy in England of your age." "Dear boy," they all begin, and then proceed to shape little lessons on language, literature, geography, history, and good manners. They conclude with admonitions to obey Maittaire, his seventy-year-old tutor, and promises of "very pretty things" to reward him for industrious study. There is irony in Lord Chesterfield's explanation of irony—"Suppose that I were to commend you for your great attention to your book, and for your retaining and remembering what you have once learned; would you not plainly perceive the irony, and see that I laughed at you?" Reasons for such laughter were to come, but it was never bitter or audible ("there is nothing so illiberal, and so ill-bred as audible laughter"). Lord Chesterfield's optimism and faith in rationalism may have diminished somewhat, but it was never extinguished completely. After his failure in making an outstanding figure of young Philip, in 1761 he began the whole process over again with his godson, to whom he wrote almost three hundred letters in a decade.

It is not the early letters to his son but the later ones—addressed to "My Dear Friend"—that have aroused controversy. A strong believer in Locke's educational theory that a man's mind is wax to be molded into shape by environmental influences, Lord Chesterfield sent his son at fourteen not to a university but on the grand tour accompanied by a new tutor, the Reverend Walter Harte, supplied with letters of introduction into the highest social circles of great European cities, spied upon by the earl's agents, and pursued by affectionate but earnest epistles from an anxious father. How earnest they were can be gauged from this excerpt written to Lausanne in 1746: "I do not so much as hint to you how absolutely dependent you are on me; and that, as I have no womanish weakness for your person, your merit must and will be the only measure of my kindness." Nevertheless, it would be unfair to observe that even if the father never displayed warmth, love, or understanding, his kindness far exceeded the boy's merit.

The controversy concerns Lord Chesterfield's realistic observations on those aspects of life that he constantly urges his son to explore:

> Search, therefore, with the greatest care, into the characters of those whom you converse with; endeavor to discover their predominant passions, their prevailing weaknesses, their vanities, their follies, and their humours, with all the right and wrong, wise and silly springs of human actions, which make such inconsistent and whimsical beings of us rational creatures. . . . This is the true knowledge of the world; and the world is a country which nobody ever yet knew by description; one must travel through it oneself to be acquainted with it.

Having well-traveled that country, Lord Chesterfield could advise his son with a somewhat cynical sophistication. A man who never knew love and who married for a dowry that would repair his fortunes, he wrote: "Women are merely children of a larger growth. . . . A man of sense only trifles with them . . . . They will greedily swallow the highest [flattery], and gratefully accept the lowest . . . [but] They have, from the weakness of men, more or less influence in all courts. It is therefore necessary to manage, please and flatter them." It is this worldly self-interest that constitutes the dominant tone of the letters, "without some dissimulation no business can be carried on at all." There was no trace of mysticism or sentimentality about him; "religion must still be allowed to be a collateral security, at least, to Virtue." But virtue, apparently, was not an end in itself. Rather, it was a means to worldly success, a dependable means, if Lord Chesterfield's own career based on honesty and integrity is any measure. Nevertheless, worldly success was the goal and though "learning, honour, and virtue are absolutely necessary to gain you the esteem and admiration of mankind, politeness and good breeding are equally necessary to make you welcome and agreeable in conversation and common life." Elsewhere he urges his son to be neat and clean, to avoid obesity, to care for his teeth, and never under any circumstances to stick his finger into his nose.

The ultimate purpose was that young Stanhope should become—at the very least—a successful diplomat; but the principal objective of that occupation was "to get into the secrets of the court at which he resides" through any means including flattery or intimacy with a king's or minister's mistresses.

On the Continent, publication of the *Letters* was met with acclaim, their greatest admirer probably being Lord Chesterfield's old friend Voltaire: "I am not certain that it is not the best book on education which has ever been written." But in England the reaction was sternly condemnatory, even virulent. One periodical declared that as a man, he was "certainly solely actuated by pride, vanity, and ambition," and in her own letters Mrs. Montagu expressed her belief that "tho' many admired, no one ever esteem'd Lord Chesterfield."

LEVIATHAN

Type of work: Philosophy of politics
Author: Thomas Hobbes (1588-1679)
First published: 1651

To appreciate the range of Hobbes' subject matter in the *Leviathan* one may first consider the entire title: *Leviathan, or the Matter, Form, and Power of a Commonwealth Ecclesiastical and Civil.* In considering the "matter, form, and power" of the commonwealth, or state, Hobbes was doing far more than describing governments as he found them. His goal was to explain the origin of political institutions and to define their powers and right limits. To this end he thought it necessary to draw an analogy between the art of nature, productive of man, and the art of man, productive of the commonwealth. In drawing the analogy he first explained man himself, giving to the description a thoroughly mechanistic bias. He then proceeded to explain the state as man's artful creation, designed to put an end to the war of all against all.

The state, "that great Leviathan," is but an "Artificial Man," wrote Hobbes. The sovereign is an artificial soul, the officers of the state are artificial joints, reward and punishment are nerves, wealth and riches are strength; the people's safety is the business of the artificial man; the laws are its reason and will; concord, its health; sedition, its sickness; and civil war, its death.

All of men's ideas originate in sense, according to Hobbes—that is, they are derived from sense impressions. All sensation is a result of external bodies pressing upon the sense organs. Imagination is "nothing but *decaying sense*," the effect of sense impressions after the external body has ceased to press upon the organs. If we want to emphasize the past cause of the impression, we call the fading image a "memory" image; but if we want to emphasize the image as one not now related to any present cause,

we call it "fancy" or "imagination."

Hobbes was led by his mechanistic psychology to deny content to such a term as "infinite." He argued that when we say something is infinite we merely show that we cannot conceive its boundaries. Consequently, such a term as "God" is used not to conceive any being, but only to honor something incomprehensible.

Common names, such as "man," "horse," and "tree" may be applied to a number of individual things, yet there is nothing universal but names. In making this claim Hobbes was denying the Platonic belief that individual objects share a certain common character, or universal, in virtue of which they are similar. According to Hobbes, then, reasoning is simply the manipulation—the addition and subtraction—of names.

The passions are the "interior beginnings of voluntary motions," writes Hobbes. Since he argued that everything can be understood in terms of bodies in motion, it is not surprising that even the emotions are simply notions inside the body. Motion toward something is desire; motion away, aversion. In terms of these two basic motions Hobbes defined the other passions.

After considering the intellectual virtues and defects, the two kinds of knowledge (knowledge of observed fact, and the conditional knowledge of science), and the powers and manners of men, Hobbes turned his analytical mind to religion. Religion, he writes, is man's invention, the result of his ignorance and fear. Religious power and dogma are used to serve the interests of the priests. It is not surprising that, with these views, Hobbes was constantly in trouble both at home and abroad.

When Hobbes finally comes to the

point of declaring that men are by nature equal, he does so with no tone of ringing idealism. He means only that the differences between men are not so marked as the similarities, and he means also that there is no natural sanction for one man's assuming authority over another. Because men are similar, they sometimes come to desire the same thing; and if they cannot both enjoy the object of their desire, they become enemies and war over the object. There are three principal causes of fights between men: competition, diffidence, and glory. While men have no common power over them to keep them all in check, they are in "that condition which is called Warre; and such a warre, as is of every man, against every man." There are many inconveniences to war, and the fact that in a state of war there is no injustice (since there is no natural law governing action) in no way makes that state of affairs satisfactory. In order to secure peace men enter upon certain agreements by which they bring about a transferring of rights. It is possible for men to make such agreements, or contracts, because they have certain natural rights to use their power however they choose in order to preserve themselves.

Having discussed men, their nature, and their rights, Hobbes argued, in the second part of *Leviathan*, that the commonwealth is brought into being in order to enable men to escape from the state of war. Loving liberty and dominion over others, men agree to make some person sovereign over them all to work for their peace and benefit. The sovereign is not bound by the contract or covenant; the contract is among those who are to be ruled. If the ruler turns out to be a despot, it must be remembered that it is better to be ruled in a commonwealth than to be in a state of nature and, consequently, a continual state of war.

Hobbes considers three kinds of commonwealth: monarchy, democracy, and aristocracy, the latter being ruled by an assembly of part of the commonwealth.

There are certain advantages to the monarchial form of government, according to Hobbes: a monarch combines the private and public interest; he is better able to consult with men who have knowledge he needs; the only inconstancy the monarch has to put up with is his own; he cannot disagree with himself; and although it is sometimes inconvenient to have power vested in one man, particularly when the monarch may be an infant because of succession, the disadvantages are no greater than they are in other forms of government.

The subjects in a commonwealth are not entirely subject to the sovereign. The basic principle is that they cannot be compelled to act against that natural inclination toward self-preservation which the commonwealth is supposed to serve. They cannot be bound to injure themselves or to wage war—although this is a dubious right since the sovereign is free to imprison or execute them for disobedience. If the sovereign is not able to protect his subjects, the subjects are absolved of obedience to him.

The civil law of a commonwealth is made up of all those rules which prescribe what is right and wrong for the subjects; and since the commonwealth itself is no lawmaker, the sovereign must be the legislator. He is not subject to civil law, and only he can abrogate the law. Since an undeclared law is no law at all, and since law is not binding unless it is clearly commanded by the sovereign, the sovereign must make the law known and understood, and he must see to it that it be known as his law. The only laws that need not be published are laws of nature, and they can be contained in one sentence: "Do not that to another, which thou thinkest unreasonable to be done by another to thy selfe."

Hobbes regarded crime as resulting from some defect of the understanding, or from some error of reasoning, or from some force of the passions. He declares that "No law, made after a Fact done, can make it a Crime," and that although ignorance of natural law is no excuse, ignorance of civil law may excuse a man provided he had not the opportunity to hear the law declared. Punishment is not fundamentally retributive in Hobbes' scheme: "A Punishment, is an Evill inflicted by publique Authority, on him that hath done, or omitted that which is Judged by the same Authority, to be a Transgression of the Law; to the end that the will of men may thereby the better be disposed to obedience."

Like anything made by men, a commonwealth can perish. Its infirmities result from what Hobbes calls an "Imperfect Institution"—errors in the creation of the commonwealth. Perhaps the sovereign is not given enough power, or every man is allowed to be a judge, or conscience is authoritative in moral judgment, or supernatural inspiration is given precedence over reason, or the sovereign is held to be subject to civil law, or it is supposed that every man has some absolute property which the sovereign cannot touch, or it is supposed that sovereign power can be divided. Other difficulties, such as the lack of money, the presence of monopolies and corrupt politicians, the popularity of certain subjects, the greatness of a town, or the invasion by a foreign power can lead to the dissolution of the commonwealth.

Part III of *Leviathan* is concerned with showing the relations between a Christian commonwealth and commonwealths in general. Hobbes uses hundreds of Biblical references, as interpreted by him, to support his conclusion that it is possible to reconcile our obedience to God with our obedience to a civil sovereign, for the sovereign is either a Christian or he is not. If he is a Christian, then, even if he may sometimes err in supposing that some act is God's will, the proper thing for the subject, who has no right to judge, is to obey. If the sovereign is an infidel, then the subject must obey because the law of nature justifies the sovereign's power in a commonwealth, and to disobey would be to disobey the laws of nature which are the laws of God. No church leader, even a Pope, can rule the sovereign; and this situation is not contrary to God's law, for the Church works through civil government.

The concluding section, "Of the Kingdome of Darknesse," argues that spiritual darkness has not been completely eliminated from the Church—by which Hobbes means the Church of Rome. His principal attack on the Church of Rome is based on his claim that the Scripture is misinterpreted in order to justify the assumption of temporal power by the Popes.

Although Hobbes maintains that his entire argument is based upon a study of nature and of man's natural inclinations, it is clear that a large part of his discourse is an expression of his own preference for absolute monarchy. On this account he tends to overlook the possibility of restraining the power of a sovereign by democratic procedures. Nevertheless, the *Leviathan* is a remarkable attempt to explain and justify the institution of government, and it remains one of the masterpieces of political thought.

LIBER AMORIS

Type of work: An autobiographical account of a love affair
Author: William Hazlitt (1778-1830)
Time: 1820 1822
Locale: London and Scotland
First published: 1823

Principal personages:
H. (WILLIAM HAZLITT), the lover, a writer
S. (SARAH WALKER), the beloved
M. W. (MICAIAH WALKER), her father, a landlord and tradesman
C. P. (PETER GEORGE PATMORE), Hazlitt's friend
J. S. K. (JAMES SHERIDAN KNOWLES), another of Hazlitt's friends

Since William Hazlitt was a writer, it was not enough that he found himself passionately attracted to his landlord's daughter; he had to write about it. *Liber Amoris, or, The New Pygmalion* appeared in 1823, slightly disguised by initials in place of names, as the anonymous account of a writer's foolish passion; but it was not long before the secret was out. A reviewer for *John Bull* claimed that the review in the *Times*, favorable to the book, had been written by Hazlitt himself, and an effort was made to picture the girl of the account as a young, innocent child and Hazlitt as an "impotent sensualist."

The fact is that *Liber Amoris* was properly subtitled *The New Pygmalion*, for Hazlitt allowed his quite natural passion for an attractive and compliant young lady to lead him into flights of creative imagination whereby he sought to give her traits of character and depth of feeling to match her physical charms. His conversations with the landlord's daughter, delightfully transcribed at the beginning of the work, show Hazlitt to have been as much dazzled by his own literary facility in expressing her charms as he was with the charmer herself, seated upon his lap day after day and returning his kisses. By the end of the affair, after he had discovered that she was no more than a flirt—and not an innocent one at that—what impressed him most of all was that she was not what she had *seemed*. What she seemed to be is what, in his writer's imagination, he

made her; and what he discovered, when he realized her true nature, was that reality does not bother to copy the images of poets, even when they write a *Liber Amoris*.

The Pygmalion theme is never explicitly developed in the book, but Hazlitt speaks of Sarah as "the statue." In the first of his letters to C. P., Esq. written from Scotland, Hazlitt wrote in a footnote, "I have begun a book of our conversations (I mean mine and the statue's) which I call *Liber Amoris*." Later, in Letter XIII, the next to last letter of Part II of the *Liber Amoris*, he wrote to Patmore again concerning Sarah: "Since I wrote to you about making a formal proposal, I have had her face constantly before me, looking so like some faultless marble statue, as cold, as fixed and graceful as ever statue did. . . ."

The book begins with a series of conversations, apparently the result of Hazlitt's attempt to re-create the substance and feeling of amatory moments spent with Sarah. Then a series of letters to Patmore carry the narrative forward, telling of Hazlitt's hopes and doubts while in Scotland awaiting a divorce from his wife. The book closes with some letters to J. S. K. which, unlike the letters to Patmore, were never actually sent but were composed to complete the book.

Hazlitt became acquainted with Sarah Walker after his separation from his wife. Sarah, the second daughter of his landlord, Micaiah Walker, a tailor, was in her late teens when he met her. According to the *Liber Amoris* account, Sarah let him kiss her the first time they met, and during the first week of their acquaintance she sat upon his knee, and, in his words to her, "twined your arms round me, caressed me with every mark of tenderness consistent with modesty. . . ."

Later Hazlitt was to tell her father that Sarah had made a habit of sitting on his knee and kissing him. The father had supposed that the occasion upon which he had surprised the two lovers together was perhaps the only time such a thing occurred, but Hazlitt, trying to win sympathy for himself when he could not convince Sarah to marry him, assured Walker that "It was a constant habit; it has happened a hundred times since, and a thousand before. I lived on her caresses as my daily food, nor can I live without them."

The conversations are convincing and lively, more self-revealing than Hazlitt probably supposed. They show a man convinced of his ability to charm with language one whom he had so often kept busy with embraces. By the brief answers which Sarah gives we can guess that she found him something of a chatterbox and wished that he would pay more attention to the physical side of love and less to the spiritual and literary aspects of the experience.

For Hazlitt the overwhelming problem of his affair with Sarah was how to reconcile their hours of intimacy with her refusal to marry him or, at least, to live with him "in friendship." He asks her for an answer; he asks his friends; he asks her mother and father. But Sarah had the answer all along, only he lacked the ability to recognize its truth: "I told you my regard could amount to no more than friendship." Of course, it was the friendship of a healthy girl who enjoyed nothing more than being fondled by the lodgers in her father's house; but Hazlitt had the conventional notion that a girl who *seems* innocent and demure makes love only because she wishes to signify an intention to accept a proposal of marriage.

The course of the affair is simply told. Hazlitt met the tailor's daughter, kissed her on their first meeting, and held her on his lap. The entertainment continued for hundreds of performances. Hazlitt, as a writer, spent a good part of the time expressing his love in elaborate, literary ways which, for the most part, Sarah failed to appreciate. He kept making the effort to win from her a declaration of love to match his own, but she insisted that he could never be more than a friend to her. He gave her various books, including several he had written—and a small bronze figure of Napoleon which she treasured because it reminded her of a man she had cared for, a nobleman who considered the social distance between himself and Sarah too great to be overcome.

After Hazlitt went to Scotland to await a divorce from his wife, he wrote entreating letters to Sarah which were either not answered or were answered perfunctorily. His doubts and hopes were expressed at great length in letters to his friend Patmore.

Upon returning to London, after the divorce, Hazlitt again tried to persuade Sarah to marry him; but on the pretext that he had insulted her in a quarrel before his journey, when he had suggested vaguely that she was easy in her favors, she not only refused to marry him but returned the books and the statuette, which he promptly smashed. He finally discovered that she was playing the same game with another gentleman, C——, and that she had been doing so during the very period when he thought he had her embraces to himself alone. His final opinion of her, contrasting with the image of her as she *seemed* to be, was that she was "a practiced, callous jilt, a regular lodging-house decoy, played off by her mother upon the lodgers, one after another, applying them to her different purposes, laughing at them in turns, and herself the probable dupe and victim of some gallant in the end."

Despite Hazlitt's literary flights shown in both the conversations and the letters, *Liber Amoris* is a convincing and compelling account of an ordinary love affair. The style is mannered, in the fashion of a time when literary elaboration of ordinary passion was as much a sport as holding the landlord's daughter on one's knee. Yet beneath the poetry and the banter there is something of the English spirit and attitude which gives a dignity to what would otherwise be too trivial to be worth writing about, whatever the joys and pains of the participants. Hazlitt shows himself to be a divided man, wordly enough to realize that the girl, for all her demureness, allowed him liberties which she could not have allowed were she all she seemed to be, yet romantic enough and idealistic enough to suppose that somehow the fault was in himself and that all he had to do was to make himself worthy of her love and esteem. In this division of self Hazlitt shows himself to be the romantic Englishman—cynical and hopeful at the same time.

It is not enough to say that the portrait of Hazlitt and his "statue" is convincing and typical. Considered as a piece of literary work, *Liber Amoris* is remarkable in that it sustains interest with material so slight. What accounts for Hazlitt's success is the spirit of the piece; it is amusing, lively, sophisticated, and revealing of human foibles—all at once. It is a minor piece, and perhaps it is better to remember Hazlitt as a critical essayist; but it is from such minor pieces that English literature acquires its distinctive flavor and enduring charm.

LIEH KUO CHIH

Type of work: Novel
Author: Feng Meng-lung (1574?-1645?)
Type of plot: Historical romance
Time of plot: 770-220 B.C.
Locale: China
First published: Probably early seventeenth century

Principal personages:
KING YU, the last king of the Western Chou dynasty
KING P'ING, the first king of the Eastern Chou dynasty
DUKE HUAN OF CH'I, the first overlord
KUAN CHUNG, a philosopher and statesman
DUKE WEN OF CHIN, an overlord
KING CHUAN OF CH'U, an overlord
DUKE HSIAO OF CH'IN, a powerful feudal lord
SHANG YANG, a statesman and political reformer
SU CH'IN, a diplomat
CHANG I, a diplomat
CHING K'O, an assassin
SHIH-HUANG-TI, "The First Emperor" of Ch'in, a tyrant

Critique:

A popularized history, based entirely on Chinese classics, the *Lieh Kuo Chih* or *Tung Chou Lieh Kuo Chih (Chronicles of Divers Feudal States under the Eastern Chou Dynasty)* contains no fictitious figures. Its *dramatis personae* are numerous, including almost all the kings, princes, feudal lords, heroes, and villains throughout China from the early eighth century to the end of the third century B.C. This period of 550 years is probably the most important in Chinese history. We see how feudalism flourished, how the seven "contending kingdoms" fought bloody wars, and how China was reunified under the tyrant Ch'in Shih-huang. Much of the political institutions and strategic ideas of the succeeding centuries had their origins in the statesmen and generals of this period, just as Lao-tzu, Confucius, and leaders of other schools, all of whom appear in the text, marked the beginnings of systematic philosophical thought in China. Side by side with the shocking accounts of political assassination, incest, and massacre, heroic actions and noble deeds are recounted, to be remembered by posterity as the supreme lessons of practical morality. The classic version of this novel is credited to Feng Meng-lung, a prolific anthologist who edited and rewrote earlier fiction and drama, interspersing them with original work of his own.

The Story:

For hundreds of years the kings of Chou ruled China. King Yu-wang (781-771 B.C.) had a beautiful concubine whom he loved dearly. But the girl always looked depressed. The king would pay any price to make her smile. One day he lighted the fire beacon, a signal to announce the approach of an enemy. As the feudal lords with their troops hurried to the rescue, they found the king drinking with his concubine. They were forced to lead their troops back. The concubine enjoyed the practical joke so much that for the first time she gave a hearty laugh.

The Marquis of Shen, father of the lawful queen, resented the treatment of his daughter and grandson by the king, and he allied himself with the barbarians. Together they marched on the capital. The fire beacon was again lighted, but this time no rescuing troops appeared. King Yu-wang was killed and the beautiful concubine carried away by the barbarians.

The capital was also sacked and destroyed. When the heir-apparent, P'ing-Wang, was raised to the throne, he moved the government to Loyang, a city to the east. This was the beginning of the Eastern Chou dynasty (770 B.C.). From that time on, the royal house was weakened, and several feudal states rose to unprecedented power. The territory in the west, the present province of Shensi, was given up to the State of Ch'in, which gradually aggrandized itself as a result of the conquest of the neighboring tribes of barbarians, and became the force to reunify China centuries later.

The first feudal lord to attain to imperial importance was Duke Huan of Ch'i (685-643 B.C.) who occupied the northeast of the present province of Shangtung. His prime minister, Kuan Chung, on whom the duke relied heavily, launched a program of economic reconstruction. With his people enjoying economic prosperity at home and placing full confidence in him, the duke began a series of diplomatic moves which successfully bound various other states by treaty and he became an overlord, the leader of the feudal lords, defender of the royal house, and protector of weaker states.

The great menace to the allied states, with the King of Chou as their nominal head, was Ch'u, occupying, roughly, the present provinces of Hupeh and Hunan, a mere viscountship in the south, generally considered barbarous, but grown so formidable in its military strength and vast in its territory that its rulers defied the royal house and called themselves kings. The utmost Duke Huan of Ch'i accomplished with regard to the potential enemy in the south, though he had chased the barbarians in the northeast up to the border of Manchuria during a military campaign to help the much harassed state of Yen, was to bring about a pact of amity. The smaller states, under the pressure of circumstances, were often compelled to choose between joining the allies led by Ch'i or paying allegiance to Ch'u.

The first severe blow to Ch'u was dealt by Duke Wen of Chin, another prince who had become an overlord. Nearly a thousand chariots of war on either side, each with its allies, were engaged in a battle at a place called Ch'engp'u (632 B.C.) and Ch'u was defeated. This was the first great battle in Chinese history, and it is said to have saved Chinese civilization. Chin (occupying the present province of Shansi) for two centuries remained a great state in the north, but the power of the duke was usurped by his hereditary ministers until he had as little authority over his retainers as did the King of Chou over the feudal lords. The retainers fought fiercely among themselves and the houses of Wei, Han, and Chao emerged as the victors. These three retainers were recognized as hereditary feudal lords by the king, in 403 B.C. In 376 B.C. they divided among them the territory of Chin.

The power and prestige of Ch'u reached its zenith under King Chuan (613-591 B.C.), who defeated Chin. A hundred years later two other states in the south, hitherto obscure, extended their influence to the north. The first was Wu (now Kiangsu) whose armies in one campaign reached as far as the capital of Ch'u (506 B.C.) but were forced to withdraw before the intervention of Ch'in from the northwest. Though it had also defeated Ch'i, the glory of Wu soon faded; it was conquered by Yueh (now Chekiang) in 473 B.C., and in 334 B.C. Yueh was annexed by Ch'u.

After endless internal disturbance within most of the states and wars among them, seven "great powers" were left: Ch'in, Ch'u, Ch'i, Wei, Han, Chao, and Yen. The smaller and weaker states gradually became extinct, to the aggrandizement of the powers. The authority of the royal house was now utterly disregarded. The potentates of the great powers followed the once-detested example of Ch'u to assume kingship in the fourth century B.C. It was an age of the test of strength, when each state had to fight with every possible resource, military, diplomatic, material, and ideological, for survival if not to win supremacy.

Of the seven, Ch'in was considered geographically unassailable. Having annexed a large territory in the west, it was ready to bid for supremacy in China. Under Duke Hsiao (361-338 B.C.), organization of the peoples, which had been remarkable, was further strengthened by the policies of the prime minister, Shang Yang. The foundations of a totalitarian empire had been laid.

The military strength of Ch'in having struck such terror into the other states, their main problem was how to deal with the power in the west. At one time an alliance of six was formed to contend against Ch'in, acting upon the strategy of the diplomat Su Ch'in, who also became the chancellor of the confederation. But Su's scheme was obstructed by his former fellow-student, Chang I, who was working hard for Ch'in. With crafty maneuvers, bribery, and threats, Ch'in succeeded in dividing the allies who were either to accept defeat or to place their inter-allied jealousy above their common cause. In 317 B.C. Su Ch'in was assassinated.

The conquest of the six states by Ch'in was delayed by the efforts of the Four Statesmen of Ch'i, Ch'u, Chao and Wei. Able administrators and diplomats, they also gained great fame as patrons who threw open their doors to the scholars and men of ability who were wandering all over China seeking employment. Their popularity and ability enabled their states to hold out against Ch'in while they lived; after their deaths, none was able to stop the advance of the conqueror.

Ching K'o of Yen made a heroic attempt to assassinate the man then sitting on the throne of Ch'in (227 B.C.). His effort failed, however, and the king of Ch'in was crowned as Shih-huang-ti, "The First Emperor," known to posterity as the builder of the Great Wall and the burner of the books, after the conquest of his six rivals (220 B.C.). The last shadow monarch of the Chou Dynasty died in 256 B.C.

THE LIFE AND DEATH OF MR. BADMAN

Type of work: Allegorical dialogue
Author: John Bunyan (1628-1688)
First published: 1680

Principal characters:
  MR. BADMAN, a sinner
  MR. WISEMAN, who tells about Badman's career
  MR. ATTENTIVE, a listener

Practically every literate speaker of English has heard of *The Pilgrim's Progress* and its author, John Bunyan. Less well-known to readers, however, are Bunyan's other writings, including *The Life and Death of Mr. Badman*. There are reasons, of course, for modern neglect of Bunyan's other works. For one, there are relatively few readers attracted to the vast bulk of seventeenth-century religious writings in our time. For another, *The Life and Death of Mr. Badman*, being a didactic work, seems to the modern reader sententious and dull. Thirdly, the moral viewpoints expressed by Bunyan in *The Life and Death of Mr. Badman* sound strange in this century, so foreign are the writer's ideas to those prevalent in our time.

Yet in one sense *The Life and Death of Mr. Badman* is a companion piece to *The Pilgrim's Progress.* The latter work shows the Christian, devoted and obedient, winning his way to the rewards of righteousness, while the former illustrates what happens to the sinner who steadfastly refuses to acknowledge his evil ways and insists upon leading a depraved existence throughout a life that can be characterized only as evil, regardless of whether one agrees wholeheartedly with Bunyan's code of ethics in its entirety. The protagonist of the story, as it is related in dialogue, is Mr. Badman. He has all the evil in his heart one could possibly ask. Unlike the typical hero of picaresque fiction, Mr. Badman has no aspect which can endear him to the reader. Bunyan expected his readers to feel that the sooner Mr. Badman received punishment the better; there is no need to shed tears over such a character.

Bunyan's technique in presenting the story of Mr. Badman is to have Mr. Wiseman, the author's spokesman, relate the story of Badman's life shortly after the sinner's death. Mr. Wiseman's listener, aptly named Mr. Attentive, not only listens carefully but also draws out the details of the narrative when Mr. Wiseman lags. The dialogue form is an old one, used for ages to bring edifying material to the reader and force him into the role of a passive participant.

Possibly the most striking characteristic in *The Life and Death of Mr. Badman* is the insistence upon moral free choice and the assurance on the part of John Bunyan that all moral responsibility rests with the individual. Bunyan had no room in his theories for environmental determinism. The idea that the environment —family, the community, society in general—could be blamed for an individual's wrongdoing could not be fitted into Bunyan's moral philosophy. In the early pages of the dialogue between Mr. Wiseman and Mr. Attentive, putting the words into Mr. Wiseman's mouth as he speaks of Mr. Badman, Bunyan wrote:

"I will tell you that from a child he was very bad; his very beginning was ominous, and presaged that no good end was in likelihood to follow thereupon. There were several sins that he was given to when he was but a little one, that manifested him to be notoriously infected with original corruption; for I dare say he learned none of them of his father or mother, nor was he admitted much to go abroad among other children that were vile, to learn to sin of them; nay, contrariwise, if at any time he did get abroad amongst others, he would be as the inventor of bad words and an example in bad actions. To them all he used to be, as we say, the ringleader and master sinner from a child."

To this kind of theory voiced by Mr. Wiseman, Mr. Attentive agrees wholeheartedly, saying that certainly evil ways come from within the individual rather than, as most people believe today, from without.

The burden of the career of Mr. Badman is that one sin begets another. As a small child Badman, who has, says Bunyan, a host of equivalents in every generation, begins by lying and stealing from other members of the household, and he goes on to invest himself with almost the entire catalogue of sinfulness. Swearing, whoring, drinking, faithlessness in marriage, hypocrisy, and many other sins are committed by Badman during his lifetime.

Each mention of a new sin as the story of Mr. Badman's life progresses sends Mr. Wiseman or Mr. Attentive off into a kind of sermon or into a series of examples.

Scholars have pointed out that the examples Bunyan used in the dialogue were often borrowed from other writers, in whose books Bunyan had found them during his own reading. Bunyan accepted the stories he used as examples as fact, just as Cotton Mather was willing to accept signs of "Divine Providences" when they helped him to prove a point to his congregation or his readers.

There is no need to wonder why Bunyan wrote this dialogue of a sinner's progress, for he makes his purpose abundantly clear in an address to the "Courteous Reader." The world, says Bunyan again and again, is full of sinful people, and Mr. Badman has his relatives in every family and household. Convinced that there are so many sinners, Bunyan hopes to spread a word that may either convert or confound. Even Bunyan's Courteous Reader is viewed by the author as a possible (even probable) sinner, and he is asked to consider carefully whether he is treading in Mr. Badman's path to perdition.

LIFE IN LONDON

Type of work: Novel
Author: Pierce Egan (1772-1849)
Type of plot: Picaresque romance
Time of plot: Early nineteenth century
Locale: London
First published: 1821

Principal characters:
CORINTHIAN TOM, a man of fashion
JERRY HAWTHORN, his cousin
BOB LOGIC, their friend

Critique:

Tom and Jerry is a title commonly given to Pierce Egan's *Life in London; or the Day and Night Scenes of Jerry Hawthorn, Esq., and his Elegant Friend, Corinthian Tom, accompanied by Bob Logic, the Oxonian, in their Rambles and Sprees Through the Metropolis*. The book is a minor masterpiece. Any student of history who wishes to know of life in Regency London must read it, for it is the best single source of its kind. Pierce Egan, a sporting gentleman who observed keenly the life around him, put into his picaresque narrative a detailed account of boxing, cock fighting, masquerades, and taverns. In this work can be found much of the slang of the day—some of it still seems new—carefully explained in footnotes. At the time of publication the innumerable puns added to the liveliness of the novel, but to most modern readers the plays on words are often obscure and they can be disregarded. Egan's comic spirit made him a forerunner of Surtees and Dickens.

The Story:

Corinthian Tom, as he was later known, had been born into a rich family with loving parents, who watched after his welfare and provided for his every want. As he grew older he was a little uneasy at their solicitude, for the gay life in the capital appealed to him; and he would have liked to savor life without restrictions of any kind. Gradually instances of the many different facets of

London life came under his observation: the hungry man who counted the trees in St. James's Park to while away the dinner hour; the rake who crossed the street to avoid his tailor; the pawnshop customers. As Tom's knowledge increased, his impatience to savor the whole of life became keener.

He became very friendly with Bob Logic, a one-time student at Oxford. That merry fellow, with a comical face and an aptitude for puns, was rich, and he had already been orphaned. With no strictures of purse or parents, Bob's life was one long prank. For a time Tom envied him.

Tom's mother died first, and when his father also passed away, Tom's grief was genuine. With rare tact, Bob left him to face his sorrow alone, but after a decent wait he turned up again with his usual jests and puns. Tom then embarked on the life he most desired under Bob's shrewd tutelage. In short order Corinthian Tom was known at boxing matches, the society parades, the opera, and in slum dens. His career was crowned by the acquisition of the most desirable mistress in town, lovely and talented Catherine. As their connection became known, inevitably she was called Corinthian Kate.

His gay life was halted, temporarily, when Tom fell ill. He called in Doctor Pleas'em, a knowing doctor with the perfect approach for gay young blades. Doctor Pleas'em prescribed a country rest for his weary patient. Searching through his invitations, Tom found one from an uncle who lived at Hawthorn Hall, and immediately he set out to visit him.

At the hall Tom met his young cousin Jerry, a strong and quick lad who was dazzled by his city relative. Soon country life worked its wonders, and on the last day of his stay Tom accompanied Jerry on a twenty-six mile fox hunt. Both young men were in at the kill. That afternoon, when an agreeable party met to say their farewells to Tom, it was decided that Jerry should return to London with his cousin to acquire a city polish.

Jerry, much impressed by the appointments of Corinthian House, was a willing pupil in learning social graces. The first step was to call in a good tailor. Tom's man was Mr. Primefit, who was the most accomplished tailor in town. Mr. Primefit had built up his vast custom by never pressing for a bill; in return, the young blades never questioned the amount of a bill when they finally paid it. In his new clothes Jerry saw his first panorama of society when Tom took him riding in Rotten Row and Hyde Park.

With Tom and Bob as guides, Jerry saw the gambler, the tradesman, the sharper—all decked in finery well beyond their purses. The lively Lady Wanton and her sister, Miss Satire, were attracted by Jerry's fresh face and manly bearing. When Miss Satire made an unkind remark about Jerry's lack of polish, Lady Wanton warmly defended Jerry. The most beautiful woman they saw was the dazzling Duchess of Hearts. With his happy felicity for knowing everyone, Tom introduced Jerry to her. Jerry was struck dumb: her lovely face, her intelligent eyes, her warm heart were too much for him to comprehend.

Another person they met was Trifle, the thinnest and slightest dandy in London. To Jerry he seemed an absolute oddity. Then a calm older woman, warm of smile and respectable of appearance, drove by with three bewitching girls.

Jerry hoped for an introduction to the charming family, for they spoke to Bob. But he learned that introductions were not in order; the woman, madam of a select bawdy house, was advertising three of her most recent acquisitions.

Jerry's rusticity wore off quickly. Every afternoon and evening Bob and Tom took him out. They attended gatherings of all sorts. One afternoon Tom proposed an evening visit to the theater. Jerry assented eagerly, but Bob begged off; the theater was a bit high-toned for him. That evening Tom and Jerry went to Drury Lane. There Tom took a quick look at the stage and a longer one at the audience. Seeing few friends, the two cousins went on to Covent Garden, where the company seemed more congenial. After a glance at the play, they pushed into the Saloon. Jerry was struck by the crowds of laughing girls who were so very friendly. Tom had to tell him that the girls were on the lookout for customers.

Although Jerry was reluctant to leave the Saloon, Tom induced him to visit a coffee house. There the raffish hangers-on decided to have a bit of fun with the two swells. In the fight that followed Tom and Jerry were acquitting themselves well when the watch broke up the riot. Unfortunately, the cousins continued to battle the watch. They were finally subdued and hauled off to jail. Released on bail, they had to appear before a magistrate the next day. Their fine was supposed to pay the watch for the damage they had done.

In turn Tom, Jerry, and Bob went to a boxing establishment, a fencing salon, the dog fights, the condemned yard at Newgate. A highlight was a masquerade supper at the opera. Jerry, attracted by a coquettish woman dressed as a nun, was importunate in trying to learn her name. Finally the nun wrote an acrostic to supply the information. With Bob's help, Jerry finally learned that his companion had been Lady Wanton.

Tom was reluctant for some time to

introduce Corinthian Kate, but he finally arranged a meeting with her for Bob and Jerry. Kate, glad to see them, presented her very good friend Sue. Jerry was interested in analyzing the two women, both beautiful. Kate was self-possessed and inclined to dramatic settings; an accomplished belle. Sue seemed much warmer and more genuinely sympathetic. While Bob played the piano for them, Jerry and Sue had a pleasant tête-à-tête. Jerry was reluctant to leave.

Tom arranged a special trip for the two ladies about which he was quite mysterious. He warned them to be dressed by eleven sharp, for the success of the trip depended on punctuality, and so the ladies were ready when Tom and Jerry called. They were whisked away in a cab to Carleton Palace. There the friends went through the succession of fine rooms and examined the appointments at their leisure.

One of their memorable jaunts was an evening spent among cadgers. Disguising themselves as beggars, they visited a tavern frequented by professional alms takers, where they saw the crippled woman descend a ladder in a lively manner without her crutches. All manner of frauds came to light in that dismal gathering.

But all pleasant excursions were drawing to an end; Bob was put in debtors' prison. Although he was as merry as ever when Tom and Jerry went to see him, he did promise to put his affairs in better order, for he was confident he would soon be released. When Jerry caught a cold which he could not seem to get rid of, Doctor Pleas'em told him that he could not expect to lead such a life indefinitely, and he must return to Hawthorn Hall for a rest. Then he could come back and plunge into London life once more. Vowing to be back soon, and asking Tom to give his best wishes to Sue, Jerry returned to the country.

LIFE IS A DREAM

Type of work: Drama
Author: Pedro Calderón de la Barca (1600-1681)
Type of plot: Romantic melodrama
Time of plot: Sixteenth century
Locale: Poland
First presented: 1635

Principal characters:
BASILIO, King of Poland
SEGISMUNDO, his son
ASTOLFO, Basilio's nephew and a duke of Muscovy
ESTRELLA, the infanta, Basilio's niece
CLOTALDO, a Polish general
ROSAURA, a Russian noblewoman disguised as a man
FIFE, her servant

Critique:

Before Calderón's *La vida es sueño* was freely adapted by Edward Fitzgerald in 1853, it had been known to most English and European readers through the medium of French translations from the original Spanish. In spite of their richness of imagination, however, Calderón's plays are still little known outside the Spanish-speaking world. All of this playwright's work has vigor and brilliance; in *Life Is a Dream*, for example, he used his Polish setting and period as freely as Shakespeare used the seacoast of Bohemia or the forest of Arden. There is also a Gothic quality in the mountain scenes which suggests the popular atmosphere of much eighteenth-century fiction, and there is considerable psychological insight into character as well. This play reveals admirably the personality of its writer, who was a soldier, an ardent patriot, an artist, and a devout son of the Church. It has also been translated as *Such Stuff as Dreams Are Made Of*.

The Story:

One night, in the wild, mountainous country between Poland and Russia, a Russian noblewoman, Rosaura, and her servant, Fife, found themselves in distress. Their horses had bolted, and they feared that they would have to make on foot the remainder of their journey to the royal court of Poland. Rosaura, for protection through that barbarous frontier country, was disguised as a man.

Their weary way brought them at last to a forbidding fortress. There they overheard a young man, chained to the doorway of the castle, deliver a heart-rending soliloquy in which he lamented the harshness of his life. Rosaura approached the youth, who greeted her eagerly, with the excitement of one who had known little of sympathy or kindness during his brief span of years. At the same time he warned her to beware of violence. No sooner had he spoken these words than a shrill trumpet blast filled the night. Rosaura tossed her sword to the captive before she and Fife hid themselves among the rocks.

Clotaldo, a Polish general and the keeper of the youth, galloped up to the young man. Seeing the sword in his prisoner's hand, he ordered his men to seek the stranger who must be lurking nearby. Apprehended, Rosaura explained that she and Fife were Russian travelers on their way to the Polish court and that they were in distress because of the loss of their horses. Fife inadvertently hinted that Rosaura was really a woman. But the sword interested Clotaldo most of all, for he recognized the weapon as one which he had owned years before and which he had left in the keeping of a young noblewoman with whom he had been deeply in love. He decided that Rosaura must be his own son, but, torn between his sworn duty to his king and his paternal obligation toward his supposed son, he decided at last to say nothing for the time being. The fact that Rosaura possessed the sword obligated him to protect the travelers and to escort them safely through the mountains.

Meanwhile, in King Basilio's royal castle, the problem of succession to the Polish throne was to be decided. To this purpose, the king welcomed his nephew Astolfo and his niece Estrella, cousins. The problem of the succession existed because it was generally believed that the true heir, King Basilio's son, had died with his mother in childbirth many years before. The need for a decision was pressing; both Astolfo and Estrella were supported by strong rival factions which in their impatience were threatening the peace of the realm.

King Basilio greeted his niece and nephew with regal ceremony and then startled them with the news that his son Segismundo was not really dead. The readings of learned astrologers and horrible portents which had accompanied Segismundo's birth had led the superstitious king to imprison the child in a mountain fortress for fear that otherwise the boy might grow up to be a monster who would destroy Poland. Now, years later, King Basilio was not sure that he had done right. He proposed that Segismundo be brought to the court in a drug-induced sleep, awakened after being dressed in attire befitting a prince, and observed carefully for evidence of his worthiness to wear his father's crown. Astolfo and Estrella agreed to that proposal.

In accordance with the plan, Segismundo, who dressed in rough wolfskins in his captivity, was drugged, taken to the royal castle, and dressed in rich attire. Awaking, he was disturbed to find himself suddenly the center of attention among obsequious strangers. Force of habit caused him to recall sentimentally his chains, the wild mountains, and his former isolation. Convinced that he was dreaming, he sat on the throne while his father's

officers and the noble courtiers treated him with the respect due his rank. When they told him that he was the heir to the throne, he was mystified and somewhat apprehensive, but before long he began to enjoy his new feeling of power.

Clotaldo, his former guard and tutor, appeared to confirm the fact that Segismundo was really the prince. The young man then demanded an explanation of his lifelong imprisonment. Clotaldo patiently explained King Basilio's actions in terms that Segismundo might understand, but the youth, blinded by the sudden change in his fortunes, could see only that he had been grievously mistreated by his father. Declaring that he would have revenge for his unwarranted imprisonment, he seized Clotaldo's sword, but before he could strike the old general Rosaura appeared out of the crowd, took the weapon from him, and reproved him for his rashness.

Segismundo, in a calmer mood, was introduced to Astolfo, whose courtly bearing and formal speech the prince could not bear. Sick of the whole aspect of the court, he ordered the guards to clear the audience hall. But again he was mollified, this time by the appearance of Estrella and her ladies in waiting. Unaccustomed to feminine society, he behaved in a boorish manner, even attempting to embrace Estrella. The courtiers advised him to behave in a manner befitting a prince, and Astolfo, who hoped to marry his beautiful cousin, cautioned Segismundo about his behavior toward the princess. Unfamiliar with the formalities of court life, Segismundo lost all patience. Holding all present responsible for his long exile, he reminded them of his exalted position and defied anyone to touch Estrella. When Astolfo did not hesitate to take her by the hand, Segismundo seized Astolfo by the throat.

At this crucial moment in Segismundo's test, King Basilio entered the throne room and saw his son behaving like a wild beast. Crushed, he feared that the forecast had been true after all. Segismundo faced his father with shocking disrespect.

Pressed for an explanation of his son's imprisonment, the king tried to prove that it had been written in the stars. Segismundo scoffed at the folly of man in putting responsibility for his actions on the disinterested heavens. Then he cursed his father and called the guards to seize the king and Clotaldo. But at a trumpet blast the soldiers quickly surrounded Segismundo himself and took him prisoner.

Having failed the test of princehood, Segismundo was drugged and returned in chains to the mountain fortress. In his familiar surroundings once more, he had full opportunity to reflect on his late experiences. When he spoke to Clotaldo about them, the old general assured him that all had been a dream. Since the prince had been drugged before he left the fortress and before he returned, he was quite convinced that he had suffered an unpleasant dream. Clotaldo assured him that dreams reveal the true character of the dreamer. Because Segismundo had conducted himself with violence in his dream, there was great need for the young man to bridle his fierce passions.

Meanwhile Rosaura, aware of Segismundo's plight and anxious to thwart the ambitions of Astolfo, who had once promised to marry her, stirred up a faction to demand the prince's release. The rebels invaded the mountains and seized the fortress· they failed, however, to seize Clotaldo, who had already returned to the royal castle to report to King Basilio. When the rebel army carried the sleeping Segismundo out of the fortress and awakened him with trumpet blasts, the unhappy prince would not be persuaded that his new experience was real, and he doubted the assurance that he had been rescued from his imprisonment. The rebel leader finally convinced him that it would be well for him to join the dream soldiers and fight with them against King Basilio's very real army, which was approaching.

Clotaldo was taken prisoner by Segismundo's forces, but the young prince, remembering the advice to curb his passions, ordered the old general's release. A great battle then took place, in which Segismundo proved his princely valor and chivalric bearing. King Basilio, defeated but refusing Clotaldo's and Astolfo's pleas to flee to safety, in admiration surrendered his crown to his son.

King of Poland in his own right, Segismundo ordered the marriage of Astolfo to Rosaura, who had, in the meantime, been revealed as Clotaldo's daughter. Estrella became Segismundo's queen. The young king made Clotaldo his trusted adviser.

Type of work: Biography
Author: Robert Southey (1774-1843)
Time: 1758-1805
Locale: England, the British colonies, the Continent, the high seas
First published: 1813

> *Principal personages:*
> VISCOUNT HORATIO NELSON, English naval hero
> EDMUND NELSON, his father
> LADY EMMA HAMILTON, his mistress
> LADY FRANCES NELSON, his wife
> MAURICE SUCKLING, Nelson's uncle, a naval captain, later Comptroller of the Navy
> SIR WILLIAM HAMILTON, English ambassador to Naples
> THOMAS TROUBRIDGE,
> ALEXANDER BALL,
> SAMUEL HOOD,
> BENJAMIN HALLOWELL,
> HYDE PARKER,
> THOMAS GRAVES,
> EARL ST. VINCENT (SIR JOHN JERVIS), and
> CUTHBERT COLLINGWOOD, English naval officers

"What has poor Horatio done, who is so weak, that he, above all the rest [of your children], should be sent to rough it out at sea? But let him come, and the first time we go into action, a cannonball may knock off his head, and provide for him at once."

Had Nelson's uncle, Captain Maurice Suckling, been prophetic in this letter to Nelson's father, the course of English history subsequent to the Napoleonic Wars (1803-1815) might well have been quite different from what it has been. The weakness of the twelve-year-old Horatio that Captain Suckling referred to was only physical. Weak though he was, Nelson had already given proof of the resoluteness of heart and nobleness of mind that were to characterize his distinguished career.

Always a stranger to fear and a companion of honor, Nelson led the exemplary life that his father foresaw for his son. Nelson's father had always marked him for success in whatever profession he might follow. Through his indomitable spirit, his seafaring abilities, and his acumen in personal relationships, Nelson was a lieutenant at nineteen, a captain at twenty-one, and an admiral before he was thirty.

From his maiden voyage to India early in his career, Nelson, reduced almost to a skeleton by tropical disease, was returned home. Dejected by his physical condition and the diminished promise of success in his career, he considered suicide for a time. But from this state of mind he suddenly rallied with a feeling bordering on the religious, so obsessed was he by the "sudden glow of patriotism . . . presented by king and country as my patron."

Southey's explanation of this fervor and determination that spurred Nelson on to become a hero is compatible in its beauty with the exquisite qualities of a man who surmounted obstacles to have his name become as well known as that of the country for which he achieved heroism:

He knew to what the previous state of dejection was to be attributed; that an enfeebled body, and a mind depressed, had cast this shade over his soul; but he always seemed willing to believe, that the sunshine which succeeded bore with it a prophetic glory, and that the light which led him on was "light from heaven."

Though heroes are often seen in an aura of celestial light and divine guidance, Nelson was most cognizant of mundane matters that need attending to, even though one confides in Providence. His readiness in political strategy was a factor in the first of his three greatest naval successes, the defeat of Napoleon's fleet at Aboukir in 1798. For more than a month Nelson's fleet had sought the French fleet in the Mediterranean. Thwarted at every attempt to get information concerning the French position or to secure supplies, Nelson turned at last to Lady Emma Hamilton, the wife of the English ambassador to Naples. Through her influence with the Queen of Naples, Nelson secured supplies at Syracuse and began again his pursuit of the French.

Contrary to his command to his men that they obey orders implicitly without questioning their propriety, Nelson, sometimes seeing circumstances in a different light from that of his superiors, did not always obey orders. In the victory at Copenhagen, in 1801, against the armed neutrality of the Baltic, Nelson, second in command, ignored his commander's order to cease action. Putting his telescope to his blind eye when he was told the signal giving the order had been raised (Nelson had lost the sight of one eye in battle at Calvi), he continued the attack, saying he could not see the signal.

Acting without orders from his commander, Sir John Jervis, Nelson was largely responsible for the defeat of the Spanish fleet at Cape St. Vincent (1797). In that engagement the enemy fleet far outnumbered the English ships, twenty-seven to fifteen. This victory destroyed a threatened invasion of England.

Another practical personal qualification contributing to Nelson's success was his ability as a leader, especially his attention to effective communication. He had marked confidence in his officers' abilities, but he was sure in every case possible that everyone knew his principles of tactics.

In keeping with his confidence in Providence, Nelson seemed obsessed with the assurance of victory. This attribute was inculcated into his men. Quite pleased with the scope of the plan of an attack against the French, one of Nelson's captains asked, "If we succeed, what will the world say?" "There is no if in the case," Nelson exclaimed. "That we shall succeed is certain: who may live to tell the story is a very different question."

After destroying thirteen French ships at Aboukir, making useless the French army in Egypt, placed there in preparation for Napoleon's projected conquest of the East, Nelson became an international hero. He was showered with congratulations, rewards, and honors by all countries which, because of his military success, had escaped Napoleon's aggression. Such accolades, received before he was thirty, were to become commonplace to England's greatest naval hero.

Southey's biography is no mere chronological recital of events. His descriptions of naval battles are sufficiently developed and detailed enough to provide the excitement of adventure stories. But in these, as in the more ordinary incidents, emphasis is on persons—their abilities and weaknesses, their hopes and disappointments. The writing has a poet's tone and spirit without poetic devices. This quality in the prose serves to convey the spirit of self-reliance, nonconformity, and courage that constitutes a hero. Clarity and conciseness are the keynotes of the style.

In his choice of biographical detail, Southey never lost sight of the fact that Nelson was first a man and then a naval hero. The strong bond of love and admiration between Nelson and his father, for example, is a warming thread throughout the book. The son's deliberate adherence to his father's counsel and the father's pride in the son's accomplishments add to the stature of the hero. It was fitting, in the light of this lifelong devotion between Nelson and his father, that a few months before the father's death the older Nelson came to accept Nelson's affair with Lady Hamilton. Perhaps in blind love for his son, he saw in his son's mistress a woman described by Southey as "a character which, both in its strength and in its weakness, resembled his own." This reconciliation meant much to Nelson because his association with Lady Hamilton had brought sorrow and displeasure to his father, especially when Nelson was separated from Lady Nelson.

Southey treats Nelson's marital situation in a matter of fact manner as another facet of the admiral's life. This is no love idyl, developed by a poet.

The affair began in Naples, where Sir William Hamilton was English ambassador and Nelson was in charge of a squadron during the French occupation of Naples (1798-1799). Nelson and the Hamiltons became inseparable friends; they returned to England together in 1800. At Sir William's death, he was holding Nelson's hand and entrusting Lady Hamilton to his care.

Nelson did arrange a pension for Lady Hamilton and Horatia Nelson Thompson, "believed to be his [Nelson's] daughter," as Southey discreetly identified the child, born to Lady Hamilton about the time Nelson was separating from Lady Nelson.

Nelson's third and last great victory was the sea battle fought off Cape Trafalgar, where in 1805 he destroyed both the French and Spanish fleets. This success culminated two years of strategic naval maneuvering and warfare, with Nelson in command of the fleet in the Mediterranean. During that time he blockaded the French fleet at Toulon for twenty-two months. The English victory at Trafalgar resulted in the capture of twenty enemy ships—not an English vessel was lost—and the end of Napoleon's power of the sea. But in that battle Nelson lost his life. His immortal words "England expects that every man will do his duty" were among his last.

Nelson's stature is admirably established in Southey's description of his death:

> The most triumphant death is that of the martyr; the most awful, that of the martyred patriot; the most splendid, that of the hero in the hour of victory; and if the chariot and the horses of fire had been vouchsafed for Nelson's translation, he could scarcely have departed in a brighter blaze of glory. He has left us, not indeed his mantle of inspiration, but a name and an example, which are at this hour inspiring hundreds of the youth of England: a name which is our pride, and an example which will continue to be our shield and our strength.

The eminence of the subject and the cogency of Southey's writing make it easy to see why the American government published a special edition of the *Life of Nelson* and issued a copy to every seaman and officer in the American navy.

Although Southey was poet laureate of England for thirty years, he is remembered for only a few of his vigorous short poems, "The Battle of Blenheim" being one of his best. Ironically, the poet is best known today for his prose writing, this model among short biographies and a classic in English literature.

THE LIFE OF SAMUEL JOHNSON, LL.D.

Type of work: Biography
Author: James Boswell (1740-1795)
Time: The eighteenth century
Locale: England
First published: 1791

Principal personages:
> SAMUEL JOHNSON, author, critic, and lexicographer
> JAMES BOSWELL, the biographer, Johnson's friend
> DAVID GARRICK,
> SIR JOSHUA REYNOLDS,
> MR. AND MRS. THRALE,
> DAVID HUME, and
> OLIVER GOLDSMITH, members of the Johnson circle

James Boswell's life of Samuel Johnson has usually been considered the greatest biography yet produced in the English language, and it has undoubtedly commanded more readers than any other biography written in English. There are more massive biographies in our literature, such as David Masson's *Life of Milton* and J. G. Lockhart's *Memoirs of the Life of Sir Walter Scott,* but none has ever achieved the critical acclaim or the popularity or the prestige lavished justly upon Boswell's biography of Samuel Johnson.

During his lifetime Boswell published three great works: *The Life of Samuel Johnson, LL.D., The Journal of a Tour to the Hebrides with Samuel Johnson, LL.D.,* and *An Account of Corsica: The Journal of a Tour to That Island; and Memoirs of Pascal Paoli.* Of these three works, the *Life of Johnson* stood out as the greatest for almost a century and a half. Within the last thirty years, however, a new estimate of James Boswell's work has had to be taken, for much of Boswell's writing was lost in manuscript until the 1920's. During the period between 1927 and 1949 Colonel Isham, an American and a collector, brought together the papers which had been stored at Malahide Castle, near Dublin, Ireland, and the Forbes collection, which had accidentally passed into the hands of one of Boswell's executors and descended to the latter's heirs. Some of the papers were published by Isham, who sold the entire collection to Yale University in 1949 and 1950. The university has published several volumes of the papers under the general title of *The Yale Editions of the Private Papers of James Boswell.* Through such volumes of Boswell's writing as *Boswell's London Journal, 1762-1763* (1950), *Boswell in Holland, 1763-1764* (1952), and *Boswell on the Grand Tour: Germany and Switzerland, 1764* (1953), Boswell has emerged as a splendid writer of journals. This fact, however, does not yet detract from his stature as the author of the biography of Johnson, nor will these newer works replace the biography as the most important of Boswell's books, even though critical opinion may be modified to grant him greater stature in literature than he once had.

We now know that the *Life of Johnson* was based upon what Boswell had recorded in copious journals which he kept during the greater part of his adult life. This is not to say, however, that the biography was merely a transcription of materials from those journals. From present knowledge of the papers it can be seen that Boswell was an artist in biography, choosing carefully what suited his needs and goals. Even those who feel that Boswell intruded himself too much into the biography must now recognize that he was at some pains to omit much material about Johnson in which he himself figured. Those who felt that Boswell intruded too much into the work possibly overlooked the fact that during Johnson's life Boswell was Johnson's friend and spent from four hundred to five hundred days with his subject, thus becoming himself a part of Johnson's life and the Johnsonian environment.

Boswell's method was to record materials about Johnson in his journals. Sometimes the material was recorded daily, but on occasion Boswell fell behind and had to rely upon his memory—a phenomenal one—to recall materials he had garnered in a period of four or five days and evenings. It is notable, too, that Boswell was careful to prompt Johnson into conversation, often asking what seem to be obvious or absurd questions in order to goad Johnson into making remarks worthy of record. One such question noted by critics is that in which Boswell asked Johnson what he would do if given the solitary care of a small infant; the question, seemingly absurd, led Johnson to reply in such fashion as to comment on rearing and educating children and to set forth a philosophy of education. The more we learn about Boswell and his work, the more we understand that he was not a mere transcriber, as critical legend held for some time, but that he was a skillful writer who shaped his materials in every way he could, instead of accepting them as he found them. The casual reader may even miss some of the more obvious points of care and artistry, such as notations on how Johnson looked and spoke when delivering comments and opinions.

Johnson was a man of many achievements. He single-handedly brought forth the first recognized dictionary of the English language; he also made himself famous as a writer by means of *The Rambler* papers, his tragedy *Irene*, his poetry, and his moral essays. As a moralist Johnson also won fame as the author of the didactic novel, *The History of Rasselas, Prince of Abyssinia*. As a critic he was famous for his *Lives of the Poets* and his preface to an edition of Shakespeare's plays. People great and small admired

Johnson, including many of the famous and remarkable Englishmen of his time, men like Hume, Reynolds, Goldsmith, and Garrick. In addition, he was a picturesque, at times even ludicrous, figure, and this fact Boswell did not attempt to hide, taking to himself the task of writing "not his panegyrick, which must be all praise, but his Life; which great and good as he was, must not be supposed to be perfect." In further defense of his way of writing biography, Boswell wrote near the beginning of his biography:

> I am fully aware of the objections which may be made to the minuteness on some occasions of my detail of Johnson's conversation, and how happily it is adapted for the petty exercise of ridicule by men of superficial understanding, and ludicrous fancy; but I remain firm and confident in my opinion, that minute particulars are frequently characteristick, and always amusing, when they relate to a distinguished man. I am therefore exceedingly unwilling that anything, however slight, which my illustrious friend thought it worth his while to express, with any degree of point, should perish.

Boswell realized, as we know from what he himself said and wrote, that the function and art of biography is to focus on the subject and keep him constantly before the reader. This Boswell did in his biography of Johnson. To do so he carefully gathered together more than what he knew at first-hand of the man who was his friend and subject. He exercised diligence and care in collecting letters written by Johnson, including the text of the famous letter to Lord Chesterfield. He collected, too, letters written about Johnson, as well as anecdotes about his subject's life, trying at the same time to establish the authenticity of these reports he had of Johnson. These materials are presented in the biography in chronological order. If the results have some defects, the defects are more or less forgivable in view of their sparseness. Seldom did Boswell record facts which later biographers needed to correct.

If the account of Johnson's life before meeting Boswell is relatively short, this fact may be excused on the ground that Boswell used only what information about Johnson's early life that he could gather and trust. Naturally, he had a much larger fund of materials from the period during which he knew Johnson personally. Some critics have noted Boswell's reluctance to interpret. Of this reluctance, it must be said that interpretation was not Boswell's way. Upon occasion he generalized upon Johnson perceptively, but he preferred, as he carefully stated, to present the particulars, rather than the generalizations. The result is that John-son is "alive" in the *Life* as few biographical subjects are, with his personality and character borne out by his own spoken and written words. On occasion the reader may feel that Johnson's written words, usually letters, have been inserted where they fit none too well, seeming to interfere with the flow of the book. And yet they are a part of the scheme Boswell worked out and put together.

Samuel Johnson has been the subject of many biographies; five, for example, appeared after Johnson's death and before Boswell's work. Others have been written since, but none has ever equaled in merit Boswell's *Life of Samuel Johnson, LL.D.*

LIFE ON THE MISSISSIPPI

Type of work: Reminiscence
Author: Mark Twain (Samuel L. Clemens, 1835-1910)
Type of plot: Regional romance
Time of plot: Mid-nineteenth century
Locale: Mississippi River region
First published: 1883

Principal characters:
MARK TWAIN
MR. BIXBY, a river pilot

Critique:

It is extraordinary that a book with so many defects should have become one of the classics of our national heritage. There is, for example, a sharp and obvious division between the first twelve or fourteen chapters and the rest of the book. It is clear that it was not written all at one time, and the effects of bad composition are evident. The chapters are badly organized and there are many labored passages. Despite this lack of craftsmanship, *Life on the Mississippi* is a vivid, dramatic, and extremely interesting collection of reminiscences. Like the mighty river with which it is concerned, the book has become part of the American tradition, part of our national pride and history.

The Story:

When Mark Twain was a boy, he and his comrades in Hannibal, Missouri, had one great ambition; they hoped to become steamboatmen. They had other ambitions, too, such as joining the circus or becoming pirates, but these soon passed. Only the ambition to be a steamboatman remained, renewed twice each day when the upriver and the downriver boats put in at the rickety wharf and woke the sleepy village to bustling life. Through the years, boy after boy left the river communities, to return later, swaggering in his importance as a worker on a steamboat. Mark Twain saw these boys often, and the fact that some of them had been considered as undeniably damned in the eyes of the pious folk shook Twain's convictions pro-

foundly. He wondered why these boys who flouted Sunday School maxims and ran away from home should win the rewards of adventure and romance that meeker town boys never knew.

Mark Twain, too, had this dream of adventure. His ambition was a lofty one. He determined to become a cub-pilot. While in Cincinnati, he heard that a government expedition was exploring the Amazon. With thirty dollars he had saved he took a boat bound for New Orleans. His intention was to travel on to the headwaters of the Amazon. But the ship was grounded at Louisville, and during the delay Mark came to the attention of Mr. Bixby, the most famous pilot on the Mississippi River. He prevailed upon Bixby to teach him how to navigate.

At first the adventure was a glorious one. But soon Mark found that the more he knew about the river, the less romantic it seemed. Though he was a dutiful student, he discovered that he could not remember everything Bixby told him, regardless of how important this information seemed to be. Furthermore, to his astonishment and despair, his instructor told him that the river was changing its course continually; that there were no such things as permanent landmarks; that the river channel was never the same, but always variable. There were times when the young cub-pilot was frightened, especially when he narrowly missed hitting another ship, or trimmed the boat too close to shore. But worse was the experience of piloting in the dead of night, with no landmarks to observe and only deep blackness all around.

Bixby claimed the secret of navigation was not to remember landmarks, which changed, but to learn the shape of the river, and then to steer by the shape in one's head.

It was undeniably an interesting life. The pilot had to be on the lookout for rafts sailing the river at night without lights. Often a whole family would be on a raft, and they would shout imprecations at the steamboat which had just barely missed dumping them all into the river. Then there was the fascinating behavior of the river itself. Prosperous towns would be isolated by a new cut-off and reduced to insignificance; towns and islands in one state would be moved up or down and into another state, or, as sometimes happened, into an area that belonged to no state at all!

The river pilot reigned supreme on his boat. The captain was theoretically the master; but as soon as the boat got under way, the pilot was in charge, and only a very foolhardy captain would have interfered. The importance of the pilot in river navigation eventually led to the formation of a pilots' association. At first the idea seemed ridiculous. But the union grew as, one by one, all the good pilots joined. As a result pilots could make their own terms with the owners. Not only were wages guaranteed, but pilots secured better working conditions, pensions, and funds for their widows and orphans. Within a few years the association was the most indestructible monopoly in the country. But its days were numbered. First of all, the railroads came in and river transportation was gradually abandoned in favor of rail traffic. Then, too, the Civil War reduced navigation to a mere trickle and dealt a deathblow to river commerce. The steamboat was no longer an important means of transportation.

From then on the river was different. It seemed very different to Mark Twain when he returned after many years away from it, and saw the changes with nostalgic regret. He traveled once more on the Mississippi, but this time as a passenger and under an assumed name. He listened tolerantly to the man who told him wild and improbable stories about the river, and to a fellow traveler who explained, very explicitly, how everything worked.

Mark Twain decided to search for a large sum of money left by a murderer whom he had met in Germany. He and his companions made plans about the ten thousand dollars soon to be in their possession, and they asked to get off their boat at Napoleon to look for it. Unfortunately, the Arkansas River, years before, had swept the whole town into the Mississippi!

On his return to the river, Mark Twain learned many things he had not known. He witnessed the vast improvements in navigation and in the construction of the boats, improvements that made navigation easier and safer. He talked to the inhabitants of Vicksburg, who described their life during the bombardment of the town by Union forces. He visited Louisiana and expressed horror at the sham castles that passed for good architecture. He read Southern newspapers and saw in them, as in so many Southern traditions, the romantic sentimentality of Sir Walter Scott, an influence that he regretted, hated, and held responsible for the South's lack of progress. He came in contact with a cheerful and clever gambler; he heard about senseless feuds that wiped out entire families; he saw new and large cities that had grown up since he had left the river; he met such well-known writers as Joel Chandler Harris and George W. Cable; he had an experience with a spiritualist who grew rich on the credulous and the superstitious; he witnessed tragedy, and lost friends in steamboat explosions.

The river would never be the same again. The age of mechanization had arrived to stay. The days of the old river pilots, such as Mr. Bixby, were now a thing of the past. America was growing up, and with that growth the color and romance of the Mississippi had faded forever.

LIFE WITH FATHER

Type of work: Short stories
Author: Clarence Day, Jr., (1874-1935)
Type of plot: Humorous satire
Time of plot: Late nineteenth century
Locale: New York City
First published: 1935

Principal characters:
CLARENCE DAY, SR.
MRS. CLARENCE DAY, his wife
CLARENCE DAY, JR., the narrator

Critique:

This narrative of personal recollections is a humorous commentary on American manners in the Victorian age. Father is a domestic tyrant whose bark is considerably worse than his bite. His crotchety behavior is the last resort of masculine aggressiveness in a woman-dominated world.

The Story:

The Day household existed under the eccentric domination of Clarence Day, Sr., a Wall Street businessman who was convinced that he was always right. His son stood in awe of him. The boy's greatest treat was to be taken to his father's office on Saturday mornings. With Father dressed formally in silk hat and tailed coat, they rode downtown on the elevated and the boy gaped curiously into the windows of flophouses and wished that he could enjoy the luxury and freedom of being a tramp. That ambition he did not reveal to his father. Once he ventured to suggest that he would like to be a cowboy, but Father retorted that cowboys were shiftless people.

Father's office seemed very mysterious to the boy, and he enjoyed the privilege of filling inkwells and running errands. Later there would be luncheon at Delmonico's. Father and his favorite waiter always chatted in French about the menu, and Father enjoyed himself greatly. But the boy did not think highly of the food. There was too little of it, scarcely enough to satisfy his appetite. Seeing the starved look on his face, Father would order a large chocolate éclair for him.

One of Father's chief worries was the fear of becoming fat. The members of his club recommended long walks, but Father was already taking long walks. Then they suggested horseback riding. Accordingly, Father became a member of the Riding Club on East Fifty-eighth Street. Apart from stabling conveniences, the club had a park for riding, really only a little ring. But it was tame enough for Father, who liked things to be orderly and suitably arranged for his use. In a very short time he felt as if the park belonged to him, and if the leaves were not raked, if papers were lying around, he would take the neglect as a personal affront.

The first horse Father bought was an independent, rebellious creature. There was little love lost between them. The climax came one morning when the horse refused to obey. It reared and reared until Father gave up in disgust and went back to the club. Since the rest of the family wanted a horse of their own, Father gave them that one. He bought another for himself.

Having never been sick, Father became very annoyed whenever anybody else was ill; and he had no sympathy whatever for people whose illnesses he considered to be simply imaginary. Whenever he was unlucky enough to catch a cold, his method of treating it was to blow his nose loudly or to sneeze. Whenever he had a sick headache, he would not eat. After he had starved out his illness, he would eat again and triumphantly light up a cigar.

Father's laws were regarded as edicts not to be challenged. Accordingly, young Clarence was amazed when anyone did not respond to Father's whims and orders. While out in the country one summer, the family ran out of ice. Because Father's wine must always be chilled, the crisis was a grave one. Nothing the family could do was successful. But when Father came home, he went down to the village, intimidated a dealer into selling him an icebox, provided he would somehow get it filled with ice, and argued the iceman into delivering a load immediately.

Father got things done in his own way. The family could never keep servants for very long. One day the cook left. Father stormed into an employment agency, looked over the assembled girls, and then, over the manager's protests, picked out the one he liked. Although she had not wanted to be a cook, the girl went with him meekly and stayed on in the Day household for twenty-six years. Her name was Margaret.

In the summer Margaret always stayed in New York to look after the house, and each year there arose the problem of a temporary cook during the time that the family was in the country. One year they hired Delia. Before long Father insisted that she was starving him to death. Delia was replaced by a Japanese. At the first meal prepared by the Japanese, Father moaned with pain and declared that he was poisoned. Margaret was hastily summoned from the city, and Father was happy again.

What really vexed Father was Mother's inability to keep household accounts according to the system he tried to teach her. The money always inexplicably disappeared, and the bills were always high. In addition, Mother was fond of charge accounts. It was so easy to buy things that way, and the first of the month seemed far off in the distance. When the bills came in, however, Father always raged—and then gave in.

When Mother went on a trip to Egypt, Father could not understand why she should want to go off to the far corners of the world just to see pyramids. When she came back with part of her expense money unaccounted for, Father was curious. At last Mother admitted that she had not spent it, but intended to keep it. Father, wanting to know what good it would do her to keep it, demanded its return. But again he lost out. Mother kept the money.

Young Clarence witnessed many examples of Father's behavior. He was urged to be prompt for breakfast and bribed with the offer of a watch. He suffered whenever Father opened his mail, particularly when the letters were from young ladies. Father could never understand that letters could ever be for anyone else. When Father finally agreed to have a telephone installed, he likewise assumed that all calls were for him. Once he was very perturbed when a young lady, thinking she was speaking to young Clarence, invited him to lunch.

Women, Father insisted, did not know anything about politics. When Mother came under the influence of Miss Gulick, an emancipated young woman, he snorted contemptuously. Though he liked to dine out with friends, he did not like company in his own house. Once he startled a group of Mother's friends by uttering a lone, monosyllabic word as he stamped past the dining-room on his way upstairs.

Because he had disliked some members of his family buried in the family plot in the cemetery, he did not wish to be buried there after his death. Mother reminded him that such matters are not important to the dead. But Father insisted that he was going to buy a new plot in the cemetery, one all for himself, and in a corner where he could get out. Mother looked at him in astonishment. She whispered to young Clarence that she almost believed he could do it.

LIGEIA

Type of work: Short story
Author: Edgar Allan Poe (1809-1849)
Type of plot: Gothic romance
Time of plot: Early nineteenth century
Locale: Germany and England
First published: 1838

Principal characters:
THE NARRATOR
LIGEIA, his first wife
LADY ROWENA TREVANION, his second wife

Critique:

Poe himself called "Ligeia" his best story. It is a tale of terror combined with pure fantasy. As always in the prose tales of this genius of American literature, plot, character, and setting are fused into one. It was Poe's literary creed that all elements should be subordinated to the total effect desired. Nowhere does he better demonstrate this belief than in the fantastic story of Ligeia. Many critics have read deeper moral significance into this Gothic work.

The Story:

He could not remember when he had first met Ligeia, and he knew nothing of her family except that it was old. Ligeia herself, once his wife, he could remember in every detail. She was tall and slender. Ethereal as a shadow, her face was faultless in its beauty, her skin like ivory, her features classic. Crowning the perfect face and body was raven-black, luxuriant hair. But her eyes, above all else, held the key to Ligeia's mystery. Larger than ordinary, those black eyes held an expression unfathomable even to her husband. It became his all-consuming passion to unravel the secret of that expression.

In character, Ligeia possessed a stern will that never failed to astound him. Outwardly she was placid and calm, but she habitually uttered words of such wildness that he was stunned by their intensity. Her learning was immense. She spoke many tongues, and in metaphysical investigations she was never wrong. Her husband was engrossed in a study of

metaphysics, but it was she who guided him, she who unraveled the secrets of his research. With Ligeia he knew that he would one day reach a goal of wisdom undreamed of by others.

Then Ligeia fell ill. Her skin became transparent and waxen, her eyes wild. Knowing that she must die, he watched her struggles against the grisly reaper, a conflict frightening in its passion. Words could not express the intense resistance with which she fought death. He had always known she loved him, but in those last days she abandoned herself completely to love. From her heart she poured fourth phrases of idolatry. And on the last day of her life she bade him repeat to her a poem she had composed not long before. It was a morbid thing about death, about the conquering of Man by the Worm. As he finished repeating the melancholy lines, Ligeia leaped to her feet with a shriek, then subsided on her deathbed. In a scarcely audible whisper she repeated a proverb that had haunted her before: that man did not yield to death save through the weakness of his own will. So Ligeia died.

Crushed with sorrow, her husband left his desolate home by the Rhine and retired to an old and decayed abbey in a deserted region in England. The exterior of the building he left in its sagging state, but inside he furnished the rooms lavishly and weirdly. He had become the slave of opium, and the furnishings took on the shapes and colors of his fantastic dreams. One bedchamber received the most bizarre treatment of all, and to this chamber he led his new bride, the blue-eyed Lady Rowena Trevanion of Tremaine.

The room was in a high turret of the abbey. It was of immense proportions, lighted by a single huge window. The pane had a leaden hue, giving a ghastly luster to all objects within the room. The walls, the floors, the furniture were all covered with a heavy, arabesque tapestry, black figures on pure gold. The figures changed as one looked at them from different angles, their appearance being changed by an artificial current of air that stirred the draperies constantly.

In rooms such as this he spent a bridal month with Lady Rowena. It was easy to perceive that she loved him but little, and he hated her with a passion more demonic than human. In his opium dreams he called aloud for Ligeia, as if he could restore her to the earthly life she had abandoned. He reveled in memories of her purity and her love.

In the second month of her marriage Rowena grew ill, and in her fever she spoke of sounds and movements in the chamber, fantasies unheard and unseen by her husband. Although she recovered, she had recurring attacks of the fever and it became evident that she would soon succumb. Her imaginings became stronger, and she grew more insistent about the sounds and movements in the tapestries.

One night in September she became visibly weaker and unusually agitated. Seeking to calm her, her husband stepped across the room to get some wine. But he was arrested midway by the sense of something passing lightly by him. Then he was startled to see on the gold carpet a shadow of angelic aspect. Saying nothing to Rowena, he poured the wine into a goblet. As she took the vessel, he distinctly heard a light footstep upon the carpet and saw, or thought he saw, three or four drops of a ruby-colored liquid fall into the goblet from an invisible source.

Immediately Rowena grew worse, and on the third night she died. As he sat by her shrouded body in that bridal chamber, he thought of his lost Ligeia. Suddenly he heard a sound from the bed upon which the corpse of his wife lay. Going closer, he perceived that Rowena had a faint color. It was unmistakable; Rowena lived. Unable to summon aid, he watched her with mounting terror. Then a relapse came, and she subsided into a death pallor more rigid than before. All night this phenomenon recurred. Rowena returned briefly from the dead, only to sink once more into oblivion. Each time he saw again a vision of Ligeia.

Toward morning of that fearful night the enshrouded figure rose from the bed and tottered to the center of the chamber. Terrified, he fell at her feet. She unwound the burial cerements from her head and there streamed down raven-black hair unknown to the living Rowena. Then the spectral figure slowly opened her eyes. He screamed in one last mad shout. He could not be mistaken. Staring at him were the full black eyes of his lost love, the Lady Ligeia.

LIGHT IN AUGUST

Type of work: Novel
Author: William Faulkner (1897-1962)
Type of plot: Psychological realism
Time of plot: Early twentieth century
Locale: Mississippi
First published: 1932

> *Principal characters:*
> JOE CHRISTMAS, a white Negro
> DOC HINES, his grandfather
> MR. MCEACHERN, his foster father
> JOANNA BURDEN, his benefactress and mistress
> JOE BROWN, alias Lucas Burch, his partner
> LENA GROVE, mother of Brown's child
> BYRON BUNCH, in love with Lena

Critique:

This novel makes a study of the race problem in the South and psychological obsession with the Civil War. It is a fascinating narrative told with little regard for strict time sequence. Sometimes the author's sentence structure becomes obscure; sometimes the exact meaning of his poetic compression is lost. But the novel is important in its vivid treatment of a theme of widespread social signficance.

The Story:

Joe Christmas was the illegitimate son of a circus trouper of Negro blood and a white girl named Milly Hines. Joe's grandfather, old Doc Hines, killed the circus man, let Milly die in childbirth, and put Joe—at Christmas time; hence his last name—into an orphanage, where the children learned to call him "Nigger." Doc Hines then arranged to have Joe adopted by a religious and heartless farmer named McEachern, whose cruelties to Joe were met with a matching stubbornness that made of the boy an almost subhuman being.

One day in town McEachern took Joe to a disreputable restaurant, where he talked to the waitress, Bobbie Allen. McEachern told the adolescent Joe never to patronize the place alone. But Joe went back. He met Bobbie at night and

became her lover. Night after night, while the McEacherns were asleep, he would creep out of the house and hurry to meet her in town.

One night McEachern followed Joe to a country dance and ordered him home. Joe reached for a chair, knocked McEachern unconscious, whispered to Bobbie that he would meet her soon, and raced McEachern's mule home. There he gathered up all the money he could lay his hands on and went into town. At the house where Bobbie stayed he encountered the restaurant proprietor and his wife and another man. The two men beat up Joe, took his money, and left for Memphis with the two women.

Joe moved on. Sometimes he worked. More often he simply lived off the money women would give him. He slept with many women and nearly always told them he was of Negro blood.

At last he went to Jefferson, a small town in Mississippi, where he got work shoveling sawdust in a lumber mill. He found lodging in a long-deserted Negro cabin near the country home of Miss Joanna Burden, a spinster of Yankee origin who had few associates in Jefferson because of her zeal for bettering the lot of the Negro. She fed Joe and, when she learned that he was of Negro blood, planned to send him to a Negro school. Joe was her lover for three years. Her reactions ranged from sheer animalism to evangelism, in which she tried to make Joe repent his sins and turn Christian.

A young man who called himself Joe Brown came to work at the sawmill, and Joe Christmas invited Brown to share his cabin with him. The two began to sell bootleg whiskey. After a while Joe told Brown that he was part Negro; before long Brown discovered the relations of Joe and Miss Burden. When their bootlegging prospered, they bought a car and gave up their jobs at the lumber mill.

One night Joe went to Miss Burden's room half-determined to kill her. That night she attempted to shoot him with an antiquated pistol that did not fire. Joe cut her throat with his razor and ran out of the house. Later in the evening a fire was discovered in Miss Burden's house. When the townspeople started to go upstairs in the burning house, Brown tried to stop them. They brushed him aside. They found Miss Burden's body in the bedroom and carried it outside before the house burned to the ground.

Through a letter in the Jefferson bank, the authorities learned of Miss Burden's New Hampshire relatives, whom they notified. Almost at once word came back offering a thousand dollars reward for the capture of the murderer. Brown tried to tell the story as he knew it, putting the blame on Joe Christmas, so that he could collect the money. Few believed his story, but he was held in custody until Joe Christmas could be found.

Joe Christmas remained at large for several days, but at last with the help of bloodhounds he was tracked down. Meanwhile old Doc Hines had learned of his grandson's crime and he came with his wife to Jefferson. He urged the white people to lynch Joe, but for the most part his rantings went unheeded. On the way to face indictment by the grand jury in the courthouse, Joe, handcuffed but not manacled to the deputy, managed to escape. He ran to a Negro cabin and found a gun. Some volunteer guards from the American Legion gave chase, and finally found him in the kitchen of the Reverend Gail Hightower, a one-time Presbyterian preacher who now was an outcast because he had driven his wife into dementia by his obsession with the gallant death of his grandfather in the Civil War. Joe had gone to Hightower at the suggestion of his grandmother, Mrs. Hines, who had had a conference with him in his cell just before he escaped. She had been advised of this possible way out by Byron Bunch, Hightower's only friend in Jefferson. The Legionnaires shot Joe down; then their leader mutilated him with a knife.

Brown now claimed his reward. A deputy took him out to the cabin where he had lived with Joe Christmas. On entering the cabin, he saw Mrs. Hines holding a new-born baby. In the bed was a girl, Lena Grove, whom he had slept with in a town in Alabama. Lena had started out to find Brown when she knew she was going to have a baby. Traveling most of the way on foot, she had arrived in Jefferson on the day of the murder and the fire. Directed to the sawmill, she had at once seen that Byron Bunch, to whom she had been sent, was not the same man as Lucas Burch, which was Brown's real name. Byron, a kindly soul, had fallen in love with her. Having identified Brown from Byron's description, she was sure that in spite of his new name Brown was the father of her child. She gave birth to the baby in Brown's cabin, where Byron had made her as comfortable as he could, with the aid of Mrs. Hines.

Brown jumped from a back window and ran away. Byron, torn between a desire to marry Lena and the wish to give her baby its rightful father, tracked Brown to the railroad grade outside town and fought with him. Brown escaped aboard a freight train.

Three weeks later Lena and Byron took to the road with the baby, Lena still searching for Brown. A truck driver gave them a lift. Byron was patient, but one night tried to compromise her. When she repulsed him, he left the little camp where the truck was parked. But next morning he was waiting at the bend of the road, and he climbed up on the truck as it made its way toward Tennessee.

LILIOM

Type of work: Drama
Author: Ferenc Molnar (1878-1952)
Type of plot: Fantasy
Time of plot: Early twentieth century
Locale: Budapest
First presented: 1909

> Principal characters:
> LILIOM, a merry-go-round barker
> MRS. MUSKAT, his employer
> JULIE, his wife
> MARIE, her friend
> WOLF, Marie's husband
> MRS. HOLLUNDER, Julie's aunt
> FICSUR, Liliom's friend
> LINZMAN, the cashier whom Ficsur suggests robbing
> LOUISE, daughter of Julie and Liliom

Critique:

This play is a popular favorite on the stages of Europe and America. The author's purpose was to tell a story of love and loyalty among the working classes. As literature the play is not profound, but as an entertainment piece it will probably enjoy a long life.

The Story:

Liliom was a barker for Mrs. Muskat's merry-go-round at an amusement park on the edge of Budapest. As a barker he was a great success, for he had a stock of funny jokes that kept the customers laughing, and he had a playful way with the girls.

One day two young servant girls, Marie and Julie, came to the merry-go-round. To Mrs. Muskat's indignation, Liliom followed Julie onto the merry-go-round and put his arm around her. Mrs. Muskat warned Julie that if she ever came near the merry-go-round again she would be thrown out, as she did not wish to lose her license because of questionable behavior in the park. Liliom, however, told Julie to come back any time and she would be welcome. Although Mrs. Muskat was reluctant to let Liliom go, she could not ignore his insolence, and she dismissed him.

Liliom, to show his independence, announced that he was going to get some beer. While he was collecting his belongings, Marie disclosed to Julie that she was in love with a man in a uniform, a porter, however, not a soldier. When Liliom returned, he turned Marie away and began to discuss love with Julie, bragging and bullying all the while. Julie showed that she was deeply in love, for she had forfeited her job by staying out so late. Two policemen looking for vagrants interrupted their conversation. After asking routine questions and warning Julie that Liliom was a notorious ne'er-do-well, the policemen continued on their rounds. Though Julie protested that she did not love Liliom, it was obvious that she did. So they were married.

They moved into a run-down photographer's shop operated by the Hollunders, mother and son, at the edge of the park. Mrs. Hollunder, Julie's aunt, provided them not only with shelter but also with food and fuel. She grumbled all the time, but she was good-hearted beneath her gruffness. Marie, meanwhile, was falling more deeply in love with Wolf, the porter. One day, while the two girls were exchanging confidences, Mrs. Hollunder came in and said that Julie's other suitor, a widowed carpenter with two children and a respectable income, still wanted to take her out of the poverty in which she lived. Julie preferred to stay where she was. Then Mrs. Muskat came and offered to take Liliom back, but he refused. He and a friend named Ficsur had a scheme for getting a great deal of money; he was no longer interested in his old job at the merry-go-round.

Ficsur was planning a robbery. Each Saturday a cashier for a leather factory passed a nearby railway embankment, with the workmen's wages in a leather bag. Liliom was to accost the man and ask him what time it was while Ficsur was to come up from behind and stab the man. Ficsur encouraged Liliom to steal a knife from Mrs. Hollunder's kitchen. Julie, knowing that the two men were up to no good, begged Liliom not to go out with Ficsur, for she had arranged to have the carpenter come that evening and offer Liliom work. After Liliom had gone, Mrs. Hollunder missed her knife and suspected Liliom of taking it. Julie lied, saying that she had gone through Liliom's pockets and had found only a pack of cards.

Liliom and Ficsur arrived at the embankment just as the six o'clock train passed. Being early, they started a game of twenty-one and Ficsur won from Liliom his share in the loot they hoped to take from the cashier. Liliom accused Ficsur of cheating. Then their victim appeared and Liliom accosted him. As Ficsur was about to strike, however, the cashier seized Ficsur's arm. He pointed a pistol at Liliom's breast. Ironically, he had come from the factory, where he had just finished paying off the workers, and if Ficsur had killed him the robbers would have got no money. As the cashier called out to two policemen in the distance, Liliom broke away and stabbed himself with the kitchen knife.

The policemen attempted to take him to a hospital, but his condition was too critical. They took him back to the photographer's studio, where he died with Julie by his side holding his hand.

Dying, Liliom had a vision. Two heavenly policemen came to him and told him to follow them. They reminded him that death was not the end, that he was not through with earth until his memory had also passed away. Then they led him to the heavenly court assigned to suicide cases. There he learned that after a period of purification by fire, suicides were sent back to earth for one day to see whether they had profited by their purification. Liliom was sentenced to sixteen years in the fires.

At the end of that time Liliom returned to earth to find his wife and sixteen-year-old daughter Louise about to lunch in the garden of their dilapidated little house. Liliom was unrecognized. Julie gave him some food. He learned from Louise that her father, a handsome man, had gone to America before she was born, and had died there. When Liliom accused her husband of having struck her, Julie denied that he had ever mistreated her, and she dismissed Liliom as an ungrateful wretch. Liliom tried to please his daughter with card tricks and with a beautiful star which he had stolen from heaven, but Louise would have nothing more to do with him. As he left he struck her hard on the hand, but the blow felt as tender as a caress to her. Her mother told her that there had been times when she, too, had experienced that sort of reaction from a blow. So Liliom left in the company of the two policemen, who shook their heads in profound regret at Liliom's failure.

THE LINK

Type of work: Drama
Author: August Strindberg (1849-1912)
Type of plot: Social criticism
Time of plot: Late nineteenth century
Locale: Sweden
First presented: 1893

> Principal characters:
> BARON SPRENGEL
> BARONESS SPRENGEL, his wife
> THE JUDGE
> THE PASTOR
> ALEXANDERSSON, a farmer
> TWELVE JURORS

Critique:

The Link, a one-act play in sixteen scenes, is one of Strindberg's briefer attempts to deal dramatically with the problems of marriage and divorce—problems which concerned him personally throughout his adult life. (He had experienced the first of his three divorces in 1891, and there are undoubtedly autobiographical connections here.) The "link," which gives the play its title, is the child of the two people who wish to be separated. The child holds them together when everything else is gone between them; the desire to prevent the child from becoming a ward of the court unites them, their old antagonisms still alive, in a common bond of enmity against the unfeeling powers of the state. In this, the play becomes something more than merely a commentary on divorce. It becomes an exposé of modern justice. Once the conflict of Baron Sprengel and his wife is placed before the court, it is no longer theirs. In the hands of the youthful Judge and the callous jurors, it is stripped of its human qualities and reduced to the cold terms of abstract argument. This is a social evil, but the ever-present moralist in Strindberg seems to imply that it is fit punishment for the sins of the erring husband and wife.

The Story:

The courtroom was crowded, for popular interest in the two cases about to be heard—a false accusation charge brought against the farmer Alexandersson by his servant girl, Alma Jonsson, and a separation suit between Baron and Baroness Sprengel—was running high. The young Judge, only twenty-seven years old, was uneasy: he was taking the bench for the first time. He conferred at length with the Pastor before opening the proceedings.

The Alexandersson-Jonsson case was first. The old farmer admitted accusing the girl of theft; he had, he claimed, caught her red-handed. There were, however, no witnesses; and, as the charges could not be proved, his accusations were false—so the girl's lawyer asserted. While the court was cleared, Judge and jury conferred. All agreed that the farmer, though actually in the right, was nevertheless technically guilty. Had he denied accusing the girl, nothing could have been done to him; by being honest, however, he had lost his case. Finally the Judge called Alexandersson in and sentenced him to a fine of a hundred crowns—enough, Alexandersson claimed, to cause the loss of his farm.

The divorce case came next. The Sprengels had planned to handle things as amicably as possible. The baron was to bring the complaint against his wife, charging her with a disposition incompatible with his. She was to have a sizable annuity and the custody of their one child, a son. The baron, however, was to retain the right to supervise the child's education. These were to be the terms, and none of the personal details of their quarrel were to be brought out.

Such was their agreement; but, once the proceedings began, they found that the agreement was not to be honored. The court, the young Judge curtly informed them, would decide the disposition of the child. Meanwhile, the separation case must be decided: the husband, as complainant, must substantiate his claim.

Confused by the attitude of the court and sensing the possibility of losing her child, the baroness responded emotionally to the planned charges of her husband. The baron, realizing that his right to have charge of the boy's education was threatened by the attitude of the court, asserted that the baroness, by her feminine methods of child-rearing, was undermining the boy's masculinity.

Here the agreement for an amicable settlement broke down completely. Under the goading of the court, the two became overt enemies. All of the sordid details were dragged into the open. The baroness, turning complainant, charged the baron with adultery and produced letters to prove her accusation. The baron met this charge with a stream of vilification, which the baroness emotionally returned. Enraged, the baron announced a countercharge of adultery. The baroness defied him to prove his accusation. The baron promised that he would.

At that point the young Judge adjourned the proceedings and sought help from the elderly Pastor. The Judge, despairing of doing justice, threatened to give up his profession. The Pastor advised him always to adhere to the strict, abstract letter of the law and never to consider the human involvements in a case—else he would go mad. Meanwhile, the baron and the baroness were exchanging personal vituperations.

When the proceedings resumed, the baroness agreed to testify under oath that she was not guilty of adultery. Technical quibblings on her right to testify followed. Then the farmer Alexandersson, probably as a false witness, piqued by the injustice done him, arose and claimed that he had actually observed the baroness' infidelities. While the validity of his testimony was being argued, the baron produced copies of incriminating letters. the originals of which the baroness had seen him destroy.

Again the court was cleared so that Judge and jury could confer. As they waited, the husband and wife realized that they both had lost, that they both had been defeated by the inhuman forces of a hostile society. Their child, they knew, would be taken from them and brought up ignobly in the name of peasant morality. This realization brought them temporarily together. The baron left to take the child to his mother, out of the court's hands.

He returned just in time to hear the verdict. The two were to be separated for a year and the child placed in the custody of a peasant couple. The baron informed his wife that he had not spirited the child away but had left him at the Pastor's house in preparation for appealing the verdict to a higher court. He predicted the wranglings and heartaches they would endure in the course of the appeal and suggested that it all was a judgment of God upon them for the years that they had lived together unmarried before the child had been born.

THE LION OF FLANDERS

Type of work: Novel
Author: Hendrik Conscience (1812-1883)
Type of plot: Historical romance
Time of plot: 1298-1305
Locale: Flanders
First published: 1838

Principal characters:
PETER DECONINCK, dean of the clothworkers' guild at Bruges
JAN BREYDEL, dean of the butchers' guild at Bruges
COUNT ROBERT DE BETHUNE, called the Lion of Flanders
COUNT GUY OF FLANDERS, Count Robert's elderly father
LADY MATILDA, Count Robert's daughter
ADOLF OF NIEWLAND, a Flemish knight in love with Lady Matilda

Critique:

Hendrik Conscience is regarded as the father of modern Flemish literature, for it was he who first used the Flemish language in his fiction, thus reviving what was a dying literary language. Writing soon after Belgium had become a nation, before his death Conscience gained recognition as a leader of culture in that country, honored by his government in many ways. His books, including *The Lion of Flanders*, his first great success, have been translated into other languages. Like other novels by Conscience, this work presents a period in the history of Flanders and the Flemish-speaking people in a manner similar to that of Sir Walter Scott in his fiction; and in its ample historical detail and pageant-like descriptions, it is typical of Conscience's work. Students of Flemish culture assert that the pictures of medieval life in Flanders are highly accurate. Others will find that plot and atmosphere combine to give the book a romantic sweep that adds to the interest and pleasure of the reader.

The Story:

At the beginning of the fourteenth century Philip the Fair ruled as King of France, along with his queen, Joanna of Navarre. At the time the French treasury was almost depleted from the cost of many wars, and Philip hoped to refill it with treasure and tax money from the rich cities of Flanders. The burghers, jealous of their privileges, refused to pay, even when asked to do so by Count Guy of Flanders, who was Philip's vassal. Count Guy found himself the victim of the king's displeasure, with his lands confiscated and his daughter Philippa imprisoned in the Louvre. In hopes of aiding Count Guy, Charles de Valois, King Philip's brother, took the Flemish barons to the king to effect a reconciliation. Despite the safe conduct guaranteed by his brother, the king imprisoned the nobles. He was led to that unworthy deed by his queen, who hated the Flemings, nobles and commoners alike. Chagrined by his royal brother's unknightly conduct, Charles de Valois broke his sword and vowed not to serve France until his brother's reign was ended.

Only one Flemish noble, Sir Diederik die Vos, nicknamed the Fox, escaped. Disguising himself as a palmer, he set out to return to his native province where he hoped to lay plans to help his fellow Flemings. The French took over Castle Wynandael, the home of Count Guy. Lady Matilda, Count Robert's daughter, fled to Bruges and found asylum in the home of Adolf of Niewland. Another of her protectors was Peter Deconinck, powerful dean of the great clothworkers' guild in the city.

At the time the Flemings were divided into three groups. One, the Lilyards, favored collaboration with the French. Another, made up chiefly of commoners, favored supporting Count Guy and independence, even though the count was the French king's prisoner; this group was known as the Clawards, after the claws of the heraldic device of Flanders, a lion. The third group, made up of nobles, held back from participation in the disagreements; because the commoners were involved they did not consider this a conflict in which they could become involved with honor.

Determined to subjugate the Flemings, Philip the Fair entered Bruges with a military force and appointed his queen's uncle governor of Flanders. After the king left a per capita tax was laid on the citizens to pay for the cost of the visit. Peter Deconinck advised his clothworkers not to pay the tax; for his rebellious counsel he was placed in prison. To Deconinck's rescue went Jan Breydel, dean of the butchers, and freed him. In retaliation the Lilyards and the French governor planned to hang both Deconinck and Breydel as the first step in forcing the guilds and the people to submit entirely. The two deans of the guilds made battle plans and met force with force. The Lilyards were forced into the confines of the castle, but at last the threat of pillage by the French forces outside the city forced the Clawards to submit. The French entered the city, freed the Lilyards, and held the people of Bruges at their mercy.

One day as Adolf of Niewland walked in the countryside outside the city walls he met Sir Diederik die Vos in the disguise of a friar. The nobleman brought word that the French vassal who guarded Count Robert de Bethune, called the Lion of Flanders, was willing to grant Count Robert freedom for a time if someone else would take his place. Adolf of Niewland agreed to do so.

Some weeks later the French, led by a disloyal clothworker, arrested Lady Matilda and prepared to take her off to prison in France. Lady Matilda had dis-

pleased Queen Joanna, and this was the queen's revenge. As soon as he learned what had happened, Jan Breydel set off to rescue Lady Matilda. Captured, he managed to escape. Returning with several hundred followers, he burned the castle at Male. A small band of French knights escaped, taking Lady Matilda with them. A short time later they met a knight in black armor who rescued the girl. The knight was Count Robert in disguise. He was so pleased with the conduct of Deconinck and Breydel that he left word that they were to be knighted at the first opportunity.

On his return to Bruges, Breydel found that many citizens were fleeing to the country, the Clawards deeming it unsafe to remain in the city. They were led by Deconinck, who hoped to join forces with some nobles who were ready to support actively the cause of Count Guy of Flanders. At a council of war Count Robert advised that they prepare as quickly as possible as large a force as they could, for the French king was gathering an army of seventy thousand men to subdue Flanders. He also brought word that his sister Philippa had been poisoned in prison.

Meanwhile, the Clawards left in Bruges were badly mistreated. On May 13, 1302, in an attempt to cow the population, the French governor and the Lilyards picked out eight men to be hanged. Only one of the eight was saved —the father of Jan Breydel, rescued by his son at the last minute. In immediate retaliation the French killed all the Clawards they could find and pillaged their homes; among the victims were the mother and sister of Jan Breydel. Then the Clawards returned to the city in force and killed seven thousand Frenchmen and many Lilyards. Only a handful of the French escaped. When the city was restored to order, Lady Matilda and Adolf of Niewland returned to the latter's home. Soon after, Lord Guy, the younger brother of Count Robert, arrived with a body of troops to help protect the city.

Philip the Fair, undaunted by the setback at Bruges, raised a large army for the invasion of Flanders. The Flemings, seeing that their land must be laid waste by the French or defended to the utmost, took an oath to stand together and gathered their forces to resist the French. Soon the two armies, each in excess of sixty thousand men, advanced to meet in battle. The Flemish took up a defensive position before the city of Courtrai. There, in full view and hearing of all, Lady Matilda and Lord Guy, her uncle, invested Peter Deconinck and Jan Breydel with knighthood, as Count Robert had commanded. The French army, meanwhile, had camped near Lille. The French leader, Count Robert d'Artois, was so eager to do battle that he failed to reconnoiter the Flemish position. His vows of bloody revenge were so terrible that part of his force deserted, preferring to fight with the Flemings rather than dishonor themselves.

The French advanced from Lille to the attack. At first the advantage was on their side, but their failure to make a reconnaissance left a trap for their cavalry. Before the city of Courtrai was a large, deep marsh, into which wave after wave of the French horsemen sank, to be ridden over by their comrades who followed and to be decimated by weapons of the Flemish forces. Even so, for a time the battle seemed to go against the Flemings, until a knight in gold appeared. He was Count Robert, the Lion of Flanders, freed again from his prison for a time and hurrying to the aid of his people. Under his leadership the Flemings won the victory. After the battle Count Robert returned to his prison, knowing that the French would not dare kill him, lest hostages held by the Flemish army be killed in reprisal. Before he left, Count Robert promised that Lady Matilda should become the bride of Adolf of Niewland. The young knight had fought bravely in the battle. Badly wounded, he was recovering in the monastery in which Lady Matilda had taken refuge.

After the battle at Courtrai, called the Battle of the Golden Spurs, Flanders was safe; trade and commerce flourished again. The French still tried to subdue the Flemish people, but several such attempts ended in failure. Philip the Fair dishonored himself in one truce to write a treaty, but additional French defeats forced him finally to give up all hope of subduing the stubborn, independent Flemish. Old Count Guy of Flanders died while waiting for the treaty to be signed and so was never released from his prison. But Count Robert, the Lion of Flanders, was set free after the signing of the treaty in 1305, and until his death seventeen years later he ruled over his free people.

THE LITTLE CLAY CART

Type of work: Drama
Author: Shudraka (fl. 100 B.C.)
Type of plot: Tragi-comedy
Time of plot: Fifth century B.C.
Locale: Ancient Hindu city of Ujjayinī
First presented: Unknown

Principal characters:
CHĀRUDATTA, an impoverished young Brāhmana
VASANTASENĀ, a courtesan in love with Chārudatta
MAITREYA, a poor Brāhmana, Chārudatta's friend
SAMSTHĀNAKA, King Pālaka's brother-in-law
ĀRYAKA, an exiled prince
SARVILAKA, a Brāhmana and a thief
MADANIKĀ, Vasantasenā's slave and confidante

Critique:

The Little Clay Cart is regarded by students of literature in the Western world as one of the two best extant Sanskrit plays, the other being Kalidasa's *Sakuntala.* Many critics have pointed out that *The Little Clay Cart* is more like Western drama than any other Sanskrit play, in structure, characterization, and tone. This similarity to Occidental drama may account for the fact that its Indian critics have been less enthusiastic than those of the Western world. *The Little Clay Cart* is noteworthy for being the only known Sanskrit play to show a courtesan in love with a Brāhmana, as it is the only known one also to contain important characters from various strata of Hindu society, not from the upper castes only. It is the seemingly realistic and vivid presentation of these characters which probably has appealed most to Western readers. In the original the title is *Mrcchakatikā.*

The Story:

Chārudatta was a Brāhmana who had impoverished himself by spending his substance on the public welfare and in helping those individuals who sought his aid. Though dwelling in poverty in a broken-down house, he still enjoyed a fine reputation in Ujjayinī as an honest and upright man of rare wisdom. This reputation eased somewhat the fact that he had been deserted by most of his friends and was embarrassed by his lack of wealth.

Although married happily and the proud father of a small son, Rohasena, Chārudatta was enamored of Vasantasenā, a courtesan of great wealth and reputation who, having seen him at a temple, was also in love with him. One evening as Chārudatta and his friend Maitreya sat discussing Chārudatta's misfortunes and the efficacy of devotion to the gods, Vasantasenā found herself pursued by Samsthānaka, a half-mad brother-in-law of King Pālaka, and one of his henchmen. The men offered to do violence to Vasantasenā, but she escaped from them in the darkness and found safety in the house of Chārudatta, where a meeting between the two increased the love they already felt for each other. The courtesan, before she left to return to her own palace, entrusted a casket of jewelry to Chārudatta, as an excuse to see him again.

During the night a thief, Sarvilaka, entered Chārudatta's house and stole the jewelry to buy his love, Madanikā, who was Vasantasenā's slave and confidante. The courtesan accepted the jewels and freed Madanikā to marry Sarvilaka, intending to see that Chārudatta should learn that the jewels had been recovered. In the meantime, Chārudatta sent a rare pearl necklace of his wife's to Vasantasenā to recompense the courtesan for the

2064

loss of the less valuable jewels. His friend Maitreya, fearing that Vasantasenā's attentions could bring only bad luck and disaster, cautioned Chārudatta against doing so. Maitreya, knowing courtesans, believed that Vasantasenā was merely scheming to take from Chārudatta the few possessions he still had.

After leaving Vasantasenā's palace with his newly freed bride, Sarvilaka learned that his friend, Prince Āryaka, had been arrested by King Pālaka and placed in a dungeon. The king, neither a popular nor a just monarch, feared that the people might rise up, as a soothsayer had predicted, to place Prince Āryaka on the throne. After Sarvilaka succeeded in freeing the prince from prison, Āryaka sought help from Chārudatta, who aided him in escaping the pursuing guards.

Vasantasenā, having proved her love for Chārudatta by becoming his mistress, met his small son and gave him some jewels with which to purchase a golden toy cart to replace the unsatisfactory clay cart Chārudatta had been able to afford. She made arrangements to meet Chārudatta in Pushpakarandaka Park, outside the city, for a day's outing, but by mistake she entered the wrong vehicle and found herself in the gharri belonging to Samsthānaka, who still pursued her and was madly jealous of the love and favors she bestowed freely upon Chārudatta. When Vasantasenā arrived at the park, she was discovered in the gharri by Samsthānaka, who at first was overjoyed at seeing her because he thought she had come to him voluntarily. When she spurned him and declared her love for Chārudatta, Samsthānaka tried to make his henchmen kill her, but they refused. Samsthānaka sent his followers away and choked her himself. Believing her dead, he hid the body under a pile of leaves. Then, hoping to escape the penalty for his crime, Samsthānaka decided to go to a court and accuse Chārudatta of murdering Vasantasenā.

When Samsthānaka first appeared at court, the judges, who knew him to be somewhat mad, refused to see him or take him seriously; but when he threatened to go to King Pālaka, the judges became frightened and sent for Chārudatta. Falsely accused, Chārudatta proclaimed his innocence. But circumstances were against him. He admitted having been in the park, and the jewels of Vasantasenā were found at his home, offering a motive for the poverty-stricken man to have killed the girl. The judges, in spite of his previous reputation, were forced to find Chārudatta guilty. Although his status as a Brāhmana exempted him from the death penalty for any crime, King Pālaka ordered Chārudatta put to death. No one knew that the body identified as Vasantasenā's was that of another woman or that Vasantasenā, befriended by a Buddhist monk, was recovering near the park from Samsthānaka's attack.

Chārudatta was taken through the city by two executioners, who stopped several times to announce the name of the condemned man and the nature of his crime. Although the people of the city loved Chārudatta, they dared not intervene on his behalf, even though he steadfastly maintained his innocence. Samsthānaka's slave tried to tell that his master had really committed the crime, but no one believed him, and so Chārudatta and his executioners, accompanied by a crowd, continued on their way to the place of execution, a cemetery south of the city. The executioners, thinking to be merciful, offered to decapitate Chārudatta, but a miracle prevented their sword from touching him, and so they prepared the victim for the slow, agonizing death by impalement upon a pike. Fortunately, Vasantasenā, seeing the excited crowd as she made her way back to the city, intervened in time. When she told who had really attacked her, though unsuccessfully, Samsthānaka was arrested. The excitement was not ended, however, for word came that Chārudatta's wife, believing herself a widow, was about to cast herself upon a funeral pyre. Chārudatta reached her in time to prevent her death, and she and Vasantasenā met and accepted one another. Word came, too, that Prince Āryaka had deposed King Pālaka and was now king. One of his first deeds was to restore Chārudatta's fortune and make him an important official of the court. Chārudatta, still a man of conscience and charity, forgave Samsthānaka's villainy and caused him to be set free.

LITTLE DORRIT

Type of work: Novel
Author: Charles Dickens (1812-1870)
Type of plot: Sentimental romance
Time of plot: Early nineteenth century
Locale: England
First published: 1855-1857

Principal characters:
LITTLE DORRIT, a child born and reared in debtors' prison
WILLIAM DORRIT, her father
FANNY, her older sister
ARTHUR CLENNAM, Little Dorrit's friend
MRS. CLENNAM, Arthur's mother and Little Dorrit's employer
MONSIEUR BLANDOIS, a blackmailer
MR. MERDLE, a banker and Fanny Dorrit's father-in-law

Critique:

This book, which has never had the popularity of most of Dickens' other novels, was the product of the author's "middle period," which came prior to his great successes with *A Tale of Two Cities* and *Great Expectations*. To a modern reader the book is dreary because of the scenes in the Marshalsea debtors' prison. In addition, the very concept of a debtors' prison is so far removed from modern experience that we have difficulty in picturing the setting. To Dickens' contemporaries, however, there was probably a great deal of interest in the sections dealing with the red tape and inefficiency of the Circumlocution Office, by which Dickens satirized the inefficiency of the British government during the Crimean War.

The Story:

Amy Dorrit, or, as she was better known, Little Dorrit, was born while her mother stayed with her father, a bankrupt, in Marshalsea debtors' prison. Although her mother died soon after, the little girl, along with her older brother and sister, continued to live in the prison. As she became older, Little Dorrit went outside the prison to do sewing, for only the debtor himself was not permitted to leave the place.

One of the women for whom Little Dorrit sewed was Mrs. Clennam, a widow carrying on a place of business, even though she had been confined to her room

by illness for fifteen years. Mrs. Clennam's son, who was forty, had gone to the Orient twenty years before and had joined his father, who looked after the company's business in the East. After his father's death Arthur Clennam returned. He told his mother that he would take his part of the inheritance and fend for himself; he did not want to remain in the business with his miserly, grasping, and rather inhuman mother. Mrs. Clennam, confronted by her son's decision, took her old clerk into partnership with her.

While he was staying at his mother's house, Arthur noticed Little Dorrit and made inquiry about her. Having been struck by the girl's sweet disposition and appearance, he went to Marshalsea debtors' prison and tried to help the Dorrit family. He even said that he would try to get Mr. Dorrit out of the place. Everyone thought such a course impossible, for some of Mr. Dorrit's debts were owed through the Circumlocution Office, a place of endless red tape, to the crown.

Arthur found that he had a confederate, though an unusual one, in a clerk named Pancks, a queer creature who collected rents for Arthur's former fiancée's father. Pancks was aided in turn by John Chivery, the son of a turnkey, who was also in love with Little Dorrit, and by Mr. Rugg, an elderly lawyer.

In addition to helping Little Dorrit by putting in motion action to have her father released from prison, Arthur aided her by getting her more sewing clients, by getting her brother out of trouble, and by sending small amounts of money to defray the expenses of the Dorrit household in the prison.

At last Pancks brought unusual advice. He had discovered that Mr. Dorrit, who had been in prison over twenty years, was the only surviving heir to a large fortune which had gone unclaimed for years. Within a short time Mr. Dorrit was released, his debts having been paid, and he immediately set himself up as a man of fortune. Mr. Dorrit and his two oldest children, determined to live up to the new social position that their fortune had given them, tried to forget everything in the past. They even convinced themselves that Arthur Clennam had insulted them and refused to have anything more to do with the man. Only Little Dorrit remained unspoiled, merely surprised at the good fortune which had been thrust upon them.

As quickly as possible the Dorrit family went to the continent, where they could successfully carry out the fiction that they had never seen a debtor's prison. Because of their money they were admitted to the society of Britons who were living away from England. Fanny Dorrit, the older of the two daughters, was pursued by Mr. Sparkle, stepson of Mr. Merdle, who was supposed to be the richest and most influential banker in England. Fanny, although not in love with Sparkle, considered with pleasure the prospect of marrying into a wealthy family. The Merdles, who saw only that the Dorrits had a fortune, agreed to the match, even though Mrs. Merdle was well aware of the fact that her son had fallen in love with Fanny when the latter was a dancer on the stage in London.

After the marriage Fanny and her husband went to live in London. Mr. Dorrit visited them there and became a close friend of Mr. Merdle. The banker even proposed to help Mr. Dorrit increase his already large fortune through shrewd and well-paying investments. Mr. Dorrit, the former debtor, was in seventh heaven because of his new prospects.

Little Dorrit wondered at the change in her family but remained her own self. She wrote to Arthur at intervals, for she, at least, was still grateful for all he had done to help her. Besides, she was in love with him.

Arthur, still in London, was trying to fathom certain mysterious people who had been seen about his mother's house and also attempting to keep his own business on solid financial ground. Neither task was easy. Mrs. Clennam was visited on two occasions by a Monsieur Blandois, whom Arthur knew to be a knave and probably a murderer. He wondered what business his mother could have with such a person. He also distrusted Flintwinch, the clerk who had become his mother's partner. Flintwinch, a grubbing miserly fellow who mistreated his wife, had taken a great dislike to Arthur.

While trying to unravel the mystery, Arthur became financially insolvent. Like many others, he had become convinced that the business ventures of Mr. Merdle were the safest and quickest way to make a fortune. As a result, he had put his money and his company's money into Merdle's ventures. When Merdle and his bank failed, Arthur became a bankrupt and was sent to the Marshalsea debtors' prison, where he was housed in Mr. Dorrit's old quarters.

Mr. Rugg and Pancks did their best to make Arthur's imprisonment a short one, but he seemed to have lost all desire to live, much less to leave the prison. Only after Little Dorrit returned to England and took up quarters within the prison, to comfort him as she had comforted her father, did Arthur take any interest in life.

Learning that Monsieur Blandois had disappeared from Mrs. Clennam's house, Pancks tracked down the man and brought him back to London. Then the reason for his attempt to blackmail Mrs. Clennam was revealed. Mrs. Clennam, realizing that she had to make known the mystery to her son unless she intended to pay blackmail, rose from her wheelchair and left her house for the first time in almost twenty years. She went to the prison to tell Arthur that he was not her child and that she had for many years been keeping money from him and from Little Dorrit.

When that mystery had been solved, and the money was forthcoming, Arthur was soon released from prison. Shortly afterward he and Little Dorrit were married. Little Dorrit, after a quarter century of misfortune, was at last about to embark upon a quiet and comfortable life.

THE LITTLE FOXES

Type of work: Drama
Author: Lillian Hellman (1905-   )
Type of plot: Social realism
Time of plot: 1900
Locale: The Deep South
First presented: 1939

Principal characters:
REGINA GIDDENS, a predatory woman
BENJAMIN HUBBARD, and
OSCAR HUBBARD, her brothers
HORACE GIDDENS, her husband
ALEXANDRA, daughter of Regina and Horace
BIRDIE HUBBARD, Oscar's wife

Critique:

The Little Foxes is usually considered the major achievement of Lillian Hellman, and many critics place it high on the list of American plays. In the first place, it is technically a well-knit piece of writing: her dialogue crackles and her characters convince; there is no extraneous matter present, so that The Little Foxes is brilliantly compact and effective theater. Secondly, in the chicanery of the Hubbard family, we have what is probably an accurate picture of one aspect of the rise of industrialism in the post-Civil War South.

The Story:

William Marshall, a Chicago businessman, came South to negotiate with Benjamin and Oscar Hubbard and their sister, the striking Regina Giddens, over matters concerning the construction of a cotton mill. The Hubbard brothers and Regina foresaw a glittering future for them all. No longer would the cotton have to come to the machines; instead, at long last, it would be the other way around. They firmly believed that millions awaited them: the Hubbards would be the richest family in the South. Ben foresaw a stable of race horses, Oscar speculated on a new home, and the hapless Birdie, whom Oscar had married for her father's cotton fields, longed to see Lionnet, her old family home, restored to its former grace and beauty. Birdie continually sought a return to the genteel, refined behavior of earlier days, before the rise of materialistic ruthfulness.

Later, certain difficulties arose. The brothers lacked seventy-five thousand dollars, Regina's third of the sum which the Hubbards were to put up. Presumably this amount would come from Horace, Regina's husband, who lay in a Baltimore hospital with a fatal heart ailment. Though Regina had given Ben and Oscar her promise that Horace would put up the money, no word had yet reached them. Horace, away five months, had failed to acknowledge Regina's demands for his return. Regina suggested, however, that he was possibly holding out for a larger share of the profits; when one's money was badly needed, one should be entitled to a bigger share of the eventual returns. After crafty manipulation, Regina extracted from Ben a promise of a greater share of the profits if she could get Horace home within two weeks. Regina immediately dispatched Alexandra, her daughter, to Baltimore.

When Horace arrived a week later, in response to his daughter's summons, the Hubbards and Regina descended on him. No one in his right mind, the argument ran, would refuse a seventy-five thousand dollar investment that would garner a million. Ben explained how water power would be cheap and how the men of the mountains and small towns would be happy to work for low wages. Thus the profits would be tremendous. But Horace, though sourly admitting that the venture was a good deal for the Hubbards, stated that he and Regina had enough money already. The truth was that Horace had had enough of his scheming wife and her equally conniving family, who, having made a sizable sum already through their exploitation of the poor, were now on their way to greater fortune in identical fashion.

Regina protested furiously, but to no avail. However, Ben and Oscar were not too upset. Oscar's son Leo, through a young banking employee, had discovered that Horace had eighty-eight thousand dollars in bonds in his safe deposit box, securities which he checked only once in six months. Assuming that Horace would never miss them for a few months, Ben had Oscar seize the bonds—more than enough to meet the sum required by Marshall—and leave for Chicago to complete negotiations. Regina, after a fierce argument with Horace, learned that Oscar had gone. Ben now held the upper hand; he simply told Regina that everything had been settled. Horace, an onlooker, was quietly amused. Now, he thought, he would not be a party to the wrecking of the town. He would at least die honestly. To the watching Alexandra's horror, Regina calmly informed him that she hoped he would indeed die as quickly as possible.

Two weeks later, Horace went to his now estranged wife's part of the house. Knowing that he was to be short-lived, he had had his deposit box brought to him, and had discovered the theft. This he told Regina, along with his accurate suspicions as to the thieves' identity. To Regina's surprise, however, he stated that he intended to say nothing unless forced

to, and then he would simply call the theft a loan. Horace planned to make a new will, leaving Regina eighty-eight thousand dollars in bonds. Thus she would eventually inherit his bonds, but she would not receive a single cent of the millions Ben and Oscar prophesied for the Hubbard family. For once Horace had tied the hands of his cunning wife.

Recalling their unhappy married life, Regina shrewishly revealed her contempt for Horace from the start. Horace, feeling an attack coming on, broke his bottle of medicine. Regina, hoping that his efforts to climb the stairs would prove fatal, cruelly refused to go upstairs for his second bottle. Horace staggered from his wheelchair and collapsed on the stair landing.

In an interview with her brothers after Horace was carried to his room, Regina revealed what she had learned from her husband. Should he die, she would blackmail them for a seventy-five percent share of the profits in exchange for the bonds. Soon word came, in the person of the silent Alexandra, that Regina's plan had worked. Horace was dead. Regina then announced her plans for seeing the judge the next day. Any jury would be swayed by a woman whose brothers had stolen from her. Regina also declared that there were not twelve men in the state whom the brothers had not cheated. A philosophical Ben gave in to Regina's demands, but as he left he was wondering what Horace, who had been in a wheelchair, was doing on the landing. Perhaps in the future he might find out. And when he did, he would let Regina know.

Realizing that Alexandra loved her father very much, Regina tried to be sympathetic. However, her saddened, sickened daughter defied her plans for their future in Chicago. Alexandra announced her final departure from Regina and the Hubbards because she believed that her father would have wanted it that way.

THE LITTLE MINISTER

Type of work: Novel
Author: James M. Barrie (1860-1937)
Type of plot: Sentimental romance
Time of plot: Mid-nineteenth century
Locale: The village of Thrums in Scotland
First published: 1891

Principal characters:
GAVIN DISHART, the little minister of Thrums
MARGARET DISHART, his mother
MR. OGILVY, the schoolmaster, Margaret's second husband, and the narrator
ROB DOW, a drunkard converted by Gavin
BABBIE, a gipsy who loves Gavin
NANNY WEBSTER, an old woman saved from the poorhouse by Babbie
LORD RINTOUL, Babbie's guardian and her betrothed

Critique:

Barrie's sensitivity and deep appreciation of human values explain the popularity of this novel. The quiet, reserved humor appeals to the intellect and the heart rather than to a ludicrous sense of buffoonery, and the frequent note of sentiment is delicate and restrained. The book displays Barrie's gift for character portrayal and his lack of self-consciousness in his whimsical, ironic style.

The Story:

Mr. Ogilvy, the schoolmaster of Glen Quharity, had not seen Margaret Dishart for eighteen years until that day when he stood in the crowd that had gathered to welcome Gavin Dishart, the new minister of Auld Licht parish in Thrums. When the dominie saw Margaret again, he knew that all her happiness lay in her son Gavin. The schoolmaster did not allow Margaret to see him, as he never would even in the disturbed days to come. He knew that he was best out of her life, that he could bring her only unhappiness. When he heard Gavin deliver his first sermon at Auld Licht, the dominie knew that the little minister, who was just twenty-one, had indeed received the "call."

Lord Rintoul's castle stood in the Spittal on the hill above Glen Quharity. It was rumored that he had in his household a young girl whom he expected to marry soon, but no one had seen the girl except the sheriff of Thrums, who stopped at the castle to tell Lord Rintoul that a detachment of militia was coming to Thrums to arrest some insurgent weavers. Dressed as a gipsy, the young bride-to-be ran to the village to warn the people that soldiers were on their way.

Gavin Dishart met her that night as he was walking through Windyghoul toward Caddam. She ran dancing and singing, and laughed at him as she darted past him toward Thrums. When Gavin caught up with her, they became rivals as Gavin attempted to calm the workers whom the gipsy had aroused against the soldiers. Her activities on the night the militia came was a topic of discussion in Thrums for days afterward—this mysterious gipsy whose origin no one could guess. Even Gavin spent more hours than was proper pondering over the girl who had brazenly claimed, when the soldiers had tried to arrest her, that she was his wife.

Gavin's next meeting with the gipsy was in the cottage of old Nanny Webster, a parish charge. This story the schoolmaster heard through village gossip. The story of how Gavin had gone with Dr. McQueen to take old Nanny to the poorhouse, and how the gipsy girl, Babbie, interrupted the proceedings

THE LITTLE MINISTER by James M. Barrie. Published by Charles Scribner's Sons.

by offering to provide Nanny with an income for the old woman's support, reached the dominie only in rumor. Most of the villagers believed that the little minister had done the good work; few knew about the gipsy's part in the story.

Gavin could have avoided ever seeing Babbie again, but he did not. He even went so far as to tell her when he would be walking through Caddam woods. Babbie was not like the people of Thrums. She horrified old Nanny with her impertinence to the little minister of Auld Licht. She embarrassed Gavin by teasing him about his height, a fact which had caused him great distress all his life. Ever on the lookout for the pair was Rob Dow, who skulked among the pines of Windyghoul spying on his beloved minister and the witch who had cast a spell on Gavin. Rob, a drunkard whom Gavin had converted, feared for his minister after he had seen the gipsy nearly succeed in her attempt to make the minister kiss her. Rob jealously guarded his secret, for he was no gossip. To his death, Rob protected the little minister who had saved him from drink.

While the dominie feared lest Margaret be hurt by this woodland courtship, Gavin was troubled by his love for the brazen gipsy. As she gradually became aware of his devotion, the gipsy girl began to love him in turn. No one had ever loved her before. Lord Rintoul only played at watching her beauty. When Gavin stated that he would marry her, Babbie protested that he would be banished from Thrums and so break his mother's heart.

One night the lovers walked together through Windyghoul. Unknown to anyone, the dominie, Mr. Ogilvy, often strolled through the same wood so that he could gaze at the manse where Margaret lived. That night he met Gavin and Babbie. Immediately sensing their relationship and thinking only of Margaret, Ogilvy stepped into the affair and there he remained until it ended, not for Gavin's sake but for Margaret's protection. There were no words exchanged that night, but each knew that the dominie was aware of the love between Gavin and Babbie.

In Windyghoul, the next day, Babbie met Micah, Rob Dow's small son. Sobbing, the child told her that his father had taken to drink again because the little minister had been bewitched by the gipsy. If only she would go away, Rob could regain his faith in the minister and stop his drinking once more. Babbie realized then that Gavin's duty called him from her. She never laid eyes again on her lover until the terrible day of the great rain.

On the day of the great rain plans were being made at the Spittal for Lord Rintoul's wedding to his young bride. On this same day there was a fight in Thrums, and false news spread that Gavin had been killed by a drunken Highland piper. When the news traveled as far as the Spittal, Babbie, alarmed for Gavin and Margaret, ran to Mr. Ogilvy to ask his aid. The schoolmaster went with her to Windyghoul, where they encountered Gavin. When the two lovers were reunited, Babbie told Gavin that this was the day of her wedding to Lord Rintoul. Again Gavin asserted that he would marry her.

They hurried away to a gipsy camp and there the gipsy king married them over the tongs. Meanwhile Lord Rintoul, searching for his bride, had followed her in time to witness the ceremony. In the confusion of the gipsy camp, Babbie cried out to Gavin that she heard Lord Rintoul's voice. As Gavin rushed to encounter his rival, Babbie was suddenly snatched away. Assuming that Lord Rintoul would bring her back to the Spittal, Gavin headed toward Glen Quharity. The increasing rain drove him to Mr. Ogilvy's house for shelter.

The dominie ordered Gavin to end his fruitless pursuit, but the little minister insisted that he would take Babbie back to the manse as his bride. Then Mr. Ogilvy had to tell Gavin about

Margaret. The schoolmaster—his name was Gavin also—had married Margaret after her first husband, Adam Dishart, had disappeared at sea. Six years after little Gavin's birth Adam Dishart had returned to claim his wife and little Gavin as his own. Mr. Ogilvy, perceiving the sorrow in Margaret's eyes as she faced the two men who claimed her, had disappeared and had sworn never to allow Margaret to know of his existence again. It was too late for the little minister and his real father to find any filial love after the schoolmaster's painful revelation. Gavin acknowledged his father, but he claimed that it was more God's will that he find Babbie again. As Gavin set out toward the Spittal, Mr. Ogilvy started toward Thrums to protect Margaret from village gossip that might reach her.

Babbie had not been captured by Lord Rintoul. Rob Dow, resolved to destroy the cause of his minister's downfall, had seized her. The gipsy eluded him during the severe storm, however, and ran to the manse to find Gavin.

Gavin, meanwhile, had lost all trace of Lord Rintoul in the rain-swept darkness. While he was making his way across the storm-flooded countryside, he came upon a ravine where some men shouted to him that Lord Rintoul was stranded on a small islet which was being washed away by the swiftly-flowing water. He could be saved if a man would jump down onto the island with a rope. Although he had no rope, Gavin jumped in the hope that he could help Lord Rintoul to maintain his foothold on the tiny piece of dwindling turf. As the villagers gathered at the brink of the ravine, their minister shouted to them that he had married Babbie the gipsy and that Mr. Ogilvy was to carry the news of his death to his mother and his wife. Then a man leaped into the ravine with a rope. It was Rob Dow, who performed his last living act to save the little minister whom he loved.

Gavin, followed by his admiring congregation, returned to the manse. There he found his mother and Babbie, who now could reveal herself, not as the wild gipsy of Windyghoul, but as the lady whom Lord Rintoul had planned to wed. Gavin and Babbie were married again under the prayers of a real minister, but Gavin always felt that he had really married her under the stars in the gipsy camp.

Mr. Ogilvy told the story of Gavin and Babbie to the eager little girl who was the daughter of the little minister and his wife. At the schoolmaster's request, Margaret Dishart had never learned of his part in Gavin's love affair. But after her death Gavin Ogilvy heard Babbie's and Gavin's daughter call him grandfather.

LITTLE WOMEN

Type of work: Novel
Author: Louisa May Alcott (1832-1888)
Type of plot: Sentimental romance
Time of plot: Nineteenth century
Locale: A New England village; New York City; Italy
First published: 1868

Principal characters:
MEG,
JO,
BETH, and
AMY, the March sisters
MRS. MARCH (MARMEE), their mother
MR. MARCH, their father
THEODORE LAWRENCE (LAURIE), a young neighbor
PROFESSOR BHAER, a tutor, in love with Jo

Critique:

Little Women is one of the best-loved books of all time, as popular today as when it was written eighty years ago. Although it is actually a children's book, it appeals to grownups as well, who see in it a mirror of their own childhood, or at least the childhood they would have preferred. The story is largely autobiographical, the March girls being Louisa's own sisters, with herself as Jo.

The Story:

The March family lived in a small house next door to the Lawrence mansion, where young Theodore Lawrence and his aged grandfather had only each other for company in the great house. Old Mr. Lawrence was wealthy and he indulged every wish of his grandson, but often Laurie was lonely. When the lamp was lit and the shades were up in the March house, he could see the four March girls with their mother in the center seated around a cheerful fire. He learned to know them by name before he met them, and in his imagination he almost felt himself a member of the family.

The oldest was plump Meg, who had to earn her living as governess of a group of unruly youngsters in the neighborhood. Next was Jo, tall, awkward, and tomboyish, who liked to write, and who spent all her spare time devising plays and entertainments for her sisters. Then there was gentle Beth, the homebody, content to sit knitting by the fire, or to help her mother take care of the house. The youngest was curly-haired Amy, a schoolgirl who dreamed of someday becoming a famous artist like Michelangelo or Leonardo da Vinci.

At Christmas time the girls were confronted with the problem of what to do with the dollar Marmee, as they called their mother, had said they might spend. At first each thought only of her own pleasure, but all ended by buying a gift for Marmee instead. On Christmas morning they insisted on sharing their breakfast with the Hummels, a poor family in the neighborhood, and for this unselfishness they were rewarded when rich Mr. Lawrence sent over a surprise Christmas feast consisting of ice cream, bonbons, and four bouquets of flowers for the table.

Many happy days followed, with Laurie, who had met Jo at a fashionable New Year's Eve dance, becoming a part of the March family circle. But in November of that same year a telegram brought a message that their father, an army chaplain in the Civil War, was

LITTLE WOMEN by Louisa May Alcott. Published by Little, Brown & Co.

critically ill. Mrs. March did not know what to do. She felt that she should go to her husband at once, but she had barely five dollars in her purse. She was hesitant about going to wealthy, irascible Aunt March for help. Jo solved the problem by selling her beautiful, long, chestnut hair, which was her only vanity, for twenty-five dollars. She made the sacrifice willingly, but that night, after the others had gone to bed, Meg, who thought Jo was asleep, heard her weeping softly. Gently, Meg asked if Jo were crying over her father's illness, and Jo sobbed that it was not her father she was crying for now, but for her hair.

During Marmee's absence dark days fell upon the little women. Beth, who had never been strong at best, contracted scarlet fever, and for a time it looked as if Jo were going to lose her dearest sister. Marmee was sent for, but by the time she arrived the crisis had passed and her little daughter was better. By the next Christmas, Beth was her old contented self again. Mr. March surprised them all when he returned home from the front well and happy. The little family was together once more.

Then John Brooke, Laurie's tutor, fell in love with Meg. This fact was disclosed when Mr. Brooke surreptitiously stole one of Meg's gloves and kept it in his pocket as a memento. Laurie discovered the glove and informed Jo. To his great surprise, she was infuriated at the idea that the family circle might be disturbed. But she was quite reconciled when, three years later, Meg became Mrs. Brooke.

In the meantime, Jo herself had grown up. She began to take her writing seriously, and even sold a few stories which helped with the family budget.

Her greatest disappointment came when Aunt Carrol, a relative of the Marches, decided she needed a companion on a European trip, and asked not Jo but the more lady-like Amy to accompany her. Then Jo, with Marmee's permission, decided to go to New York. She took a job as governess for a Mrs. Kirke, who ran a large boarding-house. There she met Professor Bhaer, a lovable and eccentric German tutor, who proved to be a good friend and companion.

Upon her return home, Laurie, who had always loved Jo, asked her to marry him. Jo, who imagined that she would always remain an old maid, devoting herself exclusively to her writing, tried to convince Laurie that they were not made for each other. He persisted, pointing out that his grandfather and her family both expected them to marry. When she made him realize that her refusal was final, he stamped off, and shortly afterward went to Europe with his grandfather. In Europe he saw a great deal of Amy, and the two became close friends, so that Laurie was able to transfer to her younger sister a great deal of the feeling he previously had for Jo.

In the meantime Jo was at home caring for Beth, who had never fully recovered from her first illness. In the spring, Beth died, practically in Jo's arms, and after the loss of her gentle sister Jo was lonely indeed. She tried to comfort herself with her writing, and with Meg's two babies, Daisy and Demi, but not until the return of Amy, now married to Laurie, did she begin to feel her old self again. When Professor Bhaer stopped off on his way to a university appointment in the Midwest, Jo was delighted. One day, under an umbrella he had supplied to shield her from a pouring rain, he asked her to marry him, and Jo accepted. Within a year old Aunt March died and willed her home, Plumfield, to Jo. She decided to open a boys' school, where she and her professor could devote their lives to instructing the young.

So the little women reached maturity, and on their mother's sixtieth birthday they all had a great celebration at Plumfield. Around the table, at which there was but one empty chair, sat Marmee, her children and her grandchildren.

When Laurie proposed a toast to her, she replied by stretching out her arms to them all and saying that she could wish nothing better for them than this present happiness for the rest of their lives.

LIVES OF THE CAESARS

Type of work: Biography
Author: Gaius Suetonius Tranquillus (c. 70-c. 140)
Time: c. 86 B.C.-A.D. 96
Locale: The Roman world
First transcribed: c. 120

Principal personages (in historical order):
JULIUS CAESAR (CAIUS JULIUS CAESAR), c. 102-44 B.C.
AUGUSTUS (CAIUS OCTAVIUS), 63 B.C.-A.D. 14
TIBERIUS (TIBERIUS CLAUDIUS NERO), 42 B.C.-A.D. 37
GAIUS CALIGULA (CAIUS CAESAR GERMANICUS), 12-41
CLAUDIUS (TIBERIUS CLAUDIUS DRUSUS), 10 B.C.-A.D. 54
NERO (NERO CLAUDIUS CAESAR), 37-68
GALBA (SERVIUS SULPICIUS GALBA), 3 B.C.-A.D. 69
OTHO (MARCUS SALVIUS OTHO), 32-69
VITELLIUS (AULUS VITELLIUS), 15-69
VESPASIAN (TITUS FLAVIUS VESPASIANUS), 9-79
TITUS (TITUS FLAVIUS SABINUS VESPASIANUS), 41-81
DOMITIAN (TITUS FLAVIUS DOMITIANUS), 51-96

Perhaps Suetonius, like other biographers and historians, made mistakes; perhaps he retained ancedotes and bits of gossip that a less lively writer would have discarded; but he made the Caesars mortal men, though some of them carried the title of god, and he showed them in defeat and victory, virtue and vice, as they were or, at least, as some men reputed them to be. So colorful are the details of murders and lustful acts that even the most extravagant of Hollywood representations of ancient Rome are calm and temperate by comparison.

The beginning of the life of Julius Caesar is missing, the account beginning in his sixteenth year, but otherwise the book is complete. Like the other biographies there is more emphasis on Julius the person and on his relationships with the people about him than there is on the great historical moments of his life. But the major events were bound to be reported in great detail in ordinary works; Suetonius performs the service of filling out the cold lines of history with an impartial account of the personal traits of the Caesars.

After the death of his father, Julius married Cornelia, daughter of the consul Cinna, who bore him a daughter, Julia. Since by this act—which allied Julius with the popular party—he irritated the dictator Sulla, he was forced to go into hiding; but Caesar's friends interceded for him and at last he was forgiven. Sulla warned, however, that Caesar would "one day deal the death blow to the cause of the aristocracy."

Brief statements are made about Caesar's campaigns in Asia and about his service in Cilicia under Servilius Isauricus. Julius then returned to Rome and began his political career by bringing a charge of extortion against Cornelius Dolabella. After Dolabella had been acquitted Caesar went to Rhodes to study oratory under Apollonius Molo. On the way he was kidnapped by pirates; after being freed upon payment of ransom, he returned to capture and punish the pirates.

Julius became military tribune and gained an increasing reputation as an orator. After the death of his wife he married Pompeia, but he divorced her on suspicion that she had committed adultery with Publius Clodius.

By his political acts Caesar made himself popular with the masses, an advantage he made secure by arranging gladiatorial shows and stage plays for their amusement. By resorting to bribery, he won the election to the office of pontifex maximus. His efforts to secure mercy for Catiline after the conspiracy was detected almost cost him his life, for the address of Marcus Cato kept the Senate committed to the extreme penalty and Julius was threatened by the Roman knights who stood as guards in the Senate.

After becoming consul in 60 B.C., Caesar made a compact with Gnaeus Pompeius and Marcus Crassus, thus securing power over the Senate.

Suetonius carefully describes the political moves by which Julius continued to increase his own power while battling for the popular party against the Senate. After the nine-year campaign in Gaul, Caesar decided that only civil war could settle the political dissension. Crossing the Rubicon, he marched on Rome. After his victory he rewarded his troops, entertained the masses with shows, and undertook a reform of the Senate and of the calendar. His victory over Pompey, who had led the opposition, made the subsequent defeat of the senatorial party an easier task. As dictator, Caesar began with reforms but ended with such an assumption of power and infallibility, together with complete disdain of the Senate, that a conspiracy was formed against him which included Brutus, Cassius, Cimber, Casca, and other friends of Caesar who had turned against him. He died by their daggers on the Ides of March, after being warned by a series of signs.

Suetonius devotes the bulk of his essay on Julius to an account of Caesar's personal characteristics. Julius is described as having been "tall of stature, with a fair complexion, shapely limbs, a somewhat full face, and keen black eyes. . . . He was somewhat overnice in the care of his person, being not only carefully trimmed and shaved, but even having superfluous hair plucked out. . . ." Lengthy consideration is given to the charge that Julius had been intimate with King Nicomedes. Suetonius writes that he will take no account of various invectives and reproaches made against Caesar

on this matter: he then proceeds to quote, with great detail, all gossip he disdains. Julius drank very little wine, according to Suetonius; he seduced many women, had love affairs with queens—including Cleopatra—excelled in the art of war, wrote his memoirs with simplicity and skill, rode a horse that was "almost human," treated his friends with kindness and consideration, and was so merciful that when he captured the pirates who had kidnapped him, he cut their throats before crucifying them. Suetonius declares that Julius Caesar "was numbered among the gods, not only by a formal decree, but also in the conviction of the common people."

The life of Augustus, like that of Julius, is first summarized by Suetonius, who then proceeds to tell of Augustus the man. Born Caius Octavius, he inherited power from Julius, although he had to join with Antony and Lepidus and fight a series of battles in order to become undisputed ruler of the Empire. The name "Augustus" was a title conferred by the Senate to honor him.

Suetonius mentions some of the acts Augustus committed while triumvir, deeds by which he incurred "general detestation." He ordered a Roman knight stabbed to death for taking notes; he so abused Tedius Afer, consul elect, that Afer "hurled himself headlong," committing suicide; he tortured Quintus Gallius because of the suspicion that Gallius had a sword under his cloak, and he tore out the man's eyes with his own hands after ordering his execution.

On the more constructive side, Augustus is credited with having built many public works, revising the wards of the city and the system of night watches, building up a library of Sibylline books after burning prophetic writings of little repute, adding to the public security, revising existing laws, rebuilding roads, and surpassing his predecessors in the magnificence of public shows.

He won the affection of the people

and the Senate, and was named "Father of his Country" by the latter. He had few friends, but he was faithful to them. He gambled and made love to other men's wives, although this latter practice is partly excused by Suetonius on the ground that it was pursued not from passion but from a desire for information about the ladies' husbands. In other respects he was temperate, furnishing his house simply and eating simple food. He is described as handsome, although he had teeth that were "wide apart, small, and ill-kept. . . ." Augustus died painlessly and without disturbance, as he had wished, from an illness.

Suetonius' treatment of the lives of the other Caesars is similar to that of Julius and Augustus, although with most of the Caesars, beginning with Tiberius, murders and sexual excesses were so common that most of the accounts are taken up with a recital of monstrous deeds. Although Nero is the most infamous of the Caesars—and probably deserves to be remembered as almost entirely depraved—it would be difficult to decide which of the others was the worst.

After a few years of attention to the duties of emperor, Tiberius openly gave way to his vices, drowning himself in wine, consorting at banquets attended by nude girls, killing those who offended him or who were about when something angered him, and finally arranging matters so that every day was execution day and every crime a capital one. He drove his sister-in-law to suicide by starvation. He devised elaborate systems of torture and, to insure the death of his victims, had them thrown over a cliff to the rocks where guards broke up the bodies with boathooks. When he died there was general rejoicing and cries of "Tiberius to the Tiber!"

After writing of some of Caligula's accomplishments—great public games, the building of public works—Suetonius comments, "So much for Caligula as emperor; we must now tell of his career as a monster." He demanded that he be worshipped as a god; he built temples to himself and invited the moon to his embraces. He lived in incest with his sisters, stole the wives of other men, and had a series of wives. He murdered his friends and those who helped him to power. He matched worthless gladiators against wild beasts, and in random fashion chose prisoners to be devoured by savage animals in the arena. He enjoyed watching executions while eating his lunch, and at a banquet he ordered the hands of a slave cut off and hung about his neck so that the wretched man could be led about the banquet hall as a warning against stealing. These are simply samples of Caligula's deeds. He was stabbed to death when he was twenty-nine years old, after almost four years of rule.

Claudius began his rule in such manner that he won the love and devotion of his subjects, and he accomplished many worthwhile objectives; but he was a cruel and suspicious man, and he died by poison.

Even a summary statement of Nero's crimes is difficult. He was cruel, vain, and lustful. Ordinary entertainment and ordinary modes of sexual intercourse were displaced by extravagant orgies of various sorts. Regarding himself as a musician and singer, he forced great audiences to listen to him for hours on end, forbidding anyone to leave, so that women sometimes gave birth to children while he performed. He enjoyed fires and burned great sections of Rome. He wandered the streets in disguise, indulging in revels and fights. Boys, men, married women, prostitutes, and wives—all fed his lust, sometimes in violent and dramatically contrived ways. He murdered his mother after several attempts, and it was Suetonius' opinion that he had something to do with the poisoning of Claudius. Hundreds of other persons—his family, his companions, and others—died by his hand or by his orders. Suetonius writes that Nero "showed neither discrimination nor moderation in putting to death whomsoever he pleased on any pretext whatsoever." When the Senate finally sent men to capture him for execution, he killed himself by cutting his own throat, but only after considerable wailing and postponement.

Nero was the last Caesar by family connection; the others bore the name "Caesar" as a designation of rank. Suetonius' account of the remaining Caesars—Galba, Otho, Vitellius, Vespasian, Titus, and Domitian—gives considerably less space to their exploits; but the style continues to be lively and informative.

LIZA OF LAMBETH

Type of work: Novel
Author: W. Somerset Maugham (1874-   )
Type of plot: Naturalism
Time of plot: Late nineteenth century
Locale: England
First published: 1897

Principal characters:
LIZA KEMP, a street girl
TOM, who loved her
JIM BLAKESTON, Liza's lover
SALLY, her friend

Critique:

Liza of Lambeth is the first novel of W. Somerset Maugham. One of the least known to readers of his more popular novels, it belongs to the school of naturalism which flourished in English fiction about the turn of the century. There is virtually no development of character, and the plot is no more remarkable than the commonplace lives of the people in the novel. Here, more than in any other of his novels, Maugham drew directly upon his own observations and experiences as a young doctor serving his interneship among the poor of the London slums. The novel is as blunt and unsparing as a clinical report.

The Story:

Liza Kemp spent most of her free time on the streets of Lambeth. She was not exactly a loose girl, but her dress and actions provoked whistles and jeers whenever she appeared. Liza's father was dead, and her mother, living on a small pension, earned enough as a charwoman to keep herself in beer. She never spoke a kind word to her daughter, although she expected Liza to hand over all her money and spend all her time with her mother. Like most girls of her class, Liza worked in a factory and made only enough money to live and to buy a few items of cheap finery.

After a gay dance in the streets of Lambeth, Liza was chased by several young men trying to kiss her. As she fled, only half in earnest, she ran straight into the arms of a stranger and was soundly kissed. Flouncing off, she found herself strangely moved by the unexpected experience. That night Tom, her earnest and persistent suitor, called on her as usual. Liza liked Tom but she did not love him, and so she tried to send him away without hurting his feelings. But Tom was stubborn. He begged her to take time to consider his proposal. When he asked her to go on an outing the next day, she refused. She did not want him to spend his money or his hopes on her.

Later her friend Sally also begged her to go on the outing. When she learned that the stranger who had kissed her would be one of the party, Liza relented, but against her better judgment. She had learned that the stranger was Jim Blakeston, a married man and the father of five children. Jim's wife went on the outing too, but Jim paid little attention to her. Instead, he spent most of his time following Liza and Tom around. Jim's actions angered Tom, but that poor young man was too much in love to blame Liza for encouraging the older man.

After the excursion Jim followed Liza home and kissed her passionately. She knew that she should be angry, but she was also flattered and pleased. From that night on Liza was lost. When Jim asked her to walk with him or to meet him at a show, she refused; then she kept the appointment anyway. Although she knew they were both wrong, she seemed powerless to withdraw from his influence. They tried to avoid people they knew, but Liza was afraid that they would be seen sooner or later. At last, grown reckless, she allowed Jim to seduce her.

The next few weeks were heaven for Liza. She loved Jim deeply, and he returned her love. But Liza knew that people were beginning to talk about her. Young men and girls yelled insults after her. Even Tom cut her once, and that fact hurt her because she knew that Tom was good and kind and she hated to lose his former opinion of her. Her love was too strong, however, to be permanently affected by the insults she received. Jim even offered to leave his wife and take her away to another part of the city, but Liza knew that they would always be in danger of being caught. She also realized that Jim loved his children and would be unhappy away from them. Furthermore, Liza felt that she could not leave her mother. Although the old woman had never been much of a mother, Liza thought it her duty to stay with her. There seemed nothing for Liza and Jim to do but to continue as they were or to part entirely. Neither could think of parting.

After Liza's friend Sally was married, her happiness made Liza even more miserable in her own shame. Later she learned that Sally's happiness was only superficial. Her husband beat her regularly, but the girl was too proud to let anyone but Liza know. Liza also had a shock. Once she was late for an appointment with Jim and he drank too much while he waited for her. When she tried to keep him from going back into the pub for more beer, he struck her in the eye. He was instantly contrite, but the damage to Liza's heart never quite mended.

Sally warned Liza one day that Jim's wife was looking for her. To avoid a public scene, Liza tried to keep clear of Mrs. Blakeston, who was much the larger and stronger of the two. In a fight, Liza realized, she would be bested. But at last they met and Mrs. Blakeston gave Liza a horrible beating. Outclassed from the beginning, the girl fought gamely. Tom and Jim appeared almost simultaneously and stopped the fight, Tom carrying Liza home tenderly and Jim threatening to kill his wife for hurting Liza.

Tom loved Liza so much that he wanted to marry her, although he knew all the gossip about her; he had cut her in the past because of his hurt. Even when she told him that she was going to have Jim's baby, Tom still wanted to have her for his wife. Liza refused him again, however; Tom was too good to be tied to a woman of her reputation.

Jim himself almost killed his wife. He was prevented from doing so only by the intervention of a neighbor woman.

Later that night Liza awoke with a burning fever and intense pain. For the next day or two she suffered terribly, and at last her mother became worried enough to send for a midwife. The woman knew at once that Liza had miscarried and was gravely ill. Although they sent for a doctor, the midwife knew that there was little hope for the girl. Tom called regularly, out of his mind with worry. Liza, when she was conscious, looked only for Jim. He came as soon as he heard about her condition, but he was too late to give any comfort to the dying girl. She lay unconscious for several hours, then quietly died. As the doctor covered her face, Jim turned away, weary and defeated.

THE LONG JOURNEY

Type of work: Novel
Author: Johannes V. Jensen (1873-1950)
Type of plot: Cultural epic
Time of plot: The Age of Man
Locale: The world
First published: 1923-1924

Principal characters:
FYR, typical of the earliest users of fire
CARL, typical of the early Stone Age man in the glacial period
WHITE BEAR, typical of the later Stone Age man
WOLF, typical of the horse-riding and horse-breeding man
NORNA GEST, typical of the man who entered the Iron Age and lingered to the fall of the Roman Empire
CHRISTOPHER COLUMBUS, typical of the Renaissance man
CHARLES DARWIN, typical of modern man

Critique:

In 1944 the Nobel Prize in Literature was awarded to Johannes V. Jensen "because of the exceptional vigor and fertility of his poetic imagination, combined with an all-embracing intellectuality and bold creative expression." All those qualities are certainly manifest in The Long Journey, a prose epic published in translation as Fire and Ice (1923), The Cimbrians (1923), and Christopher Columbus (1924). Yet to call The Long Journey a novel is to understate its value; rather, it is a great work of cultural mythology, a new integration and an ultra-sensitive reinterpretation of the progress Man has made in the world since that remote age when he first began to walk upon the earth. At least one writer has termed it a "bible of evolution." Perhaps no less comprehensive category can hold a work which ranges from before the Ice Age to the twentieth century. This work was published in Denmark as six novels over the period 1909 to 1922.

The Story:

In the north of what is now Europe, in the prehistoric days before the glaciers came from the North, Man lived in fear and trembling—in fear of the elements, the beasts of the jungles, and his own primitive leaders. Into one of those herd-like groups was born a boy who was named Fyr. As the child grew older he was seized with a desire to climb to the top of Gunung Api, a vast volcano quiet but not extinct. There on the slopes of the volcano, wandering by himself, Fyr learned to make use of the flames and their heat to keep himself warm, to cook his meat, to provide himself with a deity, and to enhance his own importance.

Attracted first by his songs and then by his person, women joined Fyr, until he, like other leaders, was the head of a primitive family group. After the women came children and, finally, other men who made themselves subservient to Fyr. Under his leadership the tribe became a band of hunters, using the pits, spears, and bows which Fyr devised for them. Wherever they went, they took with them burning wood to re-create their god and household symbol: the fire. Soon all the forest folk bowed to the authority of Fyr, bound to him by his fire and by the tools of wood and stone which he created to make their lives more bearable. One day, however, the god seemed to demand a sacrifice, and the people, making Fyr their scapegoat, placed him in the fire he had brought them. Although he was roasted and eaten, he lived on, a representative of human ingenuity

THE LONG JOURNEY by Johannes V. Jensen. Translated by A. G. Chater. By permission of the publishers, Alfred A. Knopf, Inc. Copyright, 1923, 1924, by Alfred A. Knopf, Inc. Renewed, 1952, by Alfred A. Knopf, Inc.

which they could not understand.

As ages passed, Gunung Api became extinct. Still later, the northern ice cap, beginning to move over the land, brought cold to the tropic jungles. After other ages had passed, a small band of hunters lay crouched in the same forest. The seasons were much colder, and the tribe and most of the animals had moved to the South, until a hunting expedition had brought them back to the old territory. One of their number, Carl, was the fire-tender. He was thrown out of the band, an outcast, when he let the fire die.

Carl fled to the North, somehow keeping himself alive in the winter by wrapping himself in skins and burrowing into the ground or building rude huts of stone. High on the extinct volcanic cone he traveled. Everywhere he saw only desolation and ice. He sought for the enemy of his tribe, the cold, but did not find him. He was joined in his wanderings by a dog; the animal slowly joined into a comradeship with the man, although not without some trembling and hesitancy on the part of each. As the winters passed, Carl learned to prepare for them by laying in a supply of food and building a shelter. He even learned to foretell when the great cold was coming and where he would find food and shelter as its ice and snows moved gradually to the South. When he did find an occasional human being, the encounter served only as an opportunity for Carl to eat a different kind of meat. One day he gave chase to a human being who turned out to be a woman. He captured her by the sea, and the lure of the sea was to call him again.

Carl's wife was Mam. She brought new habits of gathering and storing, as well as children. She added vegetables to Carl's diet, and their home became a permanent one. Carl was still aware of fire, a possession which he had lost and not regained. Gathering many stones, he chipped them against one another in his efforts to strike fire from them. At last,

successful, he bequeathed fire to his children.

The children of Carl and their wives added pottery work to their skills; with ceramics came boiling, a new way of cooking. Among the descendants of Carl there arose a group of priests, against whom rebels were sometimes pitted. Such a rebel was White Bear. Denied a certain woman for his wife, he killed the leader of the priestly clan. Like Carl before him, White Bear became an outcast, taking May, his woman, with him. White Bear became a seaman, building small boats and sailing them, in company with his sons, while May and the daughters remained at home to farm and care for the cattle.

White Bear began to use horses. He built a chariot, with horses to draw it. His sons, more adventurous, learned to ride. One of the sons, Wolf, became so enamored of the horses that he rode them away to become a nomad, forerunner of the Golden Horde of Genghis Khan.

Ages later a new man appeared. He was Norna Gest, son of the matriarch Gro. While he was still a young boy dwelling at the edge of the sea on an island, he built himself a dugout canoe and sailed away, carrying with him a young girl who was, after a time, to become his mate. They and their child explored a new land to the north, now Sweden, but returned to the home island in after years. Gest himself was not an ordinary mortal; he was to live as long as he kept a partially burned candle. After his return to his original home, he and his companions went on many voyages and made use of sails as well as paddles.

As years passed, Gest found he had outlived his companions. He awoke one day to find himself in a changed Sealand, a place where men were either thralls or earls. Disturbed at the changes and despised because he had taken a new wife in the person of a milkmaid, one of the thralls, he wandered sadly about the land.

Unhappy in the changed Sealand, Gest and his bondwoman-wife sailed to Sweden to found a new colony in which they were to be the leaders. With them they took new techniques of smelting and forging metals. In their new home they gradually acquired domestic animals —horses, sheep, and cattle. Their sons and daughters married, and thus the colony grew. The mother died, and one day Gest disappeared, to wander again over the globe. Unnoticed but noticing, he traveled through central Europe and floated down the Danube. He traversed the Mediterranean lands, where his life began in the early Stone Age. Finding something wanting in the lands of the South, Gest turned his face once again toward his homeland, where he became a wandering skald.

Arriving in Jutland, he was welcomed by Tole, a leader who was guardian of the ancient god of the Jutlanders. This was a wooden idol which Tole wished to enclose in a great bronze bull. Tole welcomed Gest as the bringer of skills with metals and as a man of great wisdom. The two men made plans to cast the bronze bull at the time of the great spring festivals, before the flocks and herds were taken up to the summer pastures. The bull was successfully cast, and the festivities ended with human sacrifices of slaves and thralls. Gest wandered off afoot after the festival.

In later years floods rose up in the seas about Jutland, and the younger men wished to leave the country to search for a homeland safe from the ever-encroaching sea. The entire tribe left, except for elderly Tole. With the tribe went the bronze bull, destined now to long journeying across the face of central and southern Europe.

Back and forth across the lands went the Cimbrians, enlisting other tribes in their search for better lands. At last they traveled far enough to come to the notice of the Romans.

Failing to obey the warning of the Romans to remain out of their dominions, the Cimbrians and their allies of the North became enemies of the Empire. As enemies they decided to strike at Rome itself. Victorious at first, they became proud and reckoned not at all on the strategy of the Roman generals, strategy which defeated them. In their defeat the Cimbrians and their allies were ruined. Those who were not killed or who did not commit suicide were sold into bondage to the Romans, to live miserably as captives in the South, where eventually their blood blended with the blood of their conquerors.

Norna Gest saw these things happening. Finally, knowing that his time was at an end, he once again left Rome in his boat and glided slowly toward the sea, there to burn his candle to its end.

After the fall of the Roman Empire, barbarians from the North were gradually assimilated into the Christian religion. The ancient ship of the North, inverted on land, became the Gothic cathedral, a compound of the mariner's vessel and the stately forests through which earlier man had roamed. Among the descendants of the barbaric tribes of the North were the Langobards. One of the descendants of the latter group was a man named Christopher Columbus, who was to lead mankind farther on its journey of discovery across the seas and into a whole new hemisphere then undreamed of, or at least forgotten by the descendants of the early Northmen who had once visited it.

Columbus saw himself as a veritable Christopher, one who carried the Christ into the world. While others caroused before setting out across the ocean with him, he prepared himself by attending masses in the cathedral. He had faith in divine help and a divine purpose. When the qualities which his faith gave him proved insufficient to meet the demands of leadership, he could also call upon an amazing strength of body which his northern forebears had bequeathed him.

Although he reached the islands of the West Indies, other men carried man's long journey into the New World; Columbus was doomed to be only a leader pointing the way. To later conquistadors, men like Cortés and Pizarro, went the credit for gaining the mainland for European culture. Those men faced the odds of sheer numbers when they met the strength of the late Stone Age men, the followers of Montezuma and the Incas, who still existed in America, savages caught in the lag where European culture had left them many ages before. In Mexico, for example, Cortés was to find human sacrifices and worship of volcanic spirits, examples of culture-progress which had long since ceased to exist in the Old World. The light which Columbus saw from his ship at night was a symbol of the fire worship met throughout the New World.

The Indians believed that the coming of the white men marked the return of their great sun god, Quetzalcoatl. Perhaps the god might have been Norna Gest, visiting the New World during his travels. But the savages soon lost their superstitious awe of men with fair skins and hair, and many Europeans were sacrificed on the altars of Mexico and other southern countries.

The great battle of the New World was fought in Mexico. There the journey of the European culture was most seriously threatened. In the north the Indians seemed to fade away before the white culture; in the West Indies disease had killed them like summer flies at the first autumn frost. But in Mexico there was warfare between the eagle and the serpent, symbols of Man's migrations and his conflicting cultures. Cortés and his soldiers were like eagles swooping down on the snake, insignia of the Aztecs.

Even though Cortés was temporarily successful, with the help of a woman who turned against her own people, and even though he was able to send the idol of Huitzilopochtli toppling down the long flights of stairs which led to its temple, the Spaniards were doomed to temporary defeat. Cortés had to hack his way out of Tenochtitlán while the screams of Spaniards sacrificed alive echoed in his ears.

Years later a young man named Darwin, a naturalist on H. M. S. Beagle, was to become a new symbol in man's journey from the past, through the present, into the future. Those on the Beagle thought they saw the Flying Dutchman. Perhaps that dread captain, doomed to sail forever, will become the symbol of Man's long journey as it continues. Or perhaps the long journey is now almost ended. No one knows.

THE LONG NIGHT

Type of work: Novel
Author: Andrew Lytle (1902-   )
Type of plot: Historical romance
Time of plot: 1857-1862
Locale: Alabama, Mississippi, Tennessee
First published: 1936

Principal characters:
LAWRENCE McIVOR, the narrator, William McIvor's son
CAMERON McIVOR, his grandfather, an Alabama planter
PLEASANT, Cameron McIvor's favorite son and avenger
WILLIAM, and
LEVI, Pleasant's brothers
ELI McIVOR, Pleasant's uncle
TYSON LOVELL, leader of a gang of slave speculators
LIEUTENANT ROSWELL ELLIS, Pleasant's friend
ALBERT SIDNEY JOHNSTON, Confederate general

Critique:

A remarkable first novel based in part on actual characters and events, *The Long Night* is a work of originality and true historical imagination. After the murder of his father by a gang of desperadoes modeled more or less upon the notorious Murrell gang of actual history, a young Alabaman embarks upon a grim career of revenge, but with the outbreak of the Civil War his desire for private vengeance becomes submerged in the greater and bloodier issues of that conflict. At last, facing a tragic dilemma, he makes his own desperate and separate peace and goes into hiding. In spite of minor structural defects the novel achieves its purpose with considerable stylistic vigor and imaginative power, and the account of the battle of Shiloh is a vivid piece of war reporting. In addition, the writer presents a realistic and convincing regional picture of ante-bellum life on the southern frontier. These qualities combine to give *The Long Night* its definite distinction among more conventional novels dealing with the Civil War theme.

The Story:

Lawrence McIvor was twenty-two when he heard his family's story for the first time. Just out of college, he had been summoned to his Uncle Pleasant's house deep in the coves of Winston County, Alabama. There through all of one dark winter night he listened to his kinsmen's tale of hatred and grim vengeance.

The McIvor troubles began in Georgia, at a militia muster where powerful old Cameron McIvor refused to wrestle one of the reckless Caruthers twins. Several days later Job Caruthers attacked McIvor and the planter broke the young man's arm. After his recovery Job and his brother Mebane returned a borrowed team of horses in a wind-broken condition. Furious, McIvor shot Job. The brother then started a lawsuit which left the planter almost ruined. McIvor decided to move to Texas. Pleasant, his favored son, was sixteen at the time.

The McIvors traveled by wagon, with their cattle and remaining slaves. Near Wetumpka, Alabama, they met Tyson Lovell, a wealthy landowner who offered McIvor five hundred acres of good land to crop on shares. Not long after they had settled in their new home William, the oldest son, married a storekeeper's daughter and went to live in town. Pleasant and his younger brother Levi helped their father and the hands in the fields. There was something mysterious and

THE LONG NIGHT by Andrew Lytle. By permission of the author and the publishers, The Bobbs-Merrill Co., Inc. Copyright, 1936, by The Bobbs-Merrill Co., Inc.

sinister about Lovell. After McIvor and Pleasant, tracking a lost mule, found a shack in which two neighbors named Wilson were guarding several strange slaves, the father became convinced that Lovell was a speculator, head of a gang of slave stealers and horse thieves, an organization to which most of their neighbors belonged. Lovell, becoming alarmed, tried to frighten the McIvors into leaving the country, first by having the sheriff discover two stolen slaves in the planter's smokehouse, later, after McIvor and Lovell quarreled, by swearing out a bench warrant which named McIvor an outlaw.

Defying Lovell, the planter waited for his enemy to act. William came to stay at the farm, but he was called away suddenly by false news of his wife's illness. That night Pleasant was waylaid and locked in an old church. Before daylight armed men broke into the McIvor house. While the Wilton brothers held the old planter in his bed, a man named Fox shot him.

The McIvor kin gathered in secret. A few, William among them, argued that the murderers should be punished by the law. Others clamored for an open feud. Grief-crazed over his father's death, Pleasant revealed that he had tracked the gang to its meeting place and learned the names of its forty members. After the court dismissed charges brought by McIvor's widow, she and her family quietly left the country. Pleasant, a young uncle named Eli, and Bob Pritchard, a cousin, swore to answer violent death with violence.

Pleasant and his kinsmen began to terrorize the region. A dishonest district attorney, Lovell's tool, was killed in a fall from an inn balcony. One Wilton was dragged to death by his horse. Another was found shot. Lovell's house burned, his overseer's charred body in the ruins. Fox ran away. After Sheriff Botterall's posse trapped and killed Pritchard, Pleasant resolved to kill secretly and alone. Forcing Botterall into a wild stallion's stall, he lashed the animal until

it trampled Lovell's henchman to death. Several of the gang fled to Texas, but Pleasant followed and killed them. He and Eli built a cabin in the wilds of Winston County. From there he planned to carry on his stealthy, deadly raids around Wetumpka.

Two years after his father's death he went one night to a house Lovell owned near Buyckville. In hiding, he had not known that Fort Sumter had been fired on until he found Lovell in his study and learned from his mocking enemy that the Civil War had begun. Lovell declared that the army would soon swallow the survivors of his gang; besides, Pleasant had walked into a trap. Hearing bloodhounds baying in the distance, Pleasant boasted that he still intended to make Lovell the last of his victims. After knocking the man unconscious with a pistol, he ran from the house before his trackers could surround it.

Pleasant and Eli joined the Confederate Army, and as a result Pleasant continued his work of revenge. At Corinth, while on outpost duty, he killed a sergeant and four men from Lovell's gang and arranged the bodies to make them appear as if shot by Federal scouts. Summoned to General Albert Sidney Johnston's headquarters to give his version of the attack, he met Lieutenant Roswell Ellis, on the staff of Colonel Armistead McIvor, Pleasant's cousin from Kentucky. In an army in which there were few binding distinctions of rank Pleasant and Ellis became friends. Pleasant learned that Fox, his father's murderer, had offered to have Andrew Johnson assassinated and that General Johnston had scornfully rejected the offer. Knowing that Fox was in the neighborhood, he bided his time.

The march toward Shiloh Church began through pouring rain. Two nights before the battle Pleasant and Ellis were detailed to scout duty along the Federal lines. After Ellis returned to report, Pleasant spent the night in the woods. All the next day he watched the Federal encampment and waited for the battle to begin. But there were delays in bringing up Confederate troops and equipment and the battle of Shiloh was not joined until Sunday morning, April 6, 1862. Pleasant, wandering through the acrid battle haze, found his own company in time to join in a wild charge in which Eli was killed. The Federal troops retreated. Pleasant, shot in the hand, spent the night with a wounded major from Ohio. The next day the reinforced Federal lines advanced and the Confederates, with General Beauregard in command after General Johnston's death, began their retreat to Corinth.

Pleasant was with the army at Murfreesboro when he heard that his brother William had been killed. Levi, after nursing his wounded brother, died three days later. Pleasant went to meet his mother at Chattanooga when she drove through the Federal lines to claim her sons' bodies. On his way back to Murfreesboro, Pleasant was glad to have Roswell Ellis' friendship. Ellis was of the living, and Pleasant had seen too many deaths. After Shiloh woods he was beginning, despairingly, to doubt his vows of hatred and revenge.

Scouting near La Vergne, Pleasant did not return to camp immediately because he was on the track of a Lovell man named Awsumb, but when he looked at his enemy through his gunsights he was unable to pull the trigger. On his arrival at headquarters he learned that after his failure to report at once a brigade had been sent to test the enemy strength at La Vergne. Ellis had been killed in the engagement. Pleasant felt that his delay had caused his friend's death. Ellis had given him back his humanity and he had destroyed his friend. Following dark and bloody trails of reprisal, he had loved the dead too much and the living too little, and he himself was doomed. He thought of the hills and hidden coves of Winston County. There a deserter from whatever cause he fled could hide forever.

THE LONGEST JOURNEY

Type of work: Novel
Author: E. M. Forster (1879-   )
Type of plot: Social criticism
Time of plot: Early twentieth century
Locale: England
First published: 1907

Principal characters:
RICKIE ELLIOT, a student at Cambridge
AGNES PEMBROKE, an old friend
HERBERT PEMBROKE, her brother
STEWART ANSELL, a friend of Rickie at Cambridge
EMILY FAILING, his aunt
STEPHEN WONHAM, his half-brother

Critique:

In this novel Forster is primarily concerned with the story of a sensitive young man and the problems he encounters on his introduction into the world. The author is somewhat satiric as he views his characters but, as usual, he does not present the world as a completely dreary and uninteresting place. Men, in general, are portrayed as rather weak individuals who are fighting against superior forces, but the reader is not meant completely to lose his love and respect for them. Here, in a novel which is probably autobiographical in part, we see several characters who try without success to live happily in a world of weak and misguided ideals.

The Story:

Frederick Elliot, who was a student at Cambridge and almost alone in the world, had finally attained some degree of contentment in his life after a rather unhappy childhood. He had been born with a lamed left foot which kept him from most of the normal activities of children, and he had grown up virtually without friends. Early in his life his father had begun to call him Rickie because of its close similarity to rickety, and the name had stayed with him. Besides his deformity there was another, more serious, difficulty. He found out quite early that his father and mother did not love each other

and that he was loved not at all by his father and only a little by his mother. Both his parents died when he was fifteen, leaving him comfortably well off so far as finances were concerned but without anyone who wanted to give him a home.

At Cambridge he had shown himself to be a capable student but one without any scholarly pretensions. He had made several friends among the non-athletic groups and spent much of his time in long discussions on topics of literary or philosophical interest. One day, during such a discussion, he was interrupted by the arrival of his old friends, Agnes and Herbert Pembroke, whom he had invited for the weekend. In the meantime he had completely forgotten about them. Because these two people were part of that very small group which took an interest in Rickie's career, they spent a great part of their time at Cambridge encouraging him to decide on a particular course for his life, even if he did nothing more than write, the only thing he admitted having an interest in. They pointed out that money was not important as long as he met a certain standard of ideals.

At Christmas of that same year Rickie saw his friends again. He had stayed several days with Stewart Ansell, a friend from Cambridge, but felt it was necessary to spend a part of his vacation with the Pembrokes as well. He rather dreaded this part of his vacation because Agnes' fiancé, a man whom Rickie had known at public school, was to be there. Rickie not only disliked Gerald Dawes but he also hated to witness the lovers' happiness; he felt that such happiness was forever to be denied him because of his lame foot which he considered a hereditary disorder. During this time Gerald was killed while playing football, and it was Rickie who was able to offer the most comfort to Agnes by convincing her that she *should* suffer since her love for Gerald had been the greatest thing she could ever experience.

Two years later, when she came again to visit him at Cambridge, Rickie realized that he was also in love with Agnes, although he still felt that he could never marry because of his deformity. She convinced him, however, that they should be married. Rickie was about to finish his work at Cambridge, but they felt a long engagement was necessary for him to settle himself. Ansell immediately opposed the marriage because he sensed that Agnes was not a sincere person. She laid constant claim to honesty and forthrightness, but Ansell could not be convinced that these qualities revealed the true Agnes. He knew immediately that she would force Rickie into a dull and conventional life, convincing him at the same time that he was taking the proper step.

Soon after their engagement Rickie and Agnes visited his aunt, Mrs. Emily Failing, at her country home. Rickie had never particularly liked his aunt, but since she was his only known relative he and Agnes felt that they should go to see her. Mrs. Failing was a woman who liked for people to do what she wanted and she was never happier than when they were obviously uncomfortable while carrying out her desires. While there they also saw Stephen Wonham, a young man whom Rickie had met before but whose

relation to Mrs. Failing had never been made clear. However, after Rickie had been so bold as to engage in an argument with his aunt, she informed him that Stephen was actually his brother. It was not until later that Rickie found out that Stephen was the son of his mother, whom he had loved very much, and not of his father. Not even Stephen himself knew who he was, but the matter had never greatly concerned him.

After their marriage Rickie and Agnes went to live with Herbert at Sawston School. The arrangement had been worked out between Herbert and Agnes because Herbert needed help in his duties as a house master. Although Rickie soon realized that Herbert was basically stupid and that they disagreed on many points, he adapted himself to whatever course Herbert and Agnes chose. His marriage, in which he had hoped to find certain spiritual ideals, never reached a very intimate level, and before long his life became a shell. Ansell would have no more to do with him, and he was cut off from the one intellect at the school because of Herbert's feelings and aspirations.

Two years later, after Rickie had apparently succumbed completely to the forces playing on him, Stephen Wonham again entered his life. It became apparent immediately that Agnes, who had kept up a connection with Mrs. Failing, had been instrumental in having Stephen thrown out of her house, all because of her desire to inherit the money from the estate. Rickie was furious but again he submitted. Stephen, who had finally been told the truth about himself, came to Sawston expecting to find the kind of love which he had never known before. But when Rickie refused to see him and Agnes offered him money never to say anything about his parentage, he left immediately.

Stephen wandered around London for several days doing odd jobs and supporting himself as well as he could. Before

2092

long he had saved enough money for a drunken spree. During his drunkenness, determined to wreck Rickie's house, he returned to Sawston. In the process he might have killed himself if Rickie had not saved him. By this time Rickie, under the influence of Ansell, had begun to see how foolish he had been. Now he decided to give Stephen a home. Although Stephen would have none of this idea, he managed to convince Rickie that they should go away together.

Thus Rickie began the regeneration of his soul. Unfortunately it was of short duration. On a subsequent visit to his aunt, at which time Stephen insisted on accompanying him, he again saved Stephen's life but lost his own. Stephen, who had promised not to drink, got drunk and collapsed on the railroad crossing. Rickie managed to get him off, but he himself was killed. Just before he died he realized that he had been betrayed a second time by his belief in the individual.

LOOK HOMEWARD, ANGEL

Type of work: Novel
Author: Thomas Wolfe (1900-1938)
Type of plot: Impressionistic realism
Time of plot: 1900 to 1920
Locale: North Carolina
First published: 1929

Principal characters:
EUGENE GANT
ELIZA GANT, his mother
OLIVER GANT, his father
BEN GANT, his brother
MARGARET LEONARD, his teacher
LAURA JAMES, his first sweetheart

Critique:

The work of Thomas Wolfe contains two invariable elements. One is a reliance on characters of exceptional brilliance and vitality. The other is the portrayal of a central character who is the sensitive artist isolated in a hostile world. The latter character is generally Thomas Wolfe himself. In his fiction Wolfe attempted to re-create the whole American experience in his own image, and beneath the sprawling, often chaotic mass of his novels there are firm outlines of the naked and innocent story of the American land and its people. Although his emotional range is limited to the adolescent and the romantic, he stands plainly in the succession of American writers who have expressed in their work the symbols of a haunted inner world of thought and feeling.

The Story:

Eugene, the youngest child in the Gant family, came into the world when Eliza Gant was forty-two years old. His father went on periodic drinking sprees to forget his unfulfilled ambitions and the unsatisfied wanderlust which had brought him to Altamont in the hills of old Catawba. When Eugene was born, his father was asleep in a drunken stupor.

Eliza disapproved of her husband's debauches, but she lacked the imagination to understand their cause. Oliver, who had been raised amidst the plenty of a Pennsylvania farm, had no comprehension of the privation and suffering which had existed in the South after the Civil War, the cause of the hoarding and acquisitiveness of his wife and her Pentland relations in the Catawba hill country.

Eliza bore the burden of Oliver's drinking and promiscuousness until Eugene was four years old. Then she departed for St. Louis, taking all the children but the oldest daughter, Daisy, with her. It was 1904, the year of the great St. Louis Fair, and Eliza had gone to open a boarding-house for her visiting fellow townsmen. The idea was abhorrent to Oliver. He stayed in Altamont. Eliza's sojourn in St. Louis ended abruptly when twelve-year-old Grover fell ill of typhoid and died. Stunned, she gathered her remaining children to her and went home.

Young Eugene was a shy, awkward boy with dark, brooding eyes. He was, like his ranting, brawling father, a dreamer. He was not popular with his schoolmates, who sensed instinctively that he was different, and made him pay the price; and at home he was the victim of his sisters' and brothers' taunts and torments. His one champion was his brother Ben, though even he had been conditioned by the Gants' unemotional family life to give his caresses as cuffs. But there was little time for Eugene's childish daydreaming. Eliza believed early jobs taught her boys manliness and self-reliance. Ben got up at three o'clock every morning to deliver papers. Luke had been a *Saturday Evening Post* agent since he was twelve. Eugene was put under his wing. Although the boy loathed the work, he was forced every Thursday to corner customers and keep up a continuous line of chatter until he broke down their sales resistance.

Eugene was not yet eight when his parents separated. Eliza had bought the Dixieland boarding-house as a good investment. Helen remained at the old house with her father. Daisy married and left town. Mrs. Gant took Eugene with her. Ben and Luke were left to shift for themselves, to shuttle back and forth between the two houses. Eugene grew to detest his new home. When the Dixieland was crowded, there was no privacy, and Eliza advertised the Dixieland on printed cards which Eugene had to distribute to customers on his magazine route and to travelers arriving at the Altamont station.

But although life at the boarding-house was drabness itself, the next four years were the golden days of Eugene's youth, for he was allowed to go to the Leonards' private school. Margaret Leonard, the tubercular wife of the schoolmaster, recognized Eugene's hunger for beauty and love, and was able to find in literature the words that she herself had not the power to utter. By the time he was fifteen Eugene knew the best and the greatest lyrics almost line for line.

Oliver Gant, who had been fifty when his youngest son was born, was beginning to feel his years. Although he was never told, he was slowly dying of cancer.

Eugene was fourteen when the World

War broke out. Ben, who wanted to join the Canadian Army, was warned by his doctor that he would be refused because he had weak lungs.

At fifteen, Eugene was sent to the university at Pulpit Hill. It was his father's plan that Eugene should be well on his way toward being a great statesman before the time came for old Oliver to die. Eugene's youth and tremendous height made him a natural target for dormitory horseplay, and his shy, awkward manners were intensified by his ignorance of the school's traditions and rituals. He roomed alone. His only friends were four wastrels, one of whom contributed to his social education by introducing him to a brothel.

That summer, back at the Dixieland, Eugene met Laura James. Sitting with her on the front porch at night, he was trapped by her quiet smile and clear, candid eyes. He became her lover on a summer afternoon of sunlit green and gold. But Laura went home to visit her parents and wrote Eugene that she was about to marry a boy to whom she had been engaged for nearly a year.

Eugene went back to Pulpit Hill that fall, still determined to go his way alone. Although he had no intimates, he gradually became a campus leader. The commonplace good fellows of his world tolerantly made room for the one who was not like them.

In October of the following year Eugene received an urgent summons to come home. Ben was finally paying the price of his parents' neglect and the drudgery of his life. He was dying of pneumonia. Eliza had neglected to call a competent doctor until it was too late, and Oliver, as he sat at the foot of the dying boy's bed, could think only of the expense the burial would be. As the family kept their vigil through Ben's last night, they were touched with the realization of the greatness of the boy's generous soul. Ben was given, a final irony, the best funeral money could buy.

With Ben went the family's last pretenses. When Eugene came back to the Dixieland after graduation, Eliza was in control of Oliver's property and selling it as quickly as she could in order to use the money for further land speculations. She had disposed of their old home. Oliver lived in a back room at the boarding-house. His children watched each other suspiciously as he wasted away, each concerned for his own inheritance. Eugene managed to remain unembroiled in their growing hatred of each other, but he could not avoid being a target for that hatred. Helen, Luke, and Steve had always resented his schooling. In September, before he left for Harvard to begin graduate work, Luke asked Eugene to sign a release saying that he had received his inheritance as tuition and school expenses. Though his father had promised him an education when he was still a child and Eliza was to pay for his first year in the North, Eugene was glad to sign. He was free, and he was never coming back to Altamont.

On his last night at home he had a vision of his dead brother Ben in the moonlit square at midnight; Ben, the unloved of the Gants, and the most lovable. It was for Eugene as well a vision of old, unhappy, unforgotten years, and in his restless imagination he dreamed of the hidden door through which he would escape forever the mountain-rimmed world of his boyhood.

LOOKING BACKWARD

Type of work: Novel
Author: Edward Bellamy (1850-1898)
Type of plot: Utopian romance
Time of plot: A.D. 2000
Locale: Boston, Massachusetts
First published: 1888

Principal characters:
JULIAN WEST, a traveler in time
EDITH BARTLETT, his nineteenth century fiancée
DR. LEETE, a twentieth century citizen
EDITH LEETE, his daughter

Critique:

The main value of *Looking Backward: 2000-1887* lies in its credible presentation of a socialist Utopia, and the book has served to introduce many famous people to the theory of socialism. Bellamy was not merely a follower of Marx and other economists; he rationalized for himself the case for economic revolution. The prophecies he makes for the world by A.D. 2000 are sometimes strikingly shrewd, and his judgments made of modern society are pointed and witty. Bellamy's idea was to present the ideas of socialism, as he saw them, in a way which would appeal to a wide reading public, both of yesterday and today.

The Story:

Julian West had a hard time sleeping. In order to have complete quiet he had built a sound-proof room with thick cement walls in the cellar of his house. He was also in the habit of having a quack doctor named Pillsbury put him to sleep by hypnosis.

One night he went to dinner with his fiancée's family and spent an enjoyable evening with Edith and her father, Mr. Bartlett. He went home, had the doctor give him a treatment, and went to sleep. He awoke to find strange people in the room. They asked him who he was, and when he had gone to sleep. Julian was amazed when he realized that he had been asleep one hundred and thirteen years, three months, and eleven days.

From much questioning, Julian learned what must have happened. During the night that he last remembered, his house had burned down except for the sealed room in which he slept; and apparently everyone assumed that he had died in the fire. Because of his hypnotic state, his body had remained the same. He was still a young man of thirty when he was discovered by Dr. Leete in the year 2000. Dr. Leete and his daughter, Edith, were very kind to their guest from the past and tried to explain the changes in the world since he had last seen it.

Boston was a new city with only the bay and the inlets as he remembered them. The city was beautiful, with attractive buildings and spacious parks. The strikes and labor troubles of the nineteenth century had resulted in a bloodless revolution, and now a socialized government controlled all business. There was no smoke because all heating was done by electricity. All the people were healthy and happy.

Dr. Leete tried to explain the world of A.D. 2000. There was no money. The state gave everyone, no matter what his job, a card which contained the same amount of credit for a year's expenses. There was no chance, however, for anyone to spend his credit foolishly and starve. If a person proved incapable of handling his credit card intelligently, the government took care to see that he was supervised. Julian was taken to one of the big stores to see how goods were sold. The store had nothing but samples, representing every type of material made in or imported by the United States. The buyer picked out the items he wanted, called a clerk, gave the order, and the clerk relayed the order to the central warehouse from which the item was delivered to the buyer's home before he returned from the store. Julian was much impressed with this system.

He learned from Dr. Leete how education was handled. Everyone was given a full education until he was twenty-one. A broad cultural course was taught so that there was no intellectual snobbery among the people. At twenty-one, the student went into menial service for three years. During this time he waited on tables in the large public eating houses, or did some other simple task. After three years, he was given an examination to qualify him for one of the government professional schools. If he failed, he was helped to find the job for which he was best suited and which he would most enjoy. If this job proved to be the wrong one, he could change his position. In order that all necessary jobs would be chosen by enough people to do the essential work, the jobs were arranged so as to be equally attractive. If one job was so boring that few people would want to choose it, the hours were made shorter so that enough applicants could be found. Whether a citizen was a doctor or a bricklayer, he was given the same amount of credit for his work.

Crime was treated as a mental disease; criminals were put in hospitals and treated as mental cases. Julian learned that crime had been cut down amazingly as soon as money was abolished. Theft became silly when everyone had the right and power to own the same things. At the head of the government was the President, who was controlled by Congress. Education and medicine were controlled by boards made up of older professional advisers to the President. A woman chosen by the women of the country had the power to veto any bill concerning the rights of the female population. There was no public discontent with government, and there was wonderful international cooperation.

Julian asked Dr. Leete what he had done in life, and learned that the doctor had practiced medicine until he was forty-five years old. At that time he had retired. Now he studied and enjoyed various kinds of recreation.

Edith Leete took great pleasure in showing Julian the various advances the world had made in culture since his day. She showed him how music was carried into all the homes in the country by telephone. She showed him the public libraries in which Julian learned that his old favorites were still read. Dickens was especially popular, as the new world thought him one of the wisest men in judging the sadness of the old capitalistic system. When an author wrote a book, it was published at his own expense by the government. If it proved a success, he received royalties in additional credit cards. Works of art were voted on by the public in the same way. When Julian commented that this plan would not have worked in his day because of the lack of public taste, Edith told him that with general education the taste of the people had developed greatly. Julian became very fond of Edith, and thought how strange it was that she should have the same name as his long-dead fiancée.

When Julian became worried about a means of support, Dr. Leete told him that he had arranged for him to take a college lectureship in history, as Julian knew much about the past which even historians would be delighted to learn. Knowing that he was secure in this new world, Julian asked Edith to marry him. She told him that she had always loved him.

When Julian asked how this was possible, she explained that she was the great-granddaughter of Edith Bartlett. She had found some of Julian's old love letters to the other Edith, and had been charmed by them. She had always told her parents that she would marry only a man like the lover who had written them. Julian was pleased at this unexpected turn of affairs, and the two planned to marry and live happily in the wonderful world of the twenty-first century.

LORD JIM

Type of work: Novel
Author: Joseph Conrad (Teodor Józef Konrad Korzeniowski, 1857-1924)
Type of plot: Psychological romance
Time of plot: Late nineteenth century
Locale: Ports and islands of the East
First published: 1900

<blockquote>

Principal characters:
LORD JIM, a British sailor
MARLOW, his friend
STEIN, a trader
DAIN WARIS, a native

</blockquote>

Critique:

Lord Jim first ran as a magazine serial that puzzled many readers. Conrad claimed that he had planned the narrative as a novel. Critics claimed that he had written a short story which had run away from him. The fact remains that the story is told in a unique framework. At its beginning it seems to skip haphazardly backward and forward through time at no one's direction. It is told partly by Conrad, partly in narrative by Marlow, and partly through a letter written by Marlow. The reader must solve for himself the problem of Jim's character. Certainly, Conrad was attempting to illustrate in Jim's weakness and strength the mystery of human character and to reveal the hidden springs of human conduct.

The Story:

Jim was an outcast, a wanderer. Hired as water clerk in seaports throughout the East, he would keep his job only until his identity became known. Then he would move on. The story of Lord Jim began when he determined to leave home to go to sea. Accordingly, his father obtained a berth for him as an officer candidate and he began his service. Although he loved the sea, his beginning was not heroic. Almost at once he was injured and was left behind in an Eastern port. When he recovered, he accepted a berth as chief mate aboard an ancient steamer, the *Patna*, carrying Moslem pilgrims on their way to Mecca.

The steamer was unseaworthy, her German captain a gross coward, her chief engineer liquor-soaked. One sultry night in the Red Sea the ship struck a floating object. The captain sent Jim to check.

A month later Jim testified in court that when he went to investigate he found the forward hold rapidly filling with sea water. Hearing his report, the captain declared the *Patna* would sink quickly and gave orders to abandon ship. At first Jim was determined to stand by his post. At the last minute, on sudden impulse, he jumped to join the other white men in the lifeboat they had launched. The pilgrims were left aboard the sinking vessel.

But the *Patna* had not sunk. A French gunboat overtook the vessel and towed it and the abandoned passengers into port without its chief officers aboard.

Marlow, a white man, sat at the inquiry. Later, he took up the thread of the story as he had learned it from Jim. Something in Jim was fixed to Marlow's memory so that he was forced to recall the event and to tell the story to friends as long as he lived; it became a part of his own life.

It always began the same way. First there had come a cable from Aden telling that the *Patna*, abandoned by its officers, had been towed into port. Then two weeks later the captain, the two engineers, and Jim had come ashore, their boat having been picked up by a steamer of the Dale Line. They were whisked into court at once for the investigation. The captain lost his papers for deserting his ship, and he stormed away declaring that his disgrace did not matter; he would become an American citizen.

The chief engineer went to a hospital. There, raving in delirium tremens, he declared he had seen the *Patna* go down. The *Patna* was full of reptiles when she sank, he declared. He also declared that the space under his bed was crammed with pink toads. The second engineer, his arm broken, was also in the hospital. Neither was called to testify.

Jim, with his recollection of his family and his father's teaching, as well as his own deeply established sense of honor, was a marked man for the rest of his life. Marlow told how he had dinner with Jim during the trial. The boy seemed of a different stamp from the other officers of the *Patna*. Marlow was determined to fathom the boy's spirit, just as Jim was determined to regain his lost moral identity.

Jim told Marlow how the disgraceful affair had happened. After he had investigated the damage, he had felt that the ship could not remain afloat, for her plates were rust-eaten and unable to stand much strain. There were eight hundred passengers and seven boats, and not enough time to get into the boats the few passengers who could be carried to safety. Shortly afterward he discovered the captain and the engineers making ready to desert the ship. They insisted that he join them; the passengers were doomed anyway. The acting third engineer had a heart attack in the excitement and died. Jim never knew when—or why—he had jumped into the lifeboat the other officers had launched. Jim told Marlow how they had agreed to tell the same story. Actually, he and his companions thought that the *Patna* had gone down. Jim said that he had felt relief when he had learned that the passengers were safe. The whole story made sailor-talk in all ports where seamen met and talked. After the inquiry Marlow offered to help Jim, but Jim was determined to become a wanderer, to find out by himself what had happened to his soul.

Jim began his wanderings, to Bombay, to Calcutta, to Penang, Batavia, and the islands of the East. For a time he found work with an acquaintance of Marlow's, but he gave up his job when the second engineer of the *Patna* turned up unexpectedly. Afterward he became a runner for some ship chandlers, but he left them because he had heard one of the owners discussing the case of the *Patna*. He moved on, always toward the East, from job to job.

Marlow continued his efforts to help Jim. He sought out Stein, a trader who owned a number of trading posts on the smaller islands of the East Indies. Stein made Jim his agent at Patusan, an out-of-the-way settlement where he was sure Jim might recover his balance. There, in that remote place, Jim tried to find some answer to his self-hatred. Determined never to leave Patusan, he associated with the natives, and by his gentleness and consideration became their leader. They called him Tuan Jim—Lord Jim. Dain Waris, the son of Doramin, the old native chief, was his friend.

The rumor spread in the ports that Jim had discovered a valuable emerald, and that he had presented it to a native woman. There was a story about a native girl who loved him and who had given him warning when some jealous natives came to murder him.

Marlow followed Jim to Patusan. When Marlow prepared to leave, Jim accompanied him part of the way. He explained to Marlow that at last he felt as though his way had been justified. Somehow, because the simple natives trusted him, he felt linked again to the ideals of his youth. Marlow felt there was a kind of desperateness to his conviction.

The end came when Gentleman Brown, a roving cutthroat, determined to loot Lord Jim's stronghold. He arrived while Jim was away. Led by Dain Waris, the natives isolated Brown and his marauders on a hilltop but were unable to capture them. Lord Jim returned and after a long talk with Brown became convinced that Brown would leave peaceably if the siege were lifted. He persuaded the reluctant natives to withdraw. The vicious Brown repaid Lord Jim's magnanimity by vengefully murdering Dain Waris. Lord Jim went unflinchingly to face native justice when he offered himself to the stern old chieftain as the cause of Dain Waris' death. Doramin shot Jim through the breast.

Marlow, who had watched Jim's life so closely, felt that Jim had at last won back his lost honor.

LORNA DOONE

Type of work: Novel
Author: R. D. Blackmore (1825-1900)
Type of plot: Historical romance
Time of plot: Late seventeenth century
Locale: England
First published: 1869

Principal characters:

JOHN RIDD, yeoman of the parish of Oare in Somerset
SIR ENSOR DOONE, head of the outlaw Doone clan
LORNA DOONE, his ward
CARVER DOONE, his son
TOM FAGGUS, a highwayman
JEREMY STICKLES, king's messenger
REUBEN HUCKABACK, John Ridd's great-uncle

Critique:

R. D. Blackmore, in his preface to *Lorna Doone: A Romance of Exmoor,* was content to call his work a "romance," because the historical element was only incidental to the work as a whole. Secret agents, highwaymen, clannish marauders, and provincial farmers figure against a background of wild moor country. A feeling for the old times, for great, courageous people, for love under duress made the novel popular with Victorian readers. People who have read it in their youth remember it with nostalgia, for the book has a penetrating simplicity. Told in the first person by John Ridd, the main character in the novel, it has an authentic ring, the sound of a garrulous man relating the adventures of his youth.

The Story:

John Ridd was engaged in a schoolboy fight in the yard of old Blundell's school when John Fry, employed by Ridd's father, called for the boy to summon him home. Before the two left, however, young John completed his fight by knocking out his opponent. On their way home through the moorlands they were nearly captured by members of the outlaw Doone band, who had been ravaging the countryside, stealing and killing. When John Ridd reached his father's farm, he learned that only a few days before, the Doones had set upon and murdered his father. This incident stimulated the desire for revenge by all the members of the parish of Oare, for the murdered man had been greatly respected.

John settled down to the responsibilities which the death of his father had thrust upon him. At first his time was greatly taken by farm work, as he grew and matured into the largest and strongest man in the Exmoor country. As he grew up, John learned much about the wild Doone clan. There was one Doone, however, for whom he felt no animosity. This was the beautiful child of the man supposed to be the murderer of John's father. At first sight John had been stirred by the beauty of Lorna Doone. Thereafter he was in great conflict when he understood that his passion was directed toward the girl whom he ought for his father's sake to hate.

When John's great-uncle, Master Reuben Huckaback, was attacked and robbed by the Doones, he went with John to swear out a warrant for their arrest, but he had no luck because the magistrates were unwilling to incur the enmity of the Doones.

John was drawn deeper into his relationship with Lorna Doone. At their secret meetings in Doone Valley she told him the story of her life with the out-

LORNA DOONE by R. D. Blackmore. Published by Dodd, Mead & Co., Inc.

laws; how she always had loved her grandfather, Sir Ensor Doone, but feared and lately had come to hate the rough, savage sons, nephews, and grandsons of Sir Ensor. This hatred was increased when Carver Doone cold-bloodedly murdered Lord Alan Brandir, a distant relative, who had come to take her away from the Doones.

About this time John was called to London to serve the cause of James II's tottering throne. There he disclosed all he knew of the Doones' activities and of the false magistrates who seemed to be in league with them. He was warned that Tom Faggus, a highwayman who was John's own cousin, might go to the gallows before long. He returned to his mother and his farm no penny richer or poorer than when he left, because of his refusal to accept bribes or to become the dupe of sly lawyers in the city.

In the meantime concern over Lorna, who had two suitors among the Doones themselves, had almost unhinged John's mind. He was delighted to discover that Lorna, still only seventeen, held off the two Doones. At the same time he feared more than ever his chance of winning the ward of the outlaws he was pledged to help the king destroy. However, he at last won Lorna over to his suit, and with her agreement he felt nothing could stop him.

At home the love of his sister Annie for her cousin, Tom Faggus, reminded John of his duties as his father's son and plunged him into the worries over his mother and Annie and the farm. John's mother had other plans for his marriage, but when he revealed the only course his love must take, he won her over. In the meantime Master Jeremy Stickles brought news of the rising of the Duke of Monmouth and of troubles brewing for the king.

Suddenly, Lorna's signals stopped. John made his will and descended into the Doone hideout and there at great risk discovered that Lorna had been kept in her rooms because she would not marry Carver Doone. John managed to talk to her and she pledged never to give in to her family. He narrowly escaped capture, and at the same time managed to save the life of Jeremy Stickles, king's messenger, by overhearing the outlaws as they plotted to kill Jeremy when he should be crossing the valley bridge. The Doones' plot to kill Stickles brought further plans for retaliation from the king's men.

Old Sir Ensor Doone was close to death. Before he died, he gave John Ridd and Lorna Doone his blessing and to Lorna he presented the glass necklace he had kept for her since childhood. Then John took Lorna home with him to his mother's farm. Jeremy Stickles went south to muster forces for the destruction of the Doone clan.

The counselor of the Doones took advantage of his absence to visit the Ridd farm in order to make a truce with John Ridd. His offer was rejected, but he threw trouble into the paths of the lovers by telling them that Lorna's father had murdered John's father and that his own father was the murderer of Lorna's father. Moreover, he tricked them out of Lorna's necklace, which by now, through the word of Tom Faggus, they knew to be made of diamonds.

Uncle Reuben Huckaback grew interested in having John marry his granddaughter Ruth, and took John to see the gold mine he had just bought. Upon his return, John learned that Lorna had disappeared. She had been taken away by the Dugals, who claimed her as their missing heiress.

When Tom Faggus joined the rebels against the king, John, at his sister Annie's request, went to find him and to bring him back to safety. John discovered Tom almost dead. John was taken prisoner and was nearly executed. He was saved only by the arrival of his friend, Jeremy Stickles.

John went to London and there saw Lorna. By good chance and virtue of his great strength he overcame two villains who were attempting to rob and kill a nobleman. The man happened to be Lorna's relative. In return for this deed, the king gave John the title of knight. Moreover, he had the court of heralds design a coat of arms for John's family. The coat of arms was soundly made and the queen herself paid for it, the king declining.

When John returned from London, covered with honors, he discovered the Doones had been raiding once more. Then came the long awaited revenge. The Doones were routed, their houses were burned, and their stolen booty was divided among those who put in claims for redress. The counselor revealed that it was Carver Doone who had killed John's father. The necklace was recovered.

Arrangements for the wedding of John and Lorna were made. At the end of the ceremony in the church, Carver Doone, out of his great jealousy, shot Lorna. Without a weapon in his hand, John rushed out in pursuit of Carver and found him at Barrow Down. There took place the greatest battle between two men ever told of in books. It was a fight of giants. As John felt his ribs cracking in Carver's tremendous hug, he fastened his own iron grip upon his enemy's arm and ripped it loose. Then he threw his crushed and bleeding enemy into the bog and saw Carver Doone sucked down into its black depths.

Thus the greatest enemy of John Ridd was at last destroyed and John returned to his bride to find that she might live. She did survive and in peace and plenty John Ridd lived among his friends to a hearty old age.

LOST HORIZON

Type of work: Novel
Author: James Hilton (1900-1954)
Type of plot: Adventure romance
Time of plot: 1931
Locale: Tibet
First published: 1933

> *Principal characters:*
> HUGH CONWAY, a British consul
> RUTHERFORD, his friend
> HENRY BARNARD, an American embezzler
> MISS BRINKLOW, a missionary
> CAPTAIN MALLISON, another British consul
> CHANG, a Chinese lama
> FATHER PERRAULT, the High Lama

Critique:

Shangri-La, the name for the setting of this novel, has come to mean to most Americans a place of peace and contentment. Such was the strange Utopia James Hilton described in Lost Horizon, making it seem like a real place, peopled by living beings, rather than the land of an impossible ideal.

The Story:

When Rutherford had found Hugh Conway, a former schoolmate, suffering from fatigue and amnesia in a mission hospital, Conway had related a weird and almost unbelievable story concerning his disappearance many months before.

Conway was a member of the consulate at Baskul when trouble broke out there in May, 1931, and he was considered something of a hero because of the efficiency and coolness he displayed while white civilians were being evacuated. When it was his turn to leave, he boarded a plane in the company of Miss Roberta Brinklow, a missionary; Henry Barnard, an American, and Captain Charles Mallison, another member of the consulate. The plane was a special high-altitude cabin aircraft provided by the Maharajah of Chandapore. Conway, thirty-seven years old, had been in the consular service for ten years. His work had not been spectacular and he was expecting to rest in England before being assigned to another undistinguished post.

After the plane had been in the air about two hours, Mallison noticed that their pilot was the wrong man and that they were not headed toward Peshawur, the first scheduled stop. Conway was undisturbed until he realized they were flying over strange mountain ranges. When the pilot landed and armed tribesmen refueled the plane before it took off again, Conway began to agree with Mallison and Barnard, who thought they had been kidnaped and would be held for ransom.

When Conway tried to question the pilot, the man only pointed a revolver at him. A little after midnight the pilot landed again, this time narrowly averting a crackup. Climbing out of the plane, the passengers found the pilot badly injured. Conway believed that they were high on the Tibetan plateau, far beyond the western range of the Himalaya Mountains. The air was bitterly cold, with no signs of human habitation in that region of sheer-walled mountains. The pilot died before morning, murmuring something about a lamasery called Shangri-La. As the little group started in search of the lamasery, they saw a group of men coming toward them.

When the men reached them, one introduced himself in perfect English; he was a Chinese named Chang. Following the men, Conway and his friends arrived at the lamasery of Shangri-La that evening. There they found central heat, plumbing, and many other luxuries more commonly found only in the Western Hemisphere. They were given fine rooms and excellent food. They learned that there was a High Lama whom they would not be privileged to meet. Although Chang told them porters would arrive in a few weeks to lead them back to the outer world, Conway had the strange feeling that their coming had not been an accident and that they were not destined soon to leave.

Presently Chang told them that Conway was to be honored by an interview with the High Lama. Mallison begged him to force the High Lama to provide guides for them, for Mallison had learned that Barnard was wanted for fraud and embezzlement in the United States and he was anxious to turn Barnard over to the British authorities. But Conway did not discuss their departure with the High Lama, whom he found a very intelligent, very old man. Instead, he listened to the lama's remarkable story of Father Perrault, a Capuchin friar lost in the mountains in 1734, when he was fifty-three years old. Father Perrault had found sanctuary in a lamasery and had stayed there after adopting the Buddhist faith. In 1789 the old man lay dying, but the miraculous power of some drugs he had perfected, coupled with the marvelous air on the plateau, prolonged his life. Later tribesmen from the valley helped him build the lamasery of Shangri-La, where he lived the life of a scholar. In 1804 another European came to the lamasery; then others came from Europe and from Asia. No guest was ever allowed to leave.

Conway learned then that the kidnaping of their plane had been deliberate. But, more important, he learned that the High Lama was Father Perrault and

that he was two hundred and fifty years old. The old man told Conway that all who lived at Shangri-La had the secret of long life. He had sent the pilot for new people because he believed a war was coming which would destroy all known civilization and Shangri-La would then be the nucleus of a new world. His picture of life in the lamasery pleased Conway. He was content to stay.

Conway, knowing that the others would find it hard to accept the news, did not tell them that they could never leave. Mallison continued to talk of the coming of the porters, but Barnard and Miss Brinklow announced that they intended to pass up the first opportunity to leave Shangri-La and wait for a later chance. Barnard faced jail if he returned, and Miss Brinklow thought she should not miss the opportunity to convert the lamas and the tribesmen in the valley.

The weeks passed pleasantly for Conway. He met a Frenchman called Briac, who had been Chopin's pupil. He also met Lo-Tsen, a Chinese girl who seemed quite young, but Chang told him she was really sixty-five years old. Conway had more meetings with the High Lama; at one of them the old man told Conway that he knew he was going to die at last and that he wanted Conway to take his place as ruler of the lamasery and the valley and to act wisely so that all culture would not be lost after war had destroyed Western civilization.

While he was explaining these matters, the old lama lay back in his chair, and Conway knew he was dead. Conway wandered out into the garden, too moved to talk to anyone. He was interrupted by Mallison, with the news that the porters had arrived. Although Barnard and Miss Brinklow would not leave, Mallison had paid the porters to wait for him and Conway. Mallison said that the Chinese girl was going with them, that he had made love to her and that she wanted to stay with him. Conway tried to tell Mallison that the girl was really an old woman who would die if she left the valley, but Mallison refused to listen. At first Conway also refused to leave Shangri-La, but after Mallison and the girl started and then came back because they were afraid to go on alone, Conway felt that he was responsible for them as well and he left the lamasery with them. He felt that he was fleeing from the place where he would be happy for the rest of his life, no matter how long that life might be.

Rutherford closed his manuscript at that point, for Conway had slipped away and disappeared. Later Rutherford met a doctor who told him that Conway had been brought to the mission by a woman, a bent, withered, old Chinese woman. Perhaps, then, the story was true. Convinced that Conway had headed for the hidden lamasery, Rutherford hoped that his journey had been successful, that Conway had reached Shangri-La.

LOST ILLUSIONS

Type of work: Novel
Author: Honoré de Balzac (1799-1850)
Type of plot: Naturalism
Time of plot: Early nineteenth century
Locale: Angoulême, France
First published in three parts: 1837, 1839, 1843

Principal characters:
DAVID SÉCHARD, a printer
EVE, his wife
LUCIEN CHARDON, his brother-in-law
MADAME DE BARGETON, loved by Lucien

Critique:

This longest of all Balzac's novels is a study of a hero who is too innocent even to understand all the machinations of his enemies. The tone is somber and cynical. Virtue is rewarded in a way, but chicanery is always triumphant. Although the plot is marred by the lavish details with which the past histories of the characters are presented, Balzac has achieved in this novel considerably more suspense than usual. *Lost Illusions* is perhaps the high point of the author's "Scenes of Country Life."

The Story:

Angoulême was divided into two social classes: the aristocrats of fashionable society and the bourgeois. David Séchard and Lucien Chardon were scarcely aware that they belonged to the less privileged class. Lucien was the brilliant, handsome, unstable son of a chemist. David was the sober, kind son of a printer.

David's father had sent him to Paris to learn all the latest innovations in the printing trade. The illiterate father, avaricious and mean, hoped that David would learn how to make more money from the old-fashioned printery shop of Séchard and Son. When David returned from Paris, his father quickly sold him the business at a high price and retired to his vineyard.

Partly because of his friendship for poetic Lucien and partly because of his temperament, David did not prosper. He was always discussing a grand project with Lucien or dreaming of Eve, Lucien's beautiful sister.

Lucien wrote some verses which attracted attention. Even the aristocrats of the town heard of him, and Madame de Bargeton, a woman of thirty-six married to an old husband, invited him to one of her famous evening gatherings. Eve scrimped to buy Lucien the proper clothes for the occasion. The evening was not an entire success. Few except Madame de Bargeton listened to Lucien's poetry, but he made a real conquest of his hostess.

While Lucien did his best to break into society and win the heart of Madame de Bargeton, David and Eve were quietly falling in love. David strained his resources to the utmost to furnish rooms over the print shop for his wife-to-be, a room at the rear for his mother-in-law, and a comfortable room on the street for Lucien. David had determined to promote Lucien's literary talent by supporting him.

Two days before the wedding, Lucien was surprised in Madame de Bargeton's boudoir. Her husband, old as he was, fought a duel with a man who had gossiped about Madame de Bargeton. Not wishing to face the scandal, Madame de Bargeton decided to go to Paris, and Lucien was to follow her. With a heavy heart, for he knew Lucien's weaknesses, David drove his friend at night along the Paris road. Safely away from Angoulême, Lucien joined his mistress.

David and Eve, married, settled into their new rooms. Eve was a devoted wife, though foolishly fond of her scapegrace brother. Before her child was born she began to grow uneasy. Lucien wrote very seldom and David paid little attention to his business. He was too busy working on an experiment to find a new way to make paper without rags. If he could invent a new process they would all be rich. Meanwhile the family was desperately in need, for Lucien's demands for money kept them poor. At last Eve herself took charge of the print shop.

She had her first small success when she hit on the idea of printing a *Shepherd's Calendar,* a cheap almanac to peddle to farmers. But the firm of Cointet Brothers, rivals in the printing trade, gave her so much unfair competition that she made only a small profit from her printing venture. After her baby came she had to give up her efforts for a while. David was more than ever wrapped up in his attempts to find a new process for making paper.

Meanwhile Lucien had failed completely to make his way in Paris. He had quarreled with his rich mistress, and they had parted. He could find only odd jobs as a journalist. He borrowed continually from David to lead the dissolute life of a man-about-town. Finally, when he went to live openly with Coralie, an actress, he lost all chances for any real success.

Pressed for money, Lucien forged David's name to notes for three thousand francs. When the firm of Cointet Brothers, acting as bankers, presented the notes to David for payment, he was unable to raise the money. The law suit that followed disturbed Eve so much that she had to hire a wet nurse for her baby; in that small French town she was disgraced.

Cointet Brothers promised a rich marriage to Petit-Claud, David's lawyer, if he would prolong the suit, increase the costs to David, and eventually force him into debtor's prison. During the delays Eve and David both appealed to his father for help, but the old miser refused aid to his son. He was mainly interested in collecting rent for the building where David had his shop. With all help denied, David went into hiding and worked feverishly on his paper process.

In Paris, Coralie died, leaving Lucien without a place to live. Having no money, he began the long walk home. One night he caught a ride among the trunks of a carriage and went to sleep on his precarious perch. When he awoke the carriage had stopped. As he got off he saw that he had been riding with his former mistress, Madame de Bargeton, now Madame la Comtesse Châtelet, wife of the new prefect of the district. She and her husband laughed openly as the disheveled Lucien stalked away.

A few miles from Angoulême Lucien became ill and sought refuge with a miller. Thinking him about to die, the miller sent for a priest. When Lucien begged for news of his family, the priest told him of David's troubles. Lucien hurried to town to see what he could do for the brother-in-law he had helped to ruin.

In Angoulême, Lucien was sorrowfully received by his sister. To add to the distress of David and his family, Cointet Brothers published in the paper a glowing account of Lucien's successes in Paris. There was a parade in Lucien's honor, and the du Châtelet's even invited him to dinner.

Realizing that he still had a hold over Madame du Châtelet, Lucien tried to get David released from his debts through her influence. Meanwhile, after seeing some samples of David's work, the Cointets offered to pay off his debts, buy his print shop, and develop his invention for him. The offer was intended, however, to bring David out of hiding. Then a letter from Lucien to his friend was intercepted and a forged note substituted, appointing a place of meeting. David, on the way to the meeting, was arrested and thrown into prison.

Lucien, after a despairing farewell to his sister, left Angoulême. He intended to kill himself, but on the road he was picked up by a Spanish priest, an emissary traveling between Madrid and Paris. The envoy saw promise in Lucien and offered him fifteen thousand francs in return for Lucien's promise to do as the priest wished. The Spaniard meant to acquire power through Lucien's attraction for women and his poetic fervor. The bargain sealed, Lucien sent the fifteen thousand francs to David.

The money arrived just after David had signed away his shop and his paper-making process to the Cointets. David and Eve retired to the country and in due time inherited money and a vineyard from his father. Petit-Claud, the double-crossing lawyer, became a famous prosecutor. The Cointets made a great fortune from David's process, and one of them became a deputy and a peer.

A LOST LADY

Type of work: Novel
Author: Willa Cather (1876-1947)
Type of plot: Regional realism
Time of plot: Late nineteenth century
Locale: Nebraska
First published: 1923

> *Principal characters:*
> CAPTAIN FORRESTER, a railroad constructor
> MRS. FORRESTER, his wife
> JUDGE POMMEROY, his friend and legal adviser
> NIEL HERBERT, the judge's nephew
> IVY PETERS, a shyster lawyer

Critique:

This book, which is marked by a studied attention to form, achieves an epic-like tone. In part this is derived from the theme as well as from the viewpoint of the novel. The theme expresses a feeling of admiration which most Americans share for the builders who opened the West, a herculean task which could not be done twice. The viewpoint is that of a young man whose youth claims the right of sentimental ardor which makes youth so delightful. Moreover, Miss Cather captured the tone of many women of the generation about which she was writing. Mrs. Forrester possessed more valiant self-reliance than many of her contemporaries. As such she was able to be a lost lady and still keep her own personality intact.

The Story:

The Forrester home at Sweet Water was a stopping off place for railroad magnates riding through the prairie states along the Burlington line. Old Captain Forrester liked to drive his guests from the station and watch them as they approached his estate. He enjoyed their praise of his stock farm and their delight when his charming wife met them at the front door. Everyone from railroad presidents to the village butcher boy and the kitchen maids liked Mrs. Forrester; her manner was always one of friendliness and respect.

Niel Herbert's acquaintance with Mrs. Forrester began when he fell from a tree while playing with some village boys on the captain's property and Mrs. Forrester summoned a doctor. He did not know it at the time, but Mrs. Forrester had already singled him out from the others because he was Judge Pommeroy's nephew. After his recovery he was often invited to the Forrester home with his uncle.

The boy who had caused Niel's fall was Ivy Peters. He had winged a woodpecker and then had slit its eyes. The bird had fumbled back into its hole, and Niel was trying to reach the creature to put it out of its misery when he lost his balance and fell.

During a period of hard times Niel's father went out of business and left Sweet Water. Niel stayed on to read law in his uncle's office. A few days before Christmas, Mrs. Forrester invited Niel to her home to help entertain Constance Ogden, the daughter of one of the captain's friends, who was coming to spend the holidays with the Forresters. Also included in the party was Frank Ellinger, a bachelor of forty. The dinner was a gay one. Niel decided that Constance was neither pretty nor pleasant. It was plain that she had designs on Frank Ellinger.

The following day Niel was asked to stay with Constance during the afternoon, while Mrs. Forrester and Frank took the small cutter and went after cedar for the Christmas decorations. The Blum boy, out hunting, saw Mrs. Forrester and Frank after he came upon the deserted cutter beside a thicket, but he did not give away their secret. The doings of the rich were not his concern and Mrs. Forrester had been kind to him on many occasions.

During that winter Judge Pommeroy and his nephew often went to play cards with the Forresters. One night, during a snowstorm, Mrs. Forrester revealed to Niel how much she missed the excitement and glamour of former winters at fashionable resorts. She mocked the life of quiet domesticity in which she and the captain were living.

In the spring the captain went to Denver on business and while he was gone Frank Ellinger arrived for a visit. One morning Niel cut a bouquet of wild roses to leave outside the windows of Mrs. Forrester's bedroom. Suddenly he heard from the bedroom the voices of Mrs. Forrester and Frank Ellinger. The first illusion of his life was shattered by a man's yawn and a woman's laugh.

When the captain came home from Denver, he announced that he was a poor man. Having satisfied his creditors, he had left only his pension from the Civil War and the income from his farm. Shortly afterward the captain had a stroke.

Niel continued to visit the sick man and his wife. He realized that Mrs. Forrester was facing her new life with terror she tried to hide for her husband's sake. Niel, having decided to become an architect, left Sweet Water to spend two years at school in the East. When he returned, he learned that Ivy Peters, shrewd and grasping, had become an important person in the town. Niel, who despised Peters, was disappointed to learn that Peters, now the captain's tenant, had drained the marsh where the boys had gone fishing years before. The captain himself had become wasted and old.

Most of the time he sat in his garden staring at a strange sundial he had made.

Niel learned that Mrs. Forrester, who seemed little older, was still writing to Frank Ellinger. He observed, too, that Mrs. Forrester treated Peters with easy familiarity, and he wondered how she could be on friendly terms with the pushing young lawyer.

That summer a storm flooded the fields along the creek. Niel went to Judge Pommeroy's office to read. He thought of an item he had seen in the Denver paper earlier in the day; Frank Ellinger had finally married Constance Ogden. Close to midnight Mrs. Forrester, drenched to the skin, appeared at the office. At her demand Niel made the telephone connection with Ellinger in Colorado Springs. Mrs. Forrester began to talk politely, as though complimenting Ellinger on his marriage. Then she became hysterical. When she began to scream reproaches, Niel cut the wires.

Mrs. Forrester recovered after her collapse, but the gossipy town telephone operator pieced together a village scandal from what she had managed to overhear.

Captain Forrester died in December. None of his wealthy friends attended the funeral, but old settlers and former employees came to do honor to the railroad pioneer who had been one of the heroes of the early West.

One day Mr. Ogden stopped in Sweet Water. He thought that Judge Pommeroy ought to send to Washington a claim to have Mrs. Forrester's pension increased. Niel was forced to explain that Mrs. Forrester had turned her affairs over to Ivy Peters.

After her husband's death Mrs. Forrester began to entertain Ivy Peters and other young men from the village. At her urging Niel went to one party, but he was disgusted with the cheap manners of both hostess and guests. He could not bear to see the old captain's home thus abused.

Niel felt that an era was ending. The

great old people, such as the judge and the captain and their friends, were passing, the men who had built the railroads and the towns. The old men of gallant manners and their lovely ladies had gone forever. In their place was a new type of man, the shrewd opportunist, like Ivy Peters. On the day Niel saw Peters putting his arms around Mrs. Forrester, he decided to leave Sweet Water.

As long as his uncle lived, however, he had news of Mrs. Forrester. The judge wrote that she was sadly broken. Then his uncle died and Niel heard no more for many years.

A long time afterward a mutual friend told him what had happened to his lost lady. She had gone to California. Later, she had married a rich Englishman and had gone with him to South America. She had dyed her hair and had dressed expensively in an effort to keep her youth.

Finally, one year, the G.A.R. post received a letter from Mrs. Forrester's English husband. It enclosed money for the continued care of Captain Forrester's grave. His gift was a memorial to his late wife, Marian Forrester Collins.

THE LOST WEEKEND

Type of work: Novel
Author: Charles Jackson (1903-   )
Type of plot: Psychological melodrama
Time of plot: Twentieth century
Locale: New York City
First published: 1944

Principal characters:
DON BIRNAM, an alcoholic
WICK, his brother
HELEN, his friend

Critique:

Although *The Lost Weekend* is in some respects more a case history than a novel, it is nevertheless a vivid and convincing story of a maladjusted personality. Jackson shows considerable insight into alcoholism as a social problem without destroying the personal quality of his hero's experience and the desperation of his struggle during a long weekend when he is thrown upon his own resources. In this novel the drama remains objective; the underlying cause of Don Birnam's alcoholism is dramatized rather than analyzed.

The Story:

Don Birnam was an unsuccessful writer who drank too much. Time and again, his brother Wick and his friend Helen tried to break him of the habit. They kept money out of his reach so that he could not buy liquor. They warned neighbors and bartenders against his habits. They sent him to a rest farm for the cure. But even there he managed to get something to drink.

One weekend Don was left alone while Wick went to the country. As soon as his brother had gone, Don took the money Wick had left for the housekeeper and went out to buy liquor. He went into a bar and chatted with Gloria, the hostess. He told her about his life, about his wife who was frigid, his children, and other details all equally fantastic and imaginary. He asked Gloria to meet him later. After being convinced

that he was not joking, she accepted.

That night Don went into another bar and began drinking heavily. While there, idly watching a young couple, he suddenly decided to steal the girl's purse. He would do it only as a joke, he told himself. Later he could return the purse and they would all laugh at his prank. He picked up the purse and slipped it under his coat, acting calmly and naturally all the time, but as he was walking out a waiter stopped him. Luckily, the girl did not want to press charges. Don was pushed out into the street.

He went from one bar to another. When he drifted back to Sam's bar, Gloria was angry because he had forgotten his date with her. He could not understand why she asked him about his wife and his children, because he had neither. Next morning he found that his money had disappeared and that there was no money in the apartment. He decided to pawn his typewriter. He walked up and down the streets, but all the pawnshops were closed because it was a Jewish holiday. He went home, changed his clothes, and borrowed ten dollars from a nearby merchant. He went out to drink again. Coming back, he fell down a flight of stairs and lost consciousness.

When he awoke, he was in the alcoholic ward of a hospital. With him were a doctor and Bim, a male nurse. He wanted his clothes, he insisted; he wanted to go home. At last the doctor told him that he could go if he would sign a paper absolving the hospital of all responsibility.

Leaving the hospital, Don went straight to his apartment, where he fell asleep. The ringing of the telephone awoke him. He could not remember when he had last eaten. When he tried to get up, he almost collapsed, and he sank, exhausted, into a chair. After a while he heard a key in the lock. It was Helen, coming to see how he was getting along while Wick was away. She helped him to get dressed and took him to her apartment. When the maid came in, Helen went out on an errand. Don tried to get the key to the closet, but the maid pretended that she had no idea where it was. Don was growing more and more desperate for liquor. Before Helen left the apartment, he had called to her in terror because he thought a bat was devouring a mouse in the room. His thirst was growing worse. Seeing Helen's fur coat, he seized it and ran out of the apartment. He pawned the coat for five dollars and bought several pints of whiskey. He went back to his own apartment. Afraid that Wick might return, he hid one bottle in the bathroom and suspended the other on a string outside his window.

He lay down on the bed and took a long drink of whiskey. He felt wonderful. The ordeal was over; he had come through once more. There was no telling what might happen the next time, but he saw no reason to worry now. He wondered why Wick and Helen made such a fuss about it all.

LOVE FOR LOVE

Type of work: Drama
Author: William Congreve (1670-1729)
Type of plot: Comedy of manners
Time of plot: Seventeenth century
Locale: London
First presented: 1695

Principal characters:
SIR SAMPSON LEGEND, a foolish old gentleman
VALENTINE, his son, an indigent gallant
BENJAMIN, another son, a sailor
FORESIGHT, an old man given to astrology
ANGELICA, his niece
PRUE, his daughter
MRS. FORESIGHT, his young second wife
MISTRESS FRAIL, her sister

Critique:

Love for Love, generally considered one of Congreve's finest plays, is marked by a relatively simple but not particularly original plot. For the most part, the Restoration writers of comedy seemed to be content to follow their Elizabethan and Jacobean predecessors in matters of plot and of stock characters. Whatever grossness—and it is comparatively trifling—is present in this play is far overbalanced by clever and amusing dialogue and by several pairs of well-conceived and variously-contrasted characters. Surely Ben Jonson's theory of humors is quite alive in Sir Sampson Legend's penchant for tall tales of travel and in old Foresight's obsession for prognostication.

The Story:

Young Valentine Legend, having squandered all of his money in riotous living, was destitute and deeply in debt. With no property left but his books, he declared his intention of becoming a playwright, for his love for Angelica had indeed compelled him to take desperate measures. On hearing of his intention, Jeremy, his knavish manservant, showed alarm and said that Valentine's family would surely disown him.

Among Valentine's creditors was Trapland, a lecherous old scrivener who persisted in dunning him. When Valentine, who had been joined by his friend Scan-dal, subtly threatened Trapland with blackmail concerning a wealthy city widow the old man suddenly forgot the money owed him.

Sir Sampson Legend's steward told Valentine that he could be released from all debts by signing over his rights as Sir Sampson's heir to Ben, his younger brother. If he signed, he would receive four thousand pounds in cash.

In the meantime Foresight, an old fool given to the science of prognostication, recalled Prue, his bumpkin daughter, from the country. Foresight planned to marry her to Ben Legend.

Angelica, wealthy, young, and clever, reproved her uncle for his belief in astrology. Irate, Foresight threatened to end her friendship with Valentine. Angelica, piqued, insinuated that Mrs. Foresight, the old man's young second wife, was not true to him.

Sir Sampson Legend, a great teller of tall tales of world travel, arranged with Foresight for the marriage of Ben and Prue. When Sir Sampson playfully hinted to Foresight that Mrs. Foresight might not be a faithful wife, Foresight threatened to break off the marriage agreement. Sir Sampson quickly made amends.

Valentine, seeking Angelica, encountered his father at Foresight's house. He was indignant when his father disowned him as a son and he begged his father to change his mind about the conditions under which he could be freed of debt.

When Mrs. Foresight rebuked her sister for her indiscretion in frequenting the haunts of gamesters and gallants, Mistress Frail revealed her knowledge of Mrs. Foresight's own indiscretions. Mistress Frail then declared her intention of marrying Ben and enlisted her sister's aid in the project. Prue, meanwhile, found herself charmed by Tattle, a voluble young dandy. When Mrs. Foresight and Mistress Frail encouraged Tattle to court Prue, he was mystified because he knew of the marriage arranged between Prue and Ben. Even so, he gave Prue a lesson in the art of love, a lesson which progressed as far as her bedchamber. Tattle, having grown tired of dalliance with the rude country girl, was relieved when Prue's nurse found them.

Ben, returning from a sea voyage, declared that marriage did not interest him at the moment, but he visibly changed his mind when Mistress Frail flattered him. Left alone, he and Prue expressed dislike for each other. Ben declared that he talked to Prue only to obey his father.

Scandal, in Valentine's behalf, ingratiated himself with Foresight by pretending a knowledge of astrology. His scheme succeeding, he convinced Foresight that it was not in the stars for Valentine to sign over his inheritance or for Ben and Prue to marry. Attracted to Mrs. Foresight, Scandal hoodwinked old Foresight in order to pay gallant attentions to his young wife. Meanwhile Ben and Mistress Frail confessed their love and decided to marry.

Because Scandal had reported that Valentine was ill, Angelica went to his lodgings. In spite of Scandal's insistence her acknowledgment of love for Valentine would cure the young man, she quickly detected a trick and departed. Sir Sampson and a lawyer named Buckram arrived to get Valentine's signature to the documents they had prepared. Jeremy insisted that Valentine was out of his mind. Buckram said that the signature would

be invalid under the circumstances, but Sir Sampson forced his way into his son's presence. Valentine, pretending complete lunacy, called himself Truth and declared that he would give the world the lie. After the frightened Buckram left, Valentine showed clarity of mind, but, when the lawyer was called back, Valentine again seemed to lapse into lunacy.

Mistress Frail, having learned that there was little chance of Ben's getting the whole estate, broke off their engagement. Sir Sampson, frustrated by Valentine, decided to marry and beget a new heir. Mrs. Foresight plotted with Jeremy to marry Mistress Frail, disguised as Angelica, to Valentine during one of his fits of madness. When Jeremy revealed the scheme to Valentine and Scandal, the friends, in their turn, planned to marry Mistress Frail to Tattle by means of another disguise.

After Valentine had confessed his feigned madness to Angelica, she expressed disappointment; she had thought him really mad for love of her. She then went to Sir Sampson, learned his new state of mind, and suggested that he and she go through with a mock marriage ceremony in order to bring Valentine to his senses. When foolish Sir Sampson suggested that they actually get married so that she could inherit his estate, Angelica said that his plan would not be advisable since the papers leaving the estate to Ben were already drawn up.

Jeremy tricked foolish Tattle into believing that he, disguised as a friar, might marry Angelica, who would be disguised as a nun. Prue, forsaken by Tattle, asserted that she would marry Robin, the butler, who had professed his love for her.

Mistress Frail, thinking that she was marrying Valentine, and Tattle, thinking that he was marrying Angelica, were thus tricked into wedlock. Told by Angelica that she intended to marry his father, Valentine in despair declared that he was ready to sign over his inheritance. Impressed by this indication of his love for her, Angelica tore up the bond, which Sir

2118

Sampson had given her, and she brought the doting old man to his senses by revealing that she had always intended to marry Valentine. Sir Sampson and old Foresight consoled each other; they admitted that they had acted like fools.

LOVE IN A WOOD

Type of work: Drama
Author: William Wycherley (1640-1716)
Type of plot: Comedy of manners
Time of plot: Seventeenth century
Locale: London
First presented: 1671

Principal characters:
MR. RANGER, a young man about town
LYDIA, his cousin and betrothed
MR. VALENTINE, a gallant lately returned to London
CHRISTINA, his betrothed
MR. VINCENT, a confidant of all the lovers
ALDERMAN GRIPE, an elderly usurer
MISTRESS MARTHA, his daughter
LADY FLIPPANT, his sister, in London to find a husband
SIR SIMON ADDLEPLOT, an indomitable fortune hunter
MR. DAPPERWIT, a fop and a would-be gentleman
MRS. JOYNER, a matchmaker and procuress
MRS. CROSSBITE, a blackmailer and procuress
LUCY, her daughter

Critique:

The first of three satiric comedies, *Love in a Wood; or, St. James's Park,* as it was popularly known, shows brilliantly the genius of William Wycherley, who gained his insight as an intimate in high society on both sides of the Channel. It was this play which gained for the young man the favor of a king and the love of the king's mistress, the Duchess of Cleveland.

The Story:

Lady Flippant, a widow disappointed in her efforts to find a new husband, berated her matchmaker, Mrs. Joyner, for not finding a wealthy young man to relieve her impecunious position. The lady's brother, Alderman Gripe, had grown tired of her foppish visitors, especially the witless Mr. Dapperwit.

Sir Simon Addleplot, at the suggestion of the cozening Mrs. Joyner and the double-dealing Dapperwit, disguised himself and gained employment as a clerk to the miserly Gripe in order to woo the usurer's daughter Mistress Martha and through her to secure her father's fortune. Not realizing that he had been gulled into becoming Jonas the clerk,

Sir Simon was again duped into believing that he was loved by Lady Flippant, who was really enamored of Dapperwit.

Mr. Ranger, with Mr. Vincent, his friend and confidant, was about to go into St. James's Park in search of some amorous adventure when his cousin and betrothed, Lydia, discovered his whereabouts. He avoided her, however, and dined for diversion with the gulled Sir Simon, Dapperwit, and Lady Flippant in order to watch the work of Mrs. Joyner, who had already made twenty crowns through introductions and would obtain a hundred if Sir Simon got Mistress Martha or fifty if he got Lady Flippant. The widow spurned Sir Simon, flirted with Dapperwit, and hinted at matrimony to both the young gallants, Ranger and Vincent.

Later, all promenaded through St. James's Park in the hope of discovering one another's intrigues. Lydia, recognizing Ranger, ran into the house of her friend Christina in order to avoid a compromising meeting with her betrothed. Ranger pursued her, only to become enamored of Christina, who was faithfully waiting the return to London of

Mr. Valentine, her fiancé. Christina, in order to help Lydia, had pretended to be the young woman he had pursued from the park. Her little act quickly over, she sent the impertinent Ranger away. Ranger, in despair because he had not learned the fair unknown's name, did not know that Lydia had heard his gallant speeches to Christina.

Ranger went to the home of his friend Vincent. Valentine, in danger of his life from a rival, was in hiding there; he wished no one else to know of his return from France before his loved one did. Valentine, concealed, overheard Ranger ask the name of the young woman whom he pursued into her apartment. When Vincent named the apartment as Christina's, Valentine became convinced that his beloved one had been untrue to him.

In contrast to this sequence of mistaken and confused identities, the busy Mrs. Joyner was more positive in identifying Lucy, the daughter of her friend Mrs. Crossbite, as the object of hypocritical old Gripe's lust. The solicitous mother, pleased with this development, ordered her recalcitrant daughter to give up her love for Dapperwit. When Dapperwit, thinking to cure Ranger's melancholy over Christina, brought him to see Lucy, the girl repulsed him for his infidelity and what she thought was his intention of procuring her for Ranger. The jilted fop recovered his spirits, however, when he received a message delivered by Jonas, the supposed clerk. The message held out the promise of a later assignation which might lead, Dapperwit hoped, to a wedding.

As the gallants departed, the ever-busy Mrs. Joyner brought furtive Alderman Gripe to see Lucy. His hasty lust frightened the lass, however, and she screamed. Though he dickered for the sake of salving his miserly conscience, Gripe was coerced into paying five hundred pounds of hush money to Mrs. Crossbite. Lady Flippant, at the same time, was making advances to the defenseless Dapperwit, and the nimble-footed lovers, Ranger and Lydia, were busy at double deception. Lydia denied that she had been in the park jealously searching for him; Ranger assured her that he had called for her as he had promised.

The Gripe household was at this time in an uproar. The sly old man was busily attempting to hide his shame and regain his money, and Mrs. Joyner virtuously pretended horror at the treatment he had received at the hands of Mrs. Crossbite. Jonas, meanwhile, made love to Lady Flippant, who protested only after she learned that her seducer was really Sir Simon Addleplot, the man she hoped finally to marry. So the poor man, undone by his own deceit, lost Mistress Martha through his dissembling ways and Dapperwit's roguery.

Lydia, desirous of testing Ranger, sent him a letter to which she signed Christina's name, asking the gallant to meet her that evening at St. James's Gate. The wronged Christina, however, had since learned of her lover's return, and Valentine was at that time trying to reassure himself of her innocence. Overhearing Ranger's new plans unsettled him again, though his eavesdropping on a conversation between Christina and Vincent and then on one between Christina and her supposed lover finally set his mind at rest. Lydia also confessed her part in this lovers' plot and counterplot. The two couples, thus reunited, decided that matrimony was the only sure solution to love's equation.

But the false lovers found no such easy solution, so addle-witted and dapper-plotted had their intrigues become. Sir Simon, still passing as Jonas, escorted Mistress Martha to Dapperwit; he thought their embraces inopportune and inappropriate. But Sir Simon's arrangements for a parson, a supper, and a reception in nearby Mulberry Garden were not completely wasted. Propelled to the same garden by the two scheming procuresses, Alderman Gripe married Lucy to be revenged on his son-in-law, that Dapperwit who took a bride six months pregnant. Sir Simon took widowed Lady Flippant as his wife, just as she had intended.

Thus were all the honest ladies made wives and all the bawds made honest, up in St. James's Park.

LOVE'S LABOUR'S LOST

Type of work: Drama
Author: William Shakespeare (1564-1616)
Type of plot: Comedy of manners
Time of plot: Sixteenth century
Locale: Navarre, Spain
First presented: c. 1594

Principal characters:
FERDINAND, King of Navarre
BEROWNE,
LONGAVILLE, and
DUMAINE, lords of Navarre
DON ADRIANO DE ARMADO, a foolish Spaniard
COSTARD, a clown
THE PRINCESS OF FRANCE
ROSALINE,
MARIA, and
KATHERINE, ladies attending the princess
JAQUENETTA, a country wench

Critique:

There is little wonder that *Love's Labour's Lost* is not among the popular favorites of most readers of Shakespeare. The play is slow-moving, in places dull, and it shows neither the perfection of plot nor the fineness of characterization which distinguish most of the later plays. At the same time it is filled with clever talk and it exhalts, in the romantic manner of the sonneteers, the theme of love. The note of seriousness apparent beneath the surface cleverness of the dialogue makes this play an early comedy of manners, in which the ladies try to teach the young noblemen the value of sincerity and faithfulness to vows. The foolish Armado and the stupid clown enliven many of the scenes with their wit. All in all, this drama is not a poor play; an early work, it is not so good as most readers expect from the master dramatist.

The Story:

The King of Navarre had taken a solemn vow and forced three of his attending lords to take it also. This vow was that for three years they would fast and study, enjoy no pleasures, •and see no ladies. None of the three noblemen wanted to take the vow; Berowne, in particular, felt that it would be impossible

to keep his promise. He pointed out this fact to the king by reminding him that even at that very time the Princess of France was approaching the court . of Navarre to present a petition from her father, who was ill. The king agreed that he would be compelled to see her, but he added that in such cases the vow must be broken by necessity. Berowne foresaw that "necessity" would often cause the breaking of their vows.

The only amusement the king and his lords would have was provided by Costard, a clown, and by Don Adriano De Armado, a foolish Spaniard attached to the court. Armado wrote the king to inform him that Costard had been caught in the company of Jaquenetta, a country wench of dull mind. Since all attached to the court had been under the same laws of abstinence from earthly pleasures, Costard was remanded to Armado's custody and ordered to fast on bran and water for one week. The truth was that Armado also loved Jaquenetta. He feared the king would learn of his love and punish him in the same manner.

The Princess of France arrived with her three attendants. All were fair and lovely, and they expected to be received at the palace in the manner due their rank.

But the king sent word that they would be housed at his lodge, since under the terms of his vow no lady could enter the palace. The princess, furious at being treated in this fashion, scorned the king for his bad manners. When she presented the petition from her father, she and the king could not agree, for he vowed he had not received certain monies she claimed had been delivered to him.

At that first meeting, although each would have denied the fact, eight hearts were set to beating faster. The king viewed the princess with more than courteous interest. Berowne, Longaville, and Dumaine, his attendants, looked with love on the princess' ladies in waiting, Rosaline, Maria, and Katherine. A short time later Berowne sent a letter to Rosaline, with Costard as his messenger. But Costard had also been given a letter by Armado, to be delivered to Jaquenetta. The obvious happened. Costard, mixing up the letters, gave Jaquenetta's to Rosaline and Rosaline's to the country wench.

Berowne had been correct in thinking the vow to leave the world behind would soon be broken. Hiding in a tree, he heard the king read aloud a sonnet which proclaimed his love for the princess. Later the king, in hiding, overheard Longaville reading some verses he had composed to Maria. Longaville, in turn, concealed himself and listened while Dumaine read a love poem inscribed to Katherine. Then each one in turn stepped out from hiding to accuse the others of breaking their vows. Berowne all that time had remained hidden in the tree. Thinking to chide them for their broken vows, he revealed himself at last and ridiculed them for their weakness, at the same time proclaiming himself the only one able to keep his vow. But at that instant Costard and Jaquenetta brought to the king the letter Berowne had written Rosaline, the letter Costard had mistakenly delivered to the country girl.

Then all confessed that they had broken their vows. Berowne provided an excuse for all when he declared that one could learn much by studying women and the nature of love. Their honor saved, the four determined to woo the ladies in earnest, and they made plans to entertain their loves with revels and dances.

Each lover sent his lady a token to wear in his honor. But when the ladies learned from a servant that the lovers were, for a joke, coming in disguise to woo the princess and her companions, the girls in turn planned to discomfit the king and the three lords by masking themselves and exchanging tokens. The men arrived, also masked and disguised as Russians. Each man tried to make love to the lady wearing his token, but each was spurned and ridiculed. The ladies would not dance or sing, but would only mock the bewildered gentlemen.

Finally the suitors departed, hurt and indignant at the treatment they had received. Before long they returned in their own dress. The ladies then unmasked and told of the lunatic Russians who had called on them. Although the men confessed their plot and forswore all such jokes forever, the ladies still did not stop teasing them. Since each man had made love to the wrong girl because of the exchange of tokens, the ladies pretended to be hurt that each man had broken his vows of love and constancy by protesting love for another. The poor suitors suffered greatly for their merriment before they learned that the ladies had anticipated their coming in disguise and thus had planned a joke of their own.

The king ordered a play presented for the entertainment of all. But in the midst of the gaiety word came that the princess' father, the King of France, had died. She must sail for home immediately, accompanied by her attendants. When the king and his lords pleaded with the ladies to stay in Navarre and marry them, the ladies refused to accept their serious protestations of love; they had jested too much to be believed. Each man vowed that he would remain faithful, only to be reminded of the former vows he had broken.

Then each lady made a condition which, if met, would reward her lover a year hence. The king must retire for twelve months to a hermitage and there forsake all worldly pleasures. If at the end of that time he still loved the princess, she would be his. In the same fashion the other three lords must spend a year in carrying out the wishes of their sweethearts. Even the foolish Armado was included in the plan. He joined the others, announcing that Jaquenetta would not have him until he spent three years in honest work.

Thus all the swains tried with jests and fair speech to win their ladies, but without success. Now as the price of their folly they must prove in earnest that they deserved the hearts of their beloveds.

LOVING

Type of work: Novel
Author: Henry Green (Henry Vincent York, 1905-   )
Type of plot: Domestic comedy
Time of plot: World War II
Locale: Eire
First published: 1945

Principal characters:
CHARLEY RAUNCE, an English butler
MRS. TENNANT, Raunce's employer
MRS. JACK TENNANT, Mrs. Tennant's daughter-in-law
EDITH, a maid in love with Raunce
ALBERT, Raunce's assistant

Critique:

The novels of Henry Green have not found favor with American readers as readily as they have in Great Britain. Green combines modern techniques with Dickensian humor and sly social criticism. In this novel he conducts his readers to the little known world below stairs, the world of the servants which few masters or mistresses ever see. The qualities of depth and perception revealed in this and other of Green's books have made him a novelist better known to other writers than he is to the public at large.

The Story:

The great mansion owned by Mrs. Tennant had been thrown into turmoil by the death of old Eldon, the butler. In the servants' quarters no one knew quite what arrangements would be made after his death, for the mansion and its inhabitants formed an isolated bit of England in Eire. None of the servants could guess what Mrs. Tennant, who was a widow and very vague, might do in rearranging their duties. Only the footman, Charley Raunce, kept any purpose in his behavior.

Immediately after Eldon's death, Raunce went into the butler's room and took two small notebooks, one filled with the butler's monthly accounts and the other containing a set of special memoranda about visitors to the mansion, in-formation which had helped the old man to solicit generous tips from Mrs. Tennant's guests. That same day Raunce went to his mistress and asked for the post of butler. She agreed to give him the post, but without any extra pay. Raunce knew, however, that by juggling the accounts he could make up whatever pay rise he deemed sufficient. That evening he solidified his position by successfully taking over the old butler's place at the head of the table in the servants' dining-room.

There were two upstairs maids in the Tennant mansion, Edith and Kate. Raunce insisted that Edith, with whom he was in love, continue her practice of bringing the butler his morning tea. The housekeeper, Mrs. Burch, was scandalized, but was forced to give in.

Raunce's usurpation of the old butler's position immediately upon the latter's death soon appeared a minor matter, for a scandal rocked the mansion within a few days. Mrs. Tennant's daughter-in-law, Mrs. Jack, was found in bed with a neighbor, Captain Davenport. The discovery was made by Edith, who went to open the curtains and lay out Mrs. Jack's clothes in the morning. Even though Mrs. Tennant was unaware of her daughter-in-law's indiscretion, the episode created consternation and nervousness in the servants' quarters.

LOVING by Henry Green. By permission of the publishers, The Viking Press, Inc. Copyright, 1945, by Henry Green.

To add to the uneasiness among the servants, a blue sapphire ring belonging to Mrs. Tennant disappeared. Mrs. Tennant, who was always losing valuables, did not blame the servants, but the loss made them feel ill at ease.

A few days afterward Mrs. Tennant and her daughter-in-law went to England to visit Jack Tennant, who had been given a few days' leave from military duty. The English servants almost gave their notice when they learned that they were being left in sole charge of the mansion, for they were well aware of the unfriendly attitudes of the Irish about the countryside and were also in fear of an invasion of the district by German troops. Raunce, who had a great sense of duty, as well as a realization of what a good place he had, prevailed upon them to remain, despite the general dissatisfaction.

In Mrs. Tennant's absence Raunce paid court to Edith and discovered that she was in love with him. They spent many pleasant hours together, for Raunce was kept from his duties by a sore throat and Edith spent much of her time nursing him. They, like the other servants, were worried by the absence of their mistress and by their failure to find Mrs. Tennant's missing ring. Edith finally found it, but she and Raunce were at a loss to know where to keep it until Mrs. Tennant's return. They decided to hide it in the upholstering of a chair.

Much to their dismay, the ring was taken from the chair. Shortly after they discovered its loss a second time, an investigator from an insurance company called at the mansion. All the servants refused to answer his questions, for his presence during their mistress' absence bothered them and they did not know what to say in order to protect her and her interests. The investigator left in a suspicious mood, saying that his company would not pay for the loss. After his departure the servants discovered that the initials of the insurance company

were like those of the militant, revolutionary Irish Republican Army. The discovery almost panicked them completely. Only the thought of military service and short rations in England kept them from giving up their jobs immediately.

In the remaining days before Mrs. Tennant's return, Edith learned that Mrs. Tennant's grandchildren and the cook's nephew had found the sapphire ring while playing. Not realizing the value of the piece of jewelry, the youngsters had taken it out and hidden it on the lawn. By pretending to want it as a wedding present from one of the little girls, Edith persuaded the child to bring it to her.

When Mrs. Tennant returned, the ring was restored to her, and the matter of its loss and the ugliness of the insurance investigator soon became matters of the past, almost forgotten after Raunce's helper, a young lad named Albert, gave his notice and left the mansion because Mrs. Tennant had implied that he had taken the ring in the first place. He went back to England to enter the military service and become an aerial gunner.

Raunce was made restless by the realization, brought home to him by Albert's departure, that he had no part in the war effort. He also felt remorseful because his mother, who was exposed to the bombings by the Germans, refused to come to Ireland to live with her son and Edith after their marriage. These influences, plus the many dissensions among the servants and the domestic crises that were occurring at the mansion, assumed larger and larger proportions as he thought about them. At last he admitted to Edith that he was dissatisfied and wanted to leave. His announcement made Edith unhappy, for she thought at first that he was trying to get out of marrying her.

When he convinced her that he wanted her to go with him, they decided that, unlike good servants, they would leave without giving notice to Mrs. Tennant. One night they eloped and went back to England to be married and to live.

THE LOWER DEPTHS

Type of work: Drama
Author: Maxim Gorky (Aleksei Maksimovich Peshkov, 1868-1936)
Type of plot: Naturalism
Time of plot: Late nineteenth century
Locale: Russia
First presented: 1902

Principal characters:
    KOSTILYOFF, the landlord
    VASSILISA, his wife
    NATASHA, her sister
    VASKA, a young thief
    KLESHTCH, a locksmith
    ANNA, his wife
    NASTYA, a street-walker
    THE BARON, a former nobleman
    LUKA, a tramp
    SATINE, a cardsharp
    THE ACTOR, an alcoholic

Critique:

The Lower Depths, also translated as A Night's Lodging and At the Bottom, is generally accounted the best of Gorky's plays and one of the most vital of Russia's dramatic pieces. The play was pure naturalism in its day, but to modern taste it may appear more romantic. Gorky presents little of positive affirmation, but he observes shrewdly an unfortunate people. Perhaps more than any other document, the play explains the Russian revolution of 1917.

The Story:

The cellar resembled a cave, with only one small window to illuminate its dank recesses. In a corner thin boards partitioned off the room of Vaska, the young thief. In the kitchen lived Kvashnya, a vendor of meat pies, the decrepit Baron, and the streetwalker Nastya. All around the room were bunks occupied by a succession of lodgers.

Nastya was reading a story called *Fatal Love.* She was absorbed in the novel with her head bent down. The Baron, who lived largely on her earnings, seized the book and read its title aloud. Then he banged

Nastya over the head with it and called her a lovesick fool. Satine raised himself painfully from his bunk at the noise. His memory was vague, but he knew he had been beaten up the night before. Bubnoff cruelly told him he had been caught cheating at cards. The Actor stirred in his bed on top of the stove. He predicted that some day Satine would be beaten to death.

The Actor awakened enough to remind the Baron to sweep the floor. The landlady was strict and made them clean every day. The Baron loudly announced that he had to go shopping. He and Kvashnya left to make the day's purchases.

The Actor climbed down from his bunk and declared that the doctor had told him he had an organism poisoned by alcohol. Sweeping the floor would be bad for his health.

Anna coughed loudly in her bunk. She was dying of consumption and there was no hope for her. Kleshtch, her husband, was busy at his bench, where he fitted old keys and locks. Anna sat up to call her husband. Kvashnya had left her some dumplings in the pot, and she offered them to her husband. Kleshtch agreed there was

2129

no use to feed a dying woman, and so with a clear conscience he ate the dumplings.

The Actor helped Anna down from her high bed and out to the draughty hall. The sick woman was wrapped in rags. As they went through the door, the landlord, Kostilyoff, nearly knocked them over.

Kostilyoff looked around the dirty cellar and glanced several times at Kleshtch, working at his bench. The landlord asserted loudly that the locksmith occupied too much room for two roubles a month and henceforth the rent would be two roubles and a half. Then Kostilyoff edged toward Vaska's room and inquired furtively if his wife had been in. He had good reason to suspect that Vassilisa was sleeping with Vaska.

At last Kostilyoff got up enough courage to call Vaska. The thief came out and denounced the landlord for not paying his debts, saying that Kostilyoff still owed seven roubles for a watch he had bought. Ordering Kostilvoff to produce the money immediately, Vaska sent him roughly out of the room.

The others admired Vaska for his courage and urged him to kill Kostilvoff and marry Vassilisa; then he could be landlord. Vaska thought over the idea for a time, but decided that he was too soft-hearted to be a landlord. Besides, he was thinking of discarding Vassilisa for her sister Natasha. Satine asked Vaska for twenty kopecks, which the thief was glad to give immediately; he was afraid Satine would want a rouble next.

Natasha came in with Luka. She put him in the kitchen to sleep with the three already there. Luka was a merry fellow who began to sing, but he stopped when all the others objected. The whole group sat silent when Vassilisa came in, saw the dirty floor, and gave orders for an immediate sweeping. She looked over the new arrival, Luka, and asked to see his passport. Because he had none, he was more readily accepted by the dissolute company.

Miedviedeff, who was a policeman and Vassilisa's uncle, entered the cellar to check up on the lodging. He began to question Luka, but when the tramp called him sergeant, Miedviedeff left him alone.

That night Anna lay in her bunk while a noisy, quarrelsome card game went on. Luka talked gently to the consumptive woman as Kleshtch came from time to time to look at her. Luka remarked that her death would be hard on her husband, but Anna without emotion accused Kleshtch of causing her death. She hoped for the rest and peace she had never known. Luka assured her there would be peace after her death.

The card players became louder and Satine was accused of cheating. Luka quieted the rioters; they all respected him even if they thought him a liar. He told Vaska he could reform in Siberia, and he assured the Actor that at a sanatorium he could be cured of alcoholism.

Vassilisa came in. When the others left, she told Vaska that if he would kill Kostilyoff and set her free she would give him three hundred roubles. Then Vaska would be free to marry Natasha, who at the moment was recovering from a beating given by her jealous sister. Vaska was about to refuse when Kostilyoff entered in search of his wife. He was violently suspicious, but Vaska pushed him out of the cellar.

There was a noise on top of the stove. Luka had overheard the whole thing. He was not disturbed greatly, and he even warned Vaska not to have anything to do with the vicious Vassilisa. Walking over to Anna's bunk, Luka saw that she was dead. When they got Kleshtch out of the saloon, he came to look at the body of his dead wife. The others notified him that he would have to remove the body, because in time dead people smell. Kleshtch agreed to take her outside.

The Actor began to cavort in joy, and he talked excitedly. He had made up his mind to go to the sanatorium for his health. Luka had told him he would even be cured at state expense.

In the back yard that night, as Natasha was telling romantic stories to the crowd, Kostilyoff came out and gruffly ordered Natasha in to work. When she went in, Vassilisa poured boiling water on her feet. Vaska went to the rescue of Natasha and knocked Kostilyoff down. Somehow in the brawl Kostilyoff was killed. At once Vassilisa blamed Vaska for the murder as the crowd slunk away. Natasha thought that Vaska had murdered Kostilyoff for the sake of Vassilisa. Natasha was almost in delirium as she wandered about accusing Vaska of murder and calling for revenge.

In the excitement Luka wandered off; he was never seen again. Vaska escaped a police search. Natasha went to the hospital. In the lodging things went on much as they had before. Satine cheated at cards, and the Baron tried to convince the others of his former affluence. They all agreed that Luka was a kind old man, but a great liar.

During a bitter quarrel with Nastya, the Baron stepped out in the yard. Satine and the others struck up a bawdy song. They broke off when the Baron hurried back to announce that the Actor had hanged himself. Satine thought the suicide was too bad—it broke up the song.

LOYALTIES

Type of work: Drama
Author: John Galsworthy (1867-1933)
Type of plot: Social criticism
Time of plot: Early 1920's
Locale: London
First presented: 1922

Principal characters:
FERDINAND DE LEVIS, a rich young Jew
CAPTAIN RONALD DANCY, D. S. O., retired
MABEL, his wife

Critique:

Loyalties is one of the first plays to deal honestly and openly with the problem of anti-Semitism. Galsworthy takes such pains to deal fairly with both sides of the question, however, that he comes close to destroying his own thesis. The most completely drawn character is probably Captain Dancy, a man of action trying to adjust himself to a static society and finding an outlet in anti-social behavior. Although he does not ask us to condone Dancy's behavior, Galsworthy certainly enables us to understand it.

The Story:

Having retired from His Majesty's service, young Captain Ronald Dancy, D.S.O., was at loose ends as to what to do with himself. Accustomed to a life of action, he at first absorbed himself in horses and women, but he found in neither the violent excitement he craved. His stable was so expensive that he was at last forced to give his Rosemary filly to his friend, Ferdinand De Levis, because he could no longer afford to keep her. As for his women, he decided to throw them all over and marry a woman who admired him, and who had the spirit which Ronny desired in his wife.

In spite of the fact that he was obviously penniless, Ronny managed to keep his memberships in his favorite London clubs, and friends invited him and his wife to their weekend parties in the country. At Meldon Court, the home of his old friend, Charles Winsor, Ronny

discovered that De Levis had sold for a thousand pounds the horse Ronny had given him. He was naturally embittered by the discovery, and later in the evening his resentment prompted him to bet De Levis ten pounds that he could jump to the top of a bookcase four feet high. He won his bet, but De Levis was contemptuous of a man who would indulge in such parlor games for the sake of a little money.

Around midnight, Winsor and his wife were awakened by De Levis, who announced that the thousand pounds he had received for the sale of the filly had been stolen from under his pillow. De Levis demanded an investigation. The Winsors were reluctant to incriminate either their servants or their guests, but at the insistence of De Levis the police were called.

Ronny's friends immediately arrayed themselves against De Levis for his tactlessness in handling the matter. He instantly interpreted their attitude as the result of prejudice because he was a Jew, and Ronny substantiated his conclusion by taunting De Levis with his race. Although they tried desperately to be fair, Ronny's friends had to admit that De Levis had behaved badly, and they suddenly remembered that his father had sold carpets wholesale in the city. After all, De Levis was a little too pushing; in spite of his money he did not exactly belong to the Mayfair and country set.

De Levis carried into the club to which

both men belonged the enmity aroused by Ronny's insult to his race, and he openly accused Ronny of the theft. Ronny immediately challenged him to a duel, but since such barbaric customs were no longer tolerated among gentlemen, De Levis was saved.

Ronny urged his wife Mabel to go with him to Nairobi. But she, believing in her husband's innocence, begged him to remain and fight for his good name. Realizing that to do otherwise would be an admission of guilt, Ronny consulted a lawyer and entered a suit against De Levis for defamation of character. However, the lawyer selected to defend Ronny's case was the worst choice that a man in Ronny's position could possibly have made. Old Jacob Twisden, senior partner of the firm of Twisden and Graviter, was a lawyer of the old school who believed that simple justice should take precedence over all loyalties, whether they were racial, economic, social, political, or merely personal.

In addition to the fact that he had stolen De Levis's money, Ronny had also withheld from his wife and his friends his relations with an Italian girl before his marriage. The girl's father, a wine dealer named Ricardos, had threatened to inform Ronny's wife of the relationship unless he provided for the girl. Out of fear, Ronny had been prompted to make a daring jump from his room to that of De Levis to obtain the money with which to pay Ricardos. The stolen notes were eventually identified as having passed through these different hands. When Twisden learned the true circumstances on which the case he was defending were based, he advised Ronny to drop the suit and leave the country as soon as possible. In that proposal he was seconded by Ronny's own superior officer, General Canynge, who offered Ronny a way out with a billet in the Spanish war.

When De Levis discovered that the suit was to be dropped, he appeared willing to let bygones be bygones because he felt that he had been vindicated; he wanted no money in return. But Ronny's problems were still unsolved. When he confessed to his wife the truth about all that had happened, she at first refused to believe his story. At last she agreed to follow Ronny wherever he might choose to go. Before Ronny could make his escape, however, the police arrived with a warrant for his arrest. He fled to his room and called to the officers to come and get him. Before they could reach him, he had shot himself.

What Ronny never knew was that both he and De Levis were victims of social conventions. Because Ronny belonged, his friends had been loyal. But loyalty, as they now realized, was not enough.

LUCIEN LEUWEN

Type of work: Novel
Author: Stendhal (Marie-Henri Beyle, 1783-1842)
Type of plot: Psychological romance
Time of plot: The 1830's
Locale: France
First published: 1894

Principal characters:
LUCIEN LEUWEN, a serious young man
MONSIEUR LEUWEN, his father
MADAME DE CHASTELLER, a beautiful widow
MADAME GRANDET, an ambitious woman
DR. DU POIRIER, a physician

Critique:

Published posthumously, Lucien Leuwen is a long unfinished work divided into two novels: The Green Huntsman and The Telegraph. In it Stendhal gives a subtle, penetrating analysis, Freudian in tone, of a young commoner in the difficult days after the revolution of 1830. Lucien is considered an idealized portrait of Stendhal. The novel, though rewarding, is frustrating, for Stendhal never revised the manuscript; indeed, parts of the narrative were not completed. The grand passion of Lucien for Bathilde, for example, is not concluded; from his notes we know that the author intended them to marry. Despite these imperfections the novel is regarded in France as Stendhal's third masterpiece.

The Story:

The revolution of 1830 was not a success; the armed rabble were victorious in the fighting, but afterward the rich bourgeoisie came to power. Although the king had lost much of his authority, France was not yet a true republic. The absolute monarchists remained loyal to the vanished power of the Bourbons, the people still hoped for a democratic rule, and the middle class steered a cautious, unsatisfactory path between the two extremes.

Lucien, son of a rich banker, had mild republican leanings. For daring to air his views, he was expelled from the Ecole Polytechnique, and for a time he remained idle at home. His indulgent, wealthy father tried to induce him to work in the family bank, and his mother presented him to the polite, gay society of her Parisian salon. But Lucien was dull and preoccupied. In despair his father filled his pockets with money and bade him entertain the light ladies at the Opera.

As a way out, Lucien took a commission as second lieutenant in a regiment of lancers going to maintain order in Nancy. Lucien liked his uniform with the magenta stripes, but he found his fellow officers insufferable. His lieutenant-colonel, especially, was a man of honorable reputation, but a bore. Only the soldiers in the ranks seemed genuine and unaffected.

The regiment was depressed on entering the town of Nancy. The land was flat; sewage ditches ran down the narrow, crooked streets, and the houses were mean. Lucien felt that he made an unsoldierly appearance because his mount, furnished by the regiment, was a mean-looking nag. As they passed a more pretentious house, a woman standing at an upstairs window seemed interested in Lucien, but as luck would have it, he was thrown from his horse just as he was trying to see her more clearly.

Lucien soon bought a good horse and rented a comfortable apartment, once occupied by a lieutenant-colonel who had left the regiment. In spite of his servants, his wine, and his stable, he was quite unhappy. His commanding officer, resenting his wealth, made his life miserable; the other officers had little to do with him. The townspeople held aloof from the military. One faction consisted of the aristocrats who were opposed to the moderate monarchy, and the other faction was the republican majority who smarted under any kingly rule. None of the officers was received in society; few of the enlisted men made friends with people of the suspicious working class.

Backed by his father's money and his own Parisian graces, Lucien set out determinedly to be accepted by the nobility. He cultivated the wily Dr. du Poirier, the leader of the monarchist set. Little by little Lucien was welcomed to the various salons. Only his military life irked him now. Government spies even reported that he had gone into a republican reading room; to quiet rumors of political unreliability Lucien fought and won two duels.

Several of the salons were presided over by beautiful, high-born women who accepted Lucien on friendly terms. The most beautiful of all, however, was Madame de Chasteller; and for long Lucien did not meet her. He heard of her in some detail, however, a rich widow dominated by a miserly father. She had had only one lover, so the gossips said, the lieutenant-colonel whose apartment Lucien had rented. When he finally met her, Lucien was smitten. Bathilde de Chasteller was lonely, proud, and shy.

Bathilde was an aristocrat, Lucien a commoner. As their love grew, they were both troubled. Bathilde felt that a marriage was impossible, and Lucien hesitated to try to make her his mistress. Unhappy much of the time, they were together so much that gossip soon spread. At a dinner at a country tavern, The Green Huntsman, they came to an open confession of their love.

The aristocratic young men were much displeased. They were afraid that Lucien, a commoner, would marry the rich Bathilde and take her away. Some of the more hot-headed ones proposed to challenge Lucien to a duel. Scheming Dr. du Poirier guaranteed to rid them of the hated Lucien.

Bathilde, ill for days, was under the treatment of Dr. du Poirier, and Lucien had been given permission to visit her. As he waited in the hall, the doctor brought a baby in swaddling clothes from Bathilde's chamber. From a conversation Lucien understood that Bathilde's illness had been a confinement. Sure that the lieutenant-colonel was the father, Lucien obtained leave and left Nancy.

In Paris, through his father, he secured his release from the army. Then, through his father's influence, he obtained a post as Master of Petitions in the Ministry of the Interior. Although he could not forget lovely Bathilde, Lucien threw himself into politics and soon was a valuable aid to the minister. At first he had little idea of the trickery so common in high office, but his knowledge grew rapidly. The minister had speculated successfully with money borrowed from M. Leuwen. When there was some danger the transaction would come to light, Lucien managed to hide all traces of the affair.

Another incident added to his standing. The government hired *agents provocateurs* to harass the military. One agent made the mistake of trying to intimidate a sentry, who shot him in the abdomen. Gravely wounded, the agent was taken to a hospital. Afraid that he would make a deathbed statement as to who had employed him, a government spy tried to induce a doctor to poison the wounded man. When the doctor objected, the minister gave Lucien the job of hushing up the scandal. Lucien succeeded in bribing the dying man and his wife so that they both maintained silence.

Lucien was sent to Caen to try to influence an election. On the way he was set upon by a mob and spattered with mud. Heartsick at the way people reacted to the corrupt government, he nevertheless did his best. By paying a hundred thousand francs to bribe the legitimist party, he almost prevented the election of a favored candidate.

The minister showed his displeasure by passing over Lucien on the honors list. Not willing to have his son slighted, M. Leuwen went into politics himself and became a deputy. With his wealth and charm, he soon was powerful enough to dictate who should be in the cabinet. He arranged to have the fatuous Grandet made a minister if his beautiful and ambitious wife would become Lucien's mistress. Madame Grandet accepted the proposition and soon fell really in love with Lucien.

M. Leuwen made the mistake of revealing the bargain to Lucien, who thought he had won by his own merit the most beautiful woman in Paris. He was greatly upset and even thought himself unfaithful to his lost Bathilde. Taking leave from the ministry, he left for a stay in the country.

M. Leuwen died suddenly, leaving his affairs in bad state. Lucien, insisting on paying all creditors in full, saved only a modest income for his mother and himself. He got an appointment to the embassy at Capel. He was happy in his new post, and felt only a faint melancholy for Bathilde.

THE LUCK OF ROARING CAMP AND OTHER SKETCHES

Type of work: Short stories
Author: Bret Harte (1836-1902)
Time: 1850-1865
Locale: California
First published: 1870

Relatively few authors ever achieve the astonishing literary success that Bret Harte did during his lifetime. His stories of California life, enormously popular, were in great demand by magazine editors all over the country, and the *Atlantic Monthly* bid the unheard-of amount of ten thousand dollars for the sole rights to one year of Harte's literary production.

However, this flash in the pan popularity is seldom consistent with a lasting literary reputation, and in Harte's case the line between literary value and entertainment is often thin. That Harte reached his artistic maturity at the age of thirty-one and began to decline five years later indicates this fact. During these few years Harte produced some stories of genuine literary value. The majority of them are collected in *The Luck of Roaring Camp and Other Sketches*, and it is mainly on this volume that Harte's literary reputation rests.

Harte's vision of life goes far to explain the meteoric popularity of his stories. The local color, the picturesque characters, and the trick endings all added to Harte's attraction, certainly, but they were surface attractions. The heart of his success lay in his particular vision of life and his ability to convey that vision to his readers.

Harte was, essentially, an optimist and an uplifter. This does not mean that Harte believed in a shallow doctrine of social or moral reform. Rather, he believed in the potential goodness of man and in the possibility of redemption for every sinner. Harte saw life as a purgatory for the human soul. He saw life as a test for men, as a trial in which the ultimate goal is salvation. Salvation, however, was to be achieved in this life, although, paradoxically, it was frequently to be gained at the cost of death. In other words, death, rather than being an end of

the trial, was to be seen as the final consummation of the trial, as a selfless act of devotion on the part of his heroes. Redemption for Harte was an act of selfless heroism, of love, of devotion. Such an act lifted one above the petty world of grasping self-interest and redeemed one from the sin of self-involvement. This is the spirit that pervades Harte's most memorable stories.

This spirit raises Harte's best characters from local stereotypes and picturesque caricatures to people of real feelings and semi-heroic stature, and it helps to explain Mark Twain's statement that "Bret Harte got his California and his Californians by unconscious absorption, and put both of them into his tales alive." He wove the experiences of his people into his private theme of redemption and thereby gave them life.

The people Harte wrote about were people seeking salvation from themselves, people who longed to wipe their past clean, and people who had come West to lose their identity, as is indicated by the fact that very few of his characters retained their given names. His characters have had their identities and pasts wiped clean with names like Cherokee Sal, Kentuck, Yuba Bill, Tennessee's Partner, and the Duchess. People like these were ripe material for redemption by virtue of their self-dissatisfaction. In order to be saved, one must first have sinned.

This theme is the core of Harte's most successful stories. In the title story of the collection, "The Luck of Roaring Camp," which first appeared in the *Overland Monthly* in 1868, a dissolute prostitute works out her salvation by giving birth to a baby and dying. The miners in the camp work out their salvation by giving the baby love and generous gifts in the absence of a mother.

One miner in particular, Kentuck, works out his salvation by giving his life in a futile attempt to save the baby. The baby, of course, is incidental because of its innocence. What matters is that the baby brought out the generous qualities of the people involved and thereby redeemed them from their own pettiness. In the second story of the collection, "The Outcasts of Poker Flat," the theme is the same. A gambler and two prostitutes are saved from themselves by virtue of their devotion to a pair of innocent youngsters who had eloped. In the third story, "Miggles," a pretty young woman is redeemed by virtue of her devotion to a helpless invalid.

The theme of love's power to save turns Harte's best stories into human interest tales, which Harte did a good deal to popularize. This theme was the source of Harte's uplift, optimism, and popularity.

Harte's vices as well as his virtues can be attributed to this same theme. It quickly lapses into sentimentalism, and it also tends to gloss over the sharp frictions and discordances of everyday life with a nonexistent glamor and romance. In "Brown of Calaveras" the image of gambler Jack Hamlin riding off into the rosy sunset after having handsomely refused to run away with a man's beautiful young wife certainly strikes one as unnecessarily romantic and sentimental. Again, this theme of redemption through love and death lends itself too easily to theatrical endings in which death seems to be an easy way to end the story.

At his best, however, Harte avoids these tendencies. The sentimentality of the story is balanced frequently by an ironic, humorous narrative style. In his most memorable stories Harte employs an ironic prose that maintains a distance between himself and his subject matter. This prose is clear and restrained, giving his fiction a sweet-sour flavor that blends well with his vision of things. Thus his skillful prose gives the reader the impression that his characters do not deserve one's full sympathy until they succeed in redeeming themselves. It reminds us that his characters are human and, as such, are subject to human failings. This fact does not mean that Harte is ever self-righteous. On the contrary, he was always humane in his treatment of character. It was just that he realized human limitations as well as human virtues. In his preface to *The Luck of Roaring Camp* he wrote:

> I might have painted my villains of the blackest dye. . . . I might have made it impossible for them to have performed a virtuous or generous action, and have thus avoided that moral confusion which is apt to rise in the contemplation of mixed motives and qualities. But I should have burdened myself with responsibility of their creation, which . . . I did not care to do.

Even in his preface Harte's use of irony is skillful. Actually, he was a shrewd judge of character with a talent for "the contemplation of mixed motives and qualities."

Harte put this talent to good use in his sketches. He was an admirable craftsman in blending virtue and vice, humor and pathos, the ridiculous and the sublime. He had a good eye for contrasts, particularly for the contrast between nature and man. Nature, like man, was ambivalent for Harte. On the one hand, he saw nature as serene, remote, and passionless; on the other, it could be violent, deadly, and passionate. In Harte's stories the moods of nature are usually in juxtaposition to the moods of his people. In "The Luck of Roaring Camp," for example, nature becomes still for a moment at the birth and the first cry of the baby. Later, when everything in the human realm seems calm and settled, nature in the form of a flood overwhelms the mining camp and takes several lives, including the baby's. The same occurs in "The Outcasts of Poker Flat." When the gambler, the thief, and the two prostitutes are driven out of town, everything is calm, but when these four begin to find some measure of peace, a snowstorm overwhelms them and their two innocent companions.

It has been pointed out that Harte's literary techniques were borrowed from writers like Irving and Dickens. To be sure, Harte did adapt his techniques from the Eastern writers and from Europeans. Also, he had a romantic tradition behind him. Harte was, essentially, an Easterner who had come West for his literary materials. But to hold the fact that Harte borrowed from other writers against him is to miss the point. Harte transformed these techniques with his own personal merits and limitations. He transmuted them with his own personal vision of life.

Both Harte's virtues and vices as a storyteller derive from his optimistic vision of human redemption. On the debit side, his bitter-sweet endings are patently stylized, and there is a tendency to coat his situations with sentiment. On the asset side, Harte's endings have a good measure of dramatic impact. Then, too, he frequently balances the sentiment and glamor with a healthy humor and irony. Again, Harte was an effective stylist and his sentences are sharp and lucid. Furthermore, Harte opened the field for human interest and local color stories, thus paving the way for a flourishing school of regional fiction. Finally, Harte's happy talent for characterization and caricature blended very well with his style of writing and his personal outlook on life, thus forming a fortunate fusion of form and content. For these reasons he retains an assured place in a minor tradition.

THE LUSIAD

Type of work: Poem
Author: Luis Vaz de Camoëns (1524?-1580)
Type of plot: Epic
Time of plot: Fifteenth century
Locale: Europe, Africa, and Asia
First published: 1572

Principal characters:
VASCO DA GAMA, Portuguese sea captain and explorer
VENUS, goddess of love, patroness of the Portuguese
BACCHUS, god of revelry, patron of Asia

Critique:

Descended from an ancient Galician family, Camoëns was distantly related to the hero of his epic narrative. In addition, the author had covered part of Vasco da Gama's route when he went to the Orient as an agent of the crown. On his return trip from Macao Camoëns was shipwrecked, saving nothing but a faithful Javanese slave and the manuscripts of *The Lusiad*. The poem was, like all great epics, the product of a man of action during a period of great national activity, at a time when the national spirit of Portugal had reached a high point. In the epic tradition, the poem finds the gods of Olympus siding for and against the Portuguese heroes; there is a descent into the underworld of Neptune. The "famous weapon" in this poem is the Portuguese ships' cannon. All of the other hallmarks of the epic are present, too, for those who would seek them.

The Story:

The gods and goddesses, called together by Jove, assembled on Olympus. When they had taken their places, Jove announced to them that the Fates had decreed that the men of Lusitania, or Portugal, should outdo all the great conquerors of ancient times by sailing around Africa to Asia, there to become the rulers of a new continent. Of all the assembled pantheon only Bacchus, who looked upon Asia as his own, dissented. Venus, friendly toward the Portuguese, however, took their side, aided by Mars.

Vasco da Gama was the captain chosen to head the voyage of exploration. Having sailed southward to the Cape of Good Hope, the Portuguese ships made their way around it and then sailed northward along the African coast, until they arrived at the island of Mozambique. The natives of that island pretended friendliness but tried to ambush the sailors when they put ashore for water; fortunately, the Portuguese escaped. Leaving the island behind, da Gama sailed northward along the African coast in search of India. He tried to land on another coast but there, too, the natives were unfriendly. When they tried to lay an ambush, Venus interceded on behalf of da Gama and his men.

Guided by Mercury, da Gama set sail for a point still farther north. Arriving off Mombassa, the Portuguese ships dropped sails and anchors. The Moorish King of Mombassa made the Portuguese welcome to his domain, as Jove had told Venus he would, and gave the men of Portugal needed supplies. While paying a visit to da Gama's ship, he asked the Portuguese leader to tell him about Portugal's history and the history of the voyage thus far. Da Gama was only too glad to give an account of his long and troublesome voyage and to tell of his nation's history.

Da Gama told the king where Portugal lay on the map of Europe and related how the Moors had at one time overrun the land. He described the great battles of Portuguese kings against the Moors: how the first Alphonso had first pushed the Moors back toward the shores of the Mediterranean and how his grandson, also named Alphonso, had continued the wars

2140

against the Moors and defeated with a small army five hosts of Moors under five Moorish kings. The second Alphonso was succeeded by Sancho, who, continuing the wars against the Moors, drove them from Europe and then fought against them in the Holy Land. Da Gama also told of the wars between the Spanish kings and the descendants of the great Alphonsos.

After ending his narrative of the martial history of Portugal, da Gama described his own adventures since leaving the mouth of the Tagus River. He told how his ships had sailed past the Canary Islands, past the Hesperides, and past the mouth of the mighty Congo. He told the king of the strange waterspouts they had seen, the terrible storms they had endured, and the awesome sea creatures they had met. He related how they had tried to make friends of the black people of the African coast by giving them odd knickknacks and how the blacks in return had tried to kill them after pretending friendship. Da Gama told of the experiences of one of his men, Veloso, who had wandered too far inland and had almost been killed by blacks, and how Veloso had claimed that he returned quickly only because he thought the ships in danger.

Da Gama also narrated his adventure with the spirit of the Cape of Good Hope. The spirit appeared to the Portuguese as his ships sighted the cape and told them that they were the first men to sail in those waters. In return for their daring, the spirit prophesied, some of them would have to die, and that many of these men who followed them would also die for venturing so far into strange lands. The spirit told da Gama that he was one of the Titans who had fought against Jove and that his name had been Adamastor. The Titan had pursued a nymph, a chase which ended when divine wrath changed him into a range of mountains forming the cape at Africa's foot.

Da Gama next told of the plague which had struck his crew, of the shortage of drinking water, of the loss of necessary food through spoilage. He also told of battles and ambushes in which the Portuguese fought with unfriendly natives of the east African coast.

After hearing his account of Portuguese history and da Gama's fabulous voyage, the king thought he could not do enough to show his friendliness toward the great men who represented Portugal. The Mombassans sent a pilot to da Gama and also the provisions and water necessary for a voyage across the Indian Ocean to the city of Calcutta.

Bacchus, meanwhile, was furious at the success of da Gama and his ships. Determined to prevent Asia from falling into the hands of the Portuguese, Bacchus went into the depths of the sea to the court of Neptune, there to seek the aid of the sea god. He told Neptune that the men of Portugal were despoiling his kingdom and that the Portuguese spoke of the ruler of the sea only in terms of insolence. Neptune, angered at the report, sent storms to destroy their ships, but Venus interceded once more on behalf of the Portuguese and saved them from the storms unleashed by Neptune.

The Portuguese, arriving on the Indian coast, landed on the shore near Calcutta. One of the first to meet the men of Portugal was a Mohammedan who was glad to see them because he himself was from the northwestern part of Africa. He sent word to the Emperor of Malabar, informing him of the white strangers and of the distance they had traveled. The emperor quickly gave audience to da Gama, who told the ruler that he wished to trade for products of the eastern lands. Arrangements went forward to exchange Portuguese goods for spices and other products of India. The Mohammedan peoples in India became aroused and tried to bribe the king's council to halt the trading. Failing in that plan, they tried to delay da Gama's departure, for they hoped to destroy the Portuguese ships in battle with a fleet sailing from Arabia. Da Gama outwitted his enemies, however, and set out on the return voyage before the Arabian fleet had arrived.

As the Portuguese ships sailed westward toward home, Venus moved an island into their path. Needing a rest from their travels, da Gama and his men anchored off the island and went ashore. There, under the guidance of Venus, nymphs charmed away the hours for the sailors, and the goddess herself took da Gama to a castle high on a hill and showed him a vision of the future in which he saw later Portuguese—Albuquerque, Sampoyo, Noronia, and others—completing the conquest of Asia for their king and nation.

LYSISTRATA

Type of work: Drama
Author: Aristophanes (c. 448-385 B.C.)
Type of plot: Utopian comedy
Time of plot: Fifth century B.C.
Locale: Athens
First presented: 411 B.C.

Principal characters:
LYSISTRATA, an Athenian woman
CLEONICE, her friend
LAMPITO, a Spartan woman
MYRRHINÉ, a Greek woman
A MAGISTRATE
CINESIAS, a Greek husband
OLD MEN OF ATHENS, the Chorus

Critique:

The basic assumption on which the Lysistrata is based is highly comic; indeed, Aristophanes reveals, in the very weakness of the average woman in the play, his knowledge that the supposition was not only comic but also impossible. Yet the assumption that women, by concerted determination not to lie with their men, could effect peace and government reform is not entirely comic. This idea was probably an ancient one even in the time of Aristophanes, but he was able to blend the alarming logic and the delightful illogic of it to produce an amusing if somewhat bawdily skeptical work of art. Lysistrata herself is the archetype of the militant feminist, the woman who has managed through the ages to keep alive the war of the sexes.

The Story:

The Second Peloponnesian War was in progress when Lysistrata, an Athenian woman, summoned women from Athens, Sparta, and all other Greek cities involved in the war. She wished to have them consider her carefully thought out plan for ending hostilities between Athens and Sparta. The women arrived one by one, curious about the purpose of the meeting. Since their husbands were all away at war, they looked with enthusiasm for any scheme which would bring their men back to them.

Lysistrata declared that the war would end immediately if all the Greek women refrained, from that time on, until fighting stopped, from lying with their husbands. This suggestion took the women by complete surprise, and they objected strenuously. But Lampito, a Spartan woman, liked the idea. Although the others finally agreed to try the plan, they did so without enthusiasm.

Over a bowl of Thracian wine, Lysistrata led her companions in an oath binding them to charm their husbands and their lovers, but not to lie with them unless forced. Some of the women returned to their native lands to begin their continent lives. Lysistrata went to the Acropolis, citadel of Athens.

While the younger women had been meeting with Lysistrata, the older women had marched upon the Acropolis and seized it. The old men of the city laid wood around the base of the Acropolis and set fire to it with the intention of smoking out the women, who, in turn, threatened the old men with pots of water. During an exchange of scurrilous vituperation the women threw water on their opponents.

When a magistrate and his men attempted to break open a gate of the citadel, Lysistrata, now in command, emerged and suggested that the magistrate use common sense. When the indignant magistrate ordered his Scythians to seize

Lysistrata and bind her hands, the Scythians advanced reluctantly and were soundly trounced by the fierce defenders.

Asked why they had seized the Acropolis, the women replied that they had done so in order to possess the treasury. Since they now controlled the money, and since it took money to wage war, they believed that the war must soon end.

The male pride of the old men was deeply wounded when Lysistrata declared that the women had assumed all civil authority and would henceforth provide for the safety and welfare of Athens. The magistrate could not believe his ears when he heard Lysistrata say that the women, tired of being home-bodies, were impatient with the incompetence of their husbands in matters which concerned the commonweal. For rebuking the women, the magistrate received potfuls of water poured on his head. The ineffectual old men declared that they would never submit to the tyranny of women. The women answered that the old men were worthless, that all they could do was to legislate the city into trouble.

Despite their brave talk and their bold plan, however, the women proved to be weak in the flesh, and disaffection thinned their ranks. Some, caught as they deserted, offered various excuses in the hope of getting away from the strictures imposed by Lysistrata's oath. One woman simulated pregnancy by placing the sacred helmet of Athena under her robe. Some of the women claimed to be frightened by the holy snakes and by the owls of the Acropolis. As a last desperate measure, Lysistrata resorted to a prophecy, which was favorable to their project, and the women returned reluctantly to their posts.

When Cinesias, the husband of Myrrhiné, one of Lysistrata's companions, returned from the war and sought his wife,

Lysistrata directed Myrrhiné to be true to her oath. Begging Myrrhiné to come home, Cinesias used various appeals, without success. Although Myrrhiné consented to his request for a moment of dalliance with her, she put him off with trifling excuses. At last, in spite of his pleas, she retired into the citadel.

A messenger arrived from Sparta, where Lampito and her cohorts had been successful, and declared that the men of Sparta were prepared to sue for peace. As the magistrate arranged for a peace conference, the women looked once more upon the old men of Athens with a kindness that cooled the ire of the indignant old fellows.

On their arrival in Athens, the Spartan envoys were obviously in need of the favors of their wives. Indeed, so desperate were they that they were ready to agree to any terms. Lysistrata rebuked the Spartans and the Athenians for warring upon each other; they had, she declared, a common enemy in the barbarians, and they shared many traditions. While she spoke, a nude maiden, representing the goddess of peace, was brought before the frustrated men. Lysistrata reminded the men of the two countries that they had previously been friends and allies and again insisted that war between the two was illogical. The men, their eyes devouring the nude maiden, agreed absently with everything Lysistrata said, but when she asked for an agreement contention immediately arose because one side asked for conditions unsatisfactory to the other.

The women, seeing that any appeal to reason was futile, feasted the envoys and filled them with intoxicating liquors. Sated, and eager for further physical satisfaction, the men signed a peace agreement and dispersed hastily, with their wives, to their homes.

THE MABINOGION

Type of work: Tales
Author: Unknown
Type of plots: Heroic romances
Time of plots: The Middle Ages
Locale: Arthurian Britain, mainly Wales
First transcribed: Twelfth and thirteenth centuries; first translation published, 1838-1849

Principal characters:
PWYLL, Prince of Dyved
RHIANNON, his wife
PRYDERI, their son
KICVA, Pryderi's wife
BENDIGEID VRAN, King of the Island of the Mighty, Llyr's son
BRANWEN, Llyr's daughter
MATHOLWCH, King of Ireland, Branwen's husband
MANAWYDAN, another of Llyr's sons, Pryderi's stepfather
KING MATH
GWYDION, one of King Math's warriors
LLEW LLAW GYFFES, Gwydion's favorite son
BLODEUWEDD, Llew Llaw Gyffes' elfwife
MACSEN WLEDIG, Emperor of Rome
LLUDD, King of Britain
LLEVELYS, his brother, King of France
KING ARTHUR
KILHWCH, one of King Arthur's knights
YSBADDADEN, a crafty giant
OLWEN, his daughter, loved by Kilhwch
RHONABWY, a dreamer
OWAIN, the new Knight of the Fountain
PEREDUR, one of King Arthur's knights
GERINT, another of King Arthur's knights, later a king
ENID, his wife

Critique:

Paradoxically, the title of this collection of Welsh tales, written in the twelfth and thirteenth centuries and preserved in the fourteenth-century manuscript titled *Red Book of Hergest*, is a relatively modern one. When Lady Charlotte Guest, the translator, called these tales *The Mabinogion* she used a misnomer for the most part, for her title applies only to the first four stories. These tales, among the finest of medieval literature, represent the best of Celtic culture. The world they disclose to our modern eyes is one of great heroes, black villains, incomparable battles, women of great beauty, old crones, magnificent splendor, wretched squalor, landscapes of matchless glamour, wizards, and warlocks—a world of chivalric romance and harsh brutality. Undoubtedly, this world and these stories have their roots in primitive Celtic mythology that was translated into folklore and eventually into romantic tales. Although the poet-authors are unknown, they show considerable artistry and craftsmanship in the treatment of their subjects.

The Stories:

PWYLL, PRINCE OF DYVED

Pwyll, the Prince of Dyved, was caught stealing a dying deer. In order to redeem himself Pwyll agreed to exchange lands and appearances with the chieftain who had caught him and to slay the chieftain's enemy after a year's time. That year each prince ruled the other's land wisely and well, and each remained faithful to his own true wife. At the year's end Pwyll slew the enemy, returned home on good terms with the other prince, and eventually gained the other's lands. From a hill one day Pwyll saw a lovely lady ride by. She eluded him three times, but on the fourth he spoke to her. She told him that her name was Rhiannon and invited him to her castle a year from that day. Pwyll went with his men, subdued her other suitor, and won the lady. Some time thereafter Rhiannon bore a son who disappeared the first night after his birth. The women on watch accused her of killing it, and so Pwyll made her pay a heavy penance. Meanwhile, a farmer had taken the baby from a monster. Eventually he restored the boy to Pwyll, who then released his wife from her penance and named his son Pryderi.

BRANWEN, DAUGHTER OF LLYR

Bendigeid Vran, son of Llyr and King of the Island of the Mighty, made a pact with Matholwch, King of Ireland, and gave him his sister Branwen to wed. When the King of Ireland suffered an insult at the hands of one of Bendigeid Vran's men, Bendigeid Vran made good the loss; but because of the insult Matholwch and Branwen were made to suffer heavily at the hands of the Irishmen. Bendigeid Vran learned of their treatment, sailed to Ireland, and made war on the Irish. Both sides suffered great losses. Bendigeid Vran was killed by a poisoned spear; his last request was that his head be buried in the White Mount in London. Branwen died of sorrow. Finally, only seven of Bendigeid Vran's men were left alive to bury the heads of their chief, and only five pregnant Irish women.

MANAWYDAN, SON OF LLYR

Two of the men left living after the war in Ireland were Pryderi and Manawydan, the brother of Bendigeid Vran. These two went to live on Pryderi's lands, and Manawydan married Pryderi's mother. The two men and their wives, for Pryderi had a wife named Kicva, lived pleasantly until the countryside was magically laid desolate and everyone else had disappeared. They left their lands and tried to earn a living at various trades, but were always driven off by their envious competitors. When they returned to their own lands, Pryderi and his mother entered a magic castle that vanished with them. Manawydan then tried farming, and again his crops were magically desolated. Determined to get to the bottom of the mystery, Manawydan stayed up to watch his last field. When he saw thousands of mice ravaging the field, he caught one and declared that he would hang it. Pryderi's wife tried to dissuade him along with three churchmen, but he was still determined to hang the mouse. At last the third churchman disclosed himself as the one who had cursed Manawydan and his friends in revenge for an insult from Pryderi's father years before. He promised to restore everything, including Pryderi and his mother, if Manawydan would release the mouse. Manawydan insisted that the magician never touch his lands again, and he returned the mouse, who happened to be the churchman's wife. Everything was restored, and the four companions returned to their former happiness.

MATH, SON OF MATHONWY

Gwydion's brother, Gilvaethwy, loved King Math's footmaiden, Goewin. Hoping to secure the maiden for his brother, Gwydion tricked Pryderi into exchanging some pigs for twelve phantom steeds and twelve phantom greyhounds. Pryderi and his men pursued them. While King Math and his men were preparing to fight this army, Gwydion and his brother raped the footmaiden before they returned to the fight and won the battle for King Math. The king then punished the brothers by turning them into animals for three years. After his penance Gwydion had two sons. Their mother cursed Gwydion's favorite son, named Llew Llaw Gyffes, by saying that he would never have a human wife. To thwart this curse King Math and Gwydion created for him an elfwife, Blodeuwedd, out of flowers. The wife proved unfaithful by taking a lover. Determined to get rid of her husband, she asked him how he might be killed. Foolishly, he told her and she told her lover, who tried to kill Llew Llaw Gyffes. Gwydion's son did not die, however, but was turned into an eagle. Gwydion then searched for his son, found him, and restored him to his former shape. Gwydion and Llew Llaw Gyffes then took revenge on the wife and her lover by turning her into an owl and killing him.

THE DREAM OF MACSEN WLEDIG

Macsen Wledig, the Emperor of Rome, dreamed one night of a lovely maiden in a strange and wonderful land. Awaking, he sent his messengers all over the world in search of her. After wandering in many lands they found her in a castle in Britain, and they guided the emperor to her. He found everything as it had been in his dream. The maiden accepted him, and for her maiden portion he gave her father the island of Britain and caused three castles to be built for her. Macsen Wledig lived with his wife in Britain for seven years. Meanwhile, the Romans had chosen a new emperor, who sent a note to Wledig warning him not to return. Wledig then marched on Gaul, fought his way through Italy, and reconquered Rome.

LLUDD AND LLEVELYS

Three plagues ravaged Britain. The first was a crafty foreign people; the second was a yearly midnight scream that made everything barren; and the third was the habitual disappearance of food at the king's court. Lludd, the great King of Britain, asked help from his wise and well-beloved brother, Llevelys, who was King of France. Llevelys told him to mash insects in water and sprinkle the solution over the foreigners to kill them. To get rid of the screaming dragon Lludd would have to lure it with mead, put it in a sack, and bury it in a stone coffer. To keep the food Lludd would have to capture a magician who put everyone to sleep. The king performed these tasks and Britain was rid of the plagues.

KILHWCH AND OLWEN

Kilhwch's stepmother had spitefully prophesied that Kilhwch would not have a woman until he won Olwen, the daughter of Ysbaddaden, a crafty and powerful giant. Straightway, Kilhwch, who had fallen in love with Olwen without having seen her, set out for King Arthur's court, where King Arthur accepted the young man as his knight. Kilhwch then set out to seek Ysbaddaden; with him went all of King Arthur's gallant warriors. After a long journey Kilhwch met Olwen, the most beautiful woman he had ever seen. He and King Arthur's men proceeded to Ysbaddaden's court to ask for Olwen. After fighting for three days and wounding the giant three times, Kilhwch learned that he could win Olwen and slay her father after performing forty nearly impossible tasks for the giant. By dint of brute force, cunning, and magic, Kilhwch, King Arthur, and his men succeeded in completing the tasks. Kilhwch then slew Ysbaddaden, married Olwen, and lived happily ever after.

THE DREAM OF RHONABWY

While seeking a man who had ravaged the land, Rhonabwy and his companions found themselves in a dark hall where the floors were covered with dung. After trying to talk to the strange people inhabiting the hall and failing, Rhonabwy lay down on an ox-skin and began to dream.

He dreamed of the heroic Arthurian age when men were demigods who lived in splendor in a land where life was full. He found himself in King Arthur's court watching a game between King Arthur and Owain. While the game was in progress, three servants informed Owain that his ravens were being killed by King Arthur's men, but the king insisted that the game continue. Owain told his men to raise his banner, whereupon the ravens revived and began to slaughter the men. Three servants came to tell King Arthur how his men were being killed, but Owain insisted that the game continue. At last the king begged Owain to call off the ravens. He did so and there was peace. Many men then brought tribute to King Arthur. At that point Rhonabwy awakened.

THE LADY OF THE FOUNTAIN

While at King Arthur's court Owain learned from Kynon of a powerful Knight of the Fountain who overthrew all challengers. Upon being taunted by Kai, Owain went in search of this knight, challenged him, and slew him. Then with the help of a maiden Owain escaped the angry townsmen who were seeking to avenge the death of their lord and he married the dead knight's wife. He ruled the land well for three years. Meanwhile, King Arthur and his knights had come in search of Owain. Upon arriving at the fountain, King Arthur's men all challenged the new Knight of the Fountain and were overthrown by him. The king and Owain were finally reunited, and Owain returned to King Arthur's court after promising his wife that he would return at the end of three years. Owain was reminded of his promise when his wife came to King Arthur's court and removed the ring which she had given him as a token by which to remember her. Then Owain went in search of his wife. After restoring a lady's kingdom, killing a serpent about to destroy a lion, saving the maiden who had aided him six years earlier, and killing her tor-

mentors, Owain was restored to his wife. Another feat was defeating and transforming the Black Oppressor. Thereafter Owain and his wife lived happily at King Arthur's court.

PEREDUR, SON OF EVRAWG

Peredur lived a sheltered life with his mother; nevertheless he grew up strong and swift. Although his mother did not want him to become a knight, nothing could keep him from fulfilling his desire. When he prepared to leave his mother and journey to King Arthur's court, she instructed him in the chivalric code. Peredur was an ungainly sight as he entered King Arthur's court, for he was still awkward and naïve. However, he soon showed his prowess in battle, and through many adventures he acquired polish and skill in the arts of hunting, war, and love. Many reports of his strength and bravery reached King Arthur's ears. Peredur spent his time defending and loving maidens, restoring kingdoms to the wronged, avenging insults, killing monsters and evil men, protecting the weak, and ridding the land of plagues. In short, he was a matchless knight. When, in the course of his adventures, he inadvertently caused a kingdom to wither and grow barren, he restored it to fertility by dint of strength and courage. In the end he rid the land of seven evil witches.

GERINT, SON OF ERBIN

While King Arthur and his men were hunting, Gerint rode with the queen and her maids. When a dwarf insulted Gerint and one of the maids, the knight challenged the dwarf's lord to a contest and defeated him. Afterward Gerint restored a kingdom to its proper lord and won the king's daughter, Enid, as his wife. Gerint then traveled back to King Arthur's court and received a stag head for his reward. In time Gerint, having inherited a kingdom from his father, went with Enid to rule the land. Because he devoted more time to his wife than he did to jousts or battles, his subjects complained bitterly.

When Enid learned of their grievance, she inadvertently told him. In anger, Gerint set out on a journey with his wife to prove his strength and valor. He performed superhuman feats and slaughtered belligerent knights and caitiffs in vast numbers, but he nearly died in the attempt. Finally, having proved himself to his wife and subjects, he returned home to rule once more.

MACBETH

Type of work: Drama
Author: William Shakespeare (1564-1616)
Type of plot: Romantic tragedy
Time of plot: Eleventh century
Locale: Scotland
First presented: 1606

Principal characters:
MACBETH, a Scottish thane
LADY MACBETH, his wife
DUNCAN, King of Scotland
MALCOLM, his son
BANQUO, a Scottish chieftain
MACDUFF, a rebel lord

Critique:

The Tragedy of Macbeth, one of Shakespeare's shortest dramas, is the story of a highly imaginative, ambitious and conscience-stricken nobleman whose wife drove him to murder. Macbeth, at first a man of honor and integrity, had one major flaw — ambition. When the opportunity for power was presented to him, he committed his first crime. Later he was forced into utter degradation in order to conceal that first evil step. The macabre settings of *Macbeth*, the gloomy castle and the eerie heath, are in keeping with the weird tone of the whole play.

The Story:

On a lonely heath in Scotland, three witches sang their riddling runes and said that soon they would meet Macbeth.

Macbeth was the noble thane of Glamis, recently victorious in a great battle against Vikings and Scottish rebels. For his brave deeds, King Duncan intended to confer upon him the lands of the rebellious thane of Cawdor.

But before Macbeth saw the king, he and his friend Banquo met the three weird witches upon the dark moor. The wild and frightful women greeted Macbeth by first calling him thane of Glamis, then thane of Cawdor, and finally, King of Scotland. Too, they prophesied that Banquo's heirs would reign in Scotland in years to come.

When Macbeth tried to question the three hags, they vanished. Macbeth thought very little about the strange prophecy until he met one of Duncan's messengers, who told him that he was now thane of Cawdor. This piece of news stunned Macbeth, and he turned to Banquo to confirm the witches' prophecy. But Banquo, unduped by the witches, thought them evil enough to betray Macbeth by whetting his ambition and tricking him into fulfilling the prophecy. Macbeth did not heed Banquo's warning; the words of the witches as they called him king had gone deep into his soul. He pondered over the possibility of becoming a monarch and set his whole heart on the attainment of this goal. If he could be thane of Cawdor, perhaps he could rule all of Scotland as well. But as it was now, Duncan was king, with two sons to rule after him. The problem was great. Macbeth shook off his ambitious dreams to go with Banquo to greet Duncan.

A perfect ruler, Duncan was kind, majestic, gentle, strong; Macbeth was fond of him. But when Duncan mentioned that his son, Malcolm, would succeed him on the throne, Macbeth saw the boy as an obstacle in his own path, and he hardly dared admit to himself how this impediment disturbed him.

On a royal procession, Duncan announced that he would spend one night at Macbeth's castle. Lady Macbeth, who knew of the witches' prophecy, was even more ambitious than her husband, and she saw Duncan's visit as a perfect opportunity for Macbeth to become king. She determined that he should murder Duncan and usurp the throne.

That night there was much feasting in the castle. After everyone was asleep, Lady Macbeth told her husband of her plan for the king's murder. Horrified at first, Macbeth refused to do the deed. But on being accused of cowardice by his wife, and having bright prospects of his future dangled before his eyes, Macbeth finally succumbed to her demands. He stole into the sleeping king's chamber and plunged a knife into his heart.

The murder was blamed on two grooms whom Lady Macbeth had smeared with Duncan's blood while they were asleep. But the deed was hardly without suspicion in the castle, and when the murder was revealed, the dead king's sons fled — Malcolm to England, Donalbain to Ireland. Macbeth was proclaimed king. But Macduff, a nobleman who had been Duncan's close friend, also carefully noted the murder, and when Macbeth was crowned king, Macduff suspected him of the bloody killing.

Macbeth began to have horrible dreams; his mind was never free from fear. Often he thought of the witches' second prophecy, that Banquo's heirs would hold the throne, and the prediction tormented him. Macbeth was so determined that Banquo would never share in his own hard-earned glory that he resolved to murder Banquo and his son, Fleance.

Lady Macbeth and her husband gave a great banquet for the noble thanes of Scotland. At the same time, Macbeth sent murderers to waylay Banquo and his son before they could reach the palace. Banquo was slain in the scuffle, but Fleance escaped. Meanwhile in the large banquet hall Macbeth pretended great sorrow that Banquo was not present. But Banquo was present in spirit, and his ghost majestically appeared in Macbeth's own seat. The startled king was so frightened that he almost betrayed his guilt when he alone saw the apparition. Lady Macbeth quickly led him away and dismissed the guests.

More frightened than ever, thinking of Banquo's ghost which had returned to haunt him, and of Fleance who had escaped but might one day claim the throne, Macbeth was so troubled that he determined to seek solace from the witches on the dismal heath. They assured Macbeth that he would not be overcome by man born of woman, nor until the forest of Birnam came to Dunsinane Hill. They warned him to beware of Macduff. When Macbeth asked if Banquo's children would reign over the kingdom, the witches disappeared. The news they gave him brought him cheer. Macbeth felt he need fear no man, since all were born of women, and certainly the great Birnam forest could not be moved by human power.

Then Macbeth heard that Macduff was gathering a hostile army in England, an army to be led by Malcolm, Duncan's son, who was determined to avenge his father's murder. So terrified was Macbeth that he resolved to murder Macduff's wife and children in order to bring the rebel to submission. After this slaughter, however, Macbeth was more than ever tormented by fear; his twisted mind had almost reached the breaking point, and he longed for death to release him from his nightmarish existence.

Before long Lady Macbeth's strong will broke. Dark dreams of murder and violence drove her to madness. The horror of her crimes and the agony of being hated and feared by all of Macbeth's subjects made her so ill that her death seemed imminent.

On the eve of Macduff's attack on Macbeth's castle, Lady Macbeth died, depriving her husband of all courage she had given him in the past. Rallying, Macbeth summoned strength to meet his enemy. Meanwhile, Birnam wood had moved, for Malcolm's soldiers were hidden behind cut green boughs, which from a distance appeared to be a moving forest. Macduff, enraged by the slaughter of his innocent family, was determined to meet Macbeth in hand-to-hand conflict.

Macbeth went out to battle filled with the false courage given him by the witches' prophecy that no man born of woman would overthrow him. Meeting Macduff, Macbeth began to fight him, taunting him at the same time about his having been born of woman. But Macduff had been ripped alive from his mother's womb. The prophecy was fulfilled. Macbeth fought with waning strength, all hope of victory gone, and Macduff, with a flourish, severed the head of the bloody King of Scotland.

McTEAGUE

Type of work: Novel
Author: Frank Norris (1870-1902)
Type of plot: Naturalism
Time of plot: 1890's
Locale: San Francisco and Death Valley
First published: 1899

Principal characters:
McTEAGUE, a dentist
TRINA, his wife
MARCUS SCHOULER, McTeague's friend and Trina's cousin

Critique:

McTeague, generally considered the best of Norris' novels, falls into the category of naturalism, a mode popular in the early 1900's. Two characteristics of this school were the hero of much brawn and few brains, and the influences of heredity and environment upon character. McTeague, Trina, and Marcus are drawn inevitably to catastrophe through their own inherited qualities acted upon by environmental forces. The novel is at once powerful and terrifying.

The Story:

McTeague, born in a small mining town, worked with his unambitious father in the mines. But his mother saw in her son a chance to realize her own dreams. The opportunity to send him away for a better education came a few years after McTeague's father had died. A traveling dentist was prevailed upon to take the boy as an apprentice.

McTeague learned something of dentistry, but he was too stupid to understand much of it. When his mother died and left him a small sum of money, he set up his own practice in an office-bedroom in San Francisco. McTeague was easily satisfied. He had his concertina for amusement and enough money from his practice to keep him well supplied with beer.

In the flat above McTeague lived his friend, Marcus Schouler. Marcus was in love with his cousin, Trina Sieppe, whom he brought to McTeague for some dental work. While they were waiting for McTeague to finish with a patient, the cleaning woman sold Trina a lottery ticket.

McTeague immediately fell in love with Trina. Marcus, realizing his friend's attachment, rather enjoyed playing the martyr, setting aside his own love in order that McTeague might feel free to court Trina. He invited the dentist to go with him to call on the Sieppe family. From that day on McTeague was a steady visitor at the Sieppe home. To celebrate their engagement, McTeague took Trina and her family to the theater. Afterward they returned to McTeague's flat, to find the building in an uproar. Trina's lottery ticket had won five thousand dollars.

In preparation for their wedding, Trina was furnishing a flat across from McTeague's office. When she decided to invest her winnings and collect the monthly interest, the dentist was disappointed, for he had hoped to spend the money on something lavish and exciting. But Trina's wishes prevailed. With that income and McTeague's earnings, as well as the little that Trina earned from her hand-carved animals, the McTeagues could be assured of a comfortable life.

Marcus slowly changed in his attitude toward his friend and his cousin. One day he accused McTeague of stealing Trina's affection for the sake of the five thousand dollars. In his fury he struck at his old friend with a knife. McTeague was not hurt, but his anger was thoroughly aroused.

In the early months after their wedding, McTeague and Trina were extremely happy. Trina was tactful in the changes she began to make in her husband. Gradually she improved his manners and appearance. They both planned for the time when they could afford a home of their own. Because of those plans they had their first real quarrel. McTeague wanted to rent a nearby house, but Trina objected to the high rent. Her thriftiness was slowly turning into miserliness. When McTeague, unknown to her, rented the house, she refused to move or to contribute to the payment of the first month's rent which signing of the lease entailed.

Some days later they went on a picnic to which Marcus was also invited. Outwardly he and McTeague had settled their differences, but jealousy still rankled in Marcus. When some wrestling matches were held, Marcus and the dentist were the winners in their bouts. It now remained for the two winners to compete. No match for the brute strength of McTeague, Marcus was thrown. Furious, he demanded another match. In that match Marcus suddenly leaned forward and bit off the lobe of the dentist's ear. McTeague broke Marcus' arm in his anger.

Marcus soon left San Francisco. Shortly thereafter an order from City Hall disbarred McTeague from his practice because he lacked college training. Marcus had informed the authorities.

Trina and McTeague moved from their flat to a tiny room on the top floor of the building, for the loss of McTeague's practice had made Trina more niggardly than ever. McTeague found a job making dental supplies. Trina devoted almost every waking moment to her animal carvings. She allowed herself and the room to become slovenly, she begrudged every penny they spent, and when McTeague lost his job she insisted that they move to even cheaper

lodgings. McTeague began to drink, and drinking made him vicious. When he was drunk, he would pinch or bite Trina until she gave him money for more whiskey.

The new room into which they moved was filthy and cramped. McTeague grew more and more surly. One morning he left to go fishing and failed to return. That night, while Trina was searching the streets for him, he broke into her trunk and stole her hoarded savings. After his disappearance Trina learned that the paint she used on her animals had infected her hand. The fingers of her right hand were amputated.

Trina took a job as a scrub woman, and the money she earned together with the interest from her five thousand dollars was sufficient to support her. Now that the hoard of money that she had saved was gone, she missed the thrill of counting over the coins, and so she withdrew the whole of her five thousand dollars from the bank and hid the coins in her room. One evening there was a tap on her window. McTeague was standing outside, hungry and without a place to sleep. Trina angrily refused to let him in. A few evenings later, drunk and vicious, he broke into a room she was cleaning. When she refused to give him any money, he beat her until she fell unconscious. She died early next morning.

McTeague took her money and went back to the mines, where he fell in with another prospector. But McTeague was haunted by the thought that he was being followed. One night he stole away from his companion and started south across Death Valley. The next day, as he was resting, he was suddenly accosted by a man with a gun. The man was Marcus.

A posse had been searching for McTeague ever since Trina's body had been found, and as soon as Marcus heard about the murder he volunteered for the manhunt. While the two men stood facing each other in the desert, Mc-

Teague's mule ran away, carrying on its back a canteen bag of water. Marcus emptied his gun to kill the animal, but its dead body fell on the canteen bag and the water was lost. The five thousand dollars was also lashed to the back of the mule. As McTeague went to unfasten it, Marcus seized him. In the struggle McTeague killed his enemy with his bare hands. But as he slipped to the ground, Marcus managed to snap one handcuff to McTeague's wrist, the other to his own. McTeague looked stupidly around, at the hills about a hundred miles away, and at the dead body to which he was helplessly chained. He was trapped in the parching inferno of the desert that stretched away on every side.

MADAME BOVARY

Type of work: Novel
Author: Gustave Flaubert (1821-1880)
Type of plot: Psychological realism
Time of plot: Mid-nineteenth century
Locale: France
First published: 1857

Principal characters:
CHARLES BOVARY, a provincial doctor
EMMA, his wife
LÉON DUPUIS, a young lawyer
RODOLPHE BOULANGER, a wealthy landowner

Critique:

Flaubert's genius lay in his infinite capacity for taking pains, and *Madame Bovary*, so true in its characterizations, so vivid in its setting, so convincing in its plot, is ample testimony to the realism of his work. This novel was one of the first of its type to come out of France, and its truth shocked contemporary readers. Condemned on the one hand for picturing the life of a romantic adulteress, he was acclaimed on the other for the honesty and skill with which he handled his subject. Flaubert does not permit Emma Bovary to escape the tragedy which she brings upon herself. Emma finds diversion from the monotony of her life, but she finds it at the loss of her own self-respect. The truth of Emma's struggle is universal and challenging.

The Story:

Charles Bovary was a student of medicine who married for his own advancement a woman much older than himself. She made his life miserable with her nagging and groundless suspicions. One day Charles was called to the bedside of M. Rouault, who had a broken leg, and there he met the farmer's daughter, Emma, a beautiful but restless girl whose early education in a French convent had given her an overwhelming thirst for broader experience. Charles found his patient an excellent excuse to see Emma, whose charm and grace had captivated the young doctor. But his whining wife, Héloise, soon began to suspect the true

reason for his visits to the Rouault farm. She heard rumors that in spite of Emma's peasant background, the girl conducted herself like a gentlewoman. Angry and tearful, Héloise made Charles swear that he would not visit the Rouault home again. Then Héloise's fortune was found to be non-existent. There was a violent quarrel over her deception and a stormy scene between her and the parents of Charles brought on an attack of an old illness. Héloise died quickly and quietly.

Charles felt guilty because he had so few regrets at his wife's death. At old Rouault's invitation, he went once more to the farm and again fell under the influence of Emma's charms. As old Rouault watched Charles fall more deeply in love with his daughter, he decided that the young doctor was dependable and perfectly respectable, and so he forced the young man's hand, told Charles he could have Emma in marriage, and gave the couple his blessing.

During the first weeks of marriage Emma occupied herself with changing their new home, and busied herself with every household task she could think of to keep herself from being utterly disillusioned. Emma realized that even though she thought she was in love with Charles, the rapture which should have come with marriage had not arrived. All the romantic books she had read during her early years had led her to expect more from marriage than she received, and the dead calm of her feelings was a bitter disappointment. The intimacy of marriage disgusted her. Instead of a perfumed, handsome lover in velvet and lace, she found herself tied to a dull-witted husband who reeked of medicines and drugs.

As she was about to give up all hope of finding any joy in her new life, a noble patient whom Charles had treated invited them to a ball at his chateau. At the ball Emma danced with a dozen partners, tasted champagne, and received compliments on her beauty. The contrast between the life of the Bovarys and that of the nobleman was painfully evident. Emma became more and more discontented with Charles. His futile and clumsy efforts to please her only made her despair at his lack of understanding. She sat by her window, dreamed of Paris, moped, and became ill.

Hoping a change would improve her condition, Charles took Emma to Yonville, where he set up a new practice and Emma prepared for the birth of a child.

When her daughter was born, Emma's chief interest in the child was confined to laces and ribbons for its dresses. The child was sent to a wet nurse, where Emma visited her, and where, accidentally, she met Léon Dupuis, a law clerk bored with the town and seeking diversion. Charmed with the youthful mother, he walked home with her in the twilight, and Emma found him sympathetic to her romantic ideas about life. Later Léon visited the Bovarys in company with Homais, the town chemist. Homais held little soirees at the local inn, to which he invited the townsfolk. There Emma's acquaintance with Léon ripened. The townspeople gossiped about the couple, but Charles Bovary was not acute enough to sense the interest Emma took in Léon.

Bored with Yonville and tired of loving in vain, Léon went to Paris to complete his studies. Broken-hearted, Emma deplored her weakness in not giving herself to Léon, fretted in her boredom, and once more made herself ill.

She had not time to become as melancholy as she was before, however, for a stranger, Rodolphe Boulanger, came to town. One day he brought his farm tenant to Charles for bloodletting. Rodolphe, an accomplished lover, saw in Emma a promise of future pleasure. When he began his suit, Emma realized that if she gave herself to him her surrender would be immoral. But she rationalized her doubts by convincing herself that nothing as romantic and beautiful as love could be sinful.

Deceiving Charles, Emma met Rodolphe, rode over the countryside with him, listened to his urgent avowals of love, and finally succumbed to his persuasive appeals. At first she felt guilty, but later she identified herself with adulterous heroines of fiction and believed that, like them, she had known true romance. Sure of Emma's love, Rodolphe no longer found it necessary to continue his gentle lover's tricks. He no longer bothered to maintain punctuality in his meetings with Emma; and though he continued to see her, she began to suspect that his passion was dwindling.

Meanwhile Charles became involved in Homais' attempt to cure a boy of a clubfoot with a machine Charles had designed. Both Homais and Charles were convinced that the success of their operation would raise their future standing in the community. But after weeks of torment, the boy contracted gangrene, and his leg had to be amputated. Homais' reputation was undamaged, for he was by profession a chemist, but Bovary, a doctor, was looked upon with suspicion. His practice began to fall away.

Disgusted with Charles' failure, Emma, in an attempt to hold Rodolphe, scorned her past virtue, spent money recklessly on jewelry and clothes, and involved her husband deeply in debt. She finally secured Rodolphe's word that he would take her away, but on the very eve of what was to be her escape she received from him a letter so hypocritically repentant of their sin that she read it with sneers. Then, in horror over the realization that she had lost him, she almost threw herself from the window. She was saved when Charles called to her. But she became gravely ill with brain-fever, and lay near death for several months.

Her convalescence was slow, but she was finally well enough to go to Rouen to the theater. The tender love scenes behind the footlights made Emma breathless with envy. Once more, she dreamed of romance. In Rouen she met Léon Dupuis again.

This time Léon was determined to possess Emma. He listened to her complaints with sympathy, soothed her, and took her driving. Emma, whose thirst for romance still consumed her, yielded herself to Léon with regret that she had not done so before.

Charles Bovary grew concerned over his increasing debts. In addition to his own financial worries, his father died, leaving his mother in ignorance about the family estate. Emma used the excuse of procuring a lawyer for her mother-in-law to visit Léon in Rouen, where he had set up a practice. At his suggestion she secured a power of attorney from Charles, a document which left her free to spend his money without his knowledge of her purchases.

Finally, in despair over his debts, the extent of which Emma only partly revealed, Charles took his mother into his confidence and promised to destroy Emma's power of attorney. Deprived of her hold over Charles' finances and unable to repay her debts, Emma threw herself upon Léon's mercy with all disregard for caution. Her corruption was so complete that she had to seek release and pleasure or go out of her mind.

In her growing degradation, Emma began to realize that she had brought her lover down with her. She no longer respected him, and she scorned his faithfulness when he was unable to give her money she needed to pay her bills. When her name was posted publicly for a debt of several thousand francs, the bailiff prepared to sell Charles' property to settle her creditors' claims. Charles was out of town when the debt was posted, and Emma, in one final act of self-abasement, appealed to Rodolphe for help. He, too, refused to lend her money.

Knowing that the framework of lies with which she had deceived Charles was about to collapse, Emma Bovary resolved to die a heroine's death and swallowed arsenic bought at Homais' shop. Charles, returning from his trip, arrived too late to save her from a slow, painful death.

Charles, pitiful in his grief, could barely endure the sounds of the hammer as her coffin was nailed shut. Later, feeling that his pain over Emma's death had grown less, he opened her desk, to find there the carefully collected love letters of Léon and Rodolphe. Broken with the knowledge of his wife's infidelity, scourged with debt, and helpless in his disillusionment, Charles died soon after his wife, leaving a legacy of only twelve francs for the support of his orphaned daughter. The Bovary tragedy was complete.

MADEMOISELLE DE MAUPIN

Type of work: Novel
Author: Théophile Gautier (1811-1872)
Type of plot: Sentimental romance
Time of plot: Early nineteenth century
Locale: France
First published: 1835

Principal characters:
  M. D'ALBERT, a young esthete
  ROSETTE, his mistress
  THÉODORE DE SÉRANNES, in reality Mademoiselle Madelaine de Maupin

Critique:

France, in the 1830's, was going through one of those occasional periods of high morality which at intervals excite the world, and Gautier, disgusted with the hypocrisy of many of the period's defenders, wrote this romance of passion as his challenge to the period. In a long and boastful preface he pleads the cause of moral freedom in art. The novel is highly sensual, its plot based partly on history and partly on Shakespeare's *As You Like It.*

The Story:

D'Albert was a young Frenchman of twenty-two, handsome, well-educated, artistic, and well-versed in the affairs of the world. He loved beauty, especially female beauty. All his life he had dreamed of women, but he had never met the girl of his dreams, who would combine the beauty of a Ruben's nude with that of a Titian nude. It was little wonder that he had not found her.

The one thing lacking in d'Albert's life was a mistress. One day his friend de C—— offered to take him around the town and discourse on the various ladies of his acquaintance so that d'Albert could make a choice. The expedition was a delightful one, as de C—— seemed to have precise and full information on every beauty, not only on her outward circumstances, but also on the very quality of her mind. D'Albert, after some hesitation, finally decided to lay siege to Rosette, a beautiful young woman who seemed the most likely to bring

his romantic and poetic mind down to earth.

It did not take d'Albert long to win the love of Rosette, and they were soon acknowledged lovers. Rosette was pliable, versatile, and always entertaining. She did not let d'Albert alone long enough for him to go off into musing daydreams. Variety was the spice of their love.

For five months the two continued to be the happiest of lovers, but at last d'Albert began to tire of Rosette. As soon as she noticed the cooling of his ardor, Rosette knew that she must do something different if she wished to keep his love. If he were growing tired of her in the solitary life they were leading, perhaps he would regain his interest if he saw her among a group of people. For this reason Rosette took d'Albert to her country estate for a visit. There she planned parties, dinners, and visits to keep him amused, but he remained bored.

One day a visitor, an old friend of Rosette, arrived. The guest was an extremely handsome young man named Théodore de Sérannes, whose conversation, riding, and swordsmanship all entranced d'Albert. The two men met every day and went hunting together, and the more d'Albert saw of Théodore the more fascinated he became. In time d'Albert was forced to admit to himself that he was in love with Théodore.

He was in love with a man, and yet he always thought of him as a woman. D'Albert's mind grew sick with the

2159

problem of Théodore's true identity. Some days he would be sure that Théodore was a woman in disguise. Then, seeing him fencing or jumping his horse, d'Albert would be forced to conclude that Théodore was a man. Rosette, he knew, was also in love with Théodore, and her infatuation kept her from noticing d'Albert's interest in the same young man.

One day d'Albert mentioned that his favorite play was Shakespeare's *As You Like It.* The rest of the company immediately decided to present the play. At first Rosette was chosen for the part of Rosalind, the heroine who dressed as a man in order to escape from her uncle, but when she refused to wear men's clothes the part was given to Théodore.

As soon as d'Albert saw Théodore dressed in woman's clothes, he guessed rightly that Théodore really was a woman. What he did not know was that Théodore, who was really named Madelaine de Maupin, had decided that she would have nothing to do with men until she had found a good and noble lover. She knew that as a woman she would have no chance to see men as they really were, and so she had hit upon the device of learning about them by dressing as a man. But she had found perfidy and falseness in every man she met. Mademoiselle de Maupin had with amusement seen d'Albert fall in love with her, and she had watched the tortures of his mind when he could not decide whether she was male or female.

As the rehearsals of the play went on, the parallels between the play and real life became even more amusing to both d'Albert and Mademoiselle de Maupin. At last, after the play had been presented, d'Albert wrote Mademoiselle de Maupin a letter. In it he said that he was sure she was a woman, and that he loved her deeply.

She took so long to reply to his letter that d'Albert again became afraid that she really was a man. One night, however, as d'Albert stood at a window a hand gently touched his shoulder. He looked around and beheld Mademoiselle de Maupin dressed in her costume as Rosalind. He was struck dumb with amazement. Mademoiselle de Maupin told him her story, and said that since he was the first man to see through her disguise, he should be the man to first have her as a woman.

That night d'Albert learned that she was truly the woman of his dreams. In the morning he found himself alone. Mademoiselle de Maupin had gone, leaving a letter in which she told d'Albert and Rosette that they would never see her again. She wrote to d'Albert that they had known one perfect night. She had answered his dream, and to fulfill a dream once was enough. Her letter ended by telling d'Albert to try to console Rosette for the love she had wasted on the false Théodore, and she hoped that the two would be very happy for many years to come.

THE MADRAS HOUSE

Type of work: Drama
Author: Harley Granville-Barker (1877-1946)
Type of plot: Social criticism
Time of plot: Early twentieth century
Locale: London
First presented: 1910

Principal characters:
HENRY HUXTABLE
KATHERINE, his wife
CONSTANTINE MADRAS, Katherine's brother
AMELIA MADRAS, his wife
PHILIP MADRAS, their son
JESSICA, Philip's wife
MAJOR HIPPISLY THOMAS, Philip's friend
MARION YATES, an employee at the Madras House
EUSTACE PERRIN STATE, an American, a prospective buyer of the
Madras House
MISS CHANCELLOR, and
MR. BRIGSTOCK, also employees at the Madras House

Critique:

The Madras House is a dramatic work still interesting in the contemporary theater. A problem play of the type popularized by Ibsen and Shaw at the turn of the century, it attempts to deal realistically with several related themes: the contrast between sexual honesty and sexual hypocrisy, the contrast between bourgeois respectability and real honesty in human dealings, the inevitability of social change even in connection with a long-established commercial institution like the Madras House, and the contrast in all personal relations between expressed motive and real motive. As in his other works, the playwright asked his audiences to think about themselves and the standards of the world which they at the time were far too likely to take for granted. If Granville-Barker's dramas seem a little old-fashioned to some persons today, the causes are simple: we enjoy certain freedoms because the characters on his stage talked about them at length. Further, we have had full experience of enjoying those freedoms and find that pursuit of them may at one and the same time free us from old restrictions and plunge us into new ones, ambiguities of human action that the author of The Madras House did not foresee.

The Story:

Henry Huxtable, his wife, and six spinster daughters lived in dreary middle-class respectability, supported by the income from a great store, the Madras House. Their lives were in sharp contrast to that of the sales persons who were required to "live in" at store dormitories closely supervised to make sure that the store was actually as respectable as it seemed to be. Another owner was Constantine Madras, Katherine Huxtable's brother, who had retreated from England and respectability and had lived for many years in Moslem countries.

The time had come for the sale of the Madras House; such a sale had been necessitated by confusion in family affairs. On an October Sunday, Philip Madras, Constantine's son, heard that his father had returned to England, and he was distressed by this news of the reappearance of the elderly black sheep. But this was not the only problem that Philip wished to discuss with his uncle, Henry Huxtable. The morale of the store had been upset by the discovery that one of the closely supervised girls at the store, Marion Yates, was pregnant. It was suspected that her betrayer was Mr. Brigstock, another sales person, for he had been seen kissing the disgraced girl. The old immorality of Constantine—who, it was soon learned, had lived as the master of a harem in Arabia—and the current immorality of Marion were threats to what the Huxtables called decency.

First, the Marion Yates situation was inquired into. It was immediately apparent that the young woman would refuse to name the father of her child. Instead, she planned to bear it and bring it up as her nephew or niece; the child, at least, would not be affected by family pressures for which the Huxtables stood.

Another problem that came up concerned the prospective buyer of the store, an American named State. Mr. State distressed everyone by talking in excessively naïve terms. All his phrases—such as "the Needs of the Gentler Sex" and "Woman's Noble Instinct to Perpetuate the Race"— seemed to come from his mouth in capital letters; he was a grotesque representative of an early stage of modern advertising. Furthermore, he insultingly believed that his methods were in advance of British ones and that his presence in England would change for the better the English system of merchandising.

To State's unconscious hypocrisy and to the self-conscious respectability of the Huxtables, Constantine Madras opposed himself and his own nature. At great length he defended his own pattern of life, one in which man was free to do what he liked and in which woman learned to like what man did. He pointed out that Arabian culture had not been feminized and intellectualized as, he claimed, had happened in England. To all such remarks, his hearers lent a shocked ear.

A further complication arose when Philip learned that he had a problem of his own: his wife Jessica felt neglected and was ready to fall in love with Philip's best friend, Major Thomas. For the first time Philip was forced to recognize that his wife was a woman and an individual as well as a wife. His reaction to Jessica's problem was complicated by the fact that he felt contempt for sentimentalities displayed during his mother's fruitless interview with her estranged husband Constantine.

Philip's moderately respectable soul was still more disturbed when he learned that his father was the father of Marion Yates's unborn child. But Constantine did not blush at this revelation; he merely demanded care and protection for Marion and favored the company with a discourse on English priggishness. But Constantine, in turn, was distressed when Marion refused any assistance from him. Confused by her lack of social docility and feminine meekness, Constantine retreated to a cab and, eventually, to his Arabian household.

Still unresolved was the relationship between Philip and his wife. He finally recognized her as a person. To please her as well as himself, he gave up his interest in the Madras House, leaving it to Mr. State, the American. His plan was to talk matters over with his wife and to engage in activities useful to society. Both he and Jessica found themselves united by a hope that they could work together to improve the conditions of a faulty society which the sale of the Madras House had called to their attention.

THE MADWOMAN OF CHAILLOT

Type of work: Drama
Author: Jean Giraudoux (1882-1944)
Time: A little before noon in the spring of next year
Locale: The Chaillot District of Paris
First presented: 1945

Principal characters:
COUNTESS AURELIA, the Madwoman of Chaillot
MME. CONSTANCE, the Madwoman of Passy
MLLE. GABRIELLE, the Madwoman of St. Sulpice
MME. JOSEPHINE, the Madwoman of La Concorde
THE RAGPICKER
THE PRESIDENT
THE BARON
THE BROKER
THE PROSPECTOR

In *The Madwoman of Chaillot,* Jean Giraudoux orchestrates three of his most constantly recurring themes: the inscrutability of woman, the love of humanity, and the abhorrence of materialism. For one who is familiar with all of Giraudoux's plays, the anti-war theme is implied in the latter. Stylistically, Giraudoux employs two of his favorite devices: the fantastic parable and the duality of character. The resulting impact of *The Madwoman of Chaillot* is that it possesses a remarkable unity of both form and idea, the unifying theme being the writer's love and faith in the triumph of the human entity in a time of despair.

As in several of Giraudoux's other plays, *The Madwoman of Chaillot* extends into the realm of fantasy, leaving irritating reality far behind. It differs from his other plays, however, in that it involves some forty acting parts and depends to some extent upon mere motion rather than upon typical plot complications for its effect.

The basic framework of the plot is simple. A mighty syndicate of financiers wishes to exploit the untouched deposits of oil under the streets of Paris, and they ignore humanity, beauty, and truth in the process. The free souls of Paris oppose them and eventually triumph by literally removing them from the scene.

In depicting the opposing forces in the battle for humanity, Giraudoux has weighted the scales in favor of the human element. On the one side are Presidents, Prospectors, Barons, Press Agents, Brokers, and Ladies of the Street. On the other side are the Waiter, the Little Man, the Street Singer, the Flower Girl, the Shoelace Peddlar, the Ragpicker, and other folk. In the middle, and significantly devoted to the gentle souls, is the Madwoman of Chaillot, aided by her compatriots, the Madwomen of Passy, St. Sulpice, and La Concorde. The capitalistic forces are stereotypes who function as well-oiled machinery; they are devoid of characteristics which would set them apart or elicit for them the least bit of empathic reaction. The people of Paris are all recognizable types, but each possesses some quality of individuality. Their vocations are of little concern; what matters is their love of life and mankind. The situation is basically mad, for the forces are utterly extreme.

The Madwoman tips the scales. She is both mad and frighteningly sane. Hers is an almost obligatory characterization, and Giraudoux has constructed the fabric of Countess Aurelia in such a fashion as to envelop the viewer in the sheer logic of her reasoning, making him captive of her every move. At the same time he suspends his belief in the situation through its sheer madness, so that a detachment from reality is effected. (Giraudoux's plays usually abound in under-

2163

stated truths made in situations of extreme agitation or tension.) He endows Countess Aurelia with telling powers of observation. Her comments are frequently so simply and mercilessly clear and true that we wish we might have said them ourselves. But our sanity renders us incapable of such guileless simplicity.

A less facile playwright than Giraudoux might easily have succumbed to the practice of constructing the parable with idealized characters lacking reality and acting within a metaphysical framework. Or another writer might have developed the situation realistically, carefully couching his thesis among the intricacies of plot and character relationships. Although *The Madwoman of Chaillot* is not exactly a compromise between these two extremes, Giraudoux employs the best techniques of both. In this play he shows the value of revealing two levels of thought within the same character.

Countess Aurelia's very insanity is sane, for she is caught up in a moment of fantastic ideals, of powerful and inhuman forces, of incredible economic stratagems which require sanity of a kind. Success ignores life and beauty in a headlong momentum toward some indefinable goal. The mad countess has captured and held her sanity in an attempt to love life and beauty to the fullest. For this gentle woman, time has stopped when life was at its loveliest.

The Madwoman encounters the menace in the form of the President, the Baron, the Prospector, and the Broker at a sidewalk café in the Chaillot district. Her friends are all aware that something terrible is afoot and inform her of the plot to drill for oil beneath the streets. The Prospector has sent his agent with a bomb to destroy the city architect, the only obstacle to the drilling. Pierre, the young assassin, is rescued by the Policeman as he is about to throw himself into the river rather than carry out his task. He is revived and convinced by the Madwoman that life is really worth living.

It is apparent to the Madwoman that the only way to combat the encroachment of the materialistic interests is to annihilate them. Because she and her friends have little chance of opposing them if commonly interpreted methods of justice were used, she decides upon an infallible plan and sends her confederates scurrying about on errands to help her carry it out.

She retires to her quarters in the Rue de Chaillot where she will receive the delegation of capitalists. They dare not resist her invitation, for she has informed them that a large deposit of oil rests under her basement. To prove it, she has prepared a sample; a bottle of mixed kerosene and mange cure is waiting for the Prospector, who professes to be able to detect the existence of oil deposits by merely sniffing the air.

Some years before, the Madwoman had rescued a Sewer Man who promised to show her a secret entrance from her basement into the sewers of Paris. She summons him now and he willingly presses the stone concealing the entrance. The other Madwomen, Mme. Constance, who takes her invisible lap dog with her everywhere; Mlle. Gabrielle, who talks to nonexistent friends; and Mme. Josephine, who is an expert at jurisprudence because her brother-in-law was a lawyer, all arrive for a delightful tea scene. They are indeed mad, but this in no way prejudices the trial which follows.

Mme. Josephine is called upon to conduct a court, for it is only just and proper that the financiers have a fair hearing before they are sent to oblivion. The Ragpicker agrees to speak in their defense, and a damning testimony it is, with money at the root of this materialistic evil. The verdict of the tribunal is unanimous; the accused are guilty on all charges. The Madwoman may proceed with the extermination.

The guests begin to arrive, and in a wonderful scene of comic irony each group in turn is sent through the door into the sewer. First come the Presidents, next the Prospectors, then the Press

Agents, and so on until all, like sheep, have followed the infallible nose of the Prospector down the dark stairway, never to return again.

Immediately all the wrongs of the world are righted. Giraudoux ends his play with a paean to the Madwoman of Chaillot and to life itself. The pigeons fly again; the air is pure; the sky is clear; grass sprouts on the pavements; complete strangers are shaking hands. Humanity has been saved, and the friends of friendship thank the Madwoman, the triumphant feminine force, who expresses Giraudoux's philosophy in a simple statement that any sensible woman can set right in the course of a single afternoon whatever is wrong in this muddled world.

MAGGIE: A GIRL OF THE STREETS

Type of work: Novel
Author: Stephen Crane (1871-1900)
Type of plot: Social criticism
Time of plot: Late nineteenth century
Locale: New York
First published: 1893

> *Principal characters:*
> MAGGIE, a girl of the slums
> JIMMY, her brother
> PETE, Jimmy's friend and Maggie's lover
> THE MOTHER

Critique:

The importance of *Maggie* is primarily historical, for it was the first novel to deal realistically and straightforwardly with the sordid life of the slums. It is, therefore, the first naturalistic novel in America of any real value, and in spite of its many faults of style and structure it gave rise to the naturalistic fiction of our day. For this contribution to our literature we owe Stephen Crane a great debt.

The Story:

In the slum section of New York City, Maggie and her two brothers grew up in the squalor and corruption, both moral and physical, of that poverty-stricken area. Her father usually came home from work drunk, and her mother, too, was fond of the bottle. The children were neglected. When the drunken parents ranted at each other, the children hid in terror under the table or the bed.

Somehow Maggie managed to remain untouched by that sordidness. Her younger brother died. Jimmy, her older brother, went to work after the father died. He fought, drank, and had many affairs with women. From time to time he was hounded by some of the women, who demanded support for themselves and the illegitimate children he had fathered. Jimmy brushed them aside.

When Jimmy brought his best friend home with him, Maggie fell in love. Pete, a bartender, was handsome, flashy,

and exciting. One night he took her out to show her the night life of the city. Maggie's wonder knew no bounds, for to her the experience was the height of luxury. On the doorstep she allowed Pete to kiss her goodnight. Pete was disappointed, but not discouraged. He took Maggie out again. The next time she surrendered and went to live with him.

But Pete soon grew tired of Maggie, and she was compelled to return home. In furious indignation, her mother ordered her out of the house. She had done everything, the mother insisted, to bring Maggie up to be a fine, decent girl. She had been an excellent mother and had spared no pains to keep her daughter on the path of virtue. Now her daughter would be dead to her. The neighbors joined in, denouncing Maggie. Jimmy, the seducer of other men's sisters, became indignant. He and a companion went to the bar where Pete worked, intent upon beating him up. When they failed, Jimmy contented himself by shrugging his shoulders and condemning his sister.

Maggie was now homeless and penniless. She went to see Pete, but he sent her away, irritated and fearful lest he should lose his job. She turned to prostitution, plying her trade by night, accosting poor and wealthy alike. But she did not have much luck. One night she walked forlornly and unsuccessfully in the waterfront district. Resignedly she

MAGGIE: A GIRL OF THE STREETS, by Stephen Crane. By permission of the publishers, Alfred A. Knopf, Inc.

trudged on, toward the pier and the black, murky depths of the river.

A short time later, Jimmy came home from one of his prolonged absences. Maggie, the mother wailed, was dead. With the neighbors around her, she sobbed and moaned. What the Lord had given the Lord had taken away, the neighbors told her. Uncomforted, Maggie's mother shrieked that she forgave her daughter; oh yes, she forgave Maggie her sins.

THE MAGIC MOUNTAIN

Type of work: Novel
Author: Thomas Mann (1875-1955)
Type of plot: Philosophical chronicle
Time of plot: 1907-1914
Locale: Davos, Switzerland
First published: 1924

Principal characters:

HANS CASTORP, a German engineer
JOACHIM ZIEMSSEN, his cousin
SETTEMBRINI, a patient at Davos
NAPHTA, Settembrini's friend
CLAVDIA, Hans' friend

Critique:

The Magic Mountain is a novel concerned with perspectives of history and philosophy in our time. In it the modern age has become the International Sanatorium Berghof high in the Swiss Alps, and to this institution gravitate various and conflicting currents of thought and activity in the persons of a group of invalids exiled by disease to a pinnacle of the "magic mountain." The magic it exercises in their lives is to cut them off from calendar time. Time flows through their days and years with quiet nothingness and perceptions of reality stretch into eternity. Modern ideologies and beliefs are represented by characters like the Italian humanist, the absolutist Jewish Jesuit, a German doctor, a Polish scientist, and hedonistic Mynheer Peeperkorn. The magic mountain is the sick world of Europe, and its people are various aspects of the modern consciousness.

The Story:

Hans Castorp had been advised by his doctor to go to the mountains for a rest. Accordingly, he decided to visit his cousin, Joachim Ziemssen, who was a patient in the International Sanatorium Berghof at Davos-Platz in the mountains of Switzerland. He planned to stay there for three weeks and then return to his home in Hamburg. Hans had just passed his examinations and was now a qualified engineer; he was eager to get started in his career. His cousin was a soldier by profession. His cure at the sanatorium was almost complete. Hans thought Joachim looked robust and well.

At the sanatorium, Hans soon discovered that the ordinary notions of time did not exist. Day followed day almost unchangingly. He met the head of the institution, Dr. Behrens, as well as the other patients, who, at dinner, sat in groups. There were, for instance, two Russian tables, one of which was known to the patients as the bad Russian table. A couple who sat at the latter table had the room next to Hans. Through the thin partitions, he could hear them— even in the daytime—chase each other around the room. Hans was rather revolted, inasmuch as he could hear every detail of their love-making.

There was another patient who interested him greatly, a gay Russian woman, supposedly married, named Clavdia Cauchat. Every time she came into the dining-room she would bang the door, an act which annoyed Hans a great deal. Hans also met Settembrini, an Italian, a humanist writer and philosopher. Settembrini introduced him to a Jew, Naphta, who turned out to be a converted Jesuit and a cynical absolutist. Because the two men spent their time in endless discussions, Settembrini finally left the sanatorium to take rooms in the village, in the house where Naphta lodged.

THE MAGIC MOUNTAIN by Thomas Mann. Translated by H. T. Lowe-Porter. By permission of the author and the publishers, Alfred A. Knopf, Inc. Copyright, 1927, by Alfred A. Knopf, Inc.

From the very first day of his arrival, Hans felt feverish and a bit weak. When his three weeks were almost up, he decided to take a physical examination. The examination proved that he had tuberculosis. So he stayed on as a patient. One day, defying orders, he went out skiing and was caught in a snowstorm. The exposure aggravated his condition.

His interest in Clavdia was heightened when he learned that Dr. Behrens, who liked to dabble in art, had painted her picture. Further, the doctor gave Hans an X-ray plate of Clavdia's skeletal structure. The plate Hans kept on his bureau in his room.

Most of his free time he spent with Joachim or with Settembrini and Naphta. The Italian and the Jesuit were given to all sorts of ideas, and Hans became involved in a multitude of philosophical discussions on the duration of time, God, politics, astronomy, and the nature of reality. Joachim, who was rather humorless and unimaginative, did not enjoy those talks. But Hans, since he himself had become a patient at the sanatorium, felt more at home and was not quite so attached to Joachim. Besides, it was Clavdia who interested him.

On the occasion of a carnival, when some of the restrictions of the sanatorium had been lifted, Hans declared his love for Clavdia. She thought him foolish and refused his proposal. The next day she left for Russia. Hans was in despair and became listless. Joachim grew even more impatient with the progress of his cure when the doctor told him that he was not yet well and would have to remain on the mountain for six more months. Wanting to rejoin his regiment, Joachim, in defiance of the doctor's injunctions, left the sanatorium. The doctor told Hans that he could leave too; but Hans knew that the doctor was angry when he said it, and he remained.

Before long Joachim returned, his condition now so serious that his mother was summoned to the sanatorium. He died shortly afterward. Clavdia Cauchat also returned. She had been writing to the doctor and Hans had heard of her from time to time. But she did not return alone. As a protector, she had found an old Dutchman named Mynheer Peeperkorn, an earthy, hedonistic planter from Java. Hans became very friendly with Peeperkorn, who soon learned that the young engineer was in love with Clavdia. The discovery did not affect their friendship at all, a friendship that lasted until the Dutchman died.

For a time the guests amused themselves with spiritualist seances. A young girl, a new arrival at the sanatorium, claimed that she was able to summon anyone from the dead. Hans took part in one meeting and asked that Joachim be called back from the dead. But Dr. Krokowski, the psychologist at the sanatorium, was opposed to the seances and the sessions broke up. Then Naphta and Settembrini got into an argument. A duel was arranged between the two dialecticians. When the time came, the Italian said he would fire into the air. When he did so, Naphta became more furious than ever. Realizing that Settembrini would not shoot at him, Naphta turned the pistol on himself and pulled the trigger. Dying, he fell face downward in the snow.

Hans Castorp had come to the sanatorium for a visit of three weeks. That stay turned out to be more than seven years. During that time he saw many deaths, many changes in the institution. He became an old patient, not just a visitor. The sanatorium became another home in the high, thin air of the mountaintop. For him time, as measured by minutes, or even years, no longer existed. Time belonged to the flat, busy world below.

Then an Austrian archduke was assassinated. Newspapers brought the world suddenly to the International Sanatorium Berghof, with news of war declared and troop movements. Some of the patients remained in neutral Switzerland. Others packed to return home. Hans Castorp said goodbye to Settembrini, who was his best friend among the old patients, and the disillusioned humanist wept at their parting. Hans was going back to Germany to fight. Time, the tragic hour of his generation, had overtaken him at last, and the sanatorium was no longer his refuge. Dodging bullets and bombs in a front line trench, he disappeared into the smoky mists that hid the future of Europe.

MAGNALIA CHRISTI AMERICANA

Type of work: History
Author: Cotton Mather (1663-1728)
Time: 1620-1698
Locale: New England
First published: 1702

Cotton Mather's *Magnalia Christi Americana; or The Ecclesiastical History of New England from Its First Planting, in the Year 1620, Unto the Year of Our Lord 1698* is commonly referred to, and dismissed, as a fairly authoritative and substantial picture of the Puritan theocracy in New England. It is a history of Puritanism in the New World and much of it is true; but it is the product of a dogmatic, neurotic, tyrannical clergyman who failed to discriminate between facts and legends, the laws and the superstitions, of the early colonial period. Mather gives as much prominence and weight to accounts of witches and repentant criminals as he does to the biographies of church leaders, and the entire history is conditioned by the belief that God's will was done in early New England.

If the book is taken not as a history but as an impassioned product of the Puritan character in all of its dedication and its blindness, the experience of reading the book becomes a time-experiment by which one can gaze into the working of a mind three hundred years removed from our own. Great writers do not allow such strange, backward glimpses; their comments have a timelessness that makes their minds contemporary. But Mather is no great writer, and when he speaks he reveals himself as his times made him: pedantic, intemperate, and superstitious, yet an educated, religious man. From such personalities much of the distinctive character of America developed, and if the historian uses the *Magnalia* as source material for a study of the early American character and its formative influence, more will be gained than if the book is taken as simply an account of New England Calvinism in its beginnings.

Mather was pastor of the North Church in Boston only after the book appeared; during its writing he was assistant minister. He was a prolific writer, and critics generally agree in recognizing the quantity of his work without granting any worth, other than ordinary, to its literary quality.

The *Magnalia* is divided into two volumes; the first contains three books, the second, four. The first book, titled "Antiquities," reports, in Mather's words, "the design where-on, the manner where-in, and the people where-by the several colonies of New England were planted." The second book contains the lives of the governors and the names of the magistrates of New England, and the third presents the lives of "sixty famous divines." Volume II begins with an account of the history of Harvard College, proceeds to an account of the "acts and monuments" of the New England churches, their discipline and principles, then records a number of "illustrious discoveries and demonstrations of the Divine Providence"—including "sea-deliverances . . . remarkables done by thunder . . . an history of criminals, executed for capital crimes; with their dying speeches," —and concludes with "the wonders of the invisible world, in preternatural occurrences. . . ." The last book, "A Book of the Wars of the Lord," deals with early religious controversies, with the "molestations given to the churches of New England by that odd sect of people called Quakers," with impostors who pretended to be ministers, and with an account of the Indian wars.

The historical account of the discovery and founding of New England begins with a critical consideration of the claims of various countries as discoverers of the New World. Mather finally gives the

Cabots of England the credit for the discovery of the North American continent, but he declares that regardless of who first discovered America, it was the English who did the most for the new colonies.

Mather writes of the early settlements in Florida and Virginia and of their difficult days. He then provides a dramatized recital of the voyage of the *Mayflower*. The landing at Cape Cod is taken by Mather as a sign of God's providence; had the voyagers landed somewhere along the Hudson River, he declares, they would have been massacred by the Indians.

Mather's story of the founding of the various colonies is enlivened by zestful and partly imaginary accounts of Indian raids, of storms and droughts, and of quarrels with England and among the colonists themselves. The difficulties of the early settlers are interpreted as signs of God's providence working to produce men of strong faith in a new land. To the history of the establishment of the colonies and of churches within the colonies Mather attaches an "ecclesiastical map" which is a list of the congregations and ministers in the Plymouth, Massachusetts, and Connecticut colonies in 1696. The churches were erected, Mather writes, "on purpose to express and pursue the Protestant Reformation."

After some "historical remarks" on Boston, a lecture given in 1698 and designed to warn the Bostonians that their town had fallen on evil ways and that only with the help of God could it be returned to its former state of power and piety, Mather presents the lives of the governors of the colonies, commencing with William Bradford, governor of Plymouth colony. Other governors whose lives are included are John Winthrop, governor of Massachusetts colony; Edward Hopkins, the first governor of Connecticut colony; Theophilus Eaton, governor of New Haven colony; John Winthrop (the son), governor of Connecticut and New Haven, and other successors.

His stories of the clergy are so punctuated with moralizing passages and anecdotes that it is difficult to distinguish one divine from another. Despite Mather's pious tone, it is possible to appreciate the courage and religious devotion of the colonial ministers.

Mather is at his informative best in recording the decisions of the early churchmen concerning matters of faith. He objected to the opinion that the churches of New England simply followed the doctrines professed in England. A copy is given of the "Confession of Faith" agreed upon at Boston on May 12, 1680. The predominant feature of the document is the declaration of reliance on Holy Scripture, which is taken to be the word of God, interpretable by reference to the Scripture itself. Man's corruption is definitely admitted and is related to the fall of Adam, as seduced by Satan. Christ is the mediator between God and man. Man has free will, but since he does not always will the good, he is a sinner, to be saved only by the grace of God. The laws of God are for the direction of man, but they do not bind God Himself. The report of these points of dogma is supplemented by an account of the practices of the churches concerning such matters as church membership, election of officers, ordination, and the communion of churches with one another.

Mather becomes more human, almost gay, in the section titled "Remarkables of the Divine Providence." He begins with sea-deliverances: "I will carry my reader upon the huge Atlantick, and, without so much as the danger of being made sea-sick, he shall see 'wonders in the deep.'" The first story concerns Ephraim Howe, who lost two sons during a voyage from New Haven to Boston, was buffeted by storms for weeks, was shipwrecked and forced to live on gulls, crows, and ravens, and was rescued only after his friends had died and he had been isolated on an island near Cape Sables for over three months. Other tales of deliverances after prayer include the story of a man preserved on the keel of an overturned boat, an incident of "twelve men living five weeks for five hundred leagues in a little boat," and several incidents of rescue at sea involving the calming of storm-tossed waters, the changing of wind, or the chance passage of a rescuing boat.

To his accounts of sea-deliverances Mather adds stories of other acts of God —of flocks of birds arriving to end a plague of caterpillars, of the relief of droughts and floods, of persons rescued from drowning or other dangers. Mather was impressed by wounds which would have been fatal, in his opinion, had not Divinity intervened. He tells, for example, of Abigail Eliot:

> One Abigail Eliot had an iron struck into her head, which drew out part of her brains with it: a silver plate she afterwards wore on her skull where the orifice remain'd as big as an half crown. The brains left in the child's head would swell and swage, according to the tides; her intellectuals were not hurt by this disaster; and she liv'd to be: a mother of several children.

In the hope of correcting ordinary sinners, Mather included a number of dying speeches of criminals. A verbatim report is given of the conversation between Hugh Stone, who cut his wife's throat, and a minister. The conversation was lengthy, but the criminal continued his confession of sins in a discourse and prayer almost as long as the conversation. He directed his remarks to "young men and maids," and warned that "If you sav, when a person has provok'd you, 'I will kill him;' 'tis a thousand to one but the next time you will do it."

In writing of witches, Mather had few reservations concerning the truth of the charges against them. He believed in molestations from evil spirits, as directed by Satan, and he regarded the evidence of such possession as beyond any reasonable doubt. He wrote of women who claimed to have made pacts with the devil, who rode on broomsticks and put curses on others, causing endless trouble. Execution was the proper punishment for such persons, according to Mather— although he did admit that there was "a going too far in this affair."

Perhaps the wonder is that the Christian spirit survived the passionate dogmatism and superstitions of colonial days. Mather's *Magnalia* is a curious and fascinating hodgepodge of history, didacticism, and fatal error combining to give an authentic reflection of a seventeenth-century American mind.

THE MAGNIFICENT OBSESSION

Type of work: Novel
Author: Lloyd C. Douglas (1877-1951)
Type of plot: Quasi-mysticism
Time of plot: Early twentieth century
Locale: Detroit and Europe
First published: 1929

Principal characters:
DR. WAYNE HUDSON, a famous brain surgeon
HELEN BRENT HUDSON, the doctor's second wife
JOYCE HUDSON, the doctor's daughter and Helen's school friend
ROBERT MERRICK, a physician
NANCY ASHFORD, superintendent at the Hudson Clinic

Critique:

The author accomplishes in *The Magnificent Obsession* one of the most difficult problems in novel-writing, the exposition of an idea, and he makes an excellent case for the theory of extending personality and gaining moral power by doing good for other individuals. The motive behind the novel is, of course, to prove that Christian teachings can be applied to modern life, even in the case of the selfish materialist.

The Story:

The staff at the Hudson Clinic was worried about the head of the hospital, Dr. Wayne Hudson. The doctor had suddenly become nervous and haggard, a bad condition for an eminent practicing surgeon, and his staff tried to advise the doctor to take six months away from his work. The doctor himself surprised his staff by announcing that he was about to marry his daughter's school friend, Miss Helen Brent. The couple were married within a short time and went to live at the doctor's lakeside cottage.

Soon afterward a shocking tragedy occurred at the lake. Dr. Hudson drowned because the inhalator that might have saved his life had been dispatched across the lake to resuscitate a wealthy young playboy, Robert Merrick.

While he was recuperating from his experience, young Merrick felt that the doctors and the nurses at the Hudson clinic resented him. He did not yet know that it was at the expense of the life of the hospital's chief surgeon that he himself was alive. He questioned the superintendent of the clinic, Nancy Ashford, who had been in love with her chief, Doctor Hudson, but Miss Ashford did not give him a satisfactory answer. Later, overhearing a conversation, Merrick discovered why the people at the hospital seemed to despise him. He talked again to Nancy Ashford, who told him the only way he could ever make amends would be to take Dr. Hudson's place in life by becoming a great surgeon.

After weeks of pondering on the idea of going to medical school, Merrick decided that he would try to fill Dr. Hudson's place. When he went back to Nancy Ashford to tell her of his plans, she told him the story of the doctor's many philanthropies. She also gave him a book which the doctor had written in code. After many days and nights of perseverance, the young man managed to break the cipher. When he had done so, it seemed to him that the doctor, whom he had come to look upon as an ideal, had been a lunatic, for the book was a strange, mystic tract about doing good. From Nancy Ashford he learned that the deceased doctor had been a great mystic, believing that his gift as a surgeon came to him from what he called the Major Personality. That power was earned by doing good unknown to others, philanthropy that would aid the recipient in leading a valuable life of service.

During the next few years Merrick attended the state medical school. One night, as he sat studying, he suddenly felt a call to go to a night club where he knew Joyce Hudson, the doctor's daughter, was to be. After rescuing her from a drunken scene, he took her home. There he met the doctor's widow.

That semester Merrick almost failed at medical school. Discouraged with his own efforts, he decided to experiment with the knowledge he had gained from the dead surgeon's manuscript. He aided a fellow student, Dawson, who was about to leave school because he lacked funds. Immediately he felt renewed hope and plunged into his work with enthusiasm.

Helen Hudson, the doctor's widow, had gone to Europe, where she remained three years. Near the end of that time she discovered that the cousin who was handling her affairs was dishonest. Needing funds, she wrote to Nancy Ashford to ask if her stock in the Hudson Clinic could be sold. Nancy told Merrick, now a doctor at the clinic. He sent Helen twenty-five thousand dollars and sold some of the stock for her. Toward the end of her stay in Europe Helen met Mrs. Dawson, wife of the medical student whom Merrick had helped through medical school. Merrick had asked Mrs. Dawson to learn something of Helen's financial losses so that he might put her affairs in order. After telling Mrs. Dawson her troubles, Helen discovered an envelope Mrs. Dawson had addressed to Merrick. Helen promptly disappeared.

Merrick went to the cousin who was managing Helen's financial affairs. The man had robbed Helen of about one hundred thousand dollars. Merrick made good the loss and sent the man out of the country, bringing no charges against him because he was related to Helen. Before the cousin left, he learned Mer-

rick's theory of personality projection and made up his mind to lead an honest life.

Tired from overwork, Merrick took a vacation in the country for several weeks. Then he returned to his laboratory and began a program of hard work. His meals were returned to the kitchen almost untouched. His labors were at last successful, for he perfected a scalpel which automatically cauterized by electricity. The device opened a new field of brain surgery because it prevented hemorrhage as it cut into the tissue.

About Christmas Helen returned to the United States. In Detroit she went to her trust company and asked to see the shares of stock which they held in her name. As she suspected, they had been transferred from Merrick. When she left the bank, she did not know whether to feel thankful or insulted.

Helen went from the bank to the Hudson Clinic, where she asked to see Merrick immediately. Her confusion was even greater when he told her he could not take back the money. He tried to explain the transfer of her stock, but she was in no mood for explanations. As he took her to the door they met her stepdaughter. Joyce complicated the tense situation by proposing a theater party for the next day. In order not to create gossip, both Helen and Merrick agreed to go to dinner and the theater afterward. As he handed Helen into the taxi, Merrick managed to murmur that he loved her.

The next evening at dinner Merrick asked Helen not to tell all she had done for a needy Italian family at Assisi. He added that the philanthropy would thereby lose its value if the story were told.

The following summer Merrick went to Europe to visit eminent surgeons in Vienna and to demonstrate his cauterizing scalpel to them. While he was in Paris he heard that Helen had been injured in a train wreck near Rome. Hurrying to Rome, he operated on the injured woman and saved her life. Then, in quixotic fashion, he left Rome before anyone could tell her who had performed the delicate operation. Helen guessed Merrick's identity, however, from the few words he had mumbled in her presence. Weeks later, when she discovered that he was planning to visit her, Helen, ashamed of her previous attitude toward his interest in her affairs, arranged to leave for the United States. But Merrick flew to Le Havre ahead of her, arranged for their marriage, and met her on the dock. When she saw him waiting, she walked into his arms. She did not have to be told why he had come.

THE MAHABHARATA

Type of work: Poem
Author: Unknown
Type of plot: Heroic epic
Time of plot: Remote antiquity
Locale: Ancient India
First transcribed: Fifth century B.C.(?)

Principal characters:
KING DHRITARASHTRA, father of the Kauravas
KING PANDU, his brother and father of the Pandavas
YUDHISHTHIRA,
BHIMA,
ARJUNA,
NAKULA, and
SAHADEVA, the five sons of King Pandu
DRAUPADI, wife of the Pandavas
DURYODHANA, oldest son of Dhritarashtra

Critique:

This tremendous poetic effort is one of two national epics of the Hindu peoples, the second being the *Ramayana.* In its present form in Sanskrit, the *Mahabharata* runs to some 200,000 verses in couplets (slokas), in eighteen sections or books, though there is credible evidence to assume that earlier versions were considerably less extensive. Of the present version, only about one-third to one-quarter of the whole relates to the central story, that of a civil war between two great royal houses of India. Not a unified epic poem in the sense that the *Iliad* and the *Odyssey* were conceived, the *Mahabharata* is a massive collection of fascinating heroic and mythological legends, sermon-like essays, worldly and spiritual advice to the warrior class on appropriate conduct for military prowess and reverential duties, material constituting codes of law, popular apothegms and proverbs, and moral tales for the edification of its reader audience. Authorship of the poem is nominally attributed to Vyasa, but since this name means "the arranger" or "the reviser," it seems evident that the identity of the original poet or poets has been long since lost. From the state of the poem as it now exists, it is readily apparent that succeeding minstrels, copyists, and zealous adapters have worked conscientiously to include records, fables, favorite stories of mythological characters,

rules for conduct, and the like as a means of preserving whatever they deemed most appealing and valuable for their contemporaries and posterity to know and understand about the glorious past. For these reasons the *Mahabharata* is both a history of prehistoric times and a compendium of materials that throw light on the religious, social, political, ethical, and moral ideals and practices of an old and memorable people.

The Story:

Among the descendants of King Bharata (after whose name India was called Bharata-varsha, land of the Bharatas) there were two successors to the throne of Hastinapura. Of these, the elder, Dhritarashtra, was blind and gave over the reins of government to his younger brother Pandu. But Pandu grew weary of his duties and retired to hunt and enjoy himself. Again Dhritarashtra took control, aided by the advice and example of his wise old uncle, Bhishma. Upon Pandu's death, his five sons were put under the care of his younger brother, who had one hundred sons of his own.

At first the king's household was peaceful and free from strife, but gradually it became apparent that Pandu's sons were far more capable of ruling than any of Dhritarashtra's heirs. Of the Pandavas, the name given to the five descendants of Pandu, all were remarkably able, but the oldest, Yudhishthira, was judged most promising and therefore was chosen heir-apparent to the throne of the old blind king. To this selection of their cousin as the future king, the king's own sons took violent exception. Accordingly, they persuaded their father to allow the Pandavas to leave the court and live by themselves. From a trap set by the unscrupulous Duryodhana, leader of the king's sons, the five brothers escaped to the forest with their mother. There they spent some time in rustic exile.

In the meantime King Drupada had announced that the hand of his daughter, Princess Draupadi, would be given to the hero surpassing all others in a feat of strength and skill, and he had invited throngs of noblemen to compete for his daughter's hand. In disguise, the Pandavas set out for King Drupada's court.

More than two weeks were spent in celebrating the approaching nuptials of the princess before the trial of strength which would reveal the man worthy of taking the lovely princess as his wife. The test was to grasp a mighty bow, fit an arrow, bend the bow, and hit a metal target with the arrow. Contestant after contestant failed in the effort to bend the huge bow. Finally Arjuna, third of the sons of Pandu, came forward and performed the feat with little effort to win the hand of the princess. But in curious fashion Princess Draupadi became the wife of all five of the brothers. At this time, also, the Pandavas met their cousin on their mother's side, Krishna of Dvaraka. This renowned Yadava nobleman they accepted as their special counselor and friend, and to him they owed much of their future success and power.

Hoping to avert dissension after his death, King Dhritarashtra decided to divide his kingdom into two parts, giving his hundred sons, the Kauravas, one portion and the Pandavas the other. Thus it came about that Dhritarashtra's sons ruled in Hastinapur and the five sons of Pandu in Indraprastha.

The dying king's attempt to settle affairs of government amicably resulted in peace and prosperity for a brief period. Then the wily Duryodhana, leader of the Kauravas, set another trap for the Pandavas. On this occasion he enticed Yudhishthira, the oldest of the brothers, into a game of skill at dice. When the latter lost, the penalty was that the five brothers were to leave the court and spend the next twelve years in the forest. At the end of that time they were to have their kingdom and holdings once again if they could pass another year in disguise, without having anyone recognize them.

The twelve-year period of rustication was one of many romantic and heroic adventures. All five brothers were concerned in stirring events; Arjuna, in particular, traveled far and long, visited sacred stream of the Ganges, was courted by several noble ladies, and finally married Subhadra, sister of Krishna.

When the long time of exile was over, the Pandavas and Kauravas engaged in a war of heroes. Great armies were assembled; mountains of supplies were brought together. Just before the fighting began, Krishna stepped forth and sang the divine song, the *Bhagavad-Gita*, in which he set forth such theological truths as the indestructibility of the soul, the necessity to defend the faith, and other fundamental precepts of the theology of Brahma. By means of this song Arjuna was relieved of his doubts concerning the need to make his trial by battle.

The war lasted for some eighteen consecutive days, each day marked by fierce battles, single combats, and bloody attacks. Death and destruction were everywhere—the battlefields were strewn with broken bodies and ruined weapons and chariots. The outcome was the annihilation of all the pretensions of the Kauravas and their allies to rule over the kingdom. Finally Yudhishthira came to the throne amidst great celebrations, the payment of rich tribute, and the ceremonial horse sacrifice.

Later the death of their spiritual and military counselor, Krishna, led the five brothers to realize their weariness with earthly pomp and striving. Accordingly, Yudhishthira gave up his duties as ruler. The five brothers then banded together, clothed themselves as hermits, and set out for Mount Meru, the dwelling place of the gods on high. They were accompanied by their wife Draupadi and a dog that joined them on their journey. As they proceeded, one after the other dropped by the way and perished. At last only Yudhishthira and the faithful dog remained to reach the portals of heaven. But when the dog was refused admission to that holy place, Yudhishthira declined to enter without his canine companion. Then the truth was revealed—the dog was in reality the god of justice himself, sent to test Yudhishthira's constancy.

But Yudhishthira was not content in heaven, for he soon realized that his brothers and Draupadi had been required to descend to the lower regions and there expiate their mortal sins. Lonely and disconsolate, he decided to join them until all could be united in heaven. After he had spent some time in that realm of suffering and torture, the gods took pity on him. Along with his brothers and Draupadi, he was transported back to heaven, where all dwelt in perpetual happiness.

2179

THE MAID OF HONOUR

Type of work: Drama
Author: Philip Massinger (1583-1640)
Type of plot: Tragi-comedy
Time of plot: The Renaissance
Locale: Palermo and Siena, Italy
First presented: c. 1623

Principal characters:

ROBERTO, King of Sicily
FERDINAND, Duke of Urbin
BERTOLDO, a natural brother of Roberto and a Knight of Malta
GONZAGA, a Knight of Malta, general to the Duchess of Siena
ASTUTIO, a counselor of state to the King of Sicily
FULGENTIO, the favorite of King Roberto
ADORNI, a Sicilian gentleman, in love with Camiola
AURELIA, Duchess of Siena
CAMIOLA, the "Maid of Honour"

Critique:

In *The Maid of Honour* Massinger wrote a play which, though by no means great, contains perhaps two memorable characters and a certain amount of dramatic poetry of at least the second rank. The figure of Camiola has been much admired for her noble unselfishness; and the self-sacrificing lover, Adorni, has also received a measure of praise. Although the play contains many of the improbabilities common to the drama of the period, the author's skill in dramatic construction is apparent. As Arthur Symons phrased it, Massinger was so unfortunate as to appear "at the ebb of a spent wave," after the great Elizabethans; nevertheless, his plays have experienced a certain revival of popularity as the result of the renewed interest in the Jacobean and Caroline dramatists.

The Story:

At the court of Roberto, King of Sicily, at Palermo, where the arrival of an ambassador from the Duke of Urbin was momentarily expected, the conversation of those waiting had turned to discussion of the sinister influence of Fulgentio, the king's unworthy favorite, and of the soldierly qualities of Bertoldo, the king's illegitimate half-brother. Upon the arrival of the ambassador, the political situation

was explained: the Duke of Urbin, in love with the Duchess of Siena but rejected by her, had attacked her territories. On the verge of defeat at the hands of the Sienese, he was appealing to Sicily for aid on the basis of a treaty of mutual assistance. King Roberto, however, maintained that the treaty had been rendered void by the aggressive action of the duke and that Sicily was not obligated to come to the rescue. This pacifistic attitude was abhorrent to the king's half-brother Bertoldo, who in a fiery speech accused the king of cowardice, claimed that Sicily's honor demanded intervention, and urged the nobles to follow him to the relief of the duke. The king, angered by the speech, replied that any might volunteer who wished, but that they would then cease to be his subjects and could expect no protection from him if fortune went against them.

On that same day, at the house of Camiola, the maid was being plagued by the suit of one Sylli, a man of almost unbelievable conceit. He, however, left upon the arrival of Bertoldo, who had come to say farewell and to declare his own love. But in spite of her evident love for Bertoldo, Camiola rejected his suit because, as a Knight of Malta, he was vowed to celibacy, nor could she be moved by his suggestion that a dispensation could be obtained. He left for the war with the determination to have honor as his only mistress.

The next day King Roberto learned of Bertoldo's departure with his volunteers and was displeased at the news. Fulgentio, however, was delighted, for with Bertoldo gone he could pursue his own wooing of Camiola. On his arrival at her house he behaved in an overbearing manner toward all present, particularly her other suitors, Sylli and Adorni. Sylli fainted, but Adorni was prepared to fight until restrained by Camiola. In a series of frank and witty speeches, Camiola told Fulgentio exactly what she thought of him and outlined his despicable character. He left, vowing to avenge himself by ruining her reputation by spreading scandal about her.

Meanwhile, in the territories of Siena, the forces of the Duke of Urbin were still faring badly. Bertoldo and his Sicilian volunteers had arrived, but they could not change the fortunes of war. In the ensuing battle they were captured. When Gonzaga, the Sienese general, recognized Bertoldo as a Knight of Malta, he tore the cross from his prisoner's cloak, for Bertoldo had broken the vows of the order by attacking the duchess in an unjust war. Further, when Astutio came as ambassador from King Roberto to disclaim his sovereign's part in the attack, Gonzaga agreed to accept the usual ransom for all the Sicilian nobles except Bertoldo, for whom he demanded fifty thousand crowns. Astutio bore the news that the king would pay nothing for his half-brother and had, in fact, confiscated the unfortunate man's estates. Unable to pay the ransom, Bertoldo faced a lifetime of imprisonment.

In Sicily, Adorni had challenged Fulgentio for his treatment of Camiola but the cowardly favorite had declined the challenge. On Camiola's birthday, in the midst of the celebration, Adorni entered bleeding. He had been wounded in the fight that he had finally forced upon

Fulgentio, but he had compelled the latter to sign a paper repudiating the slanders he had been spreading about Camiola. Adorni then confessed his love for Camiola, but she rejected him with the admonition that he must not aspire so high. Yet when, through the agency of the ransomed Sicilian noblemen, she learned of Bertoldo's plight, she was ready enough to send Adorni with the fifty thousand crowns to ransom the man she loved. Adorni promised to execute the commission faithfully, although he felt that he would not survive for long, and departed for Siena to bring happiness to his rival. Bertoldo, in ecstasies at the goodness of Camiola, gladly agreed to sign the contract of betrothal that she had demanded. It was his tragedy, however, to be sent for by the victorious Duchess of Siena, who had heard of his martial prowess. Almost instantly she fell violently in love with him; and he, after a short struggle against the sin of ingratitude, fell equally in love with her and promised to marry her.

While this surprising event was in progress at Siena, an equally unexpected change of fortune was taking place in Sicily. The king and his favorite arrived at Camiola's house; the former, with seeming sternness, rebuked her for disobedience in refusing Fulgentio's suit and for urging Adorni to attack him. Camiola defended her conduct and accused Fulgentio of having slandered her. King Roberto then ordered Fulgentio out of his sight, threatened him with death, and praised the behavior of Camiola. Thus the villain was discomfited.

Camiola, informed by the faithful Adorni of Bertoldo's perfidy, made plans accordingly. At a reunion in the palace at Palermo, the king forgave his half-brother and consented to his marriage to the Duchess of Siena. But Camiola entered and, after promising Fulgentio to try to secure his peace with the king, asked the monarch for justice on Bertoldo. Producing the contract of betrothal that he had signed, she made such a noble plea for her rights that even the love-smitten duchess acknowledged her superiority and yielded Bertoldo to her, while he admitted his falseness and confessed himself branded with disloyalty and ingratitude. Camiola forgave him and announced her approaching marriage. The entrance of a group of friars provided another surprise for the gathering. Camiola announced that she had determined to become the bride of the Church; by entering a religious order she was to become, in another sense, the Maid of Honour. As her last act, she gave Adorni a third of her estate and returned to Bertoldo the cross of the Knights of Malta, bidding him to redeem his honor by fighting against the enemies of the faith. As she departed for the convent, King Roberto stated admiringly that she well deserved her title of Maid of Honour.

THE MAID'S TRAGEDY

Type of work: Drama
Authors: Francis Beaumont (1584?-1616) and John Fletcher (1579-1625)
Type of plot: Revenge tragedy
Time of plot: The legendary past
Locale: Rhodes
First presented: c. 1610

Principal characters:
THE KING OF RHODES
MELANTIUS, a soldier
EVADNE, his sister
AMINTOR, his noble young friend
CALIANAX, a lord of Rhodes
ASPATIA, his daughter, betrothed to Amintor

Critique:

Although *The Maid's Tragedy* is marred by sentimentality and by improbabilities, it is a tightly constructed play that never falters in its development from beginning to end. The plot was original with Beaumont and Fletcher; it is not surprising, however, since both men were educated playwrights, that scholars have found scenes which echo Shakespeare and Valerius Maximus. Evadne bids fair to become an unforgettable female Machiavellian, but her repentance and her suicide make her, in the end, little more than a shadowy counterpart of Lady Macbeth.

The Story:

Melantius, a military hero, returned to Rhodes from the wars. There he found himself involved in a difficult situation. The King, ostensibly to show his gratitude, had given the hand of Evadne, Melantius' sister, to Amintor, a young courtier and a dear friend of Melantius. The difficulty lay in the fact that Amintor had already promised himself to Aspatia, daughter of Calianax, an old lord.

Preparations were being made for elaborate nuptial festivities. Aspatia grieved. In the royal banqueting hall, just before the presentation of the marriage masque, Melantius encountered Calianax, who insulted him. The King's entrance checked animosities. A masque followed, after which the King, wishing the wedded couple goodnight, asked Amintor to father a boy who would grow up to defend the kingdom.

As Evadne prepared to retire, Aspatia, who was present, could not share the general enthusiastic anticipation of the marriage night, and she expressed her belief that she would soon be dead of a broken heart. Amintor, coming into the apartment received a kiss from Aspatia before she departed. He suffered momentary misgivings for having forsaken her, but he forgot her when he saw Evadne. His bride, as he soon discovered, did not appear to be interested in the consummation of their marriage. In fact, she told Amintor that she hated him and would never share his bed. Threatened by Amintor, she finally confessed that she had already given herself to the King. Amintor was deeply injured when she revealed to him that the marriage was merely a means to make legitimate any children born of that affair. Determined to make the marriage seem to be normal, however, he slept in her bedchamber, on the floor.

Aspatia, meanwhile, returned to her home, where she warned her maids never to trust their hearts to men and recounted classical stories of women who, much to their distress, gave their hearts away. Old Calianax, always a coward at heart, vowed to be valiant in avenging the slight to his daughter.

The next morning Amintor, emerging from the bedchamber, encountered Melantius, whom he puzzled with ambiguous remarks about the virtues of the soldier's family. Later Amintor's assumed manner aroused the King's suspicions; in private he accused Evadne of faithlessness. To prove her steadfastness to the King, she provoked Amintor into revealing that the marriage had not been consummated. Amintor was overcome by the enormity of the way he had been treated, but he refused to draw his sword on the King. Still, he vowed to avenge the insult somehow.

Melantius, meanwhile, pondered on Amintor's peculiar behavior. Dismissing a foolish challenge from Calianax, he encountered Amintor, whom he persuaded to unburden his heart of its troubles. When Amintor revealed that Evadne was the King's mistress, Melantius, incapable of believing Amintor's story, drew his sword and threatened to kill his friend. When Amintor seemed to welcome death, Melantius, convinced, sheathed his sword and swore to avenge his sister's disgrace. But Amintor, who felt that it was he who should do the avenging, challenged Melantius to fight. Melantius refused, calmed the youth, and promised that the two could effect a scheme to right the wrongs done them.

Melantius directed his brother Diphilus to prepare his armor for battle. He also asked Calianax, the castellan of Rhodes, to deliver the garrison to him. The old man, promising permission within the hour, hastened to report the rebellion to the King.

Melantius went to Evadne and confronted her with his knowledge of her transgression. Upon asking her to name her seducer, she pretended to be insulted and suggested that he tend to his military affairs. When Melantius threatened to kill her, she confessed the truth. Then, realizing the extent of her disgrace, she promised Melantius that she would kill the King. She also expressed her remorse

to Amintor and begged him for forgiveness. Amintor kissed her and cautioned her never to sin again.

Meanwhile, at a dinner in the palace, Calianax told the King of Melantius' scheme to kill him and to escape to the fortress of Rhodes. The King, doubting, called Amintor into the dining chamber, where with leading questions he tested Amintor and Evadne, as well as Melantius, who accompanied them. Melantius maintained his poise. When the King disclosed his knowledge of the plot, Melantius continued to dissemble and stated that Calianax was an irresponsible, foolish old man. The King was convinced that Melantius was innocent. When Melantius, in asides, importuned Calianax about the fortress, the old man tried to convince the King that Melantius was making overtures under his very eyes, but the ruler suggested that someone put the weak-minded old man to bed. The thoroughly confounded lord submitted reluctantly to Melantius' demands for the fortress.

The night for revenge having come, Diphilus took command of the fortress. Amintor, encountering Melantius, asked his assistance in killing the King. Melantius, fearful lest his plans fail, reminded Amintor that the King's person was sacred.

Evadne, going to the King's bedchamber, tied the sleeping monarch to the bed. Awaking, the King thought at first that his bondage was a pretty joke of Evadne's, but he was filled with apprehension when he saw her draw a knife. Reciting his villainy toward her, she stabbed him to death; then she forgave him.

Soon afterward, the death of the King having been discovered, the King's brother Lysippus and his followers went to the citadel, where Melantius and his people were in control. Melantius affirmed his loyalty to Rhodes, but declared that if he were not given amnesty he could very easily destroy the city. Lysippus and Melantius agreed to a general amnesty.

Meanwhile Aspatia, disguised as a man, entered Amintor's apartment, where she told Amintor that she was Aspatia's long-lost brother, returned to avenge his sister. In her disguise, Aspatia challenged Amintor to a duel. When he refused, she struck him. Goaded to action, Amintor drew and wounded Aspatia.

Evadne, bloody dagger in hand, entered and told Amintor that she had killed the King. When she asked Amintor to recognize her as his wife, he, appalled, refused and left her. Evadne stabbed herself to death. Aspatia, meanwhile, had revived long enough to reveal her true identity to Amintor, who declared his unworthiness and his shame for the way that he had treated her. When Aspatia died, Amintor, having nothing more to live for and wishing to be with his true love, stabbed himself.

Melantius, entering, was so overcome by the sight of his dead sister and his dying friend that he attempted to take his own life. Calianax, upon recognizing his daughter, the dead Aspatia, was reconciled to Melantius. Lysippus, the new ruler, looked upon the scene as an object lesson to kings to be chaste.

MAIN STREET

Type of work: Novel
Author: Sinclair Lewis (1885-1951)
Type of plot: Social satire
Time of plot: c. 1910-1920
Locale: Small Midwestern town
First published: 1920

Principal characters:
CAROL KENNICOTT, an idealist
DR. WILL KENNICOTT, her husband

Critique:

To puncture the egos of smug, self-satisfied Americans who consider their home towns flawless, Sinclair Lewis wrote *Main Street*, a novel which deals with the life of Gopher Prairie, a fictitious, small, and supposedly typical Midwestern town in Minnesota. Carol Kennicott is intent upon reforming not only her husband, a doctor in Gopher Prairie, but also the town. Lewis speaks blunt truths about the inadequacies of small-town life, but his satire is rarely vicious; and if the reader sees himself or his town reflected in the author's pages, he cannot help admitting that much that Lewis says is true, uncomfortable as truth may be.

The Story:

When Carol Milford was graduated from Blodgett College in Minnesota, she determined to conquer the world. Interested in sociology, and village improvement in particular, she often longed to set out on a crusade of her own to transform dingy prairie towns to thriving, beautiful communities. When she met Will Kennicott, a doctor from Gopher Prairie, and listened to his praise of his home town, she agreed to marry him. He had convinced her that Gopher Prairie needed her.

Carol was essentially an idealist. On the train, going to her new home, she deplored the run-down condition of the countryside and wondered about the future of the northern Middle West. Will did not listen to her ideas sympathetically. The people were happy, he said. Through town after town they traveled, Carol noting with sinking heart the shapeless mass of hideous buildings, the dirty depots, the flat wastes of prairie surrounding everything, and she knew that Gopher Prairie would be no different from the rest.

Gopher Prairie was exactly like the other towns Carol had seen, except that it was a little larger. The people were as drab as their houses, as flat as their fields. A welcoming committee met the newlyweds at the train. To Carol, all the men were alike in their colorless clothes; over-friendly, over-enthusiastic. The Kennicott house was a Victorian horror. But Will said he liked it. Introduced to the townsfolk at a party held in her honor, Carol heard the men talk of motor cars, train schedules, "furriners," and praise Gopher Prairie as God's own country. The women were interested in gossip, sewing, and cooking, and most of them belonged to the two women's clubs, the Jolly Seventeen and the Thanatopsis Club. At the first meeting of the Jolly Seventeen, Carol brought wrath upon her head when she stated that the duty of a librarian was to get people to read. The town librarian staunchly asserted that her primary trust was to preserve the books.

Carol did many things which were to cause her great unhappiness. She hired a maid and paid her the over-generous sum of six dollars a week. She gave a party with an Oriental motif. Sometimes she even kicked off a slipper under the table and revealed her arches. The women frowned on her unconventional behavior. Worse, she redecorated the old Kennicott house and got rid of the mildew, the ancient bric-a-brac, the dark wallpaper. Will protested against her desire to change things.

Carol also joined the Thanatopsis Club, for she hoped to use the club as a means of awakening interest in social reform. But the women of Gopher Prairie, while professing charitable intentions, had no idea of improving social conditions. When Carol mentioned that something should be done about the poor people of the town, everyone firmly stated that there was no real poverty in Gopher Prairie. Carol also attempted to raise funds for a new city hall, but no one could see that the ugly old building needed to be replaced. The town voted against appropriating the necessary funds.

Will Kennicott bought a summer cottage on Lake Minniemashie. There Carol enjoyed outdoor life and during the summer months almost lost her desire for reform. But when September came she hated the thought of returning to Gopher Prairie.

Carol resolved to study her husband. He was well thought of in the town, and she romanticized herself as the wife of a hard-working, courageous country doctor. She fell in love with Will again on the night she watched him perform a bloody but successful operation upon a poor farmer. But Carol's praise of her husband had little effect. Will was not the romantic figure she had pictured. He accepted his duties as a necessary chore, and the thought that he had saved the life of a human being did not occur to him. His interest in medicine was identical with his interest in motor cars. Once more Carol turned her attention to Gopher Prairie.

Carol, trying to interest the Thanatopsis Club in literature and art, finally persuaded the members to put on an amateur theatrical. But enthusiasm soon waned. Carol's choice of a play, Shaw's *Androcles*, was vetoed, and *The Girl from Kankakee* put in its place. Carol considered even that choice too subtle for Gopher Prairie, but at least the town's interest in the theater had been revived.

After three years of marriage, Carol discovered that she was pregnant. Almost immediately the neighborhood became interested in her condition. When her son was born, she resolved that some day she would send little Hugh away from Gopher Prairie, to Harvard, Yale, or Oxford.

With a new son and the new status of motherhood, Carol found herself more a part of the town, but she devoted nine-tenths of her attention to Hugh and had little time to criticize the town. She wanted a new house, but she and Will could not agree on the type of building. He was satisfied with a square frame house. Carol had visions of a Georgian mansion, with stately columns and wide lawns, or a white cottage like those at Cape Cod.

Then Carol met a tailor in town, an artistic, twenty-five-year-old aesthete, with whom she imagined herself in love. She often dropped by his shop to see him, and one day Will warned her that the gossip in town was growing. Ashamed, Carol promised she would not see him again. The tailor left for Minneapolis. Carol and Will decided to take a trip to California. When they returned three months later, Carol realized that her attempt to escape Gopher Prairie had been unsuccessful. For one thing, Will had gone with her. What she needed now was to get away from her husband. After a long argument with Will, Carol took little Hugh and went off to Washington, where she planned to do war work. But hers was an empty kind of freedom. She found the people in Washington an accumulation of the population of thousands of Gopher Prairies all over the nation. Main Street had merely been transplanted to the larger city. Disheartened by her discovery, Carol had too much pride to return home.

2187

After thirteen months, Will went to get her. He missed her terribly, he said, and begged her to come back. Hugh was overjoyed to see his father, and Carol realized that inevitably she would have to return to Gopher Prairie.

Home once more, Carol found that her furious hatred for Gopher Prairie had burned itself out. She made friends with the clubwomen and promised herself not to be snobbish in the future. She would go on asking questions—she could never stop herself from doing that—but her questions now would be asked with sympathy rather than with sarcasm. For the first time she felt serene. In Gopher Prairie she felt at last that she was wanted. Her neighbors had missed her. For the first time Carol felt that Gopher Prairie was her home.

MAIN-TRAVELLED ROADS

Type of work: Short stories
Author: Hamlin Garland (1860-1940)
Time: Late nineteenth century
Locale: The Middle West
First published: 1891

In 1887, Hamlin Garland traveled from Boston to South Dakota through farming country he had not seen in three years, to visit his mother and father, whom he had not seen in six. According to his own account, the trip was a revelation. Although he had been brought up on a farm, he had never realized how wretched the life of the farmer was. The farther west he traveled, the more oppressive became the bleakness of the landscape and the poverty of its people. When he reached his parents' farm and found his mother living in hopeless misery, Garland's depression sank into bitterness, a mood which inspired a series of short stories about farm life in the Middle West, the book titled *Main-Travelled Roads*.

One of these stories, "Up the Coolly," re-creates the mood of Garland's trip under circumstances slightly similar in some respects. Howard McLane, after years spent traveling with his own theatrical troupe, returned to the West for a surprise visit with his mother and brother. He found them living in poverty on a small, unproductive farm, the family property having been sold to pay off a mortgage. Although his mother and his sister-in-law greeted him with warmth, Grant, his brother, soon made it plain that he blamed Howard for the loss of the farm, that Howard, had he shared his apparent wealth, could have saved the farm and spared his mother a great deal of misery. Howard's attempt to win the friendship of his brother resulted only in alienation until Howard finally admitted his selfishness and neglect and offered to buy the farm back. The brothers were reconciled, but the story ends in despair with Grant's refusal of assistance.

Not many of Garland's stories end on so despondent a note; in fact, most of them end hopefully, and some happily. But none of Garland's principal characters is spared a bitter sense of failure, though most of them overcome it. Thus, in "A 'Good Fellow's' Wife," Jim Sanford lost all the savings of the farmers who had invested in his bank. In "A Branch Road," Will Hannon lost the beautiful girl he loved and regained her only when she was prematurely old and wasted. And in "Under the Lion's Paw," Tim Haskins was forced to pay double for a farm because he himself had doubled its value by hard work.

Even in the stories which are lighter in tone, the characters are made to taste of the bitterness of life. Thus, in "The Creamery Man," which is about a young man's carefree courtship, Claude Williams won not Lucindy Kennedy, the lovely daughter of a prominent farmer, but Nina Haldeman, the unrefined daughter of an immigrant. And in "Mrs. Ripley's Trip," Gran'ma Ripley made a journey back East where she had been born, but not without a sense of guilt for leaving her husband, even for so short a time.

In addition to reflecting the bitterness which Garland himself felt, many of the stories set forth a disillusioning contrast between the farm life he remembered and the reality he found when he returned after a long absence. "The Return of a Private," for instance, pictures the return of a Civil War soldier to his farm. Expecting the farm to be as prosperous as he had left it, Private Smith found it "weedy and encumbered, a rascally renter had run away with his machinery . . . his children needed clothing, the years were coming upon him, he was sick and emaciated. . . ." In "God's Ravens,"

2189

Robert Bloom, who had moved to the country because he felt stifled by city life, went through an apprenticeship of misery before the country people finally accepted him and made him feel at home.

It is possible, however, to overemphasize Garland's disillusionment; practically all the stories in *Main-Travelled Roads* have a hopeful ending in that the characters' love for the land and their trust in it are ultimately justified. It is clear that Private Smith by hard work will restore his farm to its former prosperity. Robert Bloom discovers that the cause of his discontent is within himself, not in the hearts of his farmer neighbors. Tim Haskins, robbed by one man, is set on his feet by another. It is true that Garland's realistic portrayal of hardship and poverty did much to shatter any romantic illusions about an American pastoral idyl, but its somber tone was not enough to discredit the traditional view of the farmer as a doughty, virtuous frontiersman. Rather, Garland's accomplishment was to expose the pathos, perhaps tragedy, of people who felt the futility and injustice of farm life, but who were unable to change that life and so accepted it with fortitude and resignation.

Main-Travelled Roads is more than a social document. No less a figure than William Dean Howells recognized that it was important in the development of a new American literature. In an essay which was reprinted as an introduction to later editions of *Main-Travelled Roads,* he commended Garland for the social significance of his work and then went on to praise his "fine courage to leave a fact with the reader, ungarnished and unvarnished, which is almost the rarest trait in an Anglo-Saxon writer, so infantile and feeble is the custom of our art. . . ." Singled out for special praise was the ending of "A Branch Road," in which Will Hannon persuaded Agnes Dingman to leave her husband and the farm to lead a life of comfort and ease. Such an ending Howells deemed immoral but justifiable, since for these characters it was probable and realistic. Howells' judgment was sound. It is for Garland's contribution to the rise of American realism as well as for his social commentary that his works are still read.

MAJOR BARBARA

Type of work: Drama
Author: Bernard Shaw (1856-1950)
Time: Early twentieth century
Locale: London
First presented: 1905

> Principal characters:
> SIR ANDREW UNDERSHAFT, a munitions tycoon
> LADY BRITOMART UNDERSHAFT, his domineering wife
> BARBARA, their older daughter, a major in the Salvation Army
> SARAH, their younger daughter
> STEPHEN, their son, a correct young man
> ADOLPHUS CUSINS, a professor of Greek
> CHARLES LOMAX, Sarah's suitor
> SNOBBY PRICE,
> RUMMY MITCHENS,
> BILL WALKER, and
> PETER SHIRLEY, members of the lower classes

In writing *Major Barbara*, Shaw faced essentially the same problems that had confronted the earliest English dramatists, the authors of the medieval miracle and mystery plays. Like those writers, Shaw considered drama to be only a means, not an end, and like them he used drama as a means of educating the great ignorant public. But the problems confronting Shaw were considerably more formidable than those posed by the dramatization of Biblical stories. Instead of stories which were intrinsically dramatic and which provided ready-made plots, Shaw dramatized themes: philosophical themes, moral themes, social, economic, historic, and even biological themes, most of which were intrinsically non-dramatic and unentertaining. No one but a college sophomore or a genius would have dared inflict on a theater audience, intent only on an evening's entertainment, the doctrines of Nietzsche, Schopenhauer, or, for that matter, Ernest Belfort Box. This is not to deny that earlier dramatists had successfully woven philosophical themes into their plays. But in Shaw's plays the theme is not merely an integral part of the characters and action; as often as not it is a topic of conversation which the characters, sitting in their parlors or standing on the streets, discuss and explore.

Shaw's problem, then, was clear-cut:

to create characters who were so interesting and lively that the audience would not mind listening to them preach. For Shaw's characters do preach, and nowhere quite so vociferously as in *Major Barbara*.

Major Barbara is a sermon. The subject is salvation of society and salvation of the human soul; the text, blessed are the poor. As might be expected, Shaw's message is diametrically opposed to the lesson taught by Christian ethics. Shaw believed that the poor were unblessed. Since poverty was obviously the source of sin, no poor man could possibly hope to enter the kingdom of heaven. More important to Shaw, perhaps, was the fact that poverty was also the source of crime. To eliminate poverty, then, was a social as well as a moral imperative.

A play built on such a theme could easily have sunk either into the depths of naturalism or drifted into the zone of platitudinous propaganda. Instead, since Shaw was the author, the play turned out to be outrageously funny. In fact, *Major Barbara* is one of the funniest plays Shaw wrote and therefore one of the most effective.

As in all Shaw's plays, the focus is on a conflict between the forces of conventionality and the power of a superior being—the Shavian hero. Ironically, since

Shaw was a Socialist, the hero, Andrew Undershaft, is a multimillionaire capitalist, a manufacturer of munitions. Pitted against him is his daughter Barbara, a major in the Salvation Army. Undershaft is the apostle of Shaw's secular morality. Realizing that poverty breeds social discontent and thus constitutes a threat to capitalism, he uses his immense power to eliminate poverty, at least among his own workers. Barbara he recognizes to be a superior person possessed of true, but misguided, moral energy. She has deluded herself into thinking that the converts she wins through her work in the Salvation Army have truly reformed, that the Army truly wins souls to the kingdom of God. Undershaft undertakes to convert her. On the other hand, Barbara deplores her father's profession, believing that he is dedicated to the destruction rather than the salvation of mankind. She undertakes to convert him.

The battle is one-sided, short, and decisive. Undershaft merely has to show Barbara that he, a dealer in death and destruction, can buy the Army's good graces for the price of a donation. He shows that he and others like him—a distiller, for instance—provide the financial backing without which the Army would collapse. Crushed by her father's cynicism and what she considers the Army's hypocrisy, she turns in her uniform.

The play ends on a note of sardonic optimism. Undershaft's destruction of Barbara's faith is only a preliminary step; he must now convert her to his own creed. This conversion he accomplishes by taking Barbara and the rest of his family on a tour of his factory and Perivale St. Andrews, the town in which his workers live. The town turns out to be a workingman's paradise. Instead of the misery and squalor which Barbara expects, she finds prosperity and sanitation. Realizing at last that it is impossible to save hungry men's souls, she resolves to devote her energies to saving the souls of the well-fed.

Directly involved in this struggle for Barbara's soul is her suitor, Adolphus Cusins, a professor of Greek, who, to please Barbara, neglects his studies to play the bass drum in the Salvation Army band. Cusins is important, too, in the thematic structure of the play because he is the third member of the triumvirate which is to save society. Undershaft, following the tradition of his predecessors in the munitions business, disinherits his own son Stephen and adopts Adolphus as his protégé and heir. To Undershaft's power and Barbara's moral fervor, Adolphus adds intellect. In this combination, presumably, lay Shaw's hope for the salvation of society.

The minor characters serve both to act out the message of the play and to provide much of the humor. They are divided into two classes: rich and poor. The poor class is represented by the rascals and reprobates who frequent Barbara's Salvation Army shelter. Of these, by far the most typical are Snobby Price and Rummy Mitchens, both of whom feign a desire for spiritual sustenance and testify to their conversion to Christianity in return for free meals. The most pathetic is Peter Shirley, who at forty-five has been thrown out of work because he has a streak of gray in his hair. A disciple of Thomas Paine, he swallows his pride to accept a free meal only when he is starving. By far the meanest and funniest is Bill Walker, who comes to the shelter to pommel his girl friend because she deserted him when she was converted. A bully and ruffian, he provides the funniest scene of the play when, after blackening the eye of one of Barbara's young female assistants, he is shamed into an excruciating sense of guilt by Barbara's reproofs. His role as a foil to Undershaft is apparent when Bill tries to atone for the black eye by giving a donation to the Army.

The idle rich are represented by Undershaft's wife, son, younger daughter, and the latter's suitor. Lady Britomart and her son Stephen reek of conventional morality. A typical domineering mother, Lady Britomart abhors her husband's immorality but does not hesitate to capitalize on it, accepting his money to ensure her children's comfortable place in society. Stephen, though cowed at first by his mother, declares his independence toward the end of the play and is rewarded with a career in journalism by his amused father. Charles Lomax, Sarah's suitor, demonstrates the utter frivolity and vacuity of the rich. Although these are stock characters borrowed from Oscar Wilde's drawing-room comedies, they are vigorous and funny.

Shaw's success in creating such thoroughly delightful characters is the key to the success of *Major Barbara*. Without the relief of the humor which each and every character provides, the moralizing and preaching would be tedious. It is by no means certain, however, that Shaw converted anyone to his brand of secular morality by using such a dramatic technique. The play is so amusing that it is difficult to take the theme seriously. But in the process of entertaining his audiences, Shaw was able at least to acquaint them with serious ideas. Surely he did not expect to accomplish more.

THE MALCONTENT

Type of work: Drama
Author: John Marston (1576-1634)
Type of plot: Romantic comedy
Time of plot: Thirteenth century
Locale: Genoa, Italy
First presented: 1604

Principal characters:
  GIOVANNI ALTOFRONTO, disguised as the Malcontent, sometime Duke of
    Genoa
  PIETRO JACOMO, Duke of Genoa
  MENDOZA, a court minion
  FERNEZE, a young courtier
  AURELIA, Pietro Jacomo's wife
  MARIA, Altofronto's wife
  BILIOSO, an old Marshal
  MAQUERELLE, an old panderer
  CELSO, a friend of Altofronto
  EMILIA, and
  BIANCHA, Aurelia's attendants

Critique:

Although Marston called *The Malcontent* a comedy, it has more the qualities of a tragi-comedy. The pandering in connection with cuckoldry and the court toadies are treated as comedy in the Elizabethan sense; but the principal issue of the play, restoration of the rightful, and right, state leadership, is not amusing; nor is it handled as humor in this play. In style, *The Malcontent* is unsatisfying when compared with other Elizabethan dramas. Marston seems to have tried to impress his audience with his facility of language, and his use of descriptive phrases and figures of speech is extended to the point of monotony. Also, the play comes more to life in scenes implying tragedy than in those purporting comedy. Marston dedicated *The Malcontent* to Ben Jonson, his close friend and sporadic literary feudist. John Webster collaborated to the extent of developing additions for presentation on the stage by the King's Players.

The Story:

Duke Altofronto had been banished from Genoa and a political coup, staged by Mendoza with the help of the Florentines, had brought weak Pietro Jacomo to power through his marriage to Aurelia, the daughter of a powerful Florentine leader. Altofronto, disguised as the Malcontent, prepared to bide his time until the state wearied of Pietro. His devoted duchess, Maria, waited faithfully in prison for his return. Celso acted as Altofronto's secret informant on matters of state.

As the Malcontent, Altofronto was described as a likable person of marked intelligence and straightforward honesty. He would not flatter as others did. On the negative side, however, he was described as more monster than man, more discontented than Lucifer in his Fall, a man living on the vexations of others and at variance with his own soul. This mixture, making him seem most unpredictable, served Altofronto well in plotting against his adversaries. This description of the former duke came from Pietro, strangely attracted to the erratic individual known as the Malcontent. It was Altofronto who told Pietro that he was being cuckolded by Mendoza. This condition, Altofronto declared, was most unnatural in that a cuckold was a creation of woman and not of God. Altofronto used such means to torment Pietro and to inflame him against Mendoza.

Incensed by Altofronto's report of Mendoza's relationship with Aurelia, Pietro confronted the minion with accusations and threats to kill him, but Mendoza placated the duke with disparagement of women and their habits, absolving himself of Pietro's accusations by telling him that Ferneze was the offender against the duke's marital rights. To prove his point he suggested that Pietro break into Aurelia's room that night; then, should Ferneze try to escape, Mendoza would kill him. The situation resolved itself as Mendoza planned. Ferneze was discovered in Aurelia's room and was, as the minion believed, killed in his attempt to flee.

Later, when Mendoza and Aurelia were alone, they planned Pietro's murder. Aurelia promised to use her influence to have Mendoza made Duke of Genoa. Unknown to them, however, Ferneze had not been killed. Wounded, he attracted the attention of Altofronto, who revived and hid the young courtier.

Knowing that Pietro had gone hunting, Mendoza hired the Malcontent to pursue and murder the duke. Taken in by Altofronto's apparent willingness to aid him in his villainy, Mendoza outlined the remaining steps to his ultimate goal. With Pietro removed and his alliance with Aurelia established, he would be ready to make his real bid for power. The banishment of Aurelia would be an easy step because he would publicize her infidelity to the Florentines. Then he intended to marry Maria, Altofronto's imprisoned wife, whose friends would strengthen Mendoza and his faction.

Assured by Mendoza's admission that he did not love Maria, that she too was only a pawn to him, Altofronto took heart in his assurance that Maria was still true to him, as Celso had reported. Altofronto suggested to Mendoza that they hire some wretch or holy man to report that he had seen Pietro, bereft of reason because of his wife's infidelity, throw himself into the sea. Also, he offered to act as Mendoza's emissary in winning Maria's favor.

Instead of murdering Pietro, Altofronto divulged to him the plot against his life and provided him with the disguise of the hermit who was to report his suicide. Pietro, in disguise, gave a vivid description of his own anguished demise as he lamented Aurelia's unfaithfulness. Mendoza immediately banished Aurelia. He then instructed Altofronto to negotiate with Maria.

Duped by the earnestness of the supposed hermit, Mendoza sent him after Altofronto, with orders to poison the Malcontent at supper. When Altofronto returned for a letter that would admit him to Maria's quarters in the citadel, he in turn received Mendoza's instructions to poison the hermit.

Altofronto and Pietro, encountering banished Aurelia, found her in abject grief because of her indiscretions and her love for Pietro. Altofronto eased the hurt of Pietro's inadequacy in his relationship with Aurelia by reminding him that many great men have had unfaithful wives. Among them he named Agamemnon, King Arthur, and Hercules.

Maria's faithfulness to Altofronto was proved beyond doubt when Maquerelle and the disguised Altofronto waited upon her to deliver Mendoza's offer of marriage. In answer to their proposal and the promise of great riches if she would accept Mendoza, she announced that she already had a husband. Banished or in power, present or absent, Altofronto was still her true lord.

Mendoza's only remaining threat to power was Altofronto, who in the disguise of the Malcontent knew too much of the usurper's malice. To be rid of him, Mendoza planned to use the contents of one of the two boxes given him by his intended victim. These boxes, according to the giver, contained fumes that on being breathed would either put the person to sleep for twelve hours or kill him suddenly. Mendoza, not knowing the contents of either box, used the one that merely put Altofronto into a sleep resembling death. Later he appeared at a masked ball given by Mendoza to celebrate the deaths he had planned. In the meantime, spurned by Maria, Mendoza accused her of murdering the hermit—the disguised Pietro—whom Altofronto had reported dead. Condemned to die, the faithful wife welcomed death, a fate better than damnation in being married to the usurper.

At the ball Altofronto chose Maria as his partner. Revealing his identity, he asked her to remain composed so that others would not recognize him. Pietro danced with Aurelia, who, repenting of her past deeds, vowed her undying devotion to him. Then, at the signal of a musical flourish, Mendoza's three supposed victims—Altofronto, Pietro, and Ferneze—revealed themselves, to the consternation of Mendoza and the joy of the assemblage. Immediately acclaimed, Altofronto was restored to his rightful place as Duke of Genoa.

Denying Mendoza's plea to live long enough to do penance for his sins, Altofronto ordered the minion to take his own life. Aurelia and Pietro were given the blessing of the court. Maquerelle was allowed to carry on her pandering in the suburbs. Bilioso, a sycophant who chose to stand with the wrong rather than fall with the right, was summarily dismissed from any further court favor. And Altofronto and Maria were reunited in happiness.

THE MALTESE FALCON

Type of work: Novel
Author: Dashiell Hammett (1894-1961)
Type of plot: Mystery romance
Time of plot: Twentieth century
Locale: San Francisco
First published: 1930

Principal characters:
SAM SPADE, detective
BRIGID O'SHAUGHNESSY, his client
CASPER GUTMAN, her employer
WILMER, Gutman's bodyguard
JOEL CAIRO, Gutman's one-time agent
MILES ARCHER, Spade's partner
FLOYD THURSBY, Brigid's murdered accomplice

Critique:

The Maltese Falcon is a detective novel of the hard-boiled school. Its distinction lies in the fact that the detective himself becomes involved in crime through a large bribe. Written in racy, colloquial language, the book pretends to no more than pure entertainment, but it is a classic example of its type.

The Story:

Brigid O'Shaughnessy went to the office of Sam Spade and Miles Archer, detectives, to ask them to trail a Floyd Thursby. Archer, who undertook the job, was killed the first night. About an hour later Thursby himself was killed in front of his hotel. The police were inclined to suspect Spade of the murder of his partner, for it was known that Iva Archer had been wanting a divorce so that she could marry Spade.

Brigid left word at Spade's office that she wanted to see him. She had changed hotels because she was afraid. She said she could not tell Spade the whole story, but that she had met Thursby in the Orient and that they had arrived in San Francisco the week before. She said she did not know who killed Thursby.

When Spade returned to his office, Joel Cairo was waiting for him. He asked Spade where the statuette of the black bird was and offered five thousand dollars for the recovery of the ornament. That night Spade was trailed by a small young man in a gray overcoat and cap. Spade eluded his pursuer long enough to slip into Brigid's hotel unseen. There he learned that Brigid was connected in some way with a mysterious black bird, an image of a falcon. Later she went with Spade to his apartment, to meet Cairo. She told Cairo that she did not have the prize, that he would have to wait possibly a week for its return.

When the police arrived to question Spade about his relations with Iva, they discovered Cairo and Brigid in the apartment. Spade introduced Brigid as an operator in his employ and explained that he had been questioning Cairo about the murders of Archer and Thursby. After Cairo and the police had gone, Brigid told Sam that she did not know what made the falcon so important. She had been hired to get it away from a Russian named Kemidov in Constantinople.

Next morning, before Brigid was awake, Spade went out to get groceries for breakfast and incidentally to search her hotel room for the falcon, which he failed to find. He was certain that Brigid knew where the falcon was. Brigid was afraid of what Cairo might do, however, and Spade arranged for her to stay a few days at the home of his secretary.

Because, in explaining to Cairo how Thursby was killed, Brigid had outlined the letter G in the air, Spade knew that there was some special significance attached to the letter. He again saw the young man trailing him in the corridor of a hotel and went up to him. Spade said that someone would have to talk, and G might as well know it. Shortly afterward a Mr. Gutman called and asked Spade to go see him. Spade told him that Cairo was offering him ten thousand dollars, not five, for the return of the falcon. Gutman laughed derisively; the bird was obviously worth an enormous fortune. Angry because Gutman would tell him no more, Spade left, saying he would give Gutman until five-thirty to talk.

From a taxi driver Spade learned that Brigid had gone to the Ferry Building and not to his secretary's house and that she had stopped on the way to buy a newspaper. When he returned to Gutman's hotel, he learned that the falcon was an old ornament, made in Malta, encrusted with precious gems and covered with black enamel for protection. Gutman had traced it to the Constantinople home of Kemidov, where Gutman's agents had got it. Now Gutman was wondering where it was.

Next day Spade searched Cairo's hotel room and found that the ships' schedules had been torn out of a newspaper of the day before. He bought a copy of the paper and saw that the ship *La Paloma* had arrived from Hongkong. Remembering that Brigid had mentioned the Orient, he associated her going to the Ferry Building with the arrival of the ship. Later he learned that Cairo had checked out of his hotel room. Meanwhile Spade had gone aboard the *La Paloma* and had learned that Gutman, Cairo, the strange young man, and Brigid had had a long conference with Jacobi, the captain.

While Spade was telling his secretary of his discoveries, a man came in, held out a bundle to Spade, and dropped over dead. Spade opened the package and discovered the falcon. Spade was sure that the man was Jacobi. He had his secretary call the police while he checked the package in a station nearby. The key he mailed to his post-office box. He then went to answer a distress call from Brigid, but she was not in her room. Instead, Spade found Gutman's daughter, who sent him to the suburbs on a wild-goose chase. When he returned to his apartment, he met Brigid waiting outside, obviously frightened. Opening the door, he found Gutman, the young man, and Cairo waiting for him.

Spade realized that his wild-goose chase had been planned to get him out of the way long enough to give these people a chance to find Jacobi before he returned. Since they were all together, Spade said he would give them the falcon in return for ten thousand dollars and someone on whom to blame the murders. He suggested the young man, whose name was Wilmer, as the suspect. Spade explained that if Wilmer were hanged for the murder of Thursby, the district attorney would drop the case, taking it for granted that Jacobi had been murdered by the same person. Gutman, sure that Thursby had killed Archer, finally consented to make Wilmer the victim.

Gutman produced ten one-thousand-dollar bills. Then Spade called his secretary and asked her to get the claim check from the post-office and redeem the falcon. After she had delivered the package to Spade's apartment, Gutman untied it and, to make sure he had the genuine falcon, began to scratch away the enamel. The falcon was a lead imitation. Kemidov had tricked him. Spade gave back nine thousand dollars. Then he called the police and told them that Wilmer had killed Jacobi and Thursby.

Knowing that Gutman would tell about his and Brigid's part in the plot, Spade made Brigid confess to him that she had drawn Archer into an alley that first night and had killed him with a pistol borrowed from Thursby. He told Brigid that he intended also to turn her over to the police. He had to clear himself of suspicion of killing his partner, and he could not let a woman stand in his way.

THE MAN AGAINST THE SKY

Type of work: Poetry
Author: Edwin Arlington Robinson (1869-1935)
First published: 1916

One of the most difficult of American poets to pigeonhole is Edwin Arlington Robinson. If critics try to file him away under the label of the prolix and wordy poets, he refutes them with the sparkling simplicity of such character sketches as "Bewick Finzer" and "Richard Cory"; if they decide he is coldly intellectual, they need only read *Tristram* to discover a warm and passionate love story; if they try to stuff him into that compartment occupied by poets who take themselves too seriously, such witty masterpieces as "Miniver Cheevy" and "Mr. Flood's Party" will laugh at them forever. Yet in spite of these many talents, Robinson has somewhat grudgingly been given the status of a major American poet, and critics who specialize in "modern" poetry tend to omit him from their discussions or to brush him off with a word or two. Possibly the very fact that he cannot be pigeonholed and does not belong to any school or movement accounts for this strange neglect. And strange neglect it is, for Robinson is one of the most interesting and readable poets of our time.

In *The Man Against the Sky*, the early volume that first brought him the critical acclaim that now seems to be waning, Robinson is at his best; and nearly all the types of poetry he was to write are skillfully represented here. Only his talent for handling long narratives, as found in his Arthurian trilogy and his novels in verse, such as *Cavender's House*, is lacking, and perhaps even this aspect of this work is foreshadowed in miniature by "Llewellyn and the Tree," the triangle story of a man, his shrewish wife, and Fate.

The light touch that created Miniver Cheevy and Mr. Flood introduces us in this volume to "Old King Cole":

No crown annoyed his honest head,
No fiddlers three were called or needed;
For two disastrous heirs instead
Made music more than ever three did.

The story of the old man cursed with two wild and worthless sons is essentially a tragic one, but Robinson lets the old fellow take such a merry and philosophical attitude toward his troubles that the reader is amused rather than saddened. This effect is a variation on a well-known skill of Robinson's: in his character sketches he celebrates people who would ordinarily be judged as failures and charmingly turns defeat into a contented, if not glorious, triumph. Robinson is likely to be remembered best for these short poems which are alive with strange and interesting characters. In *The Man Against the Sky* we first meet Flammonde, that "Prince of Castaways" who comes to Tilbury Town "from God knows where." Flammonde finally is able to make the townspeople see the good points in a woman of bad reputation, to help them raise money for the education of a gifted boy, and to patch up a quarrel between two citizens of the town. But Flammonde himself remains a mystery, an apparent failure in life. In "The Gift of God" we are introduced to the fond and foolish mother who in her dreams ennobles a son who is just an average young man; but her triumph comes in the very nobility of that dream. "The Poor Relation" is less subtle than many of Robinson's sketches, but it is an effective portrait of an old woman who is "unsought, unthought-of, and unheard." And, of course, there is Bewick Finzer, the man of wealth whose brain crumbles when he loses all his money; a sad reminder to the more fortunate, he comes begging for loans:

Familiar as an old mistake,
And futile as regret.

Still another fine short poem is "John Gorham," but this one differs from Robinson's other sketches in its ballad-like form. Two young people, Gorham and Jane Wayland, speak to each other in alternating stanzas; they break off their romance in most surprising fashion.

The *pièce de résistance* of the volume is the long dramatic monologue, "Ben Jonson Entertains a Man from Stratford." Using the few known facts of Shakespeare's life and the many hints found in the plays and sonnets, the poet gives us as fine a characterization of Shakespeare as can be found anywhere. Robinson's setting is a simple one: Ben Jonson meets an alderman from Stratford and treats him to a few drinks in a London tavern. While drinking, Ben talks about "this mad, careful, proud, indifferent Shakespeare." The poem is centered around the bard's very human wish to retire to the finest house in Stratford and live out his life as a country squire. In developing this theme, Robinson credits Ben with some astute observations on Shakespeare's skill as a playwright, on his troubles with women, on the contrast between his simple ambitions and his tremendous success as a writer, and on his feelings toward "a phantom world he sounded and found wanting." Part of the pleasure in reading this poem comes from recognizing the sources from which Robinson has drawn his material; for instance, Shakespeare's troubled love life derives from the recorded facts of his strange marriage to Anne Hathaway and from the "dark lady" of the sonnets; for Shakespeare's outlook on life Robinson draws chiefly on the graveyard scene in *Hamlet,* an interesting source because Robinson has definitely "weighted" his poem so that it becomes a sort of literary triple-play—Shakespeare to Jonson to Robinson—and he makes Robinson the key man. Here is a passage in which Jonson, when he meets Shakespeare

"down Lambeth way," quotes the bard as philosophizing in a gloomy mood. This could undoubtedly be Shakespeare speaking, but might it not also be pure Robinson?

"Your fly will serve as well as anybody,
And what's his hour? He flies, and flies,
   and flies,
And in his fly's mind has a brave ap-
   pearance;
And then your spider gets him in her
   net,
And eats him up and hangs him up to
   dry.
That's Nature, the kind mother of us
   all.
And then your slattern housemaid
   swings her broom,
And where's your spider? And that's
   Nature, also.
It's Nature, and it's Nothing. It's all
   Nothing. . . ."

This type of philosophy has its counterpart in the title piece of Robinson's volume. The poet has been called a "muddy thinker," but a careful reading of "The Man Against the Sky" reveals not muddiness but the honest outlook of a man who, like so many others, is unsure of the meaning of birth, life, and death. Robinson is not the first to suggest that man, in his search for the answer to the riddle, will find that the problem is a personal one, that "mostly alone he goes." Robinson places his Man on a hill against the red glare of the sunset and then speculates on the forces that brought him there and the fate that lies ahead of him:

Whatever dark road he may have taken,
This man who stood on high
And faced alone the sky,
Whatever drove or lured or guided
   him,—
A vision answering a faith unshaken,
An easy trust assumed of easy trials,
A sick negation born of weak denials,
A crazed abhorrence of an old condi-
   tion,
A blind attendance on a brief ambi-
   tion,—
Whatever stayed him or derided him,
His way was even as ours;

And we, with all our wounds and all
our powers,
Must each await alone at his own
height
Another darkness or another light. . . .

Aside from its philosophical import, this poem also illustrates well the style that is so definitely Robinson's: without straining, he combines a colloquial rhythm that is smooth and offhand with a scholarly choice of words that does not fear the polysyllable. In "The Man Against the Sky" such words as "atrabilious" and "hierophants" are slipped in as if they were inevitable.

The Man Against the Sky is not a perfect volume by any means. There are flat poems (after all, the level of "Eros Turannos" and "Bewick Finzer" is a difficult one to sustain) and even in some of the best ones there are lines that string together a series of what might be called "bland" words, the kind that get a poem started or keep it moving but contribute almost nothing of connotative value. Robinson's diction is usually so effective that these lapses seem especially egregious. Sometimes, too, Robinson sacrifices the exact word in order to make a rhyme; for example, in the third stanza of "Old King Cole" the poet has chosen "affair" to rhyme with "pair"; the choice tends to blur the meaning. These objections are minor ones, however, when set against the overall effectiveness of the volume. It seems certain that Robinson, aided by a universality that lifts him above any school, movement, period, or region (the New England flavor blends in like a tart but unobtrusive spice) will survive his current critical neglect and emerge as one of the finest of American poets.

MAN AND SUPERMAN

Type of work: Drama
Author: Bernard Shaw (1856-1950)
Time: c. 1900
Locale: England and Spain
First presented: 1905

Principal characters:

JACK TANNER, an eloquent anarchist and social philosopher
ANN WHITEFIELD, his ward and pursuer
ROEBUCK RAMSDEN, her co-guardian
OCTAVIUS ROBINSON, her suitor
VIOLET ROBINSON, Octavius' sister
HECTOR MALONE, her husband
HENRY STRAKER, Jack's chauffeur
MENDOZA, a bandit
DON JUAN
DOÑA ANA DE ULLOA, a Spanish noblewoman
DON GONZALO, her father
THE DEVIL

Frequently the subtitles of Shaw's plays are just as informative as the prefaces. They are often just as clever; they are always more to the point. Such is the case with *Heartbreak House,* which is subtitled *A Fantasia in the Russian Manner on English Themes; Fanny's First Play, An Easy Play for a Little Theatre;* and *"In Good King Charles's Golden Days," A True History that Never Happened.* So, too, with *Man and Superman,* which is subtitled simply but significantly *A Comedy and a Philosophy.* For *Man and Superman,* though it was written early in Shaw's career, represents the culmination of Shaw's theory that the drama is but a device—a trick, if you like—for getting the public to listen to one's philosophy: social philosophy, political philosophy, economic philosophy—Shavian philosophy. With the possible exception of *Back to Methuselah, Man and Superman* is Shaw's most philosophical play.

In its simplest terms, the philosophical meaning of the play is that in the war between the sexes, woman always emerges conqueror, even if man, her antagonist, be a superman; that in a battle between instinct and intelligence, instinct always wins. To develop this theme, Shaw claimed to have written a modern, philosophical interpretation of the Don Juan

story, which means that Don Juan is reincarnated as a Shavian hero in England at the turn of the century. The closest resemblance between Shaw's hero and the libertine celebrated in music and literature lies in their names: John Tanner, Don Juan Tenorio. Any other similarity is purely coincidental, for Shaw transformed literature's most notorious libertine into a man of moral passion, a Nietzschean superman who lives a life of pure reason in defiance of the traditions of organized society. As a Shavian hero, Tanner is, of course, impeccably moral, even chaste. The philosophical meaning of the play arises from the fact that Tanner, representing the good man, is unsuccessful in defending his chastity. Pitted against a scheming female who embodies the sexual, maternal drive, Tanner is forced to surrender his control of sexual instinct. He capitulates and marries. In effect, he commits moral suicide by succumbing to conventionality.

On one level, this theme is worked out in a contrived, almost trivial, but nevertheless hilarious plot. In his will, Ann Whitefield's father appointed Jack Tanner and Roebuck Ramsden joint guardians of his daughter. Ramsden objects to sharing the guardianship on the grounds that Tanner, as the author of "The Revolutionist's Handbook and Pocket Companion," is an anarchist and profligate; Tanner objects on the grounds that Ramsden is a prig and a hypocrite. Both, however, accede to the wishes of the deceased, little realizing that Ann had dictated the terms of the will in an elaborate scheme to make Tanner her husband. Upon realizing that Ann has designs on him, Tanner flees to the Continent, is detained by bandits, is ultimately caught by the pursuing Ann. They agree to marry.

On another, more esoteric level, the philosophical implications of the theme are developed at length. Tanner has a dream—a play within the play—which turns out to be no less than a Platonic dialogue: "Don Juan in Hell." In this scene, four of the principals are re-embodied as historical or mythical personages and are universalized as moral forces. Tanner appears as Don Juan, the man of moral passion; Ann, as Doña Ana de Ulloa, the eternal maternal female; Ramsden, as Don Gonzalo, the man of pleasure; and Mendoza (leader of the bandits), as the Devil. These four engage in a debate which Don Juan, speaking for Shaw, monopolizes with a series of lengthy monologues. Herein the theme of the play is recapitulated in abstract but certain terms. The subject is Man. The end of man, Don Juan argues, is the cultivation of intellect, for only by exercising it dispassionately can man discover his purpose, and discovering it, fulfill it. Therefore, the good man, the man of moral passion, will eschew anything that subverts the life of reason. Woman, however, will not be eschewed, and it is woman, with her relentless desire to propagate, and marriage, the instrument by which she domesticates, that undermine man. If man surrenders to woman, he is doomed.

The conclusion of the play is, then, a gloomy one for Shaw. By marrying Ann, Tanner admits that woman, bolstered by the "Life Force," is bound to triumph; that man, even the superman, is bound to abandon the pursuit of his own goal to serve woman in her goal of perpetuating the race.

Although the ending is gloomy and the dream play verbose, the prevailing tone of the play is comic and light. In spite of its philosophy, the drama is playable—including the dream play—principally because Shaw succeeded in making his characters gloriously human and therefore funny. Tanner, for instance, is moral, intensely moral; but he is fallible, even a bit ridiculous, as Ann delights in proving when she punctures his eloquent utterances with the charge of political aspiration. Ann herself is as engaging a heroine as any in Shaw's plays. An incorrigible liar, an inveterate hypocrite, she is charming because she is thoroughly female.

The minor characters were just as obviously invented to fit into the thematic framework of the drama, but they too contribute to the fun. Both Ramsden and Mrs. Whitefield represent the authority of the old order which Tanner is trying to overthrow; both, however, have distinctly comic personalities. Believing that a man's duty lies in protecting the weaker sex, Octavius serves primarily as a foil to Tanner but provides many laughs as a lovesick youth. Mendoza, the bandit; Straker, the impudent chauffeur; and Malone, the senile American millionaire —all figure in Shaw's design. All, moreover, as humorous persons, relieve the tedium of that design.

Considered as a whole, with the "Epistle Dedicatory," which serves as a preface, and "The Revolutionary's Handbook," which is an appendix of sorts, *Man and Superman* is one of Shaw's most important plays. It is not Shaw's masterpiece, nor is it his best play. It is too obviously a piece of propaganda for such accolades. It is, however, central to Shaw's philosophy, and philosophy is always central to Shaw's plays.

THE MAN OF FEELING

Type of work: Novel
Author: Henry Mackenzie (1745-1831)
Type of plot: Sentimental romance
Time of plot: Mid-eighteenth century
Locale: England
First published: 1771

Principal characters:
MR. HARLEY, a very sensitive young Englishman
MISS WALTON, a rich heiress
EDWARDS, a farmer befriended by Harley
MISS ATKINS, a prostitute befriended by Harley
HARLEY'S AUNT

Critique:

In the last half of the eighteenth century the function of the English novel was the study of man and his manners, particularly the emotions and sentiments of a man of great sensibility. Such is the subject matter of Henry Mackenzie's *The Man of Feeling.* In addition, this novel is a splendid example of the studied formlessness of many late-eighteenth-century novels. In it the reader finds such peculiarities as editorial notes which state that the first fourteen chapters are missing, as well as the addition of so-called "Fragments" at the end of the story. The pretended incompleteness is actually not present, and the entire story is actually told, although in a somewhat disjointed fashion. Like so many of his contemporaries in the field of fiction, Mackenzie filled his novel with the loneliness of the delicate mind, the unhappiness of love beyond one's station, the vainglory of riches, the hardships of the poor, and the glorification of benevolence.

The Story:

One day, in early September, a rural clergyman took hunting with him a friend from town. When they stopped to rest, the friend found some indecipherable initials carved on the bark of a tree. The curate said they were probably the work of a young man named Harley, a former resident of the parish. The clergyman added that he had in his possession a manuscript telling the greater part of Harley's story, a work he thought of no great value, and so he used the papers for wadding in his gun. The manuscript had been found among the possessions of a former parishioner, a friend of Harley's. Upon request, the clergyman gave the bundle of disconnected papers to his friend, who after his return to town pieced together the melancholy story which the rambling narrative unfolded.

Mr. Harley, an orphan reared by a maiden aunt, was descended from a good family among the country gentry in England. Passing years had taken toll of the family's fortunes, however, until he had only a very modest income derived from his small estate by the time he reached manhood. The young man, who was extremely virtuous, did not feel that he needed any more money, but his friends insisted that he could, with very little trouble, secure the use of some adjoining lands belonging to the crown. At his friends' insistence, and because he was very much in love with Miss Walton, an heiress, Harley set out for London to attempt to get a lease to the lands, which would give him a handsome increase to his fortunes in return for a cheap rental.

Once in London, Harley had some amazing adventures, partly because he was willing to believe all people good until he found them bad and partly because he wished to help anyone who needed aid from another human being. These adventures took place over several weeks, for Harley found that the baronet who was to help him in his suit for the lease was not an easy man to see. On the occasion of one visit to see the baronet, Harley met a young man who pretended to be quite a man about town. Harley, who wished to know more about London, spent the evening with the young man, only to learn that the fellow was a former footman who served as a pander for several wealthy men.

A short time later an unnamed friend of Harley's invited him to go with a party to the asylum at Bedlam. There Harley was much affected by the insane, particularly by a young woman who had gone mad after her lover's death; she touched Harley's heart when she cried out that he resembled her dead lover. As the party left the young lady, a gentleman offered to tell Harley about some of the inmates. Harley assented, only to find within a few minutes that his guide was himself a madman who imagined himself to be an Oriental potentate.

A few evenings later Harley went for a walk through the park. While there, he met an elderly gentleman who invited him to partake of a glass of cider at a nearby public house. Harley, impressed by the gentleman's attitude of benevolence to a beggar, agreed. Once in the house, Harley was invited to take a hand in a friendly game of cards, during which the old gentleman and an accomplice swindled the good-hearted Harley out of a substantial sum of money. Leaving the place and still unaware of the swindle, Harley was accosted by a prostitute who begged him for something to eat and drink. Harley, hating to see another human in distress, let himself open to severe criticism by taking the girl, a Miss Atkins, to a brothel where she might get some nourishment. When she poured out a tale of seduction to him, he agreed to help her if he could, and promised to see her the following day.

The next morning he went to see Miss Atkins. She told him she wanted only to return to her father, a retired army officer. Just as she had finished telling her story, her father appeared. He misjudged the scene and almost did violence to Harley and his daughter. A fainting spell on the part of Miss Atkins gave Harley a chance to explain everything to the father, who then forgave his daughter and took her back into his good graces.

Harley's London adventures were cut short by a notice from the baronet that someone else had been granted the crown lands Harley sought. The successful petitioner turned out to be the pander Harley had met at the baronet's house. Discouraged, Harley took a coach to return home.

The coach took Harley to within a day's walk of his home. From there, rather than wait for a public conveyance, the young man set out for his house on foot. On the way he met an elderly soldier, who turned out to be a farmer named Edwards, whom Harley had known as a child. Edwards told Harley how it was he happened to be in the garb he wore. The enclosure acts by Parliament had given Edwards' landlord an excuse to move the farmer and his family from a good farm to a poor one. Bad crops had climaxed the poor man's ill luck, and he and his married son had been forced to become tenants on a tiny, depleted bit of ground. As if that were not enough, a press gang had seized Edwards' son. The only way to secure the younger man's release had been for Edwards himself, an old man, to enter the service in his son's place, after buying off the officials with the little money he had left.

While a soldier in the East Indies, Edwards had befriended an aged Hindu, who made him a present of some gold. Upon his release from the service, Edwards had returned to England and was now on his way to visit his son. When he and Harley arrived in Edwards' old neighborhood, they found that disaster was still striking at the old fellow, for his son and daughter-in-law had died, leaving two small children. Harley promised the old man a farm on his own estates, and, with the two orphans, Harley and Edwards continued their journey.

Home once more, Harley saw the old gentleman comfortably established on a small farm. But unhappiness soon overtook Harley himself. Miss Walton, with whom he was very much in love, was affianced by her father to a rich man. Harley, although he had never declared his love to Miss Walton or anyone else, was heartbroken. He took to his bed with a severe illness. After many weeks of illness, the doctors and his friends despaired of his life. Miss Walton herself, hearing of his illness, came to visit him, hoping to cheer up the young man, for whom she had a great deal of esteem, more, indeed, than anyone had ever guessed.

A very tearful and touching scene occurred when Miss Walton appeared at Harley's sickbed. Harley, knowing he was near death, told Miss Walton of his love for her. Even though she was promised to another, she told of her love for him, whereupon she fainted and he died. He was buried near his mother, as he had once told his aunt he wished to be. For her part, Miss Walton remained single, preferring not to marry after Harley's death. For many years she was often seen walking or reading near the place where Harley's house had stood.

THE MAN OF MODE

Type of work: Drama
Author: Sir George Etherege (1634?-1691)
Type of plot: Comedy of manners
Time of plot: The 1670's
Locale: London
First presented: 1676

Principal characters:
DORIMANT, a young man about town
LADY LOVEIT, Dorimant's mistress
BELLINDA, in love with Dorimant
YOUNG BELLAIR, Dorimant's friend
OLD BELLAIR, Young Bellair's father
EMILIA, in love with Young Bellair
HARRIET WOODVILL, a young countrywoman of fortune who
loves Dorimant
SIR FOPLING FLUTTER, a dandy

Critique:

Most critics give Sir George Etherege credit for trying to do for the manners of fashionable London what Molière had done for the manners of fashionable Paris; that is, to portray the follies of the time in such a way as to give some hope of improving them. So true was the picture of the times in *The Man of Mode, Or, Sir Fopling Flutter,* that the London wits tried to attach the names of real people to the characterizations: Dorimant for Rochester and Sir Fopling Flutter for Mr. Hewitt. That such an attempt was made is assuredly a tribute to the author's capture of the very spirit of the age. Those who would carp at the play for immorality, particularly with respect to the love affairs of Dorimant, must keep in mind the fact that the author portrayed only what he saw in the world about him. One should search the play, not for virtue, but for realism and wit.

The Story:

One morning Dorimant was lounging in his room when an orange-woman made her appearance. In the course of buying some fruit, Dorimant, who had a remarkable reputation as a lover, discovered that a young woman of quality and fortune from the country had fallen in love with him at sight, despite her mother's attempts to keep her daughter away from thoughts of loving any heartless man of the fashionable world. Dorimant, although he was in the process of dropping one mistress, Lady Loveit, and taking on a new one named Bellinda, was interested. Shortly afterward he received his friend Bellair, a fop who was very much in love with a young woman named Emilia and wished to marry her instead of the wealthy bride his father had picked out for him. The father's choice was Harriet, the girl who had been so taken with Dorimant.

To complicate matters for young Bellair, his father had arrived in town to hasten the marriage. Lodging in the same house with Emilia, and not knowing his son's affection for the girl, the old gentleman had fallen in love with her and wished to make her his own bride. Young Bellair, with the help of his aunt, Lady Townley, hoped to win his father's consent to marriage to Emilia.

Meanwhile Lady Loveit, Dorimant's mistress, was beside herself at the neglect she suffered at the hands of her lover. She complained bitterly to Bellinda, not knowing that it was Bellinda who had won the recent attentions of Dorimant and was about to become his mistress.

True to his promise to Bellinda, Dorimant came that afternoon and notified Lady Loveit that he was finished with her. His actions frightened Bellinda, although the deed was done at her request. At Lady Woodvill's lodgings that day, the lady herself was preparing Harriet to meet young Bellair, for Harriet's mother was as anxious for her daughter to marry him as his father was for the match. That Harriet did not wish to marry him made little difference to the mother. When the two young people met, they quickly made their dislike of the match known to one another. Then they proceeded to make a mock love scene for the benefit of the parents, to throw the oldsters off the track.

That same afternoon Bellinda and Dorimant met at the home of Lady Townley. Dorimant made Bellinda promise to have Lady Loveit walk on the Mall that evening so that Dorimant could confront her with Sir Fopling Flutter, a fool of a fop, and accuse her of being unfaithful. As they spoke, Sir Fopling Flutter entered the company and proceeded to demonstrate what a fool he was by the oddities and fooleries of his dress, deportment, and speech.

That evening young Bellair and Harriet went walking on the Mall. There they met Dorimant, who was forced to leave upon the appearance of Harriet's mother. Lady Loveit appeared, tried to make Dorimant jealous by flirting, but only succeeded in bringing Dorimant's reproaches on her head.

Later that same night there was a party at Lady Townley's house. Dorimant was one of the group, under the alias of Courtage, so that Harriet's mother would not realize that he was the gallant who was trying to woo her daughter. Under his false name Dorimant succeeded in ingratiating himself with the mother. Harriet, trying to hide her love and admiration from him, showed that her wit was as sharp as Dorimant's. Sir Fopling Flutter joined the party late and made himself more of a fool in everyone's eyes than he had been before.

By the time the party broke up, it was five o'clock in the morning. Dorimant had to hurry home in order to keep a rendezvous he had made with Bellinda, for she had promised to spend part of the night with him in his rooms. In the morning she was almost caught there, as she was ready to leave, when several of Dorimant's friends appeared. Bellinda escaped by going down the back stairs and stepping into a sedan chair. Her danger was not past, however, for the carriers, accustomed to taking Lady Loveit from Dorimant's house, took Bellinda to the former's lodging. Lady Loveit, still awake, saw Bellinda step from the chair. Only quick wit on the part of Bellinda, who told the men to say they had picked her up elsewhere, prevented her assignation with Dorimant from being known to Lady Loveit. The woman did not suspect that Bellinda was her rival.

A few minutes afterward Dorimant arrived and berated Lady Loveit in highhanded fashion, only to be embarrassed when Bellinda appeared from an adjoining room. He was so discomfited that he could only mutter excuses and leave the house.

Early that morning, at Lady Townley's house, young Bellair and Emilia were married, the bridegroom taking that drastic step before his father could force him into marriage with Harriet. As the ceremony was ending, Lady Woodvill, Harriet, old Bellair, and an attorney arrived. They had come to meet with young Bellair and to sign the marriage contract between the two families. Not knowing what to do, Lady Townley temporarily hid the clergyman in a closet. In the confusion of the moment, Emilia asked Harriet if she were in love with Dorimant. Harriet refused still to admit that she was, saying that she only hated to think of leaving the pleasures of the town to be made a prisoner in the country. At that point, while the others were off in another room to go over the terms of the marriage contract, Dorimant himself arrived. When he confessed his love to Harriet, she admitted also that she was in love with him.

The others then returned. Old Bellair, anxious to have the marriage celebrated, called for a parson. The clergyman, released from the closet, declared that he had already performed one ceremony when he married young Bellair to Emilia. Old Bellair was thunderstruck.

Just then Lady Loveit and Bellinda arrived in pursuit of Dorimant. He made his excuses to Lady Loveit by telling her that he intended to marry Harriet and thus improve his fortunes. Lady Loveit, who knew the value of money, admitted that under the circumstances she could only wish him well. Bellinda was grateful because his excuse concealed her affair with him and kept her honor intact. Lady Woodvill, overhearing the conversation, was furious with Dorimant for capturing Harriet's heart, but when she learned that his intentions were honorable and that he was the same Courtage whom she had admired the evening before, she was mollified to the extent of inviting him to visit the Woodvill estate in Hampshire.

Old Bellair, not to be outdone in graciousness, gave his grudging blessing to his son, who had gone against his will in marrying Emilia. The only person completely dismayed was Lady Loveit, who vowed that she would never again trust a man or go out in society.

THE MAN WHO WAS THURSDAY

Type of work: Novel
Author: Gilbert Keith Chesterton (1874-1936)
Type of plot: Symbolic allegory
Time of plot: Early twentieth century
Locale: London
First published: 1908

Principal characters:
LUCIAN GREGORY, an anarchic poet
GABRIEL SYME, a poet-policeman
THE SECRETARY, Monday in the council
GOGOL, Tuesday
MARQUIS DE ST. EUSTACHE, Wednesday
PROFESSOR DE WORMS, Friday
BULL, Saturday
SUNDAY

Critique:

At first the reader takes *The Man Who Was Thursday* for a pleasant adventure tale, but the allegory soon becomes more evident. The story, a fable in keeping with Catholic thought and idiom, is concerned to point out the place of Sunday as the true Sabbath. Chesterton himself does not try to make the meaning of the allegory explicit and clear; the reader is expected to supply his own interpretation. For those not interested in religious morality, the chief interest of the story lies in the rapid-moving, adventurous plot. Chestertonian puns and epigrams add to the humor of the book.

The Story:

Gregory was in the habit of declaiming his anarchistic views at his pleasant garden parties where his sister acted as hostess. Among the ladies particularly he seemed a thrilling poet, but his anarchism was surely only a pose. By chance Syme visited one of the parties and disagreed thoroughly with Gregory. In Syme's view the real wonder lay in order; anarchists hoped only to shock others—and deceive themselves—by their nihilistic views.

The dispute grew so warm that Gregory invited Syme to see for himself that there were real anarchists who were intent on destroying the world. Syme swore never to tell the authorities in return for Gregory's revelations.

The two took a cab to a slum restaurant. There Syme was surprised to eat an excellent dinner. Then Gregory took him down a subterranean passage lined with firearms to a council room filled with bombs. This room was the meeting place of the group of anarchists to which Gregory belonged. There was to be an election that night, and Gregory was sure that he would be elected to the post of Thursday on the Central Anarchist Council, the inner ring presided over by the redoubtable Sunday.

Before the meeting convened, however, Syme confided that he was really a detective. Gregory was filled with confusion and made a poor speech to the assembly. The members grew suspicious of Gregory's private convictions and elected Syme to act as Thursday on the Council.

Syme had become a detective in an unusual way. One day he met a policeman who had gone to school at Harrow. The policeman said he was one of the new force recruited to combat intellectuals who were out to destroy law and order. Syme, interested, wished to join the new force. He was taken to a pitch dark room in Scotland Yard, where a man he could not see gave him a job.

Now, as an elected member of the inner council, he was taken down the Thames

River on a tug. Landing, he was met at the top of the stairs by the Secretary, who took him to the meeting being held on a balcony in open view. There huge, menacing Sunday was presiding at the banquet table. As Syme surveyed the crowd, he was struck by the crooked grins of the members.

The business at hand was the assassination of the Tsar of Russia and the President of France. The bombing was to be done by the dapper Marquis de St. Eustache, called Wednesday. Suddenly Sunday shut off debate and announced that there was a spy present. Bull was appointed to take care of the council's business alone, and Sunday then unmasked Gogol as a police spy. Gogol left hurriedly.

As Syme left the meeting, he was shadowed by the aged Professor de Worms. In spite of his best efforts, de Worms easily kept up with him. Then in a tavern, de Worms told him that he was really a young actor disguised as the professor. He was another police spy.

The two fellow spies resolved to visit Bull, who was apparently the man in charge of plots. In Bull's apartment they persuaded him to take off his dark spectacles. From his kindly eyes they deduced that he was in reality no anarchist; Bull confessed that he too was a police spy.

The three Scotland Yard men decided to cross the Channel and prevent St. Eustache from bombing the tsar and the president. They came upon St. Eustache in a café in Calais. Syme, having decided to insult the Frenchman and provoke him to a duel, tried to pull his nose. The angry man's challenge was accepted. Because the duel was to be fought near a railroad station, Syme thought the place had been chosen so that St. Eustache could board a Paris train immediately afterward. Hoping that St. Eustache would miss the train, Syme did his best to prolong the duel.

St. Eustache grew impatient and offered to end the duel by letting Syme pull his nose. Then, as the train came, St. Eustache pulled off his own nose and removed his wig; he too was a police spy.

A menacing masked mob got off the train, led by the Secretary, and gave chase to the men from Scotland Yard. The four confessed spies began to run.

The chase was a mad one. The pursued used horses and a car to seek safety with the police, but the well-disciplined mob kept up with them. At last the spies were crowded onto a pier. Arrayed against them was the mob, firing rifles and pistols. To their horror they saw the police also lined up against them with their enemies.

But, as matters turned out, the Secretary was still another Scotland Yard man, attempting to capture the others because he wanted to thwart the bombing. The five returned to London, where they picked up Gogol. They were determined to confront Sunday, the leader.

When they found him, Sunday began to run with surprising speed and grace. He used several hansom cabs and a fire engine in his flight, and he even commandeered an elephant from the zoo. On the outskirts of London he jumped into the basket of a balloon and floated out of their reach.

The six spies pursued Sunday in spite of the rough countryside. When his balloon came to earth, they thought they had overtaken him at last. A servant met them, however, and showed them to a carriage. They were taken to a nearby castle and royally received. A valet laid out costumes for them symbolizing the days of the week. Syme was given a gown embellished with a sun and a moon, for according to Genesis the Lord created the sun and the moon on Thursday.

They learned that Sunday had been the Scotland Yard official who had employed them all. By now the huge Sunday seemed beneficent. At a party in the garden the councilors were seated on thrones. Sunday was gowned in pure white, symbolizing the sanctity of the Sabbath. He lectured them on the Sabbath as a holy day; they should use it to gather strength and comfort for the week's work. When Gregory came to the party he was denounced as the real enemy—he was an intellectual anarchist.

MAN WITH A BULL-TONGUE PLOW

Type of work: Poetry
Author: Jesse Stuart (1907-   )
First published: 1934

Jesse Stuart's *Man with a Bull-Tongue Plow* is a book of regional and personal poetry come freely from the heart of its author, a book by a man informed with great natural wisdom and one on intimate terms with life close to the land.

> I am a farmer singing at the plow
> And as I take my time to plow along
> A steep Kentucky hill, I sing my song—
> A one-horse farmer singing at the plow.

Thus he describes himself, introduces himself to the reader in the opening lines of this book of 703 sonnets which, taken together, tell not only Stuart's own story, but the story of the hill country of eastern Kentucky, past and present, people among whom Stuart grew up and still lives.

These are poems written without artifice, and Jesse Stuart speaks the literal truth when he writes lines like these:

> I do not sing the songs you love to hear;
> My basket songs are woven from the words
> Of corn and crickets, trees and men and birds.
> I sing the strains I know and love to sing.
> And I can sing my lays like singing corn,
> And flute them like a fluting gray cornbird;
> And I can pipe them like a hunter's horn—
> All of my life these are the songs I've heard.

Here in these simple, unpretentious, yet profoundly moving sonnets, Stuart has caught the land we love, the people we know, the moments of beauty which are man's lot in his journey through life. Here are the warmth of the sun and the wind's voice in the leaves, the cloying musk of the grainfields, the honest sweat of the plowman, the vespers of the birds, the talking of mountain brooks.

He writes here with great sincerity in a book of such remarkable achievement for a first work, that critical comparison of Stuart with Burns is perfectly apropos. Yet Stuart speaks in his own tongue; he is that rarity among American writers—an original, in the pages of whose book beats the pulse of the soil under the creative passion of a poet who knows that, of all the possessions of man, his land is the last to pass away. This book celebrates the poet's deep and abiding love of his native earth. It is one rich in bucolic scenes, filled with the beauty of Jesse Stuart's land, and replete with portraits of men and women who have lived and died in that part of America. It is a book about all mankind, wherever men have tilled the soil, and these sonnets are distinguished for that universality which is the province of all great art.

Man with a Bull-Tongue Plow is a book of unabashed emotion. The pure music, the great gusto and joy of living which are so evident here are designed for every reader—not alone the one who is devoted to poetry. Open the book anywhere; the lines draw and hold you with their clarity, their simplicity, their instant application to life as you yourself know it, their humility and beauty. Listen to Jesse Stuart sing his love of life:

> Ah, we get out to work in early April.
> We brave our bodies to the wind and sun.
> We swing the plow around the rugged hill
> From break of day until the setting sun.

We break the earth to plant in corn and cane.
We canvas burley-beds upon the hill.

Season follows season in these poems. In August "the whispering of the corn/Is fine to hear on any summer morn," and sunset brings "red-evening clouds" "Riding at ease above the corn and timber." Here is a picture of autumn:

When golden leaves begin to shiver down
Among the barren brush beneath the trees,
And scarlet leaves and yellow and light-brown
Begin to play in wind and pepper down
To earth—these clean and frosted leaves drip down.
Then it is time the corn is in the stack,
Potatoes in the hold—hay in the mows.
This is the time rust has grown on the plows;
The time to haul the pumpkins to the shed,
Since frosts have come and pumpkin vines are dead.

Winter is the season when "We saw the crows go flying cross the land,/Up in the icy heavens with the leaves,/We saw the crows fly over gray-starved land/When winter winds sighed in the last year leaves." In Jesse Stuart's world the lives of men are joined to the great cycle of nature:

Fields will be furrowed time and time again.
They will be furrowed by tall men unborn
As they were furrowed by men now forlorn
In dust—— And fences will be built again
By men like me and fields be cleaned of brush
By men like me only to grow again.

There is a natural roughness in these poems, from a technical perspective; but it is this very quality of the primitive which gives them their greatest strength.

In the spontaneity, the wonder, the resignation to sadness, the joy in earth's beauty so patent in these poems lies their essential effectiveness. They see life whole. They span man's time, from birth to death. There is no mawkishness, no sentimentality here. They are faithful to a world where happiness and grief are alike the welcome experience of every man who is whole in his mortality, who understands that life is the greatest privilege he may know, and who knows by this understanding that he ought to spend life as profitably as he can. This is the theme of "Marcus Phelps":

I hate to leave the world, for I have found
Such joy in life—So many things to love:
The sky, the wind and dead leaves on the ground
And wild geese flying through the clouds above.
I've loved the color of the autumn leaves,
And color of the frozen corn-field stones;
And I have loved a winter wind that grieves
And dwindling autumn water's monotone.
Earth is too great to lose—earth is too vast!
Life is too great to lose—life is too vast!
I hate to part with life and things I love;
I hate to leave the earth and skies above.
And life must pass, but surely Earth will last.
All life must end—the ending must be vast.

Whether he writes of nature or of man—and they are not distinguished in *Man with a Bull-Tongue Plow* by any sharp demarcation—Stuart celebrates simple existence, praising all of life and all of death. His book is not only filled with songs about the deeply satisfying beauty of the land, but also with epitaphs setting forth in terse lines the lives of the men and women of the hill country, be

2214

they successful lives, or failures, happy lives, or sad—lines like these:

I always loved Kentucky's lonesome water,
And when I went away I wanted to return.
Just something to Kentucky's lonesome water
Makes me remember and my burnt heart burn—

Though *Man with a Bull-Tongue Plow* is a regional book, it is limitless in its application. It should take ultimate rank as one of the finest, most spontaneous of books about man and his earth. This rugged, painfully honest collection of sonnets, with its clean, powerful lines, with its roughness and its gentleness, with its sincere, wholly natural verse has an everlasting freshness. It is a book through the pages of which ring the song of the high hills and the rune of mountain water, through which the heartbeats of men and women mingle with the pulse of earth. These are poems of life and love and death, by a poet in love with life, a poet filled with the humbling wonder and beauty of earth and sky, and a man filled with respect for his fellow men and understanding of their lives.

Open *Man with a Bull-Tongue Plow* at any page and read poems of singular simplicity and great power—and hear the turning of the soil beneath the blade, hear the wind in the treetops, and keep pace unforgettably with man eternally making his mortal mark upon his little plot of earth.

THE MAN WITHOUT A COUNTRY

Type of work: Short story
Author: Edward Everett Hale (1822-1909)
Type of plot: Historical romance
Time of plot: Nineteenth century
Locale: United States and the high seas
First published: 1863

Principal character:
PHILIP NOLAN

Critique:

Written originally as propaganda for the bitterly-contested presidential campaign of 1864, *The Man Without a Country* has become a classic of our literature. No story better expresses the spirit of American nationalism. Cut off from his native land, Philip Nolan wished himself dead rather than to experience the exile which he was forced to endure because of his youthfully rash statement and deed.

The Story:

Few people noticed in the newspaper columns of 1863 the report of the death of Philip Nolan. Few people would have recognized his name, in fact, for since Madison's administration went out in 1817, it had never been mentioned in public by any naval officer and the records concerning his case had been destroyed by fire years before his death.

When he was a young officer in Texas, Philip Nolan met Aaron Burr and became involved in Burr's infamous plot against the United States Government. When Burr's treason was revealed and the rebels were brought to trial, Nolan was indicted along with some of the lesser figures of the plot. Asked at his trial whether he had any statement to make concerning his loyalty to the United States, Nolan, in a frenzy, cursed the name of his country. Shocked, Colonel Morgan, who was conducting the court-martial, sentenced Philip Nolan never again to hear the name of his native land.

The Secretary of the Navy was requested to place the prisoner aboard a naval ship with a letter to the captain

explaining Nolan's peculiar punishment. For the remainer of his life Nolan and this letter went from one ship to another, Nolan traveling alone, speaking only to officers who guarded their country's name from his ears. None of the officers wanted to have him around because his presence prevented any talk of home or of politics. Once in a while he was invited to the officers' mess, but most of the time he ate alone under guard. Since he wore an army uniform with perfectly plain buttons, he became known as "Plain Buttons."

The periodicals and books he read had to be edited in order to delete any naming of or allusion to the United States. One incident was marked well by those who witnessed it. Some officers were gathered on deck one day reading aloud to one another Scott's *Lay of the Last Minstrel.* When it came his turn, Nolan took up the poem at the section which contained the lines, "This is my own, my native land!" He colored, choked, and threw the book into the water as he ran to his room. He did not emerge for two months.

Nolan altered considerably as time passed, and he lost the bragging air of unconcern he had assumed at first. After the incident of the poem he became shy and retiring, conversing with few people and staying in his quarters most of the time. He was transferred from ship to ship, never coming closer than a hundred miles to the land whose name he was forbidden to hear. Once Nolan came close to gaining his freedom from this bondage of silence. It happened during a naval battle with a British ship. A good

2216

shot from the enemy struck one of the ship's guns, killing the officer in charge and scattering the men. Unexpectedly Nolan appeared to take command of the gun, heroically ignoring his own safety and aiding in the defeat of the English ship. He was highly praised by the captain, who promised to mention him in his naval report. Nolan's case had been so forgotten in Washington that there seemed to be no orders concerning him. His punishment was being carried on simply by repetitious habit and naval form.

During his extensive studies Nolan kept scholarly notebooks. For diversion he began to collect organic specimens of wild life, which were brought to him by ship's men who went ashore. He was never known to be ill, and often he nursed those who were. So the expatriate passed his years, nameless, friendless, loveless. If there were any record of him in Washington, no evidence of such papers could ever be uncovered. So far as the government was concerned, Nolan did not exist. Stories about the lonely man circulated through mess halls, but many were untrue.

During the last fifteen years of his life Nolan aged rapidly. The men whom he had known when he first began his endless journey in 1807 had retired, and younger men took their places on the ships. Nolan became more reserved than ever, but he was always well regarded by those who knew him. It is said that young boys idolized him for his advice and for his interest in them.

Constantly the men were on guard never to reveal to their prisoner any news about the United States. This secrecy was often difficult to maintain, for the nation was growing rapidly. With the annexation of Texas there arose a strained incident. The officers puzzled over the removal of that state from Nolan's maps, but they decided that the change would give him a hint of westward expansion. There were other inconvenient taboos. When the states on the west coast joined the Union, the ships which bore Nolan had to avoid customary landings there. Although Nolan suspected the reason for this change in his habitual itinerary, he kept silent.

When Nolan lay dying, the captain of the ship came to see him. He found that Nolan had draped the stars and stripes around a picture of Washington. On one bulkhead hung the painting of an eagle grasping the entire globe in its claws, and at the foot of the bed was a map of the United States which Nolan had drawn from memory. When the dying man asked for news from home, the captain, who liked and pitied Nolan, told him about the progress of the United States during the more than fifty years of Nolan's exile. Seeing Nolan's joy at the news of his country, the captain could not bring himself, however, to tell the dying man that the United States was engaged in the Civil War.

Philip Nolan died in 1863. His last request was that he be buried at sea, his only home.

MANETTE SALOMON

Type of work: Novel
Authors: Edmond (1822-1896) and Jules (1830-1870) de Goncourt
Type of plot: Naturalism
Time of plot: Nineteenth century
Locale: Paris
First published: 1867

Principal characters:
NAZ DE CORIOLIS, a young painter
ANATOLE BAZOCHE, his close friend, another painter
MANETTE SALOMON, a model, Coriolis' mistress
GARNOTELLE, a painter of the classical school
CHASSAGNOL, a painter of the modern school

Critique:

This novel is representative of the mature fiction of the Goncourts, pioneers of the naturalistic movement in France. Here they treat with characteristically minute detail the Parisian artists' world, personifying its many facets by following the careers of several young painters. As in the earlier Charles Demailly, the major theme concerns the effect of love on the creative powers of an artist, in this case the painter Coriolis. But here the writers have disciplined their talents to convey more successfully the sense of actual life: they set one detail beside another with deliberate lack of emphasis and kaleidoscopic swiftness; they expunge all trace of the melodramatic or unrealistic from events. Interest focuses on the psychological delineation of the artistic temperament and on aesthetic theory itself. The vividly pictorial style is admirably suited to the milieu of the plot, for it constantly transmutes into language the painter's vision of the world.

The Story:

From the Paris zoo one had a magnificent view of the city. Visitors to the zoo were startled one day by a young man, who seemed to be a guide, pointing out landmarks below in terms which might have been used to describe the zoo itself. The young man, Anatole Bazoche, delighted in such pranks; he was studying art at Langibout's studio and kept everyone in constant uproar.

The son of a stolid bourgeoise widow, he had become an artist over her protests; although he had talent, he was content to dissipate it in bright, superficial paintings. His gift for farce symbolized the age, which, disillusioned and effete, laughed at everything. Art had become restless eclecticism, turning increasingly to a romanticism that was essentially literary.

In the same studio were Chassagnol, a compulsive talker who hoped for a new vision; Garnotelle, a quiet little peasant who tried earnestly to follow rules for good painting; and Naz de Coriolis. Of Italian and Creole descent, Coriolis was feared for his temper and pride, and envied for his money. Caring for nothing but his painting, he remained aloof from all but Anatole.

Coriolis, becoming dissatisfied with this Bohemian world, filled with talk and pranks, decided to travel in the Near East for a time. As he and Anatole sat talking before his departure, a woman brought her child to his door and asked if he needed a model. Taken by the child's extraordinary beauty, he caught her up in his arms. As he swung her down again, she pulled his gold watch and chain to the floor. Laughing, he let her keep it.

Garnotelle, who had left the studio, won the Prix de Rome for his careful (if mediocre) academic art. Cut off from his funds by his mother, Anatole, experiencing a series of ups and downs, took on

2218

any hack jobs that came his way until his uncle invited him to go to Marseilles and from there to Constantinople. Unfortunately, the uncle became jealous of Anatole's charm and left him in Marseilles. He joined a circus after helping in a cholera epidemic. Then he met Coriolis, now on his way back to Paris. Coriolis, who had inherited great wealth, generously invited Anatole to share a studio with him. There the two began painting. Coriolis had vowed never to marry; he felt that marriage and fatherhood destroy the artist because they attach creativity to a lower order of things. He knew, too, that his lazy, Creole temperament needed even more discipline than most.

Coriolis' first paintings, fruits of his travels, were not favorably received. Volatile, filled with light, they did not conform to the fashionable critical notions of Near Eastern landscapes. Naïvely astonished, Coriolis discovered that critics and public preferred Garnotelle's sterile work. Determined to prove his own worth as more than an exotic colorist, he set himself to painting nudes.

During his search for a model he saw a young Jewish girl, Manette Salomon, and through Anatole he obtained her services. Manette was absolute perfection; her body had a pliant beauty that seemed the quintessence of the female. Coriolis, obsessed by her beauty, wanted to keep her all to himself, but she, a true Parisian Bohemian, wanted only to be free. Her frank, ignorant nature delighted him; her serenity gave him peace. Jealous, he once followed her, but she went only to the synagogue. This experience made him suddenly aware of her Jewishness, a strange, foreign element akin to something he had found in his travels. One day, however, he saw a watch chain she had and realized that she had been the child he had admired so long ago. Remembering her benefactor, she tenderly vowed never to leave him.

Coriolis' painting of Manette, in which he captured her glorious flesh tones, was a huge success, and its purchase by a museum restored his faith in himself. Feeling herself famous, Manette began to change: the praise of the picture Coriolis had painted of her raised a feeling of pride in her that was almost love. Like most artists, Coriolis thought of his mistress as a charming, necessary little animal.

Soon afterward he fell ill and Manette nursed him back to strength, never leaving his side. To speed his convalescence, Coriolis went with Manette and Anatole to the country near Fontainebleau. Manette, completely city bred, was delighted by her strange new world and plunged into it eagerly. Coriolis found nature soothing and inspiring, yet he grew bored and missed the comforts of his studio. Anatole luxuriated in the freshness of the countryside, falling under its spell, but livened his stay by tricking, mocking, and entertaining the other guests at the little inn.

Manette, accepted by this bourgeois group as Coriolis' wife, found her new status attractive and ignorantly believed this bourgeois world worthy of entering. Then a new arrival, sensing her true relationship to Coriolis, snubbed her. Hurt and resentful, Manette wanted to leave. The three moved to a small house near the landscapist Crescent and his wife, an ample, friendly woman who took Manette to her heart. The two young artists learned from the old peasant Crescent. But Mme. Crescent, learning that Manette was Jewish, cooled toward her, sensing (partly through peasant superstition, partly through a kind of animal instinct) something hidden, profound, and destructive in the girl's nature. Shortly thereafter, Coriolis, who could not agree with the moralistic basis of Crescent's art, decided to return to Paris.

After their return to Paris, Manette became pregnant and her body took on new languor. When Coriolis' son was born, Manette acquired a new outlook on life. The carefree Bohemian had become the mother; her stubborn pride and greed for success came to the fore.

Coriolis had begun to work again, this time on a new kind of painting—an attempt to create art through the truth of life. He did not mean to imitate photography but to make of the harmonies available in painting a re-creation unfolding the inner realities of contemporary life. His two paintings, particularly one of a wedding, were scoffed at. Manette, seeing his failure, cooled toward him.

Coriolis, doting on his son, watched him play and sketched him. As time passed, however, he was unable to work and sank into inactivity and despair. He could not understand a world which rewarded Garnotelle, now supremely fashionable with his superficial, heartless paintings.

Manette decided that for the sake of their child and her own growing desire for respectability, Coriolis should rid himself of such Bohemian friends as Anatole and Chassagnol, and of the failures which they encouraged, and model himself on Garnotelle. She set about arousing Coriolis' suspicions concerning Anatole and herself. She then persuaded Coriolis to go to the country for his lingering cough, taking the child and some new servants, her relatives. There was no room for Anatole. Coriolis, meanwhile, had grown more and more dependent on Manette, counting on her to run his home, tend his wants, and make his decisions. He was too weak to struggle against her.

Left alone, Anatole became a true Bohemian, living from day to day on handouts and forgetting his art entirely.

On Coriolis' return, Manette set about alienating his friends in earnest. They ceased to visit him, cutting him off from valid artistic communication. Though

Manette understood the artist's life and was able to adapt herself to it, she was fundamentally ignorant. Her ambitions were for money and success. To her, art was a business; to Coriolis, a religion. Yet he did not oppose her. Her mother came to live with them and feminine domination began to affect his health; but as his psychosomatic illness increased, so did his dependence on Manette. He painted as she wanted him to and became filled with self-loathing. Always eager for more money, she persuaded him to sell some of his "failures." Surprisingly, a connoisseur recognized their true artistic merit and purchased them at a fantastically high price. Again Coriolis was famous.

In despair, he turned on Manette, accused her of destroying a number of his canvases, and ordered her out of the house. She calmly went on as though she had never heard him—she had beaten him. A broken man, he was still strong enough in his belief to refuse a medal he had won for a wedding picture because he felt he was unworthy of the award. Manette scornfully removed herself still further from him. But he could not leave her.

Sometime later, Anatole heard that Garnotelle had married a princess, with Coriolis as the best man. He saw Coriolis from afar, with Manette and several dreadful bourgeois types following him. Though love had long been over between Manette and Coriolis, they were married and her ambitions fulfilled. Coriolis painted almost nothing and became increasingly ill.

Anatole, visiting the zoo again, watched the lions in their cages. He lazed on the grass, feeling himself a part of all nature and completely free.

MANFRED

Type of work: Poem
Author: George Gordon, Lord Byron (1788-1824)
Type of plot: Romantic tragedy
Time of plot: No set time
Locale: The Alps
First published: 1817

Principal characters:
MANFRED, a lonely, guilt-haunted magician
A CHAMOIS HUNTER
THE ABBOT OF ST. MAURICE

Critique:

Manfred is Byron's first great poem of revolt, and readers familiar with the poet's life will find in Manfred an embodiment of the autobiographical urge which prompted much of Byron's poetry. The rationalization of his social ostracism, his failure to cope with the outraged virtue of English society, and, more directly, his disturbance at being separated from Augusta Leigh lay behind his romantic brooding in this particular poem. There are parallels between *Manfred* and Goethe's *Faust*: the wild mountain scenery, the ability of a man of learning to summon other-world spirits, the symbolic adventures of the hero, and the philosophical references. Only in the end is Manfred unlike Faust. Because he has not contracted with evil, he dies free of hell's power. If one can separate the poem from its author, *Manfred* becomes a study of an isolated individual who cannot seek deliverance from any external social machinery, but who must work out his own destiny.

The Story:

Alone in a Gothic gallery at midnight, Manfred meditated deeply about his life. He had undergone many experiences, but none had profoundly affected him. When he called upon the spirits of the universe to appear before him, none came. Three times he summoned them. At the third call, a summons in the name of his own cursed soul, the spirits arose.

The first was the Spirit of Air. The Spirit of Interior Fire next appeared, followed by the Spirit of Ocean. The spirits of Earth, Exterior Fire, and Night arose in succession, each demanding to know what the mortal magician wished. Finally the star, Manfred's own star of ill-fated destiny, joined the spirits.

Manfred's reply was that he desired forgetfulness. When the Spirit of Air sought further explanation, Manfred could not reveal what he wanted to forget. Surely, he insisted, spirits that controlled earth, sky, water, mountains, winds, night, and destiny, could bring the oblivion he sought. But the spirits replied that they had no powers beyond their own realms. When Manfred, failing in his hopes, asked the spirits to take bodily forms, the seventh spirit, the star of his destiny, took the shape of a beautiful woman. At sight of her Manfred, hinting at a former love, attempted to hold her, but she vanished, leaving him senseless. In her place came a formless voice, the voice of himself as a magician, uttering a long incantation, mysterious and despairing.

Next morning, alone on a cliff of the Jungfrau Mountain, Manfred mourned the failure of his magic powers to assist him. Marveling at the surrounding beauty of the mountain, he weighed the possibility of leaping from the cliff. A passing hunter saw the lonely man and wondered what Manfred was doing so high on the mountain, where even the best hunters could not climb. Fearing that Manfred would lose his footing when the morning mist arose, the hunter approached him cautiously, for Manfred appeared to be tottering. Actually Manfred was about to jump when the hunter caught hold of him and led him down the steep slope.

In his cottage in the Bernese Alps, the hunter urged Manfred to rest a while before journeying on. Manfred, refusing guidance, declared that he would go on alone. When the hunter offered Manfred his best wine, Manfred exclaimed in horror that he saw blood, symbolic of Manfred's alienation from social contact, on the rim of the cup. The hunter, thinking Manfred mad, suggested that the wretched man seek comfort in contemplation and in the Church. Manfred, spurning the suggestion, said that he wished he were mad, for then his mind would be tortured by unrealities instead of the truths which now beset him. He envied the hunter's simple life, but when the hunter, noting Manfred's high-born appearance, wonderingly asked if his guest would then wish to change stations in life, Manfred replied that he would not wish any human to suffer his own wretchedness. To this the hunter said that surely a man capable of such tenderness could not harbor a soul belabored by evil. Manfred, departing, protested that the evil was not within himself; he had destroyed those whom he loved.

Below, the Witch of the Alps answered Manfred's summons that she share the loveliness of nature with him. To her he described his past spiritual life, when he had lived among men but not with them. Preferring solitude, he had studied ancient mysteries and had loved and destroyed with love a woman said to have resembled him. The Witch promised to aid him if he would swear obedience to her, but he refused her offer and she left him.

The three destinies and Nemesis gathered for a festival in the Hall of Arimanes, Spirit of Evil, Prince of Earth and Air. Manfred, daring to approach, was recognized as a magician. He told them he had come in quest of Astarte, the symbol of his sin. When she had been summoned from her tomb, she prophesied only that the next day would end his despair.

Back in his castle, Manfred felt a sublime calm. The Abbot of St. Maurice, having heard that Manfred had practiced witchcraft, arrived to save his soul. To Manfred's bitter assurance that his sins lay between heaven and himself, the abbot urged that Manfred turn to the Church for help. Manfred explained that he had always lived alone and would remain alone. The abbot mourned that he could not help such a noble man.

While the servants gossiped about their master's strange behavior, Manfred stood alone in his tower. There the abbot came once more in a last vain attempt to save Manfred. Warned that a dangerous spirit was approaching, the abbot insisted that he would confront the spirit, who had come to summon Manfred. Manfred, however, defied the summons; he was willing to die but not to join the spirits of hell, to whom he owed nothing.

As the demon disappeared, Manfred died, still lonely and unconquerable to all but death itself.

MANHATTAN TRANSFER

Type of work: Novel
Author: John Dos Passos (1896-   )
Type of plot: Impressionistic realism
Time of plot: World War I
Locale: New York City
First published: 1925

Principal characters:
ELLEN THATCHER, an actress
CONGO, a French sailor who later became a wealthy bootlegger
GUS McNIEL, a milkman who later became an assemblyman
JIMMY HERF, a newspaper reporter
GEORGE BALDWIN, a lawyer
JOE HARLAND, a drunk
JOE O'KEEFE, a young labor organizer
STAN EMERY, whom Ellen loves

Critique:

In this novel Dos Passos presents a panoramic portrait of New York City. The book is composed of many episodes in the lives of many different characters. Some of the episodes are connected; others stand by themselves. The author's style is abrupt; the scene shifts without warning. The complexity of the plot realistically reflects the complexity of metropolitan life.

The Story:

Ed Thatcher and his wife Susie had their first child, a girl named Ellen. After the birth of the child, Susie became neurotic; she wanted to die.

Congo and Emile, two French boys, came to New York to make their fortunes. Emile married a widowed Frenchwoman who owned a delicatessen. Congo did not like New York and went to sea again.

Gus McNiel, a milkman, was run over by a train. George Baldwin, a young lawyer, took Gus' case against the railroad and obtained a settlement for the injured man. While Gus was in the hospital recovering from the accident, George had an affair with Gus' wife, Nellie.

Jimmy Herf arrived from Europe with his widowed mother, who was in delicate health. One evening she had a heart attack; not long afterward she died. Jimmy's rich Uncle Jeff and Aunt Emily Merivale then became his legal guardians. One evening at their house Jimmy met Joe Harland, the drunken black sheep of the family, who had won and lost several fortunes on Wall Street.

Susie Thatcher died, and Ed worked hard for little Ellen. He stayed at the office until late each evening, working and dreaming of all the fine things he would do for his daughter some day. Ellen grew up, went on the stage, and married John Oglethorpe, a competent but lazy actor. Her married life was unhappy, for she discovered that her husband was a homosexual.

Jimmy Herf's Uncle Jeff tried to get him interested in business, but Jimmy would have none of it. He got a job as a reporter and became acquainted with Ruth Prynne, a young actress who lived in the boarding-house where Ellen and John Oglethorpe stayed.

George Baldwin had forgotten Nellie McNiel. He was now interested in Ellen. One afternoon, as he and Ellen sat together at tea, a drunken college boy stopped at their table. George introduced him to Ellen as Stan Emery.

Joe Harland, the black sheep relative of the Merivales and Jimmy Herf, was now forty-five and almost broke. He spent his last money on a few shots of whiskey to bring back memories of the old prosperous days on Wall Street.

Ellen and Stan fell in love. When she was with him, she was happy. But when she went home to John, she was miserable. Ellen decided that she and John could no longer live together. She packed her things and moved to a hotel.

Stan Emery came to Jimmy Herf's room. Stan was on a long drunk after being expelled from college. Later in the day they met John and Ellen drinking tea together. Stan left, but Jimmy stayed to talk with Ellen.

George Baldwin sat at breakfast with his wife, Cecily. He had married her for social position; they were not happy. Cecily knew of his other affairs. George did all he could to keep her from leaving home because a scandal would ruin him in the business world.

Ellen moved from her hotel to an apartment. She was supporting herself well now, for she had become a success on Broadway.

Joe Harland had finally got a job as a night watchman. One evening he was visited by a young labor organizer, Joe O'Keefe. The older man warned him against getting mixed up in labor troubles. But O'Keefe said that Gus McNiel, now an assemblyman, was on the side of labor.

Harry Goldweiser, a rich Broadway producer, fell in love with Ellen. He asked her to marry him. She refused, but in a friendly way, for her career depended upon Goldweiser.

Gus McNiel retained George Baldwin as his lawyer throughout his rise to political power. George warned him against getting mixed up with labor because, as a member of a conservative law firm, George could not help Gus with labor troubles.

Ellen wanted Stan to stop drinking so much, but he would not reform. Drink was the only means by which he could adjust himself to the world.

One evening Ellen went out to dinner with George Baldwin. Everyone was excited about the beginning of the World War. But George could think only of Ellen, and in a fit of rage he threatened her with a gun. Gus Mc-Niel, who was nearby, took away the gun and hushed up the incident. Jimmy Herf, who had been talking to the bartender, Congo, took Ellen outside and sent her home in a taxi.

Ellen finally obtained a divorce from John, and Harry Goldweiser renewed his attentions. One evening Ellen and Harry met Stan dancing with a girl named Pearline. Stan revealed that he and Pearline had been on a long drunk and had been married. Later Stan came home drunk, disgusted with his life and with Pearline. He poured kerosene around the apartment and set fire to it. Pearline returned just in time to see the firemen carry Stan from the burning building.

Ellen was crushed by Stan's death, for he was the only man she had really loved. To be with Jimmy Herf gave her some comfort because he had been Stan's friend. But Jimmy wanted to be more than a friend to Ellen; he still loved her. She told him that she was going to have Stan's baby; she wanted to leave show business and rear the child. But she had an abortion instead. Ellen and Jimmy went to Europe to do Red Cross work during the war. Finally they were married. They returned from France with their baby.

Joe O'Keefe came back from the war with a chip on his shoulder. He thought the veterans deserved a bonus because they had lost out on the big money at home. He had another reason for feeling bitter: somewhere overseas he had caught syphilis.

George Baldwin's home life was still troubled. Having post-war political ambitions, he turned against his old friend,

2224

Gus McNiel, and ran for mayor on a reform ticket. Meanwhile Jimmy and Ellen drifted apart. Jimmy became despondent and quit his job. George Baldwin finally got a divorce. He proposed to Ellen. Too weary of her muddled life to resist him, she accepted his proposal.

One night Jimmy Herf was walking the streets when a car drew up beside him and stopped. In it was the Frenchman, Congo, now a wealthy bootlegger. He took Jimmy home with him and tried to cheer him up. Late one evening after a party Jimmy Herf wandered down by the river. As he waited for a ferry to take him from Manhattan, he realized that he felt gay and happy for the first time in many months. Morning found him walking along a concrete highway, penniless but still happy. He did not know where he was going; he knew only that it would be a long way.

MANON LESCAUT

Type of work: Novel
Author: Abbé Prévost (Antoine François Prévost d'Exiles, 1697-1763)
Type of plot: Sentimental romance
Time of plot: 1700
Locale: France and New Orleans
First published: 1731

Principal characters:
MANON LESCAUT, a courtesan
THE CHEVALIER DES GRIEUX, her lover
TIBERGE, his friend
M. DE G— M—, a wealthy nobleman
M. LESCAUT, Manon's brother

Critique:

The Story of Manon Lescaut and the Chevalier des Grieux is an early example of the sentimental romance and as such it has had a considerable influence on romantic fiction in different literatures. The book is not widely read today, but the popular operatic version of the story is familiar enough. Despite its importance in the history of fiction, the modern reader is apt to be out of sympathy with its swashbuckling hero and its sentimental heroine. The Abbé Prévost would have the reader sympathize with these characters, but many readers will feel that the pair received much less misfortune than their conduct deserved.

The Story:

While the young Chevalier des Grieux was a student of philosophy at Amiens, he became friendly with a fellow student named Tiberge. One day he stood idly with his friend and watched the arrival of the Arras coach. Among the passengers was a beautiful young girl who attracted the chevalier's attention. Politely introducing himself, he learned that her name was Manon Lescaut and that she had come to Amiens under the protection of an elderly man. Against her will she was to enter a convent. She accepted the chevalier's offer to set her free from such an irksome life, and after skillfully and untruthfully disposing of her escort she went with the young student to an inn. On the morrow they planned to flee to Paris. Tiberge argued with his friend against this folly, but the chevalier was hopelessly infatuated. In Paris he and Manon took a furnished apartment, where for three weeks they were absorbed in each other.

The idyll came to an end when the young lover discovered that his mistress had also bestowed her affections on M. de B—. But the chevalier's love for Manon was so great he forgave her. Then three lackeys, sent by the chevalier's father, came to the apartment and took the young man home. There his father tried in vain to persuade him that Manon had behaved treacherously. Finally the father locked his son in his room for a period of six weeks. During this time Tiberge came to visit him, bringing him news that Manon was being kept at the expense of M. de B—. Finally Tiberge persuaded the young man to enroll at the Seminary of Saint-Supplice as a student of theology. With his father's permission, he entered the school where he became an outstanding student. Manon was present to hear his declamation at the public disputation at the Sorbonne, and after the ceremonies she came to visit him. A single passionate embrace made him forget his future in the Church. The chevalier escaped from school without any money; his mistress furnished the funds to set up quarters at Chaillot, outside Paris.

Then began a life of extravagance and riotous living far beyond their slender means. In Paris they met Manon's brother, M. Lescaut of the Royal Guards, who did not scruple to install himself in their house. When a fire destroyed all their money and possessions, the brother suggested that Manon sell her charms to some free-handed nobleman. The chevalier rejected this proposal, but consented to become a professional gambler in order to support Manon. He borrowed from Tiberge enough money to begin his career as a card cheat. For a time his luck held, but their period of prosperity ended when a maid and a valet fled with all the valuable possessions of the new household. Urged by her brother, Manon consented to become the mistress of the old and wealthy M. de G—M—, who had promised her a house, servants, and a large sum of money.

The young couple decided to play on Manon's protector by introducing the chevalier into the household as her brother. Having duped the man to make his settlement on Manon, they ran away with the jewels and money he had given her. But they were followed by the police, apprehended, and imprisoned—Manon at the Common Hospital; the chevalier at Saint-Lazare.

Once lodged at Saint-Lazare, the chevalier began to plan his escape. He cultivated his superiors and made a show of reading theology. M. de G—M—, hearing of the chevalier's studious habits, came to visit him. But when the young man heard, for the first time, that Manon was also imprisoned, he seized the old man by the throat and tried to throttle him. The monks stopped the fight and saved the old man's life.

The chevalier now wrote to Tiberge, asking his old friend to visit Saint-Lazare. To Tiberge he entrusted a note addressed to M. Lescaut. Using a pistol which Manon's brother brought him soon afterward, the chevalier escaped, killing a turnkey in his flight. Later, by bribing the attendants at the hospital, he was able to arrange for Manon's escape. Manon, wearing men's clothing, was safely conveyed to her brother's house, but just as the happy pair descended from the carriage M. Lescaut was shot by a man whose fortune the guardsman had won at cards. Manon and the chevalier fled to the inn at Chaillot to escape apprehension for the murder.

In Paris the next day the chevalier borrowed a hundred pistoles from Tiberge. He also met M. de T—, a friend, whom he invited to Chaillot for supper. During the meal the son of old M. de G—M— arrived at the inn. The impetuous young chevalier wanted to kill him at once to get revenge on the father, but M. de T— persuaded him rather to meet young de G—M— in a friendly manner over the supper table. The young man was charmed with Manon, and like his father offered to maintain her handsomely. But Manon and her lover had made plans to deceive the gullible young man, in order to get revenge on his father. She accepted his rich presents. The chevalier planned to have street ruffians capture and hold the infatuated young man while Manon and the chevalier enjoyed the supper and the bed de G—M— had arranged for himself and his mistress. But the young man's father learned of the scheme and Manon and the chevalier were surprised by the police, who hurried them off to the Chatelet.

The young chevalier then appealed to his father, whose influence was great enough to secure his son's release. He refused to interest himself in Manon, however, and she was sentenced to exile on the next shipload of convicts to be sent to the penal colony in Louisiana. After a feeble attempt to rescue her from the prison guards, the chevalier accompanied his mistress on the trip from the prison to Havre-de-Grace. He also gained permission to accompany her on the voyage to America. On shipboard and on their arrival in New Orleans they passed as man and wife.

In New Orleans they settled in a rude shelter. After the chevalier secured honorable employment, Manon desired above all things that they become legally man and wife. The chevalier appealed to the governor for permission to marry and admitted his earlier deceit. The governor refused, for his nephew M. Synnelet, had fallen in love with Manon. As a result, the chevalier fought a duel with Synnelet. Thinking that he had killed his opponent, he and Manon left the colony, but on the journey Manon, ill from fatigue, died in a lonely field. The chevalier was disconsolate.

Tiberge followed his friend to America and persuaded him to return to France. Back home, the chevalier resolved to turn to God in penance.

MAN'S FATE

Type of work: Novel
Author: André Malraux (1895-   )
Type of plot: Social criticism
Time of plot: 1927
Locale: Shanghai, China
First published: 1933

Principal characters:
 CH'EN, a Chinese terrorist
 KYO, a Communist organizer of French and Japanese parentage
 GISORS, Kyo's father
 MAY, Kyo's German wife
 BARON DE CLAPPIQUE, a French adventurer
 KATOV, a Russian revolutionist
 HEMMELRICH, a German revolutionist
 FERRAL, a French businessman
 KÖNIG, chief of Chiang Kai-shek's police

Critique:

Man's Fate is in part an eye-witness account of a troubled period of crisis in China's troubled history. Malraux, himself a revolutionary at the time, was first of all a literary artist in the writing of this novel. His characters are the melting pot of cosmopolitan Shanghai. The episodic plot is significant chiefly as an illustration of leftist dialectics in modern fiction.

The Story:

The Reds, a revolutionary group with a nucleus of Moscow agents, had made a temporary alliance with Chiang Kai-shek, their immediate object being to control Shanghai with the help of the Kuomintang. But the alliance was an uneasy one, for neither side trusted the other. The Reds had completed their plans to seize Shanghai, ostensibly as part of Chiang Kai-shek's campaign, but they intended to put a Communist in control before the Blue army arrived. On their part, the Blues hoped to use the Communists to seize the city and afterwards disperse the revolutionaries.

Ch'en, the terrorist, stood ready to strike through the mosquito netting and kill the sleeper in the bed. Nerving himself for his first murder, he plunged his dagger into the man's heart. Quickly from the dead man he took a paper which would authorize the delivery of arms now aboard the *Shantung*, at anchor in the harbor. The Reds counted on these arms to seize control of the city before government troops arrived.

Ch'en took the document to Hemmelrich's phonograph shop, where Kyo was waiting. There they all congratulated him, Kyo, Katov, and Hemmelrich. Kyo and Katov tested their new code of paralleled phonograph records. One record gave an innocent language lesson, the other gave a loud hiss which covered all but the key words on the first record. Satisfied with their work, they planned a final check of their revolutionary cells. Hemmelrich refused to go with them; his wife and child were sick.

Kyo and Katov visited their two hundred units. A general strike at noon would paralyze the city. At the same time saboteurs would wreck the railway so that the government could not send reinforcements from the battle front. Other groups would take over police stations and army posts and seize all firearms. With the grenades already on hand, they would be equipped to resist even tanks.

MAN'S FATE by André Malraux. Translated by Haakon M. Chevalier. By permission of the author's agent William Aspenwall Bradley, Paris, his publishers, Messrs. Gallimard, Paris, and of Random House, Inc. Copyright, 1934, by Harrison Smith and Robert Haas, Inc.

Kyo went to the Black Cat, a night club where he knew he could find de Clappique. The Frenchman was drunk, but he had to be trusted. De Clappique was commissioned to take a forged order to the *Shantung*, directing her to shift anchorage.

Tired and tense, Kyo went home. Gisors, his father, was still awake, and Kyo told him a few details of the plan. Then May, Kyo's wife, came home exhausted from her hospital work. She was one of the few women doctors in all Shanghai, a woman with advanced views on marriage relationships. She and Kyo quarreled because of her affair with another doctor. During the quarrel de Clappique came to report that the *Shantung* had moved. A messenger recalled Kyo to headquarters.

Dressed as government soldiers, Kyo and Katov with ten others boarded the *Shantung* and got the arms, but only after seizing the captain and holding him prisoner. Now the revolutionaries could plan with confidence.

Meanwhile Ferral, head of the French Chamber of Commerce, decided to throw his support to Chiang Kai-shek. After giving orders to send funds to the Blues, he retired with his mistress Valérie. It was arranged that she would see him the following night at her hotel. He was to bring her a pet bird in a cage. At the appointed time Ferral asked for Valérie at the hotel desk. To his surprise, she was out. A young Englishman was also waiting for her with a caged bird. To revenge himself, Ferral bought the entire stock of a pet store —forty birds and a kangaroo, and set them loose in Valérie's room.

The uprising took place as planned. Ch'en seized one police station with ease and armed his small band. The second station was better defended, and grenades failed to dislodge officers barricaded on the top floor. Ch'en set fire to the building, killing the resisters as well as his own wounded comrades.

The feeble central government could not fight both Chiang and the Reds at the same time. While the government forces were occupied with the Blues, the Reds easily took control of the city.

Two days later the Blues under Chiang approached Shanghai. The general had been shrewd enough to send his first division, composed largely of Communists, to another front; consequently the Communists found themselves confronting an unsympathetic Blue army which in turn took over the city. Many of the Communists were arrested. When Moscow ordered all armed Communists to surrender their weapons to Chiang's police, dissension broke out among the Reds. Many of the Chinese deserted the Moscow party and embarked on a terroristic campaign of their own.

Ch'en conceived the idea that he must kill Chiang in order to free China. With two companions he lay in wait to throw a bomb into the general's car. His first attempt having failed, Ch'en went to Hemmelrich's shop. Hemmelrich refused to shelter him. In a second attempt, Ch'en threw himself with his bomb under the automobile. The car was wrecked and Ch'en was killed, but Chiang was not in the car.

Chiang's police destroyed Hemmelrich's shop, accidentally killing his wife and baby. Believing his cowardice was the cause of Ch'en's action and the subsequent riot, Hemmelrich seized a rifle and joined the rioters. He was quickly killed by Chiang's police.

Now in complete control, Chiang's police chief, König, began to round up the Communists, Katov among them. When the word went out that Kyo was to be arrested, Gisors begged de Clappique to intervene because the baron was König's good friend. Instead of warning Kyo, de Clappique lingered in a gambling house until after Kyo had been arrested. Later de Clappique went to König to ask for Kyo's release. The Frenchman was given only forty-eight hours to leave China.

In prison Katov gave his cyanide tablet to Kyo, who poisoned himself. Katov and his revolutionary group were executed.

Each of the survivors sought safety in his own way. Gisors returned to Japan to teach painting. May went to Moscow to practice medicine. By disguising himself de Clappique got aboard the same French liner that was taking Ferral back to France. So the Communists and their sympathizers were destroyed by relentless Chiang and the vacillating policy of Moscow. Yet there was good news from China for the survivors; the quiet work of revolution had already started again.

2231

MANSFIELD PARK

Type of work: Novel
Author: Jane Austen (1775-1817)
Type of plot: Social criticism
Time of plot: Early nineteenth century
Locale: Northamptonshire, England
First published: 1814

Principal characters:
FANNY PRICE, a poor relation at Mansfield Park
SIR THOMAS BERTRAM, owner of Mansfield Park
LADY BERTRAM, his wife
TOM,
EDMUND,
MARIA, and
JULIA BERTRAM, Fanny's cousins
MRS. NORRIS, a busybody
HENRY CRAWFORD, a self-centered young gentleman
MARY CRAWFORD, his sister
MR. RUSHWORTH, Maria Bertram's suitor
MR. YATES, a young man of fashion

Critique:

Mansfield Park is the most obviously didactic of Jane Austen's novels: virtue is universally rewarded and vice just as certainly punished. The characterization, also, is inclined more to black and white than is true of her greater works. As always, the feminine characters are more convincing than the men. The heroine, Fanny Price, is appealing and sweet, while Mrs. Norris is a masterly satirical sketch of the universal type of busybody.

The Story:

Of the three Ward sisters, one had married very well to a baronet, one very badly to a lieutenant of the marines, and one neither too badly nor too well to a clergyman. The fortunate sister, Lady Bertram, agreed at the instigation of the clerical sister, Mrs. Norris, to care for one of the unfortunate sister's nine children. Accordingly, Fanny Price, ten years old, and a shy and sensitive child, came to make her home at Mansfield Park. Among her four Bertram cousins, Tom, Edmund, Maria, and Julia, Fanny found a real friend only in Edmund. The others usually ignored her except when she could be of use to them, but Edmund comforted her, and advised her. He alone seemed to recognize her good qualities—

cleverness, grace, and a pleasant disposition. Besides Edmund's attentions, Fanny received some of a very different kind from her selfish and hypocritical Aunt Norris, who was constantly calling unnecessary attention to Fanny's dependent position.

When Fanny was fifteen, Sir Thomas Bertram went to Antigua to look after some business affairs. With him went his oldest son, who was inclined to extravagance and dissipation, and the family was left to Edmund's and Lady Bertram's care. During Sir Thomas' absence, his older daughter, Maria, became engaged to Mr. Rushworth, a young man who was rich and well-connected but extremely stupid.

Another event of importance was the arrival in the village of Mary and Henry Crawford, the sister and brother of Mrs. Grant, whose husband had become the rector after the death of Mr. Norris. Both of the Bertram girls liked Henry immensely, but since Maria was engaged, he rightfully belonged to Julia. They also became close friends with Mary Crawford, who in turn attracted both Tom, now returned from abroad, and Edmund.

Fanny regretted the Crawfords' coming, for she saw that Edmund, whom she herself loved, was falling in love with the shallow, worldly Mary, and that her cousin Maria was carrying on a most unseemly flirtation with Henry. The less observant, like Mrs. Norris, saw only what they wished to see and insisted that he was paying particular attention to Julia.

At the suggestion of Mr. Yates, a pleasure-loving friend of Tom, the young people decided to engage in some private theatricals and chose for their entertainment the sentimental "Lovers' Vows." Fanny opposed the scheme from the start, for she knew Sir Thomas would have disapproved. Edmund tried to dissuade the others, but finally let himself be talked into taking a part because there were not enough men for all the roles. Rehearsals and preparations went forward, the plan growing more elaborate as it progressed. However, the unexpected return of Sir Thomas put an end to the rehearsals. The house was soon cleared of all theatrical gear, including Mr. Yates, whose trifling, affected ways Sir Thomas had disliked immediately.

Maria, willing to break her engagement to Mr. Rushworth, had hoped her father's return would bring a declaration from Henry. Instead of declaring himself, he announced his departure for a stay in Bath. Although her pride was hurt, Maria resolved that Henry Crawford should never know she had taken their flirtation seriously. She was duly married to Mr. Rushworth.

Julia went to Brighton with the Rushworths. With both the Bertram sisters gone, Henry began an idle flirtation with Fanny and ended by falling in love with her. One of his plans for winning her favor was a scheme for getting her beloved brother William, who had just visited her at Mansfield Park, a promotion in the navy. Although Fanny was grateful for this favor, she refused him promptly when he proposed. In doing so, she incurred the serious displeasure of her uncle, Sir Thomas, who regarded

as sheer perversity the sentiments which made her turn down such an advantageous match. Even Edmund encouraged her to change her mind, for he was too preoccupied with his attachment to Mary Crawford to guess that Fanny had more than a cousinly regard for him. Edmund had just been ordained as a clergyman, a step which Mary Crawford had ridiculed, and he was not sure she would accept him as a husband. He persisted in believing, however, that her frivolous dislike of the clergy was only a trait she had acquired from worldly friends, and that her opinion could be changed.

About this time Fanny went to Portsmouth to visit her family. The stay was a depressing one, for she found her family, with the exception of William, disorderly and ill-bred, by Mansfield Park standards. Also, several catastrophes occurred at Mansfield Park to make her long to be helpful there. Tom, the oldest son, had such a serious illness that his recovery was uncertain; Maria, now Mrs. Rushworth, ran away with Henry, who forgot his love for Fanny long enough to commit an irrevocable indiscretion; and Julia eloped with Mr. Yates. The Bertram family, crushed under this series of blows, at last realized Fanny's value and dearness to them, and welcomed her back to Mansfield Park with tenderness that touched her deeply.

Mrs. Norris, as spiteful as ever, said that if Fanny had accepted Henry Crawford as she should have, he would never have run away with Maria. But Sir Thomas gave Fanny credit for seeing Henry's character more clearly than he had, and forgave her for having refused Henry. He blamed himself for Maria's downfall, for he realized he had never taken the trouble to know his children well.

But good came from all this evil. Tom's illness sobered him, and he proved a better son thereafter. Mr. Yates, though not a great match for Julia, had more income and fewer debts than Sir Thomas had anticipated, and seemed inclined to settle down to quiet domesticity. Henry and Maria separated after spending a few unhappy months together. Sir Thomas refused to receive her at Mansfield Park, but provided a home for her in another part of the country. There Mrs. Norris went to live with her favorite niece, to the great relief of everyone at Mansfield Park.

Edmund had finally realized Mary Crawford's frivolous and worldly nature when she treated his sister's and her brother's affair quite lightly. Her levity shocked him, and made it easier for him to give up thoughts of an unsuitable marriage. Eventually he fell in love with Fanny, who had loved him so long. They were married and lived at the parsonage near Mansfield Park.

THE MARBLE FAUN

Type of work: Novel
Author: Nathaniel Hawthorne (1804-1864)
Type of plot: Allegorical romance
Time of plot: Mid-nineteenth century
Locale: Rome
First published: 1860

Principal characters:
MIRIAM, an artist
HILDA, another artist, friend of Miriam
KENYON, an American sculptor
DONATELLO, a young Italian

Critique:

A romance filled with moral and symbolic overtones and undertones, *The Marble Faun,* or, *The Romance of Monte Beni* exhibits Hawthorne's preoccupation with the problem of evil. Hawthorne himself was a complex person, and some of the psychological concerns of his own character are reflected in this novel. The book is a study of the birth of the human conscience, the consequences of a sin committed by a simple, pagan spirit who through his unthinking deed releases a new sense of intellectual and moral responsibility. *The Marble Faun* is one of the American classics, eloquent testimony to the ability and insight of one of our greatest native writers.

The Story:

Nothing at all was known about Miriam. In the artistic world of Rome, she lived without revealing anything about herself and without arousing the curiosity or suspicion of those living around her. With a New England girl, Hilda, and Kenyon, a sculptor, she enjoyed a friendship which even her mysterious origin did not shadow, so complete was their understanding and trust of one another.

One day the three friends, accompanied by Donatello, a young Italian, saw a statue of the faun by Praxiteles. Struck by the resemblance of the statue to Donatello, they asked jokingly to see if the Italian also had pointed ears under his golden locks. Indeed, Donatello was very much like a faun in his character. He had great agility, cheerfulness, and a sunny nature unclouded by melancholy or care. He was deeply in love with Miriam.

On another occasion, the trio went to visit the catacombs. While there, Miriam disappeared for a moment. When she came back, she returned with a strange individual whom she had met inside one of the tombs. This person followed her for months to come. No one knew anything about him. He and Miriam had conversations together, and he spoke of the hold he had on her, of their life together in a mysterious past. Miriam became more and more unhappy. She told Donatello—who was ever ready to defend her—that he must go away, for she would bring doom and destruction upon him. But Donatello stayed, as ardent as ever.

Her persecutor appeared everywhere, followed her wherever she went. One day Miriam went to Hilda and left a packet for Hilda to deliver on a certain date to the address she would find written on the outside. Shortly afterward, the friends went out one night and climbed the Tarpeian Rock, over which the old Romans used to throw their criminals. As they were getting ready to return home, Miriam's persecutor appeared. Miriam went with him, followed by Donatello. Donatello attacked the man and with the stranger secure in his grasp looked at Miriam. Her eyes gave him his answer. He threw the tormentor over a cliff to his death.

United by this crime, Miriam and Donatello also became united in love. But they did not know that Hilda had witnessed the murder, that she was suffering because of it. They had all agreed to visit the Church of the Capuchins the following afternoon in order to see a painting which supposedly bore a resemblance to Miriam's tormentor. But Hilda did not keep the appointment. The others went, to find a mass for the dead in progress. The dead man was Miriam's persecutor. Later, when Miriam went to see Hilda, the American girl told Miriam that their friendship was over.

Donatello, too, had changed. He was no longer the unworried faun, but a person with a very guilty conscience. He began to avoid Miriam, even to hate her. He left Rome and went back to his ancestral home. Kenyon went there to visit his friend. Hilda stayed in Rome by herself, lonely, distraught.

At Donatello's country home, Kenyon learned the local tradition about his friend's family, a legend that Donatello was, in fact, descended from a race of fauns who had inhabited the countryside in remote times. He learned, too, of Donatello's feeling of guilt, but he, unaware of the killing, did not know the reason for Donatello's changed spirit. When Miriam followed Donatello to his home, he would not see her. Kenyon told her Donatello still loved her, however, and she agreed to meet both of them later on. When they met in the city square, Miriam stood quietly, waiting for Donatello to speak. At last he spoke her name, and she went to him. So they were united once more, but the union was haunted by their sin.

In the meantime Hilda had gone to deliver the packet Miriam had left in her keeping. The address was that of one high in the affairs of the government. Kenyon looked for Hilda everywhere, for he had seen her but briefly since his return. Realizing at last that he was in love with her, he was worried about her disappearance. During the carnival season he met Donatello and Miriam, who promised him he would soon see Hilda again. He did, on the day the carnival was at its height and the streets were filled with a merry-making throng.

Hilda told him her story. Her knowledge of the crime had weighed so heavily upon her that at last she had gone to confession in St. Peter's and had poured out the tale to a listening priest. Later she had delivered the packet, as Miriam had requested her, and afterward she had been detained in a convent until the authorities were satisfied she had taken no part in the murder on the Tarpeian Rock. She had just been released from her strange captivity. While they stood talking, there was a commotion in the crowd nearby. The police had seized Donatello and were taking him to jail.

For his crime Donatello was sentenced to prison. Miriam was not brought to trial, for her only crime had been the look in her eyes which had told Donatello to murder her persecutor. But Miriam's history was finally revealed. Although she herself was innocent, her family had been involved in a crime which made its name infamous. She had gone to Rome and attempted to live down the past, but evil had continued to haunt her, and the past had reappeared in the form of a tormentor who had dogged her footsteps, threatening to make her identity known to the world, until Donatello had thrown him over the cliff.

Kenyon and Hilda were married. Once again they saw Miriam, kneeling in the Pantheon before the tomb of Raphael. As they passed, she stretched out her hands to them in a gesture that both blessed them and repulsed them. They left her to her expiation and her grief.

MARCHING ON

Type of work: Novel
Author: James Boyd (1888-1944)
Type of plot: Historical romance
Time of plot: The Civil War period
Locale: North Carolina
First published: 1927

Principal characters:
JAMES FRASER, a farm boy
STEWART PREVOST, a rich planter's daughter
COLONEL PREVOST, her father
CHARLES PREVOST, her brother

Critique:

When James Boyd wrote *Marching On*, he obviously had two motives: one, to depict the spirit of the soldiers who fought heroically for a lost cause, and, two, to show how the spirit of one boy, James Fraser, kept marching on to the point where he could hold up his head proudly among those he had once thought of as his superiors. Both parts of the plot have been developed in an interesting and challenging manner. *Marching On* is not one of the best-known Civil War novels, but it is a good story, well told.

The Story:

When James Fraser fell in love with Stewart Prevost, he loved her in a hopeless way. He was the son of a poor farmer who lived in the swamps of North Carolina, and Stewart was the daughter of Colonel Prevost, a gentleman planter. Although Colonel Prevost was always courteous and friendly with the Frasers, his friendliness was reserved; James knew that he must keep his place.

James loved his father and mother, both hard-working, God-fearing people who toiled endlessly with meager reward. But he felt that he must somehow rise above their station in life, that he must gain an equal footing with the planters and other gentlemen toward whom he was forced to show a servile attitude. On nights when he was filled with despair and confusion, he slipped out of the house and played his fiddle. Into his music he could pour his dreams without fear of ridicule.

James first saw Stewart when he delivered a load of wood to her father. She said only a few words in greeting, but to James the words were as beautiful as the ringing of bells. During the next weeks he saw her often; it seemed to him that she was always on the road leading to the plantation as he passed with a load of wood. When he was alone, he cursed himself for a fool; no girl in Stewart's position would purposely seek out an awkward, uncouth farm boy. He swore to himself that he would avoid her. At last Stewart began to talk with him about life. When he told her that he would like to go away and work on the railroad, she offered to give him money to start him on his way. He bitterly decided that she only wanted to get rid of him.

For a few days James avoided the plantation. Then his pride forced him to call at Stewart's home and ask to see her. Colonel Prevost answered the door and went to call Stewart. He returned to tell James that Stewart was busy—and would be busy in the future. Trying to save his dignity, the boy stumbled blindly down the steps. The next morning he told his father and mother that he was going away.

James went to Wilmington and took a job on the railroad. His interest in machines and his determination to succeed made him an excellent worker. He lived well and sent money home each week. He made friends, but the vision of Stewart would not leave him and he was lonely. The men with whom he associated were all concerned over the coming election, for they believed that there would be trouble if Abraham Lincoln were elected. Everywhere he went, abolition and war were the main topics of conversation. Not long after Lincoln had been elected, the Secession began.

In April, after Fort Sumter had been attacked, James went home to join the company being formed by Colonel Prevost. Stewart's brother Charles was to be the captain, for he had attended Virginia Military Institute. On the night before the company was to leave the plantation James wrote Stewart a note and asked her to meet him. His love was greater than his pride, and for that he would always be grateful; Stewart swore to him that her father had never told her that James had come to see her once before, and she said regretfully that her offer of money had been thoughtlessly given. She promised to write to him, and she asked him to look after her brother Charles, for she had a premonition that he would be killed.

The next three years were later to seem to James like one continuous nightmare. Their company engaged in battle with the Yankees only three or four times, but the men marched and marched until they slept as they walked. Most of the time they were starving. When their shoes wore out, they wrapped their swollen feet in rags. Still they went on. Charles was killed. Although James killed the men who had attacked Charles, he feared that Stewart would not forgive him for failing in his promise. He wrote her, but it was two years before her answer reached him. By that time he was a prisoner. Her letter was the only thing that kept him sane during his years in prison. All the prisoners were gaunt and sick, unbelievably thin and emaciated. The Yankees were fairly

kind, but there was not enough food and clothing for anyone in those terrible years. James tried to keep a record of the number of days he had been a prisoner, but the problem was too great for his fuzzy mind. To him only Stewart's letter was real.

Released at last in an exchange of prisoners, James went immediately to the Prevost plantation. He was dirty and in rags and too weak to walk without help, but Stewart drew him like a magnet. When he climbed the long steps to her house, she was waiting for him at the top.

James stayed at the plantation until he was stronger. Stewart told him she loved him and would marry him. Although Colonel Prevost was courteous and gracious, James knew that the old gentleman still considered him little better than a poor white cracker and would be glad when he went to his own home. At last James went back to his father and mother.

James had been home only a short time before he learned that the Union army was attacking a town close to the plantation. Because the Fraser farm was off the main path of the soldiers, he went to the plantation to bring Stewart and her father home with him. The colonel could not believe that Southern troops would be defeated again and he did not want to leave his house. While James was there, the old man apologized for his attitude and told the boy that he was pleased that Stewart was going to marry him. He honored James by showing him a picture of Stewart's dead mother, his most prized treasure.

The town fell. James and Stewart went to his home, with the colonel's promise that he would follow them as soon as he had arranged for the protection of his slaves and overseers. But he never came. James returned to the plantation after he had taken Stewart to safety. There he found that Yankees had ransacked the house and killed the colonel as he tried to save his wife's picture. Filled with a desire to avenge the colonel's death, James started down the road after the troops. He wanted to kill any Yankee he saw. He had an opportunity to kill three of them, but he suddenly changed his mind when he saw that the men were released prisoners. They had fought for what they thought was right, just as he had. He could think of them only as brothers who had suffered in the same war. He put his gun away and gave them the little food he had. Then he started back to Stewart. He was going home.

MARDI

Type of work: Novel
Author: Herman Melville (1819-1891)
Type of plot: Symbolic allegory
Time of plot: Mid-nineteenth century
Locale: The islands of the Western Pacific
First published: 1849

Principal characters:

THE NARRATOR, later called TAJI, a young American sailor, mistaken for
   a god by the islanders
YILLAH, a blonde native, beloved of Taji, symbolizing Good
HAUTIA, a dark native queen, in love with Taji, symbolizing Evil
JARL, Taji's sailor companion
SAMOA, a native companion
MEDIA, a native king
YOOMY, Media's minstrel
BABBALANJA, Media's court philosopher

Critique:

Mardi and a Voyage Thither was Herman Melville's answer to those people who refused to believe that his first two travel books—*Omoo* and *Typee*—were anything but sailor's yarns that Melville had spun for the credulous. Actually, those books were based on Melville's own adventures in the South Seas. In this book, a true romance, he thought he might make people take fiction for fact, since they had been so obstinate in taking fact for fiction in earlier volumes. The second part of *Mardi*, the account of a mystical voyage through the world, is so filled with symbols that one finds it difficult to state what much of the symbolism means. Obviously the moral teaching of the novel is that one should avoid the vanity of human wishes—a message painted in such vivid colors that one loses sight of the didacticism. The characters, most of them supposedly Polynesian, discuss for Melville almost every topic thought of, from a belief in the hereafter for whales to Spanish customs and manners.

The Story:

The Narrator of the story, a young American sailor, was picked up at Ravavai, a Pacific island, by a whaling vessel, the *Arcturion*. The voyage of the *Arcturion* was not a successful one, and when the ship began to head for the cold climate of the Bay of Kamchatka, the young Narrator and his special friend in the forecastle, Jarl, decided to leave the ship. Knowing the captain would not land them anywhere, they provisioned a small boat and in it escaped from the ship under cover of darkness.

Heading westward, the two men hoped to reach some hospitable islands. After sailing for many days they came upon a drifting ship that seemed to be a derelict. Finding it in fairly seaworthy condition, they boarded it. The following morning a native man and woman were found in the rigging, where they had hidden from the Narrator and Jarl. With the help of the natives, who had escaped with the ship from an unfriendly tribe of islanders after the latter had killed the ship's crew, the Narrator and Jarl continued their voyage in search of land.

After many days of voyaging the vessel was becalmed. In the storm which followed, the vessel was wrecked. Jarl and the Narrator, with the native man, Samoa, set out in a little whaleboat. The native woman had been killed during the storm.

Many days later they saw a sail in the distance. Taking up their oars to aid the force of the sail, they slowly closed in on the craft they had spotted. As they drew

2240

close, they saw it was a strange arrangement of two native canoes with a platform built over them. After some discussion between the native priest in charge of the craft and the Narrator, the sailor and Samoa boarded the native vessel. Once aboard the craft, they discovered a beautiful blonde girl, but they had to force a passage through the natives in order to regain the whaleboat. In the scuffle they took two of the natives prisoners. From the natives they learned that the blonde girl was the priest's prisoner. Going back aboard the native craft, the sailor and Samoa rescued the girl and escaped with her from the natives.

The girl, whose name was Yillah, wished to return to her native islands. The Narrator soon fell in love with her, and the girl, in native fashion, returned his affection. The Narrator then decided that he would remain with her on her island home.

Sighting a group of islands at last, the party headed for the nearest beach. Before they reached the shore, however, natives swam out to the whaleboat and gave them an excited welcome. Towing the boat into shallow water, the natives picked it up and carried it ashore on their shoulders. The visitors were completely puzzled by their reception until they learned that the Narrator had been mistaken for the natives' god, Taji, who, according to an ancient prophecy, would one day revisit them in human form. The natives also thought that the other three occupants of the whaleboat were semi-deities whom Taji had brought from another world for companionship.

Media, king of the atoll, made the guests welcome, and Taji, as the Narrator was now called, decided to make the best of his position, as long as his godhood put him under no particular constraints. He and Yillah, housed in a splendid grass house, lived a life of tranquil happiness, doing no more than the islanders, who in their turn had little to do to make life comfortable. Then, suddenly, unhappiness struck the island and Taji. He awoke one

morning to find Yillah gone without a trace.

Within a few days of Yillah's disappearance, Taji received a visit from a portentously disguised messenger, who gave the young sailor a set of flower symbols from Queen Hautia, the dark queen of a group of distant islands.

The natives interpreted the flower symbols from Hautia to mean that the queen loved Taji, wished his presence, and bade him not look for Yillah, his lost love. Not to be dissuaded, however, Taji, accompanied by King Media and a party of his courtiers, including Yoomy the poet-singer and Babbalanja the philosopher, set sail in a huge, ornate native canoe in search of Yillah.

Before the voyagers had journeyed far on the ocean they met a black canoe containing more emissaries sent to Taji from Queen Hautia. The messengers, again using flower symbols interpreted by Yoomy, bade Taji forget his quest of the fair love and turn his canoe toward the kingdom of Hautia. Taji refused and continued on his quest.

His first stop was on the island of Juam, where Taji made a friend of King Donjalolo, a monarch who tried to escape reality by moving from one bower to another in his island kingdom and by taking no heed of anyone's happiness but his own and that of people who were in his company. Donjalolo aided Taji in his quest by sending messages throughout his island kingdom to ask for news of Yillah. After the petty princes had come to Donjalolo's court to report that they knew nothing of the girl, Taji decided to set out once more in the canoe, in the company of Media and his courtiers, to continue his search for his lost love. Again, this time in more menacing fashion, he was accosted at sea by a canoe-load of emissaries from Queen Hautia, who demanded that he go to her immediately. Again Taji refused.

After many days and· nights, during which Taji and his companions had lengthy conversations on many branches of knowledge and philosophy, they touched at an island where they visited the temple of Oro and learned of the Polynesian prophet, Alma, who had many years before, according to legend, brought peace, serenity, and love to the islands.

Continuing their voyage through the archipelago of Mardi, representing the world and all its ideas, Taji and his party visited Vivenza, modeled on the United States, passed the Cape of Capes, saw many other islands, regaled one another with many philosophical conversations during the long hours at sea, and were finally becalmed. After the calm a death-cloud passed them. Following that adventure they landed at Serenia, a land which proved too quiet and too good for them.

At last the only place left to look for Yillah, who had not been found on any one of the many atolls Taji and his companions had visited, was the bower of Queen Hautia herself. Babbalanja the philosopher, who remained in Serenia, told Taji he would never find the unattainable Yillah, but Taji went on until three emissaries from Queen Hautia met him and guided him to her land. Taji found himself entranced by Hautia, who seemed in some strange way connected with Yillah, though she invited him to sin. But still he asked in vain for word of Yillah. He was left in that land by the companions of his travels.